D0192487

SACRED SPACE

SACRED SPACE

The Prayer Book 2021

from the website www.sacredspace.ie

Prayer from the Irish Jesuits

LOYOLA PRESS.
A JESUIT MINISTRY

Chicago

LOYOLA PRESS.
A JESUIT MINISTRY

3441 N. Ashland Avenue
Chicago, Illinois 60657
(800) 621-1008
www.loyolapress.com

Scripture quotations are from the *New Revised Standard Version Bible: Catholic Edition*, copyright © 1989, 1993 National Council of the Churches of Christ in the United States of America. Used by permission. All rights reserved.

Cover art credit: Tanor/iStock/Getty Images.

ISBN-13: 978-0-8294-5016-3

Printed in the United States of America.
20 21 22 23 24 25 26 27 28 29 Versa 10 9 8 7 6 5 4 3 2 1

Contents

Sacred Space Prayer

Bless all who worship you, almighty God,
from the rising of the sun to its setting:
from your goodness enrich us,
by your love inspire us,
by your Spirit guide us,
by your power protect us,
in your mercy receive us,
now and always.

Preface

In 1999 an Irish Jesuit named Alan McGuckian had the simple—but at the time radical—idea of bringing daily prayer to the Internet. No one imagined that his experimental project would grow into a global community with volunteers translating the prayer experience into seventeen different languages.

Millions of people, from numerous Christian traditions, visit www.sacredspace.ie each year, and what they find is an invitation to step away from their busy routines for a few minutes a day to concentrate on what is really important in their lives. Sacred Space offers its visitors the opportunity to grow in prayerful awareness of their friendship with God.

Besides the daily prayer experience, Sacred Space also offers Living Space, with commentaries on the Scripture readings for each day's Catholic Mass. The Chapel of Intentions allows people to add their own prayers, while Pray with the Pope joins the community to the international Apostleship of Prayer. In addition, Sacred Space provides Lenten and Advent retreats, often in partnership with Pray as You Go, an audio prayer service from the British Jesuits.

The contents of this printed edition, first produced in 2004, are taken directly from our Internet site. Despite the increased use of Sacred Space on mobile devices, many people want a book they can hold and carry, and this book has proven especially helpful for prayer groups.

I am delighted to bring you the *Sacred Space* book, and I pray that your prayer life will flourish with its help.

Yours in Christ
Paul Campbell SJ

Introduction to *Sacred Space: The Prayerbook 2021*

Someone wrote that, just as there are many rooms in the Father's house, there are many rooms in our personal world: the mental room (for reading and decision-making, for tuning in to wisdom and insight), the emotional room (for love, affection, fear, and many other emotions) and the spiritual (where we find meaning and where we pray). A fourth might be the physical (for exercise, dieting, and looking after the body).

In Sacred Space we offer nourishment for wisdom, emotions, and prayer.

Praying Sacred Space each day has its positive effect. One person writes: "I am truly grateful for Sacred Space which is an integral and much-loved part of my prayer life." Another: "it is a blessing to read your commentaries each morning and to receive the spiritual nourishment you generously provide." Regular use of the prayer material of Sacred Space gives us a regular meeting with the Lord, an essential element of prayer.

The words of Jesus are divine words with the human voice; Scripture is a privileged place to meet God, so the material of Sacred Space is Scripture-based. Each day's Gospel reading from the Roman Catholic lectionary is provided. We read it slowly, even aloud, maybe more than once. We allow the word reach from our head to our heart. The short commentaries give sometimes an interpretation of the Gospel reading, other times maybe a prayer. We use them as they are helpful, as we use the other parts of each day's prayer.

In the "mental room" we feed the mind with some insights on prayer and the Christian life from different authors, which are included in the weekly introduction. We also find there a structure to begin the prayer for each day, ending with conversation with the Lord.

Sacred Space is a help to prayer of the heart, beginning with the word of Jesus. It encourages us to find God in all the experiences of our lives, and also in our joys, hopes, fears, and in everything that goes to make up who we are. We approach prayer just as we are, sharing this with the Lord. We hear the words of Jesus and notice that his words are spoken from his heart, from his love for us. He enters into the emotional space of our lives with his love, into the mental space with his wisdom, and into the spiritual space with his invitation to follow him, "the way, the truth and the life."

Maybe as we bring all of our life to our prayer, we will know what it is "to find God in all things," in the words of St. Ignatius.

With all this, we ask, "what is prayer for?" One good answer is that praying is putting on the mind and heart of Jesus Christ and of God. Prayer opens us to receive the greatest gift of all, the love of God. Asked once how a person knows if they are "praying right," a guide just remarked, "Our prayer is right for each of us if it makes us fuller followers of Jesus Christ." In the words of Blessed John Sullivan, the Irish Jesuit: "In prayer don't mind the scaffolding, get at God."

We hope that you find the material for each day leads you into deeper prayer, either on the www.sacredspace.ie website or in *Sacred Space: The Prayerbook 2021*. All prayer leads us into the community of Jesus' disciples, so maybe we can pray for all who make Sacred Space their daily prayer and know we are part of this worldwide community of praying people, of many denominations and faiths.

Donal Neary, SJ

How to Use This Book

During each week of the liturgical year, begin by reading the section entitled "Something to think and pray about each day this week." Then proceed through "The Presence of God," "Freedom," and "Consciousness" steps to prepare yourself to hear the Word of God in your heart. In the next step, "The Word," turn to the Scripture reading for each day of the week. Inspiration points are provided in case you need them. Then return to the "Conversation" and "Conclusion" steps. Use this process every day of the year.

The First Week of Advent
November 29—December 5, 2020

Something to think and pray about each day this week:

The terms *spiritual* and *religious* are often used interchangeably and most often when people identify themselves as "spiritual but not religious." Joseph and Mary, as they are depicted in the Christmas story in Matthew's Gospel, appear deeply spiritual. They use inner resources to overcome difficulties; these difficulties and challenges don't have to be spelled out to those of us familiar with the account of Jesus' birth. These inner resources open them to occasions when God's promptings and grace help nudge them into a safer place, even though at times comfort might tempt them to sit still in the same spot for a while.

However, the narrative in Matthew shows how deeply they are immersed in the religion of their days. Quotes from the Old Testament show how these moments are part of something greater and of which they are an important part. The two, religion and spirituality, are one. One definition of spirituality that I cannot forget is that it is the art of making connections. In our prayers and in our ponderings we try to connect with someone or something that can help us make our paths straight and find our own Immanuel, or God who is with us (Matthew 1:23). If we remain solely spiritual (if that can be done), then we are left with nothing to connect to, and good religion helps us connect deeply through its rituals, peoples, wisdom, and traditions.

Alan Hilliard, *Dipping into Advent*
Messenger Publications, 2019

The Presence of God

Dear Jesus, I come to you today longing for your presence. I desire to love you as you love me. May nothing ever separate me from you.

Freedom

Lord, grant me the grace to be free from the excesses of this life. Let me not get caught up with the desire for wealth. Keep my heart and mind free to love and serve you.

Consciousness

Where do I sense hope, encouragement, and growth in my life? By looking back over the past few months, I may be able to see which activities and occasions have produced rich fruit. If I do notice such areas, I will determine to give them time and space in the future.

The Word

God speaks to each of us individually. I listen attentively, to hear what he is saying to me. Read the text a few times, then listen. (Please turn to the Scripture on the following pages. Inspiration points are there should you need them. When you are ready, return here to continue.)

Conversation

What is stirring in me as I pray? Am I consoled, troubled, left cold? I imagine Jesus standing or sitting at my side, and I share my feelings with him.

Conclusion

Glory be to the Father, and to the Son, and to the Holy Spirit,
As it was in the beginning, is now, and ever shall be,
World without end. Amen.

Sunday November 29
First Sunday of Advent
Mark 13:33–37

Beware, keep alert; for you do not know when the time will come. It is like a man going on a journey, when he leaves home and puts his slaves in charge, each with his work, and commands the doorkeeper to be on the watch. Therefore, keep awake—for you do not know when the master of the house will come, in the evening, or at midnight, or at cockcrow, or at dawn, or else he may find you asleep when he comes suddenly. And what I say to you I say to all: "Keep awake."

- Advent begins today. We spend this time preparing for the coming of Christ into our world. He is here already, of course, but he wants to come closer. Let me be one of his points of entry by keeping awake to open the door when he knocks.

- What has Christ put me in charge of? How am I doing? Will I be delighted to see him when he comes?

Monday November 30
St. Andrew, Apostle
Matthew 4:18–22

As he walked by the Sea of Galilee, he saw two brothers, Simon, who is called Peter, and Andrew his brother, casting a net into the lake—for they were fishermen. And he said to them, "Follow me, and I will make you fish for people." Immediately they left their nets and followed him. As he went from there, he saw two other brothers, James son of Zebedee and his brother John, in the boat with their father Zebedee, mending their nets, and he called them. Immediately they left the boat and their father, and followed him.

- Simon Peter and Andrew heard the voice of Jesus as he walked by; James and John, while at their work, heeded and responded. Jesus speaks to them not in a time of retreat but meeting them at their work. What does it mean for me to work in a way that keeps me tuned in to a message that is for my salvation?

- In their everyday tasks, the apostles saw metaphors for how they would be as disciples of Jesus. Are there ways God speaks to me in my ordinary chores? How might God address me in the language of every day?

Tuesday December 1
Luke 10:21–24

At that same hour Jesus rejoiced in the Holy Spirit and said, "I thank you, Father, Lord of heaven and earth, because you have hidden these things from the wise and the intelligent and have revealed them to infants; yes, Father, for such was your gracious will. All things have been handed over to me by my Father; and no one knows who the Son is except the Father, or who the Father is except the Son and anyone to whom the Son chooses to reveal him."

Then turning to the disciples, Jesus said to them privately, "Blessed are the eyes that see what you see! For I tell you that many prophets and kings desired to see what you see, but did not see it, and to hear what you hear, but did not hear it."

- Jesus is rejoicing because the seventy disciples whom he sent out have returned. They are ecstatic about the great things they have done in his name. Whenever I spread the word of God, I too am sharing in the mission of Jesus, and this should give me great joy.

- Our sense of wonder is strongest when we are children and the whole world is new. As we grow older, we become world-weary. We look without seeing and listen without hearing. I ask the Holy Spirit to make me sensitive to God's self-revelation in the everyday events of my life.

Wednesday December 2
Matthew 15:29–37

After Jesus had left that place, he passed along the Sea of Galilee, and he went up the mountain, where he sat down. Great crowds came to him, bringing with them the lame, the maimed, the blind, the mute, and many others. They put them at his feet, and he cured them, so that the crowd was amazed when they saw the mute speaking, the maimed whole, the lame walking and the blind seeing. And they praised the God of Israel.

Then Jesus called his disciples to him and said, "I have compassion for the crowd, because they have been with me now for three days and have nothing to eat; and I do not want to send them away hungry, for they might faint on the way." The disciples said to him, "Where are we to get enough bread in the desert to feed so great a crowd?" Jesus asked them, "How many loaves have you?" They said, "Seven, and a few small fish." Then, ordering the crowd to sit down on the ground, he took the seven loaves and the fish; and after giving thanks he broke them and gave them to the disciples, and the disciples gave them to the crowds. And all of them ate and were filled; and they took up the broken pieces left over, seven baskets full.

• Jesus "called his disciples to him." God calls us constantly; we seek him only because he sought us. Our love is a response to his preexisting love for us. Can I go to God in the confidence that he has compassion for me, as he had for the crowd? That he will heal, nourish, and sustain me, as he did the crowd?

• Jesus did not conjure the loaves and fish out of thin air. He took what was offered to him and multiplied it greatly. We must never think we have little to give others. As St. Teresa of Ávila reminds us, "Christ has no body now but yours. No hands, no feet on earth but yours. Yours are the eyes through which he looks compassion on this world. Yours are the feet with which he walks to do good. Yours are the hands through which he blesses all the world."

Thursday December 3
Matthew 7:21, 24–27

"Not everyone who says to me, 'Lord, Lord,' will enter the kingdom of heaven, but only one who does the will of my Father in heaven."

[Jesus said to his disciples,] "Everyone then who hears these words of mine and acts on them will be like a wise man who built his house on rock. The rain fell, the floods came, and the winds blew and beat on that house, but it did not fall, because it had been founded on rock. And everyone who hears these words of mine and does not act on them will be like a foolish man who built his house on sand. The rain fell, and the floods came, and the winds blew and beat against that house, and it fell—and great was its fall!"

• St. Ignatius also taught that love is expressed more in deeds than in words. Without good deeds there is no real life at all!

• This is our life: listening to the word of God and doing it. We are building up the Church, the Body of Christ, founded on the rock of Peter.

Friday December 4
Matthew 9:27–31

As Jesus went on from there, two blind men followed him, crying loudly, "Have mercy on us, Son of David!" When he entered the house, the blind men came to him; and Jesus said to them, "Do you believe that I am able to do this?" They said to him, "Yes, Lord." Then he touched their eyes and said, "According to your faith let it be done to you." And their eyes were opened. Then Jesus sternly ordered them, "See that no one knows of this." But they went away and spread the news about him throughout that district.

- The start of this encounter is in public. There are crowds around Jesus, and the blind men are caught up in the general emotion. They shout at Jesus, using a formal title, "Son of David," as though he was a powerful messianic figure dispensing health to crowds. Jesus waits until he is in the house, where he can meet the blind men in person and question their faith.

- Lord, you do not meet me as one of a multitude but face-to-face, on my own, where you can test the truth of my words, free from the illusions of mass emotion.

Saturday December 5
Matthew 9:35–10:1, 5a, 6–8

Then Jesus went about all the cities and villages, teaching in their synagogues, and proclaiming the good news of the kingdom, and curing every disease and every sickness. When he saw the crowds, he had compassion for them, because they were harassed and helpless, like sheep without a shepherd. Then he said to his disciples, "The harvest is plentiful, but the laborers are few; therefore ask the Lord of the harvest to send out laborers into his harvest."

Then Jesus summoned his twelve disciples and gave them authority over unclean spirits, to cast them out, and to cure every disease and every sickness. These twelve Jesus sent out with the following instructions: . . . "As you go, proclaim the good news, 'The kingdom of heaven has come near.' Cure the sick, raise the dead, cleanse the lepers, cast out demons. You received without payment; give without payment."

- Jesus, in this Gospel account I see you engaging with vigilant eyes and ears to the cry of the suffering world of your day. To them you were the compassionate one, bringing balm to the wounded places of their lives.

- Lord, the cries of the poor and brokenhearted are evident in the mass migration daily beamed into my living room. Let me not forget that you summon me today to be your eyes, your ears, and your hands of compassion. May I respond with loving compassion to all who come to me.

The Second Week of Advent
December 6–12, 2020

Something to think and pray about each day this week:

She was sitting in the pew beside him. They were a young couple. From the rings on their fingers, one could presume they were married. From the time the Mass started, her leg was going like blazes. It wouldn't stay still. It seemed like all the nervous energy of her life was concentrated in her right leg, and it just kept hopping up and down. Funnily enough, the opening prayer of the Mass for the Advent liturgy urged us to "resolve to run forth." . . . she looked like she was going to run forth out of the pew any time and break the land speed record!

Her leg didn't get a rest even when she sat down . . . . her knee was hopping up and down as she picked at the threads on those fashionable jeans that have holes in them. At one stage during the Mass, she put her head on his shoulder . . . . he tried to shrug her away but she put her head back. He pecked her on the forehead. It was a gentle kiss, and for a few moments the leg stopped.

I once heard someone say that the coming of Jesus to the world was akin to the Father kissing us. An intimate expression of his love, care, and concern for us, and the promise that he can do more and we can do more together. It's a love like this that gets our legs going like blazes in the right direction.

Alan Hilliard, *Dipping into Advent*
Messenger Publications, 2019

The Presence of God

Dear Jesus, as I call on you today, I realize that often I come asking for favors. Today I'd like just to be in your presence. Draw my heart in response to your love.

Freedom

God my creator, you gave me life and the gift of freedom. Through your love I exist in this world. May I never take the gift of life for granted. May I always respect others' right to life.

Consciousness

Dear Lord, help me remember that you gave me life. Teach me to slow down, to be still and enjoy the pleasures created for me. To be aware of the beauty that surrounds me: the marvel of mountains, the calmness of lakes, the fragility of a flower petal. I need to remember that all these things come from you.

The Word

The word of God comes down to us through the Scriptures. May the Holy Spirit enlighten my mind and my heart to respond to the Gospel teachings. (Please turn to the Scripture on the following pages. Inspiration points are there, should you need them. When you are ready, return here to continue.)

Conversation

What feelings are rising in me as I pray and reflect on God's word? I imagine Jesus himself sitting or standing near me, and I open my heart to him.

Conclusion

I thank God for these moments we have spent together and for any insights I have been given concerning the text.

Sunday December 6
Second Sunday of Advent
Mark 1:1–8

The beginning of the good news of Jesus Christ, the Son of God.

As it is written in the prophet Isaiah,
"See, I am sending my messenger ahead of you,
     who will prepare your way;
the voice of one crying out in the wilderness:
     'Prepare the way of the Lord,
     make his paths straight,'"

John the baptizer appeared in the wilderness, proclaiming a baptism of repentance for the forgiveness of sins. And people from the whole Judean countryside and all the people of Jerusalem were going out to him, and were baptized by him in the river Jordan, confessing their sins. Now John was clothed with camel's hair, with a leather belt around his waist, and he ate locusts and wild honey. He proclaimed, "The one who is more powerful than I is coming after me; I am not worthy to stoop down and untie the thong of his sandals. I have baptized you with water; but he will baptize you with the Holy Spirit."

- Mark paints a picture of a man, Jesus, who spends his public life doing good but is then betrayed, abandoned, captured, and crucified. How can this be the Good News of Jesus Christ? I ask to be shown how Jesus' love transforms the pain and brings about the salvation of our world.

- I mingle with the crowds listening to John the baptizer. I know that he too suffered a violent death. Where is the good news in that? The good news is that he plays his part in the plan of salvation and bears steady witness to the light. In the wilderness of my life, I ask that I may always witness to light and truth and love.

Monday December 7
Luke 5:17–26

One day, while he was teaching, Pharisees and teachers of the law were sitting nearby (they had come from every village of Galilee and Judea and from Jerusalem); and the power of the Lord was with him to heal. Just then some men came, carrying a paralyzed man on a bed. They were trying to bring him in and lay him before Jesus; but finding no way to bring him in because of the crowd, they went up on the roof and let him down with his bed through the tiles into the middle of the crowd in front of Jesus. When he saw their faith, he said, "Friend, your sins are forgiven you." Then the scribes and the Pharisees began to question, "Who is this who is speaking blasphemies? Who can forgive sins but God alone?" When Jesus perceived their questionings, he answered them, "Why do you raise such questions in your hearts? Which is easier, to say, 'Your sins are forgiven you,' or to say, 'Stand up and walk'? But so that you may know that the Son of Man has authority on earth to forgive sins"—he said to the one who was paralyzed—"I say to you, stand up and take your bed and go to your home." Immediately he stood up before them, took what he had been lying on, and went to his home, glorifying God. Amazement seized all of them, and they glorified God and were filled with awe, saying, "We have seen strange things today."

- What an interesting, colorful, humorous, and yet life-changing scene! The man's friends are not easily put off. They use team effort and creativity to ensure that their paralyzed friend meets Jesus. An encounter happens that heals not only his body but also frees him from the paralysis of sin.

- Lord, forgiveness is a pressing need for all. Help me to do all I can to bring people to meet you and know your healing forgiveness. But let me do it sensitively!

Tuesday December 8
The Immaculate Conception of the Blessed Virgin Mary
Luke 1:26–38

In the sixth month the angel Gabriel was sent by God to a town in Galilee called Nazareth, to a virgin engaged to a man whose name was Joseph, of the house of David. The virgin's name was Mary. And he came to her and said, "Greetings, favored one! The Lord is with you." But she was much perplexed by his words and pondered what sort of greeting this might be. The angel said to her, "Do not be afraid, Mary, for you have found favor with God. And now, you will conceive in your womb and bear a son, and you will name him Jesus. He will be great, and will be called the Son of the Most High, and the Lord God will give to him the throne of his ancestor David. He will reign over the house of Jacob forever, and of his kingdom there will be no end." Mary said to the angel, "How can this be, since I am a virgin?" The angel said to her, "The Holy Spirit will come upon you, and the power of the Most High will overshadow you; therefore the child to be born will be holy; he will be called Son of God. And now, your relative Elizabeth in her old age has also conceived a son; and this is the sixth month for her who was said to be barren. For nothing will be impossible with God." Then Mary said, "Here am I, the servant of the Lord; let it be with me according to your word." Then the angel departed from her.

- Mary, the young girl of no status, from the village of Nazareth, an utterly insignificant place, is singled out, called, chosen, and overshadowed with God's Spirit. Her response moves from one of fear to total trust in God's inscrutable designs.

- "Mary has always been proposed to the faithful by the Church as an example to be imitated, not precisely in the type of life that she led and much less for the sociocultural background in which she lived and which scarcely exists anywhere today. Rather she is held up as an example to the faithful for the way in which in her own particular life she fully and responsibly accepted the word of God and acted on it, and because charity and the spirit of service were the driving force of her actions. She is worthy of imitation because she was the first and most perfect of Christ's disciples." (Pope Paul VI)

Wednesday December 9
Matthew 11:28–30

"Come to me, all you that are weary and are carrying heavy burdens, and I will give you rest. Take my yoke upon you, and learn from me; for I am gentle and humble in heart, and you will find rest for your souls. For my yoke is easy, and my burden is light."

- Here we see Jesus as the epitome of the Beatitudes for he presents himself as gentle and humble in heart. We see this in the way that throughout the Gospels he is comfortable with our limitations as human beings, and also in the way he invites us to face the greatness he shares with us.

- Be with Jesus for some time as he invites you to rest with these two sides of yourself that he wants you to live happily with. In doing this Jesus promises that you will find rest for your soul.

Thursday December 10
Matthew 11:11–15

"Truly I tell you, among those born of women no one has arisen greater than John the Baptist; yet the least in the kingdom of heaven is greater than he. From the days of John the Baptist until now the kingdom of heaven has suffered violence, and the violent take it by force. For all the prophets and the law prophesied until John came; and if you are willing to accept it, he is Elijah who is to come. Let anyone with ears listen!"

- John proclaimed the gospel, allowing his disciples to leave him to follow Jesus. I think of what it might mean to be less so that Jesus might be more.

- I ponder on what Jesus said about the greatness of John. I think of what he had seen and heard so that I might profit from understanding what Jesus valued.

Friday December 11
Matthew 11:16–19

"But to what will I compare this generation? It is like children sitting in the marketplaces and calling to one another,

'We played the flute for you, and you did not dance;
we wailed, and you did not mourn.'

For John came neither eating nor drinking, and they say, 'He has a demon'; the Son of Man came eating and drinking, and they say, 'Look, a glutton and a drunkard, a friend of tax-collectors and sinners!' Yet wisdom is vindicated by her deeds."

- Matthew once again brings Jesus and John before us. There is a sense of dissatisfaction in the people. They are childish in their response! Neither one meets their demands or their criteria. Both cause the people to feel uncomfortable and disturbed. So they reject them out of hand.

- Lord, I recognize something of my own response to people here. I am not always open to listening and accepting those who are different. I can so easily judge, dismiss, and reject people. I need your help today.

Saturday December 12
Luke 1:26–38

In the sixth month the angel Gabriel was sent by God to a town in Galilee called Nazareth, to a virgin engaged to a man whose name was Joseph, of the house of David. The virgin's name was Mary. And he came to her and said, "Greetings, favored one! The Lord is with you." But she was much perplexed by his words and pondered what sort of greeting this might be. The angel said to her, "Do not be afraid, Mary, for you have found favor with God. And now, you will conceive in your womb and bear a son, and you will name him Jesus. He will be great, and will be called the Son of the Most High, and the Lord God will give to him the throne of his ancestor David. He will reign over the house of Jacob forever, and of his kingdom there will be no end." Mary said to the angel, "How can this be, since I am a virgin?" The angel said to her, "The Holy Spirit will come upon you, and the power of the Most High will overshadow you; therefore the child to be born will be holy; he will be called Son of God. And now, your relative Elizabeth in her old age has also conceived a son; and this is the sixth month for her who was said to be barren. For nothing will be impossible with God." Then Mary said, "Here am I, the servant of the Lord; let it be with me according to your word." Then the angel departed from her.

- The angel said to Mary, "You will conceive and bear a son," not "Are you willing to conceive and bear a son?" That is how God's will comes to us; sometimes in the things that happen to us, other times in what we choose, and often in a mixture of both.

- Nothing is impossible to God! In difficult times, it is good to remember that God is fully in charge of our world. Everything happens according to his plan. There is always hope.

The Third Week of Advent
December 13–19, 2020

Something to think and pray about each day this week:

We are more than halfway there. May God continue to guide the journey—the Advent trail for you and all.

Maybe we can spend a bit of time with those far distant travelers, the "wise" ones, on their journey (Matthew 2:1-12). We don't need to get too deeply involved in the history or the geography of it, apart from seeking directions, but let us acknowledge today their thirst for salvation and their search for the Savior.

With the best will in the world, they finished up in the wrong place. Herod's palace was certainly not the place to find the Messiah. Herod's world allowed neither space nor time for such wonderings. It was headquarters, and the feeling was there was no need to look anywhere else for power. This was the place from which you sought an appointment, the place you came to behold royalty and the trappings of power. Here you found servants and security, dancers and musicians, fools and sages, and maybe, above all, ego.

Into this place they came, seeking (as we do) to find the Messiah. The question threw Herod and his court into confusion. Advisers were brought in, people who knew the text but not its purpose, people who dealt in facts and not in faith, and they arrived at a consensus around where Christ was to be found. It was, for them and Herod, a destination, a spot on a map, but for the Wise Kings, it was neither—it was destiny, fulfillment of a promise, a dream come true. But all this was beyond Herod. The wise ones left the palace behind, the king in his confused glory, and realized the truth—that same truth we are seeking—that Christ lives among people, totally accessible for those who wish to come into his presence.

At times though, in our confusion, we might well continue to seek him in the wrong place.

Vincent Sherlock, *Let Advent Be Advent*
Messenger Publications, 2017

The Presence of God
At any time of the day or night we can call on Jesus.
He is always waiting, listening for our call.
What a wonderful blessing.
No phone needed, no e-mails, just a whisper.

Freedom
Lord, grant me the grace to have freedom of the spirit. Cleanse my heart
and soul so that I may live joyously in your love.

Consciousness
Knowing that God loves me unconditionally, I look honestly over the
past day, its events, and my feelings. Do I have something to be grateful
for? Then I give thanks. Is there something I am sorry for? Then I ask
forgiveness.

The Word
The word of God comes down to us through the Scriptures.
May the Holy Spirit enlighten my mind and my heart
to respond to the Gospel teachings:
to love my neighbor as myself,
to care for my sisters and brothers in Christ.
(Please turn to the Scripture on the following pages. Inspiration points
are there, should you need them. When you are ready, return here to
continue.)

Conversation
I know with certainty that there were times when you carried me, Lord.
There were times when it was through your strength that I got through
the dark times in my life.

Conclusion
Glory be to the Father, and to the Son, and to the Holy Spirit,
As it was in the beginning, is now, and ever shall be,
World without end. Amen.

Sunday December 13
Third Sunday of Advent
John 1:6–8, 19–28

There was a man sent from God, whose name was John. He came as a witness to testify to the light, so that all might believe through him. He himself was not the light, but he came to testify to the light. . . .

This is the testimony given by John when the Jews sent priests and Levites from Jerusalem to ask him, "Who are you?" He confessed and did not deny it, but confessed, "I am not the Messiah." And they asked him, "What then? Are you Elijah?" He said, "I am not." "Are you the prophet?" He answered, "No." Then they said to him, "Who are you? Let us have an answer for those who sent us. What do you say about yourself?" He said, "I am the voice of one crying out in the wilderness, 'Make straight the way of the Lord,'" as the prophet Isaiah said.

Now they had been sent from the Pharisees. They asked him, "Why then are you baptizing if you are neither the Messiah, nor Elijah, nor the prophet?" John answered them, "I baptize with water. Among you stands one whom you do not know, the one who is coming after me; I am not worthy to untie the thong of his sandal." This took place in Bethany across the Jordan where John was baptizing.

- John knew that his role was to bring people to Christ. So is ours. We try to live our lives right so that people will be able to know through us that faith in Christ makes all the difference.

- John knew that his baptism was preparatory; it was only with water. Jesus baptized each of us with the Holy Spirit. The Holy Spirit dwells in us; he leads and guides us; we try to be open to his powerful work in our hearts.

Monday December 14
Matthew 21:23–27

When he entered the temple, the chief priests and the elders of the people came to him as he was teaching, and said, "By what authority are you doing these things, and who gave you this authority?" Jesus said to them, "I will also ask you one question; if you tell me the answer, then I will also tell you by what authority I do these things. Did the baptism of John come from heaven, or was it of human origin?" And they argued with one another, "If we say, 'From heaven,' he will say to us, 'Why then did you not believe him?' But if we say, 'Of human origin,' we are afraid of the crowd; for all regard John as a prophet." So they answered Jesus, "We do not know." And he said to them, "Neither will I tell you by what authority I am doing these things."

- Jesus was no stranger to the controversy and conflict of the religious establishment. They held a fixed view of how the Messiah should come. They demanded to know the source of his authority. He leaves them grappling in their stubbornness of heart.

- St. John of the Cross grappled with the mystery of who Jesus was. His life was spent contemplating the mystery of the Beloved. He wrote, "in the evening of life we will be examined in love." Lord, let me not seek to tame your word or curtail the Spirit. Rather keep me open today to holy mystery.

Tuesday December 15
Matthew 21:28–32

"What do you think? A man had two sons; he went to the first and said, 'Son, go and work in the vineyard today.' He answered, 'I will not'; but later he changed his mind and went. The father went to the second and said the same; and he answered, 'I go, sir'; but he did not go. Which of the two did the will of his father?" They said, "The first." Jesus said to them, "Truly I tell you, the tax-collectors and the prostitutes are going into the kingdom of God ahead of you. For John came to you in the way of righteousness and you did not believe him, but the tax-collectors and the prostitutes believed him; and even after you saw it, you did not change your minds and believe him."

- The Gospel reminds us of something we often forget: words can be meaningless. Promises are empty when not followed by action. The first son is arrogant, but his action shows his goodness. The second son sounds cooperative but fails to keep his promise.

- Do I make promises to others that quickly go out the window? My good intentions are no good to the person I intended to help but didn't. Could I say: "I'm sorry, I won't be able to do that for you," instead of promising what I already know is not going to happen?

- Let me take a few moments of silence to read over the Gospel text again and see if anything comes to my attention. And I could make a prayer, asking for help to be honest in speaking of my intentions.

Wednesday December 16
Luke 7:18b–23

John summoned two of his disciples and sent them to the Lord to ask, "Are you the one who is to come, or are we to wait for another?" When the men had come to him, they said, "John the Baptist has sent us to you to ask, 'Are you the one who is to come, or are we to wait for another?'" Jesus had just then cured many people of diseases, plagues, and evil spirits, and had given sight to many who were blind. And he answered them, "Go and tell John what you have seen and heard: the blind receive their sight, the lame walk, the lepers are cleansed, the deaf hear, the dead are raised, the poor have good news brought to them. And blessed is anyone who takes no offense at me."

- John has been tossed into prison. As he languishes there, the oil of his lamp is burning out. He wonders, did he get it right? Was his ministry a waste? Is Jesus the one he believed him to be?

- Lord, I can identify with John. I too find the wick of my lamp can sputter, the flame quiver, when things don't go my way. My desire for a world of peace and justice is met by a world of violence and injustice. This Advent day, refill my inner lamp and let me walk in faith and trust.

Thursday December 17
Matthew 1:1–17

An account of the genealogy of Jesus the Messiah, the son of David, the son of Abraham.

Abraham was the father of Isaac, and Isaac the father of Jacob, and Jacob the father of Judah and his brothers, and Judah the father of Perez and Zerah by Tamar, and Perez the father of Hezron, and Hezron the father of Aram, and Aram the father of Aminadab, and Aminadab the father of Nahshon, and Nahshon the father of Salmon, and Salmon the father of Boaz by Rahab, and Boaz the father of Obed by Ruth, and Obed the father of Jesse, and Jesse the father of King David.

And David was the father of Solomon by the wife of Uriah, and Solomon the father of Rehoboam, and Rehoboam the father of Abijah, and Abijah the father of Asaph, and Asaph the father of Jehoshaphat, and Jehoshaphat the father of Joram, and Joram the father of Uzziah, and Uzziah the father of Jotham, and Jotham the father of Ahaz, and Ahaz the father of Hezekiah, and Hezekiah the father of Manasseh, and Manasseh the father of Amos, and Amos the father of Josiah, and Josiah the father of Jechoniah and his brothers, at the time of the deportation to Babylon.

And after the deportation to Babylon: Jechoniah was the father of Salathiel, and Salathiel the father of Zerubbabel, and Zerubbabel the father of Abiud, and Abiud the father of Eliakim, and Eliakim the father of Azor, and Azor the father of Zadok, and Zadok the father of Achim, and Achim the father of Eliud, and Eliud the father of Eleazar, and Eleazar the father of Matthan, and Matthan the father of Jacob, and Jacob the father of Joseph the husband of Mary, of whom Jesus was born, who is called the Messiah.

So all the generations from Abraham to David are fourteen generations; and from David to the deportation to Babylon, fourteen generations; and from the deportation to Babylon to the Messiah, fourteen generations.

• There are surprises in this list of Jesus' ancestors. Matthew's genealogy is revolutionary for his time, in that it features five women. In addition, four of the women were Gentiles. Add to that the presence of some notable sinners, such as Judah and King David, and the intention is clear. It is to highlight the inclusivity of Jesus' mission.

• Paul says in Galatians 3:28–29: "There is neither Jew nor Gentile, neither slave nor free, nor is there male and female, for you are all one in Christ Jesus. If you belong to Christ, then you are Abraham's seed, and heirs according to the promise."

Friday December 18
Matthew 1:18–25

Now the birth of Jesus the Messiah took place in this way. When his mother Mary had been engaged to Joseph, but before they lived together, she was found to be with child from the Holy Spirit. Her husband Joseph, being a righteous man and unwilling to expose her to public disgrace, planned to dismiss her quietly. But just when he had resolved to do this, an angel of the Lord appeared to him in a dream and said, "Joseph, son of David, do not be afraid to take Mary as your wife, for the child conceived in her is from the Holy Spirit. She will bear a son, and you are to name him Jesus, for he will save his people from their sins." All this took place to fulfill what had been spoken by the Lord through the prophet: "Look, the virgin shall conceive and bear a son, and they shall name him Emmanuel," which means, "God is with us." When Joseph awoke from sleep, he did as the angel of the Lord commanded him; he took her as his wife, but had no marital relations with her until she had borne a son; and he named him Jesus.

- The Spirit (or Breath) of God was seen as the source of all creation and of all human life. So, just as God created all that exists in the heavens and the earth, now, through the power of God's Spirit, Jesus is conceived in Mary's womb by a particular, concrete, and special case of God's creativity.

- The birth of any child brings with it a sense of awe and wonderment. Can I share a sense of awe and wonderment at the incredible fact that God becomes human in a baby boy?

Saturday December 19
Luke 1:5–25

In the days of King Herod of Judea, there was a priest named Zechariah, who belonged to the priestly order of Abijah. His wife was a descendant of Aaron, and her name was Elizabeth. Both of them were righteous before God, living blamelessly according to all the commandments and regulations of the Lord. But they had no children, because Elizabeth was barren, and both were getting on in years.

Once when he was serving as priest before God and his section was on duty, he was chosen by lot, according to the custom of the priesthood, to enter the sanctuary of the Lord and offer incense. Now at the time of the incense offering, the whole assembly of the people was praying outside. Then there appeared to him an angel of the Lord, standing at the right side of the altar of incense. When Zechariah saw him, he was terrified; and fear overwhelmed him. But the angel said to him, "Do not be afraid,

Zechariah, for your prayer has been heard. Your wife Elizabeth will bear you a son, and you will name him John. You will have joy and gladness, and many will rejoice at his birth, for he will be great in the sight of the Lord. He must never drink wine or strong drink; even before his birth he will be filled with the Holy Spirit. He will turn many of the people of Israel to the Lord their God. With the spirit and power of Elijah he will go before him, to turn the hearts of parents to their children, and the disobedient to the wisdom of the righteous, to make ready a people prepared for the Lord." Zechariah said to the angel, "How will I know that this is so? For I am an old man, and my wife is getting on in years." The angel replied, "I am Gabriel. I stand in the presence of God, and I have been sent to speak to you and to bring you this good news. But now, because you did not believe my words, which will be fulfilled in their time, you will become mute, unable to speak, until the day these things occur."

Meanwhile, the people were waiting for Zechariah, and wondered at his delay in the sanctuary. When he did come out, he could not speak to them, and they realized that he had seen a vision in the sanctuary. He kept motioning to them and remained unable to speak. When his time of service was ended, he went to his home.

After those days his wife Elizabeth conceived, and for five months she remained in seclusion. She said, "This is what the Lord has done for me when he looked favorably on me and took away the disgrace I have endured among my people."

- Elizabeth was barren and God intervened to show his power. Where is my life barren, empty? Where do I want God to intervene for me?

- Zechariah doubted the angel's message and was punished for it. I ask for God's help with my own doubts and difficulties.

The Fourth Week of Advent/Christmas
December 20–26, 2020

Something to think and pray about each day this week:

They walk to the back of their home
The shed is alive . . . .
Shepherd boys
A young drummer
A smiling mother
Others, they're told, on the way.

The animals there too
Breathing warmth on one so new
The man who had knocked and asked for a bed
The one that was almost sent on his way
But then—the change of heart
The shed was offered
The right thing to do of course
Especially when they saw the young woman
A breath away from giving birth to new breath
How could you leave them in the cold?
The two of them there now
No longer two but three
On bended knee
He looked at his Infant guest
Thankful he'd done his best
And walked back to the house
She looked at him
And smiled
"Now," she said
"aren't you glad you cleaned the shed?"
He was.
We are.

It was the only way to prepare . . . .
To clean
Be clean
Fit for a King.
Amen!

Vincent Sherlock, *Let Advent be Advent*
Messenger Publications, 2017

The Presence of God
As I sit here, the beating of my heart,
the ebb and flow of my breathing, the movements of my mind
are all signs of God's ongoing creation of me.
I pause for a moment and become aware
of this presence of God within me.

Freedom
It is so easy to get caught up
with the trappings of wealth in this life.
Grant, O Lord, that I may be free
from greed and selfishness.
Remind me that the best things in life are free:
Love, laughter, caring, and sharing.

Consciousness
Knowing that God loves me unconditionally, I can afford to be honest
about how I am.
How has the day been, and how do I feel now? I share my feelings openly
with the Lord.

The Word
Lord Jesus, you became human to communicate with me.
You walked and worked on this earth.
You endured the heat and struggled with the cold.
All your time on this earth was spent in caring for humanity.
You healed the sick, you raised the dead.
Most important of all, you saved me from death.
(Please turn to the Scripture on the following pages. Inspiration points are
there, should you need them. When you are ready, return here to continue.)

Conversation
Sometimes I wonder what I might say if I were to meet you in person,
Lord.
I think I might say, "Thank you" because you are always there for me.

Conclusion
I thank God for these moments we have spent together and for any insights I have been given concerning the text.

Sunday December 20
Fourth Sunday of Advent

Luke 1:26–38

In the sixth month the angel Gabriel was sent by God to a town in Galilee called Nazareth, to a virgin engaged to a man whose name was Joseph, of the house of David. The virgin's name was Mary. And he came to her and said, "Greetings, favored one! The Lord is with you." But she was much perplexed by his words and pondered what sort of greeting this might be. The angel said to her, "Do not be afraid, Mary, for you have found favor with God. And now, you will conceive in your womb and bear a son, and you will name him Jesus. He will be great, and will be called the Son of the Most High, and the Lord God will give to him the throne of his ancestor David. He will reign over the house of Jacob forever, and of his kingdom there will be no end." Mary said to the angel, "How can this be, since I am a virgin?" The angel said to her, "The Holy Spirit will come upon you, and the power of the Most High will overshadow you; therefore the child to be born will be holy; he will be called Son of God. And now, your relative Elizabeth in her old age has also conceived a son; and this is the sixth month for her who was said to be barren. For nothing will be impossible with God." Then Mary said, "Here am I, the servant of the Lord; let it be with me according to your word." Then the angel departed from her.

- Theologians constructed a theory of original sin, and another theory to explain how Mary was exempt from the curse of Adam: the Immaculate Conception. In prayer I'd rather remember the old Irish poem:

  Queen of all queens, oh wonder of the loveliness of women,
  Heart which hath held in check for us the righteous wrath of God;
  Strong staff of light and fosterer of the Bright Child of heaven,
  Pray thou for us as we now pray that we may be forgiven.

- Repeating a phrase in prayer may make it go deep within us. It's like a favorite piece of music that we can hum over and over again. It is part of us. "I am the servant of the Lord" was such a phrase for Mary, spoken first at one of the biggest moments in her life. In dry times of prayer, a sentence like that can occupy mind and heart and raise us close to God.

Monday December 21
Luke 1:39–45

In those days Mary set out and went with haste to a Judean town in the hill country, where she entered the house of Zechariah and greeted Elizabeth. When Elizabeth heard Mary's greeting, the child leaped in her womb. And Elizabeth was filled with the Holy Spirit and exclaimed with a loud cry, "Blessed are you among women, and blessed is the fruit of your womb. And why has this happened to me, that the mother of my Lord comes to me? For as soon as I heard the sound of your greeting, the child in my womb leaped for joy. And blessed is she who believed that there would be a fulfillment of what was spoken to her by the Lord."

- Birth, the gift of life from God, fruitfulness was always sacred to the people of Israel; and the mothers had a special place down through sacred history—as the bearers of life. Mary and Elizabeth outdo one another, as it were, in giving thanks.

- But this particular case is special, unique. Jesus, the child that Mary is carrying, is recognized by the child in Elizabeth's womb—John leaps in recognition of the one whom both mothers revere as "Lord" (John himself being of miraculous origin from an elderly mother).

- And above and beyond what is happening to each mother, earthshaking events are in store; the Lord (long awaited) has finally come to visit his people, to be victorious over enemies, to exult with joy over those who are his own.

Tuesday December 22
Luke 1:46–56

And Mary said,
"My soul magnifies the Lord,
   and my spirit rejoices in God my Savior, for he has looked with favor on the lowliness of his servant.
   Surely, from now on all generations will call
      me blessed;
for the Mighty One has done great things for me,
   and holy is his name.
His mercy is for those who fear him
   from generation to generation.

He has shown strength with his arm;
he has scattered the proud in the thoughts of
their hearts.
He has brought down the powerful from their thrones,
and lifted up the lowly;
he has filled the hungry with good things,
and sent the rich away empty.
He has helped his servant Israel,
in remembrance of his mercy,
according to the promise he made to our ancestors,
to Abraham and to his descendants for ever."

And Mary remained with her for about three months and then returned to her home.

- This glorious prayer, the Magnificat, is charged with dynamite. It points to a society in which nobody wants to have too much while others have too little. The hungry are fed and the lowly are raised up.

- Lord, may I never be seduced by sweet devotion while I have more than I need and others have less.

Wednesday December 23
Luke 1:57–66

Now the time came for Elizabeth to give birth, and she bore a son. Her neighbors and relatives heard that the Lord had shown his great mercy to her, and they rejoiced with her.

On the eighth day they came to circumcise the child, and they were going to name him Zechariah after his father. But his mother said, "No; he is to be called John." They said to her, "None of your relatives has this name." Then they began motioning to his father to find out what name he wanted to give him. He asked for a writing tablet and wrote, "His name is John." And all of them were amazed. Immediately his mouth was opened and his tongue freed, and he began to speak, praising God. Fear came over all their neighbors, and all these things were talked about throughout the entire hill country of Judea. All who heard them pondered them and said, "What then will this child become?" For, indeed, the hand of the Lord was with him.

- The neighbors and relatives who attended the circumcision had their well-worn expectation about the child's name. But they had to learn that it is God who chooses the name and the destiny of this child. Perhaps, with every child, God moves the world in a new direction?

- How do I stay open to the God of surprises, to the Spirit who moves at will? Is my comfort zone too well defended for me to be surprised by grace?

Thursday December 24
Luke 1:67–79

Then his father Zechariah was filled with the Holy Spirit and spoke this prophecy:

"Blessed be the Lord God of Israel,
 for he has looked favorably on his people and
  redeemed them.
He has raised up a mighty savior for us
 in the house of his servant David,
as he spoke through the mouth of his holy prophets from of old,
 that we would be saved from our enemies and from the hand of all
 who hate us.
Thus he has shown the mercy promised to our ancestors,
 and has remembered his holy covenant,
the oath that he swore to our ancestor Abraham,
 to grant us that we, being rescued from the hands of our enemies,
might serve him without fear, in holiness and righteousness
 before him all our days.
And you, child, will be called the prophet of the Most High;
 for you will go before the Lord to prepare his ways,
to give knowledge of salvation to his people
 by the forgiveness of their sins.
By the tender mercy of our God,
 the dawn from on high will break upon us,
to give light to those who sit in darkness and in the shadow of death,
 to guide our feet into the way of peace."

- Zechariah, released from his silence, bursts forth in profound praise, proclaiming the activity of God at work in our world's history. The savior is coming! His own son will act as witness and light-bearer to the loving kindness and mercy of the great and holy one.

- Lord, as I move into Christmas Eve, remind me again of how mercy is the dominant theme of how you walk with us. You are forever tender toward me. Help me to grow daily in the awareness of your mercy and tenderness, constantly at work in my life.

Friday December 25
The Nativity of the Lord

John 1:1–18

In the beginning was the Word, and the Word was with God, and the Word was God. He was in the beginning with God. All things came into being through him, and without him not one thing came into being. What has come into being in him was life, and the life was the light of all people. The light shines in the darkness, and the darkness did not overcome it.

There was a man sent from God, whose name was John. He came as a witness to testify to the light, so that all might believe through him. He himself was not the light, but he came to testify to the light. The true light, which enlightens everyone, was coming into the world.

He was in the world, and the world came into being through him; yet the world did not know him. He came to what was his own, and his own people did not accept him. But to all who received him, who believed in his name, he gave power to become children of God, who were born, not of blood or of the will of the flesh or of the will of man, but of God.

And the Word became flesh and lived among us, and we have seen his glory, the glory as of a father's only son, full of grace and truth. (John testified to him and cried out, "This was he of whom I said, 'He who comes after me ranks ahead of me because he was before me.'") From his fullness we have all received, grace upon grace. The law indeed was given through Moses; grace and truth came through Jesus Christ. No one has ever seen God. It is God the only Son, who is close to the Father's heart, who has made him known.

- This is the "Christmas Gospel." Christmas is not simply the celebration of the birth of the baby Jesus but also the awesome mystery of the Incarnation of God. God pitched his tent among us and remains among us as a human being forever.

- The world did not know him. His own people, the leaders of the Jews, did not accept him. We have accepted him, and our vocation is to make his light shine for the whole world.

Saturday December 26
St. Stephen, Martyr
Matthew 10:17–22

Beware of them, for they will hand you over to councils and flog you in their synagogues; and you will be dragged before governors and kings because of me, as a testimony to them and the Gentiles. When they hand you over, do not worry about how you are to speak or what you are to say; for what you are to say will be given to you at that time; for it is not you who speak, but the Spirit of your Father speaking through you. Brother will betray brother to death, and a father his child, and children will rise against parents and have them put to death; and you will be hated by all because of my name. But the one who endures to the end will be saved.

- It can seem strange to celebrate St. Stephen, who was martyred, right after Christmas Day when our dominant emotion is joy in the birth of Christ. The point, however, is that this is why Christ came to earth, to save us from our sins by his death on the cross.

- Christian joy is that strange thing, not an emotion, but a deep peace that remains even in the midst of great opposition and difficulty. This will always be part of the Christian life.

The First Week of Christmas
December 27, 2020—January 2, 2021

Something to think and pray about each day this week:

He was every inch of what you'd expect a wise man to be. Tall, ponderous, intuitive and generous with those who weren't wasting his time. His professional life was lived as a professor of sociology and a priest. He lived through the horrors of the Rwandan genocide and he lives through it still as he endeavors to reason with the tremendous evils he witnessed. I can still hear the quiver in his voice when, twenty years after the genocide, he said, "You know that humanity has crossed a line when fathers can murder their own children." In truth he saw the slaughter of many innocents. He paused and said nothing for quite a while.

A few weeks later I was reading up on the genocide. The author, another priest, said that "tribal identities became more important than baptismal identity." Either we are all the same as children of God and we demand to both give and receive mutual respect, or we create tribes where we make ourselves more important or more valuable than others who occupy the same space.

Alan Hilliard, Dipping into Advent
Messenger Publications, 2019

The Presence of God

"Be still, and know that I am God!" Lord, your words lead us to the calmness and greatness of your presence.

Freedom

If God were trying to tell me something, would I know?
If God were reassuring me or challenging me, would I notice?
I ask for the grace to be free of my own preoccupations
and open to what God may be saying to me.

Consciousness

In the presence of my loving Creator, I look honestly at my feelings over the past day: the highs, the lows, and the level ground. Can I see where the Lord has been present?

The Word

In this expectant state of mind, please turn to the text for the day with confidence. Believe that the Holy Spirit is present and may reveal whatever the passage has to say to you. Read reflectively, listening with a third ear to what may be going on in your heart. (Please turn to the Scripture on the following pages. Inspiration points are there, should you need them. When you are ready, return here to continue.)

Conversation

Remembering that I am still in God's presence,
I imagine Jesus standing or sitting beside me,
and I say whatever is on my mind, whatever is in my heart,
speaking as one friend to another.

Conclusion

Glory be to the Father, and to the Son, and to the Holy Spirit,
As it was in the beginning, is now, and ever shall be,
World without end. Amen.

Sunday December 27
The Holy Family of Jesus, Mary and Joseph
Luke 2:22–40

When the time came for their purification according to the law of Moses, they brought him up to Jerusalem to present him to the Lord (as it is written in the law of the Lord, "Every firstborn male shall be designated as holy to the Lord"), and they offered a sacrifice according to what is stated in the law of the Lord, "a pair of turtledoves or two young pigeons."

Now there was a man in Jerusalem whose name was Simeon; this man was righteous and devout, looking forward to the consolation of Israel, and the Holy Spirit rested on him. It had been revealed to him by the Holy Spirit that he would not see death before he had seen the Lord's Messiah. Guided by the Spirit, Simeon came into the temple; and when the parents brought in the child Jesus, to do for him what was customary under the law, Simeon took him in his arms and praised God, saying,

"Master, now you are dismissing your servant in peace,
according to your word;
for my eyes have seen your salvation,
which you have prepared in the presence of all
peoples,
a light for revelation to the Gentiles
and for glory to your people Israel."

And the child's father and mother were amazed at what was being said about him. Then Simeon blessed them and said to his mother Mary, "This child is destined for the falling and the rising of many in Israel, and to be a sign that will be opposed so that the inner thoughts of many will be revealed—and a sword will pierce your own soul too."

There was also a prophet, Anna the daughter of Phanuel, of the tribe of Asher. She was of a great age, having lived with her husband for seven years after her marriage, then as a widow to the age of eighty-four. She never left the temple but worshiped there with fasting and prayer night and day. At that moment she came, and began to praise God and to speak about the child to all who were looking for the redemption of Jerusalem.

When they had finished everything required by the law of the Lord, they returned to Galilee, to their own town of Nazareth. The child grew and became strong, filled with wisdom; and the favor of God was upon him.

- The Holy Spirit is very important for St. Luke, and that Spirit is never far away. This text links him closely to Simeon, helping the old man to recognize and praise God, and to bless the parents of Jesus. What about me? The Holy Spirit dwells in me too: I am his temple! But is he perhaps only a quiet lodger whom I hardly notice? Have I locked him up? Can he become my mentor whom I look to for advice and support? Can the Spirit and I create life together?

- The early Christians announced important decisions by saying, "It has seemed good to the Holy Spirit and to us . . ." (Acts 15:28). Lord, make me sensitive to the Spirit's promptings as I make my decisions. Then things will go well for me.

Monday December 28
The Holy Innocents
Matthew 2:13–18

Now after they had left, an angel of the Lord appeared to Joseph in a dream and said, "Get up, take the child and his mother, and flee to Egypt, and remain there until I tell you; for Herod is about to search for the child, to destroy him." Then Joseph got up, took the child and his mother by night, and went to Egypt, and remained there until the death of Herod. This was to fulfill what had been spoken by the Lord through the prophet, "Out of Egypt I have called my son."

When Herod saw that he had been tricked by the wise men, he was infuriated, and he sent and killed all the children in and around Bethlehem who were two years old or under, according to the time that he had learned from the wise men. Then was fulfilled what had been spoken through the prophet Jeremiah:

"A voice was heard in Ramah,
    wailing and loud lamentation,
Rachel weeping for her children;
    she refused to be consoled, because they are no
        more."

- Another sad feast, remembering Herod's bloodthirsty massacre and the heartbreak of the babies' mothers. As we recover from Christmas, other parts of the world—even of our own country—are suffering bombs, bloodshed, bereavements. Lord, keep my heart open to the griefs that confront me.

- This terrible scene evokes the genocides and atrocities that still make the news. I pray with compassion for all who are affected by violence and cruelty.

- Herod's action was motivated by his pride and self-seeking. As I pray for all leaders, I ask God to heal me of any false image I have of myself.

Tuesday December 29
Luke 2:22–35

When the time came for their purification according to the law of Moses, they brought him up to Jerusalem to present him to the Lord (as it is written in the law of the Lord, "Every firstborn male shall be designated as holy to the Lord"), and they offered a sacrifice according to what is stated in the law of the Lord, "a pair of turtledoves or two young pigeons."

Now there was a man in Jerusalem whose name was Simeon; this man was righteous and devout, looking forward to the consolation of Israel, and the Holy Spirit rested on him. It had been revealed to him by the Holy Spirit that he would not see death before he had seen the Lord's Messiah. Guided by the Spirit, Simeon came into the temple; and when the parents brought in the child Jesus, to do for him what was customary under the law, Simeon took him in his arms and praised God, saying,

"Master, now you are dismissing your servant in peace,
    according to your word;
for my eyes have seen your salvation,
    which you have prepared in the presence of all
        peoples,
a light for revelation to the Gentiles
    and for glory to your people Israel."

And the child's father and mother were amazed at what was being said about him. Then Simeon blessed them and said to his mother Mary, "This child is destined for the falling and the rising of many in Israel, and to be a sign that will be opposed so that the inner thoughts of many will be revealed—and a sword will pierce your own soul too."

- Simeon was one of those known as The Quiet in the Land, Jews who did not look for a military Messiah, and had no dreams of armies or power, but believed in a life of constant watchfulness and prayer until God should come. There is a double surprise here: the delight of Simeon at being able to welcome the Promised One; and the astonishment of Mary and Joseph at what was being said about their boy.

- Lord, may I too open my eyes in grateful amazement when I see your interventions in my life.

Wednesday December 30
Luke 2:36–40

There was also a prophet, Anna the daughter of Phanuel, of the tribe of Asher. She was of a great age, having lived with her husband for seven years after her marriage, then as a widow to the age of eighty-four. She never left the temple but worshiped there with fasting and prayer night and day. At that moment she came, and began to praise God and to speak about the child to all who were looking for the redemption of Jerusalem.

When they had finished everything required by the law of the Lord, they returned to Galilee, to their own town of Nazareth. The child grew and became strong, filled with wisdom; and the favor of God was upon him.

- The redemption of Jerusalem was such a long time coming, so many centuries. Think how many old women in Israel looked forward in vain over all those years. How blessed was Anna that she saw the Savior just before she died. Think how blessed we are to have the Savior near us every day of our lives.

- Jesus spent thirty of his thirty-three years on earth living an ordinary life with his parents in Nazareth. These "hidden years" reveal to us the fundamental value of our ordinary day-to-day lives. Every day is crucial, with such richness and potential, which we need to consider seriously.

Thursday December 31

John 1:1–18

In the beginning was the Word, and the Word was with God, and the Word was God. He was in the beginning with God. All things came into being through him, and without him not one thing came into being. What has come into being in him was life, and the life was the light of all people. The light shines in the darkness, and the darkness did not overcome it.

There was a man sent from God, whose name was John. He came as a witness to testify to the light, so that all might believe through him. He himself was not the light, but he came to testify to the light. The true light, which enlightens everyone, was coming into the world.

He was in the world, and the world came into being through him; yet the world did not know him. He came to what was his own, and his own people did not accept him. But to all who received him, who believed in his name, he gave power to become children of God, who were born, not of blood or of the will of the flesh or of the will of man, but of God.

And the Word became flesh and lived among us, and we have seen his glory, the glory as of a father's only son, full of grace and truth. (John testified to him and cried out, "This was he of whom I said, 'He who comes after me ranks ahead of me because he was before me.'") From his fullness we have all received, grace upon grace. The law indeed was given through Moses; grace and truth came through Jesus Christ. No one has ever seen God. It is God the only Son, who is close to the Father's heart, who has made him known.

- As our year draws to a close, today's Scripture brings us back to the beginning of all time. As we stand on the threshold of another year, we take time to recall the greatest event of all: God has entered our world, not just for a day's visit, but has made it his permanent dwelling.

- Lord, let me set aside some time today, to reflect back on how the light of your presence has impacted my life during this past year. Let me be grateful and give thanks for all I have received from you directly and through the gift of other people.

Friday January 1
Mary the Mother of God
Luke 2:16–21

So they went with haste and found Mary and Joseph, and the child lying in the manger. When they saw this, they made known what had been told them about this child; and all who heard it were amazed at what the shepherds told them. But Mary treasured all these words and pondered them in her heart. The shepherds returned, glorifying and praising God for all they had heard and seen, as it had been told them.

After eight days had passed, it was time to circumcise the child; and he was called Jesus, the name given by the angel before he was conceived in the womb.

- This is the octave day of Christmas, dedicated as a solemnity to Mary, the Holy Mother of God. The Gospel invites us to join the shepherds as they visit the newborn child in Bethlehem, and to share in their wonder and joy. Have our celebrations over the Christmas season brought us closer to Jesus and his mother? Or have we found it difficult to find oases of quiet time in which to enter deeply into the mystery of it all?

- We cannot but be aware that this is also New Year's Day. How do we feel about entering a new phase of our journey through life? Are we in an expectant and hopeful mood, or are we apathetic or despondent? Whatever our feelings may be, it would be good to share them with God and ask his blessing on the days and months ahead.

Saturday January 2
John 1:19–28

This is the testimony given by John when the Jews sent priests and Levites from Jerusalem to ask him, "Who are you?" He confessed and did not deny it, but confessed, "I am not the Messiah." And they asked him, "What then? Are you Elijah?" He said, "I am not." "Are you the prophet?" He answered, "No." Then they said to him, "Who are you? Let us have an answer for those who sent us. What do you say about yourself?" He said, "I am the voice of one crying out in the wilderness, 'Make straight the way of the Lord,'" as the prophet Isaiah said.

Now they had been sent from the Pharisees. They asked him, "Why then are you baptizing if you are neither the Messiah, nor Elijah, nor the prophet?" John answered them, "I baptize with water. Among you stands one whom you do not know, the one who is coming after me; I am not worthy to untie the thong of his sandal." This took place in Bethany across the Jordan where John was baptizing.

- "Who are you?" I put labels on people and think I know them. But can I even fathom the mystery of my own being? I cannot put an easy label on John the Baptist. He is a voice in the stillness of the desert. He points beyond himself. He doesn't want to be an achiever. May he stir up in me a longing to look for the One who is coming.

- Loving Father, who are you? I see in Jesus that you are pure gift of everlasting love. You are Mystery, beyond me. But in you I know my real worth and the value of everyone and everything in my life.

The Epiphany of Our Lord/
The Second Week of Christmas
January 3–10, 2021

Something to think and pray about each day this week:

Driving home one evening, I was enthralled by a radio documentary which related recordings of the last place in Ireland to receive electricity, or the "lectric," as it was called in the local dialect. The location was aptly called The Black Valley in County Kerry.

The producers went ahead of the installation and interviewed people who were full of frightened expectation as the cables made their way closer and closer to the last door in the country to receive this new form of power. An elderly couple were in the last house on the road and, being a proud homeowner, all she was worried about was having a clean house to welcome their new guest who promised to transform their lives. As the presenter talked, you could hear her scrubbing, moving, washing, and replacing over and over again. The familiar sound of a tin pail full of water and a mop sloshing around a stone floor only served to increase the sense of excited anticipation.

When the "lectric" was eventually installed, the switch in the house was flicked and, lo and behold, despite all the cleaning and polishing the brazen "lectric" bulb revealed dirt, cobwebs, and dust in places they didn't even know existed in their humble abode. There was utter embarrassment and discomfort all round.

We don't see light, but light helps us see. The opening of St. John's Gospel is called the prologue, and it tells us that Jesus is the "light that shines in the darkness and the darkness has not overcome it." He is described as the light because his ways, insights, and teachings help us see the world and our existence in a refreshingly unlimited manner. Sometimes his light, like the "lectric," may also show us where we have to tidy up our lives!

Alan Hilliard, *Dipping into Advent*
Messenger Publications, 2019

The Presence of God
"I am standing at the door, knocking," says the Lord. What a wonderful privilege that the Lord of all creation desires to come to me. I welcome his presence.

Freedom
I will ask God's help
to be free from my own preoccupations,
to be open to God in this time of prayer,
to come to know, love, and serve God more.

Consciousness
In God's loving presence I unwind the past day,
starting from now and looking back, moment by moment.
I gather in all the goodness and light, in gratitude.
I attend to the shadows and what they say to me,
seeking healing, courage, forgiveness.

The Word
Now I turn to the Scripture set out for me this day. I read slowly over the words and see if any sentence or sentiment appeals to me. (Please turn to the Scripture on the following pages. Inspiration points are there, should you need them. When you are ready, return here to continue.)

Conversation
Sometimes I wonder what I might say if I were to meet you in person, Lord.
I think I might say, "Thank you" because you are always there for me.

Conclusion
I thank God for these moments we have spent together and for any insights I have been given concerning the text.

Sunday January 3
Epiphany of the Lord (USA)
Matthew 2:1–12

In the time of King Herod, after Jesus was born in Bethlehem of Judea, wise men from the East came to Jerusalem, asking, "Where is the child who has been born king of the Jews? For we observed his star at its rising, and have come to pay him homage." When King Herod heard this, he was frightened, and all Jerusalem with him; and calling together all the chief priests and scribes of the people, he inquired of them where the Messiah was to be born. They told him, "In Bethlehem of Judea; for so it has been written by the prophet:

'And you, Bethlehem, in the land of Judah,
    are by no means least among the rulers of Judah;
for from you shall come a ruler
    who is to shepherd my people Israel.'"

Then Herod secretly called for the wise men and learned from them the exact time when the star had appeared. Then he sent them to Bethlehem, saying, "Go and search diligently for the child; and when you have found him, bring me word so that I may also go and pay him homage." When they had heard the king, they set out; and there, ahead of them, went the star that they had seen at its rising, until it stopped over the place where the child was. When they saw that the star had stopped, they were overwhelmed with joy. On entering the house, they saw the child with Mary his mother; and they knelt down and paid him homage. Then, opening their treasure chests, they offered him gifts of gold, frankincense, and myrrh. And having been warned in a dream not to return to Herod, they left for their own country by another road.

- The story told in today's Gospel is about people being called to follow their star in order to find the fullness of life only Jesus can give. "I came that they may have life, and have it abundantly" (John 10:10). You may not have thought much about the nature of the star you follow. With a view to clarifying this, it may be worthwhile to ask yourself what you want for your children, your family, or your friends.

- Having done this, you might talk to Jesus about whether this is what he wants for you, the star he wishes you to follow.

Monday January 4
Matthew 4:12–17, 23–25

Now when Jesus heard that John had been arrested, he withdrew to Galilee. He left Nazareth and made his home in Capernaum by the lake, in the territory of Zebulun and Naphtali, so that what had been spoken through the prophet Isaiah might be fulfilled:

"Land of Zebulun, land of Naphtali,
on the road by the sea, across the Jordan, Galilee of the Gentiles—
the people who sat in darkness
have seen a great light,
and for those who sat in the region and shadow of death
light has dawned."
From that time Jesus began to proclaim, "Repent, for the kingdom of
heaven has come near." . . .

Jesus went throughout Galilee, teaching in their synagogues and proclaiming the good news of the kingdom and curing every disease and every sickness among the people. So his fame spread throughout all Syria, and they brought to him all the sick, those who were afflicted with various diseases and pains, demoniacs, epileptics, and paralytics, and he cured them. And great crowds followed him from Galilee, the Decapolis, Jerusalem, Judea, and from beyond the Jordan.

- Here we are at the beginning of Jesus' ministry. He leaves Nazareth and settles in Capernaum, a busy fishing and trading center on the Sea of Galilee. His call to repentance is identical to that of John the Baptist.

- He is a late starter, a young man in a hurry. His hero, John, has been imprisoned, and he realizes his time may be short. He ministers to large crowds, proclaiming the Good News of the reign of God, healing all kinds of sickness and exorcising demons.

- Do I catch the excitement and enthusiasm of the crowds, come from far and wide?

Tuesday January 5
Mark 6:34–44

As he went ashore, he saw a great crowd; and he had compassion for them, because they were like sheep without a shepherd; and he began to teach them many things. When it grew late, his disciples came to him and said, "This is a deserted place, and the hour is now very late; send them away so that they may go into the surrounding country and villages and buy something for themselves to eat." But he answered them, "You give them something to eat." They said to him, "Are we to go and buy two hundred denarii worth of bread, and give it to them to eat?" And he said to them, "How many loaves have you? Go and see." When they had found out, they said, "Five, and two fish." Then he ordered them to get all the people to sit down in groups on the green grass. So they sat down in groups of hundreds and of fifties. Taking the five loaves and the two fish, he looked up to heaven, and blessed and broke the loaves, and gave them to his disciples to set before the people; and he divided the two fish among them all. And all ate and were filled; and they took up twelve baskets full of broken pieces and of the fish. Those who had eaten the loaves numbered five thousand men.

- The people of God had always looked forward to the coming of the Messiah or Savior—who would usher in an era of plenty with a feast for God's family. And this is what Jesus here provides.
- We are fortunate to be living in this golden age, when God—in Jesus—is ready to shower abundance upon us. We thank him for his gifts.

Wednesday January 6
Mark 6:45–52

Immediately he made his disciples get into the boat and go on ahead to the other side, to Bethsaida, while he dismissed the crowd. After saying farewell to them, he went up on the mountain to pray.

When evening came, the boat was out on the lake, and he was alone on the land. When he saw that they were straining at the oars against an adverse wind, he came towards them early in the morning, walking on the lake. He intended to pass them by. But when they saw him walking on the lake, they thought it was a ghost and cried out; for they all saw him and were terrified. But immediately he spoke to them and said, "Take heart, it is I; do not be afraid." Then he got into the boat with them and the wind ceased. And they were utterly astounded, for they did not understand about the loaves, but their hearts were hardened.

- Jesus is praying—speaking with his Father. Is he perhaps thinking about the best way to get through to people regarding what his coming is really about? Is he perhaps recalling the great demonstration that was his feeding of the five thousand? However in the minds of the people, that was seen only as the beginning of a political campaign. And the disciples were little better. So now he is about to intervene on a different level: he saves the disciples from the storm simply to show that he himself is strong enough for his cause to succeed without having to rely on the popular mood.

- Jesus is strong enough to carry out his plan for my life, without having to rely on people who "have influence."

Thursday January 7
Luke 4:14–22a

Then Jesus, filled with the power of the Spirit, returned to Galilee, and a report about him spread through all the surrounding country. He began to teach in their synagogues and was praised by everyone.

When he came to Nazareth, where he had been brought up, he went to the synagogue on the sabbath day, as was his custom. He stood up to read, and the scroll of the prophet Isaiah was given to him. He unrolled the scroll and found the place where it was written:

"The Spirit of the Lord is upon me,
because he has anointed me
to bring good news to the poor.
He has sent me to proclaim release to the captives
and recovery of sight to the blind,
to let the oppressed go free,
to proclaim the year of the Lord's favor."

And he rolled up the scroll, gave it back to the attendant, and sat down. The eyes of all in the synagogue were fixed on him. Then he began to say to them, "Today this scripture has been fulfilled in your hearing." All spoke well of him and were amazed at the gracious words that came from his mouth.

- God defends those whom nobody else defends. Jesus was looking at families that struggled to survive, at people dispossessed of their land, at starving children, at prostitutes and beggars. He never said they were good or virtuous; he said only that they were suffering unjustly. God takes their side! Do I?

- Lord, open my heart to the broken body of Christ revealed in my suffering brothers and sisters. Make me hunger for justice and work for peace. May your compassion be a constant burning fire in my life.

Friday January 8
Luke 5:12–16

Once, when he was in one of the cities, there was a man covered with leprosy. When he saw Jesus, he bowed with his face to the ground and begged him, "Lord, if you choose, you can make me clean." Then Jesus stretched out his hand, touched him, and said, "I do choose. Be made clean." Immediately the leprosy left him. And he ordered him to tell no one. "Go," he said, "and show yourself to the priest, and, as Moses commanded, make an offering for your cleansing, for a testimony to them." But now more than ever the word about Jesus spread abroad; many crowds would gather to hear him and to be cured of their diseases. But he would withdraw to deserted places and pray.

- An energy point for Jesus was his prayer, and we find that at key times of his life, he prayed: before calling the twelve; at the time of temptation and the struggle at his Passion and death; and very often as part of his daily life he went to quiet places to pray. His ministry needed the support and life-giving energy of his relationship with his Father. Our life of love needs the energy of prayer. Prayer enhances family life, friendship, and work or ministry for others. When we bring the love and commitments of our lives to prayer, something happens to bring us deeper into the source of our convictions and commitments to God and others.

Saturday January 9
John 3:22–30

After this Jesus and his disciples went into the Judean countryside, and he spent some time there with them and baptized. John also was baptizing at Aenon near Salim because water was abundant there; and people kept coming and were being baptized—John, of course, had not yet been thrown into prison.

Now a discussion about purification arose between John's disciples and a Jew. They came to John and said to him, "Rabbi, the one who was with you across the Jordan, to whom you testified, here he is baptizing, and all are going to him." John answered, "No one can receive anything except what has been given from heaven. You yourselves are my witnesses that I said, 'I am not the Messiah, but I have been sent ahead of him.' He who has the bride is the bridegroom. The friend of the bridegroom, who stands and hears him, rejoices greatly at the bridegroom's voice. For this reason my joy has been fulfilled. He must increase, but I must decrease."

- This reading marks a stage in the transition from the preaching and ministry of John the Baptist to that of Jesus.

- Some of John's disciples had joined Jesus at John's prompting, "Look, here is the Lamb of God!" (John 1:36). Those that remained with John now seem to be upset that "all" are going to Jesus. John, however, knows that his duty to arrange everything for the wedding of his friend Jesus to his bride, the people of Israel, has been fulfilled. With his mission accomplished, he can retire with joy. He would soon suffer martyrdom (Mark 6:14–29).

- In my life, is Jesus increasing, becoming more and more?

January 10–16, 2021

Something to think and pray about each day this week:

There is a favorite preacher's story that goes like this: a member of a certain parish, who previously had been attending Mass regularly, suddenly stopped going. After a few weeks the priest decided to visit him. It was a cold evening and the priest found the man alone at home, sitting before a blazing coal fire.

Guessing the reason for the priest's visit, the man welcomed him, led him to a big chair near the fireplace and waited. The pastor made himself comfortable but said nothing. In the heavy silence, he just sat and looked at the fire.

After a few minutes, the priest took the fire tongs, carefully picked a brightly burning coal from the fire and placed it to one side of the hearth, all on its own. Then he sat back in his chair, still silent. Both of them watched the coal. Gradually, the coal's flame diminished, there was a momentary glow and then its fire went. Soon it was cold and dead. The priest got up again, picked up the cold, dead coal and put it back in the middle of the fire. Immediately it began to glow once more with the light and warmth of the burning coals around it.

The moral was simple. A single lump of coal cannot burn on its own; it takes many lumps of coal to make a fire that does not go out. No Christian can burn for God for very long without the constant support of the rest of the Church.

—Paul O'Reilly, SJ, *Hope in All Things*

The Presence of God

"Come to me, all you who are weary and are carrying heavy burdens, and I will give you rest." Here I am, Lord. I come to seek your presence. I long for your healing power.

Freedom

God is not foreign to my freedom. The Spirit breathes life into my most intimate desires, gently nudging me toward all that is good. I ask for the grace to let myself be enfolded by the Spirit.

Consciousness

I remind myself that I am in the presence of the Lord. I will take refuge in his loving heart. He is my strength in times of weakness. He is my comforter in times of sorrow.

The Word

I take my time to read the word of God slowly a few times, allowing myself to dwell on anything that strikes me. (*Please turn to the Scripture on the following pages. Inspiration points are there, should you need them. When you are ready, return here to continue.*)

Conversation

Jesus, you always welcomed little children when you walked on this earth. Teach me to have a childlike trust in you. Teach me to live in the knowledge that you will never abandon me.

Conclusion

Glory be to the Father, and to the Son, and to the Holy Spirit,
As it was in the beginning, is now, and ever shall be,
World without end. Amen.

Sunday January 10
The Baptism of the Lord
Mark 1:7–11

He proclaimed, "the one who is more powerful than I is coming after me; I am not worthy to stoop down and untie the thong of his sandals. I have baptized you with water; but he will baptize you with the Holy Spirit."

In those days Jesus came from Nazareth of Galilee and was baptized by John in the Jordan. And just as he was coming up out of the water, he saw the heavens torn apart and the Spirit descending like a dove on him. And a voice came from heaven, "You are my Son, the Beloved; with you I am well pleased."

- Jesus' baptism gives us a window into a powerful religious moment. Jesus knows his identity. The imprint of the Spirit has sealed his life. Lord, remind me that I too bear your seal of approval. I am marked by your Spirit, called to participate in your mission as your beloved son or daughter.

- John knows his identity and his place in the unfolding plan of God. He is the instrument who points people beyond himself toward Jesus. Who are the "John the Baptist" figures in my own life?

Monday January 11
Mark 1:14–20

Now after John was arrested, Jesus came to Galilee, proclaiming the good news of God, and saying, 'the time is fulfilled, and the kingdom of God has come near; repent, and believe in the good news."

As Jesus passed along the Sea of Galilee, he saw Simon and his brother Andrew casting a net into the lake—for they were fishermen. And Jesus said to them, "Follow me and I will make you fish for people." And immediately they left their nets and followed him. As he went a little farther, he saw James son of Zebedee and his brother John, who were in their boat mending the nets. Immediately he called them; and they left their father Zebedee in the boat with the hired men, and followed him.

- Jesus begins his ministry by calling a group to follow him. He gives his disciples a mission: to catch people for the kingdom of God. He chooses as his companions very ordinary people, those with no wealth or position. What is striking is that they have no certainties, little knowledge of him, and yet they risk all for him.

- Lord, you continue to call ordinary people—like me. In all my human interactions may I bring your good news to others.

Tuesday January 12
Mark 1:21–28

They went to Capernaum; and when the sabbath came, he entered the synagogue and taught. They were astounded at his teaching, for he taught them as one having authority, and not as the scribes. Just then there was in their synagogue a man with an unclean spirit, and he cried out, "What have you to do with us, Jesus of Nazareth? Have you come to destroy us? I know who you are, the Holy One of God." But Jesus rebuked him, saying, "Be silent, and come out of him!" And the unclean spirit, throwing him into convulsions and crying with a loud voice, came out of him. They were all amazed, and they kept on asking one another, "What is this? A new teaching—with authority! He commands even the unclean spirits, and they obey him." At once his fame began to spread throughout the surrounding region of Galilee.

- Jesus taught with authority, and the authority came from his person. We see what it can mean to be fully human: compassionate, fearless, loving, with a passion for justice and awareness of what is in the human heart. It is by watching him and pondering his words and behavior that I too will learn what it is to be human.

Wednesday January 13
Mark 1:29–39

As soon as they left the synagogue, they entered the house of Simon and Andrew, with James and John. Now Simon's mother-in-law was in bed with a fever, and they told him about her at once. He came and took her by the hand and lifted her up. Then the fever left her, and she began to serve them.

That evening, at sunset, they brought to him all who were sick or possessed with demons. And the whole city was gathered around the door. And he cured many who were sick with various diseases, and cast out many demons; and he would not permit the demons to speak, because they knew him.

In the morning, while it was still very dark, he got up and went out to a deserted place, and there he prayed. And Simon and his companions hunted for him. When they found him, they said to him, "Everyone is searching for you." He answered, "Let us go on to the neighboring towns, so that I may proclaim the message there also; for that is what I came out to do." And he went throughout Galilee, proclaiming the message in their synagogues and casting out demons.

- The first recorded hours of Jesus' ministry are a whirlwind of activity. We are meant to catch on to the fact that when Jesus enters human lives, things change fast and for the better, for those who are open. A new creation is here! Everyone is meant to get in on it.

- What do I need from Jesus? Am I just a spectator in the scene, or am I fighting to get close to him? His presence brings wholeness; do I need that? People become more alive; do I need that? Simon's mother-in-law gets the energy to serve; do I need that? Let it not be true that "everyone is searching for him"—except me.

Thursday January 14
Mark 1:40–45

A leper came to him begging him, and kneeling he said to him, "If you choose, you can make me clean." Moved with pity, Jesus stretched out his hand and touched him, and said to him, "I do choose. Be made clean!" Immediately the leprosy left him, and he was made clean. After sternly warning him he sent him away at once, saying to him, "See that you say nothing to anyone; but go, show yourself to the priest, and offer for your cleansing what Moses commanded, as a testimony to them." But he went out and began to proclaim it freely, and to spread the word, so that Jesus could no longer go into a town openly, but stayed out in the country; and people came to him from every quarter.

- Again in this Gospel we find Jesus moved with pity. Leprosy was a living death: the sufferer was isolated from family and community and had to cry out "Unclean, unclean!" when anyone approached. Touching the leper made Jesus ritually unclean also. There are no lengths to which Jesus will not go to help this man. He touches him, speaks to him, and gives him freedom to be fully human again.

- I spend a few moments with the leper before his cure, and then meet him afterward. What might he say to me about faith in Jesus? About my pity for others in need? Whom do I touch?

Friday January 15
Mark 2:1–12

When he returned to Capernaum after some days, it was reported that he was at home. So many gathered around that there was no longer room for them, not even in front of the door; and he was speaking the word to them. Then some people came, bringing to him a paralyzed man, carried by four of them. And when they could not bring him to Jesus because of the crowd, they removed the roof above him; and after having dug through it, they let down the mat on which the paralytic lay. When Jesus saw their faith, he said to the paralytic, "Son, your sins are forgiven." Now some of the scribes were sitting there, questioning in their hearts, "Why does this fellow speak in this way? It is blasphemy! Who can forgive sins but God alone?" At once Jesus perceived in his spirit that they were discussing these questions among themselves; and he said to them, "Why do you raise such questions in your hearts? Which is easier, to say to the paralytic, 'Your sins are forgiven,' or to say, 'Stand up and take your mat and walk'? But so that you may know that the Son of Man has authority on earth to forgive sins"—he said to the paralytic—"I say to you, stand up, take your mat and go to your home." And he stood up, and immediately took the mat and went out before all of them; so that they were all amazed and glorified God, saying, "We have never seen anything like this!"

- What might have been a simple healing turns into a tense theological confrontation. It is Jesus who instigates this by forgiving the paralytic's sins (which he wasn't asked to do). The scribes who are present consider this to be blasphemy. Only God can forgive sins. Jesus then uses his power to heal the body as a sign that he has authority to heal the soul also. Mark is already signaling the charge for which the Jewish authorities will later seek the death penalty for Jesus: blasphemy.

- Note that the paralytic depends on his friends to bring him to Jesus. It is their faith that Jesus acknowledges and responds to. The paralytic himself never utters a word throughout.

Saturday January 16
Mark 2:13–17

Jesus went out again beside the lake; the whole crowd gathered around him, and he taught them. As he was walking along, he saw Levi son of Alphaeus sitting at the tax booth, and he said to him, "Follow me." And he got up and followed him.

And as he sat at dinner in Levi's house, many tax-collectors and sinners were also sitting with Jesus and his disciples—for there were many who followed him. When the scribes of the Pharisees saw that he was eating with sinners and tax-collectors, they said to his disciples, "Why does he eat with tax-collectors and sinners?" When Jesus heard this, he said to them, "Those who are well have no need of a physician, but those who are sick; I have come to call not the righteous but sinners."

- This whole story leads up to the arresting statement with which today's Gospel ends. Jesus has come, "not to call the righteous but sinners." Far from being a situation to be avoided, the company of "sinners" is precisely what Jesus needs to seek out. They are the most in need of his healing. This teaching applies today to the Church, to our parishes, workplaces, and homes. How inclusive is our attitude toward others? Would we have felt comfortable at Levi's dinner party?

January 17–23, 2021

Something to think and pray about each day this week:

For the Christian, prayer is about the relationship with God, and in particular with Jesus. It is your deepest self opening to God. It is to listen to him in his presence. To pray is to be loved by him and to speak to him in confidence. In prayer, all masks can be removed. God can come to you only when you are willing to be known as you are. One time you will be happy, the next you will be sad. It is possible that you are angry, with God or with a human being. You may also express anger in your prayer.

Prayer is not inborn. It is something you can learn. Luckily you don't have to invent it all by yourself. Christians have been praying for two thousand years. So a lot of know-how has been developed. If you are looking for what can help you pray, it is good to let yourself be inspired by that.

There are as many different ways of praying as there are people. Some people like to pray with texts, whether or not from the Bible. Others like to pray without words. You can pray alone or with others. In a quiet, secluded place or in the middle of the hustle and bustle of the city. Some like to pray for a long time. For others, the shorter the better. A good way of praying is a way that, at that moment, helps you live more connected with God. This can change over time. What helps you get to God today may not work as well tomorrow. This is not strange. That goes for most of a person's life.

—Nikolaas Sintobin SJ, *Did Jesus Really Exist?*
and 51 Other Questions

The Presence of God

"Be still, and know that I am God!" Lord, your words lead us to the calmness and greatness of your presence.

Freedom

Everything has the potential to draw forth from me a fuller love and life. Yet my desires are often fixed, caught on illusions of fulfillment. I ask that God, through my freedom, may orchestrate my desires in a vibrant, loving melody rich in harmony.

Consciousness

I exist in a web of relationships: links to nature, people, God.
I trace out these links,
giving thanks for the life that flows through them.
Some links are twisted or broken; I may feel regret, anger, disappointment.
I pray for the gift of acceptance and forgiveness.

The Word

I read the word of God slowly, a few times over, and I listen to what God is saying to me. (*Please turn to the Scripture on the following pages. Inspiration points are there, should you need them. When you are ready, return here to continue.*)

Conversation

Jesus, you speak to me through the words of the Gospels. May I respond to your call today. Teach me to recognize your hand at work in my daily living.

Conclusion

I thank God for these moments we have spent together and for any insights I have been given concerning the text.

Sunday January 17
Second Sunday in Ordinary Time
John 1:35–42

The next day John again was standing with two of his disciples, and as he watched Jesus walk by, he exclaimed, "Look, here is the Lamb of God!" The two disciples heard him say this, and they followed Jesus. When Jesus turned and saw them following, he said to them, "What are you looking for?" They said to him, "Rabbi" (which translated means Teacher), "where are you staying?" He said to them, "Come and see." They came and saw where he was staying, and they remained with him that day. It was about four o'clock in the afternoon. One of the two who heard John speak and followed him was Andrew, Simon Peter's brother. He first found his brother Simon and said to him, "We have found the Messiah" (which is translated Anointed). He brought Simon to Jesus, who looked at him and said, "You are Simon son of John. You are to be called Cephas" (which is translated Peter).

- What are the deepest longings of my restless heart? What am I aiming for and trying to get out of life? I have so often only half-heard the invitation of Jesus to come closer, to make my home with him. His person, his teaching, and his style disturb me to the core of my being.

- Jesus, you say to me, "You would not be looking for me unless you had already found me." Help me find you ever more deeply in my times of prayer.

Monday January 18
Mark 2:18–22

Now John's disciples and the Pharisees were fasting; and people came and said to him, "Why do John's disciples and the disciples of the Pharisees fast, but your disciples do not fast?" Jesus said to them, "The wedding-guests cannot fast while the bridegroom is with them, can they? As long as they have the bridegroom with them, they cannot fast. The days will come when the bridegroom is taken away from them, and then they will fast on that day.

"No one sews a piece of unshrunk cloth on an old cloak; otherwise, the patch pulls away from it, the new from the old, and a worse tear is made. And no one puts new wine into old wineskins; otherwise, the wine will burst the skins, and the wine is lost, and so are the skins; but one puts new wine into fresh wineskins."

- A religious tradition was to fast when something was missing—to remind us that we are waiting for God in life, to ask for something, or to be rescued in bad times. Here Jesus is proclaiming that the one they were waiting for has come. Rejoicing rather than a penitential fast would be the appropriate response. Sometime in the future will be a time for fasting; the listeners are left wondering what this might be. We know ourselves that life is a rhythm of death and resurrection, with its times for rejoicing and times of sadness. The bridegroom has come: Jesus the Son of God. This is for our safety in bad times to come.

- The life of religious people is always open to scrutiny and examination from outside. I pray that my way of living communicates gospel values. I take care not to come to uncharitable judgments about the way others live.

- God calls me to growth and new life. I pray that I may receive all the goodness God has to offer, being made anew in the image of God.

Tuesday January 19
Mark 2:23–28

One sabbath he was going through the cornfields; and as they made their way his disciples began to pluck heads of grain. The Pharisees said to him, "Look, why are they doing what is not lawful on the sabbath?" And he said to them, "Have you never read what David did when he and his companions were hungry and in need of food? He entered the house of God, when Abiathar was high priest, and ate the bread of the Presence, which it is not lawful for any but the priests to eat, and he gave some to his companions." Then he said to them, "The sabbath was made for humankind, and not humankind for the sabbath; so the Son of Man is lord even of the sabbath."

- Lord, when human need was crying out to you, the law took second place. It seems so obvious that the sabbath, and law, are made for humankind, not vice versa. But it took courage as well as clarity of mind to state the obvious.

Wednesday January 20
Mark 3:1–6

Again he entered the synagogue, and a man was there who had a withered hand. They watched him to see whether he would cure him on the sabbath, so that they might accuse him. And he said to the man who had the withered hand, "Come forward." Then he said to them, "Is it lawful to do good or to do harm on the sabbath, to save life or to kill?" But they were silent. He looked around at them with anger; he was grieved at their hardness of heart and said to the man, "Stretch out your hand." He stretched it out, and his hand was restored. The Pharisees went out and immediately conspired with the Herodians against him, how to destroy him.

• Lord, when you celebrated the Sabbath by healing, the Pharisees responded by plotting to kill you. You were stressing that God does not want to make our lives more difficult, and does not impose arbitrary rules on us.

• The great commandment is the law of love. Would people who know me be able to say that I follow the law of love?

Thursday January 21
Mark 3:7–12

Jesus departed with his disciples to the lake, and a great multitude from Galilee followed him; hearing all that he was doing, they came to him in great numbers from Judea, Jerusalem, Idumea, beyond the Jordan, and the region around Tyre and Sidon. He told his disciples to have a boat ready for him because of the crowd, so that they would not crush him; for he had cured many, so that all who had diseases pressed upon him to touch him. Whenever the unclean spirits saw him, they fell down before him and shouted, "You are the Son of God!" But he sternly ordered them not to make him known.

• The magnetism of Jesus is revealed here. Ordinary unimportant people offer him an enthusiastic reception. They approach him with one desire: to touch him and be healed. Loving energy flows out from Jesus.

• Am I easy about joining this enthusiastic crowd of poor people? Can I admit that I too need the healing touch of the Son of God? Do I radiate healing to others?

Friday January 22
Mark 3:13–19

He went up the mountain and called to him those whom he wanted, and they came to him. And he appointed twelve, whom he also named apostles, to be with him, and to be sent out to proclaim the message, and to have authority to cast out demons. So he appointed the twelve: Simon (to whom he gave the name Peter); James son of Zebedee and John the brother of James (to whom he gave the name Boanerges, that is, Sons of Thunder); and Andrew, and Philip, and Bartholomew, and Matthew, and Thomas, and James son of Alphaeus, and Thaddaeus, and Simon the Cananaean, and Judas Iscariot, who betrayed him.

Then he went home.

- I may think I have chosen Jesus, but in fact he has chosen me. Like the apostles, I am chosen to be part of his mission. Imagine the apostles, having been chosen, looking at one another, and James and John turning to Andrew and asking, "Who's this Thaddeus guy?" They could well have been uneasy at rubbing shoulders with a reformed tax collector such as Matthew, and a fanatical nationalist such as Simon.

- The Lord's choice of followers may surprise me, and at times I may have difficulties with them, but they are chosen, with their faults, just as I am.

Saturday January 23
Mark 3:20–21

And the crowd came together again, so that they could not even eat. When his family heard it, they went out to restrain him, for people were saying, "He has gone out of his mind."

- The intensity or passion with which Jesus lived and served people shocked his family and led them to say, "He has gone out of his mind."

- You might like to spend time in prayer with Jesus, reflecting about how passionate he is about your life, about appreciating who you are for him, and about realizing his dream for you. Talk to him about this and tell him how it excites you, but also how it alarms you, as it did his own family.

The Third Week in Ordinary Time
January 24–30, 2021

Something to think and pray about each day this week:

Creation manifests the divine. The divine can be encountered in sub-atomic particles, in the world of Nature, and in deep space (Romans 1:19–20; *Laudato Si'*, 18). As we explore our world we find that the divine is inventive, dynamic, pulsating, unpredictable. A great fountain of love, beauty, and energy is endlessly being poured out on vast galaxies and on tiny fairy flies and on ourselves.

Early Christian theologians struggled to offer an image of the Author of Creation. Rather than picturing the three divine Persons seated on thrones—as were the emperors and their consorts of that time—they chose the image of dance to suggest a glorious procession of mutual love, a whirling and joyous ecstasy. We may imagine heaven, not as an endless choir practice on a wet Sunday afternoon, but as the unrestricted and all-inclusive joy of dancing in a transfigured universe. Even an initial awareness of the infinite imagination and power of God who plays in creation shows that ours is already a dancing universe.

We are part of the unfathomable weave of the universe, immersed in its deep mystery. Its dance has already begun: it has always been in process. Each of us has a role in it. Jesus and his Father are working (John 4:34) for the good of all creation and we can tune in to their signals and do likewise. Thomas Merton says that every moment and every event in every person's life plants seeds of spiritual vitality in their hearts. This is the divine at work on Earth: this is grace, and grace is everywhere. All is sacred, and so are we. We must not desecrate our Common Home. We belong to the great Creation Story, to a whole that is infinitely greater than ourselves. We are called even now to share with all of creation "in the freedom of the children of God" (Romans 8:21).

So let's put on our dancing shoes and learn the steps of the cosmic dance!

—Brian Grogan SJ, *Creation Walk: The Amazing Story of a Small Blue Planet*

The Presence of God
What is present to me is what has a hold on my becoming.
I reflect on the presence of God always there in love,
amidst the many things that have a hold on me.
I pause and pray that I may let God
affect my becoming in this precise moment.

Freedom
By God's grace I was born to live in freedom. Free to enjoy the pleasures
he created for me. Dear Lord, grant that I may live as you intended, with
complete confidence in your loving care.

Consciousness
To be conscious about something is to be aware of it.
Dear Lord, help me remember that you gave me life.
Thank you for the gift of life.

The Word
God speaks to each of us individually. I listen attentively to hear what he
is saying to me. Read the text a few times, then listen. (*Please turn to the
Scripture on the following pages. Inspiration points are there, should you need
them. When you are ready, return here to continue.*)

Conversation
I begin to talk with Jesus about the Scripture I have just read. What part
of it strikes a chord in me? Perhaps the words of a friend—or some story
I have heard recently—will rise to the surface in my consciousness. If so,
does the story throw light on what the Scripture passage may be saying
to me?

Conclusion
Glory be to the Father, and to the Son, and to the Holy Spirit,
As it was in the beginning, is now and ever shall be,
World without end. Amen.

Sunday January 24
Third Sunday in Ordinary Time
Mark 1:14–20

Now after John was arrested, Jesus came to Galilee, proclaiming the good news of God, and saying, "The time is fulfilled, and the kingdom of God has come near; repent, and believe in the good news."

As Jesus passed along the Sea of Galilee, he saw Simon and his brother Andrew casting a net into the lake—for they were fishermen. And Jesus said to them, "Follow me and I will make you fish for people." And immediately they left their nets and followed him. As he went a little farther, he saw James son of Zebedee and his brother John, who were in their boat mending the nets. Immediately he called them; and they left their father Zebedee in the boat with the hired men, and followed him.

- Two things make it difficult to hear how Jesus invites each of us to be with him as his companions and to share in his work. One is our limitations and consequent feeling of insignificance. The second is how exalted Jesus is as God, even though the same Jesus walked our earth.

- If you wish to pray with this reality, be with Jesus in a quiet place and let him call you by name. Let him first call you to be with him as his friend and then to share in his work.

Monday January 25
The Conversion of St. Paul, Apostle
Mark 16:15–18

And he said to them, "Go into all the world and proclaim the good news to the whole creation. The one who believes and is baptized will be saved; but the one who does not believe will be condemned. And these signs will accompany those who believe: by using my name they will cast out demons; they will speak in new tongues; they will pick up snakes in their hands, and if they drink any deadly thing, it will not hurt them; they will lay their hands on the sick, and they will recover."

- At one point, Jesus said that it was to the lost sheep of the house of Israel (of the Jewish people) that he had been sent. But in this scene, as he leaves this earth and ascends into heaven, he tells his followers to set no bounds to their preaching; they are to take on the whole pagan world.

- St. Paul was to be the great example of carrying out Jesus' commission. We celebrate today this special call, which followed his conversion to the cause of Christ. From now on, nobody is to be considered out of bounds when it comes to spreading Jesus' message.

Tuesday January 26
Mark 3:31–35

Then his mother and his brothers came; and standing outside, they sent to him and called him. A crowd was sitting around him; and they said to him, "Your mother and your brothers and sisters are outside, asking for you." And he replied, "Who are my mother and my brothers?" And looking at those who sat around him, he said, "Here are my mother and my brothers! Whoever does the will of God is my brother and sister and mother."

- In this Gospel story we have a revelation of what intimacy means for Jesus. The crowd, according to the norms of the time, thought of family as the chief place where you would experience it, but Jesus finds it primarily in the intimacy or union that God wants with us.

- In prayer, try to engage Jesus in conversation about the way he wants to be intimate with you. Spend time with his words, "I no longer call you servants, because a servant does not know his master's business. Instead, I have called you friends, for everything that I learned from my Father I have made known to you" (John 15:15).

Wednesday January 27
Mark 4:1–20

Again he began to teach beside the lake. Such a very large crowd gathered around him that he got into a boat on the lake and sat there, while the whole crowd was beside the lake on the land. He began to teach them many things in parables, and in his teaching he said to them: "Listen! A sower went out to sow. And as he sowed, some seed fell on the path, and the birds came and ate it up. Other seed fell on rocky ground, where it did not have much soil, and it sprang up quickly, since it had no depth of soil. And when the sun rose, it was scorched; and since it had no root, it withered away. Other seed fell among thorns, and the thorns grew up and choked it, and it yielded no grain. Other seed fell into good soil and brought forth grain, growing up and increasing and yielding thirty and sixty and a hundredfold." And he said, "Let anyone with ears to hear listen!"

When he was alone, those who were around him along with the twelve asked him about the parables. And he said to them, "To you has been given the secret of the kingdom of God, but for those outside, everything comes in parables; in order that 'they may indeed look, but not perceive, and may indeed listen, but not understand; so that they may not turn again and be forgiven.'"

And he said to them, "Do you not understand this parable? Then how will you understand all the parables? The sower sows the word. These are the ones on the path where the word is sown: when they hear, Satan immediately comes and takes away the word that is sown in them. And these are the ones sown on rocky ground: when they hear the word, they immediately receive it with joy. But they have no root, and endure only for a while; then, when trouble or persecution arises on account of the word, immediately they fall away. And others are those sown among the thorns: these are the ones who hear the word, but the cares of the world, and the lure of wealth, and the desire for other things come in and choke the word, and it yields nothing. And these are the ones sown on the good soil: they hear the word and accept it and bear fruit, thirty and sixty and a hundredfold."

- If your word is like a seed, Lord, then it is an organism, with a life of its own. My part is to receive it, give it roots and depth so that it survives hardships, and protect it from the thorns of multiple cares and desires. If I allow your word some space in my life, there is no limit to the fruit it may bear.

Thursday January 28
Mark 4:21–25

He said to them, "Is a lamp brought in to be put under the bushel basket, or under the bed, and not on the lampstand? For there is nothing hidden, except to be disclosed; nor is anything secret, except to come to light. Let anyone with ears to hear listen!" And he said to them, "Pay attention to what you hear; the measure you give will be the measure you get, and still more will be given you. For to those who have, more will be given; and from those who have nothing, even what they have will be taken away."

- More sayings of Jesus, with a combination of plain common sense and obscurity. We understand first that Jesus wants his close followers to let the light of his teaching shine out. Others may choose to remain in the dark, indifferent or hostile.

- The second half of the passage is obscure. It seems to mean that just as the wealthy keep accumulating riches and the poor are consistently deprived, so those with spiritual insight will be further enlightened, while those without it will only fall into worse ignorance.

- Do I allow the light of Christ to shine out before others?

Friday January 29
Mark 4:26–34

He also said, "The kingdom of God is as if someone would scatter seed on the ground, and would sleep and rise night and day, and the seed would sprout and grow, he does not know how. The earth produces of itself, first the stalk, then the head, then the full grain in the head. But when the grain is ripe, at once he goes in with his sickle, because the harvest has come."

He also said, "With what can we compare the kingdom of God, or what parable will we use for it? It is like a mustard seed, which, when sown upon the ground, is the smallest of all the seeds on earth; yet when it is sown it grows up and becomes the greatest of all shrubs, and puts forth large branches, so that the birds of the air can make nests in its shade."

With many such parables he spoke the word to them, as they were able to hear it; he did not speak to them except in parables, but he explained everything in private to his disciples.

- Lord, your images of the kingdom are alive and organic. It has its own pattern of growth, a tiny plant that grows into a massive tree with room for every creature. Let me never imagine that I am the architect or builder of your kingdom. Enough for me to be patient, a seed growing slowly, animated by your Spirit.

- Simple things we say or do can have a big influence. One person can affect many, even without knowing it. The kingdom of God grows of its own impetus in the world, and nobody can stop it, like good seed growing underground. God is the God of here, there, and everywhere. Seeds may sprout anywhere in the field, and the kingdom can find its way into the lives of individuals and communities in ways that may surprise us. The mustard seed becomes a tree for all; the kingdom of God is for every man, woman, and child. Have you ever brought something of the kingdom of God—of love and peace, prayer and faith, justice and hope—when you didn't recognize it? Let that fill your mind and heart with gratitude as you pray.

Saturday January 30
Mark 4:35–41

On that day, when evening had come, he said to them, "Let us go across to the other side." And leaving the crowd behind, they took him with them in the boat, just as he was. Other boats were with him. A great gale arose, and the waves beat into the boat, so that the boat was already being swamped. But he was in the stern, asleep on the cushion; and they woke him up and said to him, "Teacher, do you not care that we are perishing?" He woke up and rebuked the wind, and said to the sea, "Peace! Be still!" Then the wind ceased, and there was a dead calm. He said to them, "Why are you afraid? Have you still no faith?" And they were filled with great awe and said to one another, "Who then is this, that even the wind and the sea obey him?"

- Take your place in Jesus' boat and allow yourself to be drawn into the whole experience. Let the drama unfold. How do you feel when the waves pour into the boat, threatening to sink her? Do you cry out to Jesus and find him unresponsive because he is asleep? After a while he wakes and calms the wind and the sea; and chides the disciples for their lack of faith. Do you share their awe as they realize that they are in the presence of some extraordinary power? Are you as faithless as they are when storms arise in your life and Jesus seems distant and unconcerned?

January 31—February 6, 2021

Something to think and pray about each day this week:

I used to think my deepest desires were as remote as the stars, and this perception contributed to depressive symptoms, i.e., a sense of darkness and gloom, which are common in the general public. Now, by looking at my concrete realities, I'm realizing that what I really want is actually within my reach. I am learning that I need to place my feet firmly on the ground in order to wish, long for, and yearn.

"The desires and longings which we have," said Bernard Lonergan, "for what is beautiful, for what makes sense, for what is true, for what has value, and for what has ultimate value are at the heart of what it means to be human."

In this effort to be more human, it helps me to think about a time in my life when I lacked true desire. In 2017, I completed a six-month internship in the civil service. In my career, I felt dry, unmotivated, lacking in joy.

So, I let myself be guided by my inner compass, which has slowly pointed in the right direction. Now, I yearn to promote the psychological and spiritual needs of the general public, and one way I do this is through keeping a blog on mental health, which I find sustaining. I am close to the heart of my deepest desires without exploding, and what a beautiful balanced thing that is.

It is often tempting to make up our own mind on ordinary considerations in our family. If we want to be self-reliant, we may hang tight, be tough, and carry on. While a certain resolve may be admirable, we do not become part of the bigger picture of building up the kingdom of God if we willfully push through life with our blinkers on. Choosing to follow a common mission of goodness, beauty, truth, intelligibility, and love surely satisfies our deepest desires.

—Gavin Thomas Murphy, *Bursting Out in Praise:*
Spirituality and Mental Health

The Presence of God
What is present to me is what has a hold on my becoming.
I reflect on the presence of God always there in love,
amidst the many things that have a hold on me.
I pause and pray that I may let God
affect my becoming in this precise moment.

Freedom
By God's grace I was born to live in freedom. Free to enjoy the pleasures
he created for me. Dear Lord, grant that I may live as you intended, with
complete confidence in your loving care.

Consciousness
To be conscious about something is to be aware of it.
Dear Lord, help me remember that you gave me life.
Thank you for the gift of life.

The Word
God speaks to each of us individually. I listen attentively to hear what he
is saying to me. Read the text a few times, then listen. (*Please turn to the
Scripture on the following pages. Inspiration points are there, should you need
them. When you are ready, return here to continue.*)

Conversation
I begin to talk with Jesus about the Scripture I have just read. What part
of it strikes a chord in me? Perhaps the words of a friend—or some story
I have heard recently—will rise to the surface in my consciousness. If so,
does the story throw light on what the Scripture passage may be saying
to me?

Conclusion
Glory be to the Father, and to the Son, and to the Holy Spirit,
As it was in the beginning, is now and ever shall be,
World without end. Amen.

Sunday January 31
Fourth Sunday in Ordinary Time
Mark 1:21–28

They went to Capernaum; and when the sabbath came, he entered the synagogue and taught. They were astounded at his teaching, for he taught them as one having authority, and not as the scribes. Just then there was in their synagogue a man with an unclean spirit, and he cried out, "What have you to do with us, Jesus of Nazareth? Have you come to destroy us? I know who you are, the Holy One of God." But Jesus rebuked him, saying, "Be silent, and come out of him!" And the unclean spirit, throwing him into convulsions and crying with a loud voice, came out of him. They were all amazed, and they kept on asking one another, "What is this? A new teaching—with authority! He commands even the unclean spirits, and they obey him." At once his fame began to spread throughout the surrounding region of Galilee.

- At some point in their lives, people may feel themselves being brought to their knees by urges and forces that are too strong for them. They need to turn to a power above and beyond themselves.

- Jesus, with that power behind him, comes close to each of us—in his teaching, in the Christian community, in the Church.

Monday February 1
Mark 5:1–20

They came to the other side of the lake, to the country of the Gerasenes. And when he had stepped out of the boat, immediately a man out of the tombs with an unclean spirit met him. He lived among the tombs; and no one could restrain him any more, even with a chain; for he had often been restrained with shackles and chains, but the chains he wrenched apart, and the shackles he broke in pieces; and no one had the strength to subdue him. Night and day among the tombs and on the mountains he was always howling and bruising himself with stones. When he saw Jesus from a distance, he ran and bowed down before him; and he shouted at the top of his voice, "What have you to do with me, Jesus, Son of the Most High God? I adjure you by God, do not torment me." For he had said to him, "Come out of the man, you unclean spirit!" Then Jesus asked him, "What is your name?" He replied, "My name is Legion; for we are many." He begged him earnestly not to send them out of the country. Now there on the hillside a great herd of swine was feeding; and the unclean spirits begged him, "Send us into the swine; let us enter them." So he gave them permission. And the unclean spirits came out and entered the swine; and the herd, numbering about two thousand, rushed down the steep bank into the lake, and were drowned in the lake.

The swineherds ran off and told it in the city and in the country. Then people came to see what it was that had happened. They came to Jesus and saw the demoniac sitting there, clothed and in his right mind, the very man who had had the legion; and they were afraid. Those who had seen what had happened to the demoniac and to the swine reported it. Then they began to beg Jesus to leave their neighborhood. As he was getting into the boat, the man who had been possessed by demons begged him that he might be with him. But Jesus refused, and said to him, "Go home to your friends, and tell them how much the Lord has done for you, and what mercy he has shown you." And he went away and began to proclaim in the Decapolis how much Jesus had done for him; and everyone was amazed.

- Do you ever experience yourself being tormented by guilt from the past, by inability to do what you wish to do, or by fear of the future? Do you feel sometimes that you are living in a tomb, in a lifeless situation? If so, you can identify with the unfortunate demoniac. You might feel that Jesus is at a distance, but run to him and beg him to liberate you. He wants you to be free and will heal you. Then you too can "go home to your friends and tell them how much the Lord has done for you."

Tuesday February 2
The Presentation of the Lord
Luke 2:22–40

When the time came for their purification according to the law of Moses, they brought him up to Jerusalem to present him to the Lord (as it is written in the law of the Lord, "Every firstborn male shall be designated as holy to the Lord"), and they offered a sacrifice according to what is stated in the law of the Lord, "a pair of turtle-doves or two young pigeons."

Now there was a man in Jerusalem whose name was Simeon; this man was righteous and devout, looking forward to the consolation of Israel, and the Holy Spirit rested on him. It had been revealed to him by the

Holy Spirit that he would not see death before he had seen the Lord's Messiah. Guided by the Spirit, Simeon came into the temple; and when the parents brought in the child Jesus, to do for him what was customary under the law, Simeon took him in his arms and praised God, saying,

> "Master, now you are dismissing your servant in peace,
> according to your word;
> for my eyes have seen your salvation,
> which you have prepared in the presence of all peoples,
> a light for revelation to the Gentiles
> and for glory to your people Israel."

And the child's father and mother were amazed at what was being said about him. Then Simeon blessed them and said to his mother Mary, "This child is destined for the falling and the rising of many in Israel, and to be a sign that will be opposed so that the inner thoughts of many will be revealed—and a sword will pierce your own soul too."

There was also a prophet, Anna the daughter of Phanuel, of the tribe of Asher. She was of a great age, having lived with her husband for seven years after her marriage, then as a widow to the age of eighty-four. She never left the temple but worshiped there with fasting and prayer night and day. At that moment she came, and began to praise God and to speak about the child to all who were looking for the redemption of Jerusalem.

When they had finished everything required by the law of the Lord, they returned to Galilee, to their own town of Nazareth. The child grew and became strong, filled with wisdom; and the favor of God was upon him.

- Jesus was destined to be sign that would be opposed. We are his followers and can also expect opposition. Let us try to welcome it and grow through it.

- Mary was told that a sword would pierce her heart. She welcomed it and accepted it. Let us try to welcome the pain that comes our way, as from God, and accept it willingly.

Wednesday February 3
Mark 6:1–6

He left that place and came to his home town, and his disciples followed him. On the sabbath he began to teach in the synagogue, and many who heard him were astounded. They said, "Where did this man get all this? What is this wisdom that has been given to him? What deeds of power are being done by his hands! Is not this the carpenter, the son of Mary and brother of James and Joses and Judas and Simon, and are not his sisters here with us?" And they took offense at him. Then Jesus said to them, "Prophets are not without honor, except in their home town, and among their own kin, and in their own house." And he could do no deed of power there, except that he laid his hands on a few sick people and cured them. And he was amazed at their unbelief.

Then he went about among the villages teaching.

- Even after all the miracles of healing that Jesus worked, he still was not accepted in his own town. As he taught in the synagogue, there his hearers were amazed that this ordinary man whom they knew as the carpenter could attain such wisdom, and they rejected him.

- Lord, I pray that I may recognize your presence in the ordinary encounters of my day and notice the ways through which you desire to nourish me and give me life, because you are present in all things.

Thursday February 4
Mark 6:7–13

He called the twelve and began to send them out two by two, and gave them authority over the unclean spirits. He ordered them to take nothing for their journey except a staff; no bread, no bag, no money in their belts; but to wear sandals and not to put on two tunics. He said to them, "Wherever you enter a house, stay there until you leave the place. If any place will not welcome you and they refuse to hear you, as you leave, shake off the dust that is on your feet as a testimony against them." So they went out and proclaimed that all should repent. They cast out many demons, and anointed with oil many who were sick and cured them.

- Jesus calls the apostles and sends them on a mission to announce the message of repentance, cure the sick, and cast out demons. Notice how he sends them out in pairs, instructing them to trust in the providence by taking nothing for their journey. They were to be dependent entirely on God and the presence of God in one another. Their goal was to go from house to house bringing the Good News.

- Lord, I pray that, strengthened by the power of the Holy Spirit, I may radiate the light of your love to those I encounter in my daily life. Help me to have a deeper understanding of the needs of others, and give me the courage to witness to the joy of my faith.

Friday February 5
Mark 6:14–29

King Herod heard of it, for Jesus' name had become known. Some were saying, "John the baptizer has been raised from the dead; and for this reason these powers are at work in him." But others said, "It is Elijah." And others said, "It is a prophet, like one of the prophets of old." But when Herod heard of it, he said, "John, whom I beheaded, has been raised."

For Herod himself had sent men who arrested John, bound him, and put him in prison on account of Herodias, his brother Philip's wife, because Herod had married her. For John had been telling Herod, "It is not lawful for you to have your brother's wife." And Herodias had a grudge against him, and wanted to kill him. But she could not, for Herod feared John, knowing that he was a righteous and holy man, and he protected him. When he heard him, he was greatly perplexed; and yet he liked to listen to him. But an opportunity came when Herod on his birthday gave a banquet for his courtiers and officers and for the leaders of Galilee. When the daughter of Herodias came in and danced, she pleased Herod and his guests; and the king said to the girl, "Ask me for whatever you wish, and I will give it." And he solemnly swore to her, "Whatever you ask me, I will give you, even half of my kingdom." She went out and said to her mother, "What should I ask for?" She replied, "The head of John the baptizer." Immediately she rushed back to the king and requested, "I want you to give me at once the head of John the Baptist on a platter." The king was deeply grieved; yet out of regard for his oaths and for the guests, he did not want to refuse her. Immediately the king sent a soldier of the guard with orders to bring John's head. He went and beheaded him in the prison, brought his head on a platter, and gave it to the girl. Then the girl gave it to her mother. When his disciples heard about it, they came and took his body, and laid it in a tomb.

- This is one of the most horrific scenes in the Gospels. St. Mark is trying to prepare us weak disciples for the passion of Jesus. We are to become strong in face of the world's evil. Whose head is being cut off today? The heads of the voiceless, the dispossessed, the victims of war, the aborted, prisoners of conscience?

- St. Ignatius asks me to consider what I can do about such evil. If I were the soldier in the story, would I simply do what I am told, or would I refuse and end up being beheaded myself? I ask John the Baptist for the courage to protest against injustices.

Saturday February 6
Mark 6:30–34

The apostles gathered around Jesus, and told him all that they had done and taught. He said to them, "Come away to a deserted place all by your-selves and rest a while." For many were coming and going, and they had no leisure even to eat. And they went away in the boat to a deserted place by themselves. Now many saw them going and recognized them, and they hurried there on foot from all the towns and arrived ahead of them. As he went ashore, he saw a great crowd; and he had compassion for them, because they were like sheep without a shepherd; and he began to teach them many things.

- Lord, there are times when I want to get away from the crowds, when I feel oppressed by company. There are other times when I just wish that somebody knew that I exist; I can have too much of aloneness. If I can reach you in prayer, and know that you are more central to me than my own thoughts, I feel at peace, as the apostles must have felt.

The Fifth Week in Ordinary Time
February 7–13, 2021

Something to think and pray about each day this week:

At the Our Father section of the Mass one rainy Sunday, I could see a rush of people coming into the porch and into the church. I thought they might be slipping in to offer a prayer but then realized it was to shelter from a downpour. They sheltered and moved on when the shower was over. Mass continued.

It suddenly struck me—a good distraction—that we have those who come into the church just for shelter for a few minutes; they are the ones who come to find some peace, silence, and often consolation at bad times. People who have sporadic attendance at Mass come often to pray or to just sit there to get something of what the Lord offers when he says, "Come to me, all who labor and are overburdened and I will give you rest." They may come to pray at the tomb of a holy person or a favorite shrine or to light a candle.

The funeral is one of these shelter occasions also. Why do many who hardly come near a church at any other time want the service of the church at that time, either for themselves or their family? We know in the heart also that there is something in the ritual, in the community, and in the prayer that shelters us from the worst despair of life, that there is no hope.

In our churches there are many people at worship and at prayer. Many people come and return, many are regular. Some come and go, others stay and take part. All are welcome.

—Donal Neary, SJ, *The Sacred Heart Messenger*

The Presence of God
"Be still, and know that I am God!" Lord, your words lead us to the calmness and greatness of your presence.

Freedom
"In these days, God taught me as a schoolteacher teaches a pupil" (St. Ignatius). I remind myself that there are things God has to teach me yet, and I ask for the grace to hear them and let them change me.

Consciousness
How am I really feeling? Lighthearted? Heavyhearted? I may be very much at peace, happy to be here. Equally, I may be frustrated, worried, or angry. I acknowledge how I really am. It is the real me whom the Lord loves.

The Word
God speaks to each of us individually. I listen attentively to hear what he is saying to me. Read the text a few times, then listen. (*Please turn to the Scripture on the following pages. Inspiration points are there, should you need them. When you are ready, return here to continue.*)

Conversation
Do I notice myself reacting as I pray with the word of God? Do I feel challenged, comforted, angry? Imagining Jesus sitting or standing by me, I speak out my feelings, as one trusted friend to another.

Conclusion
I thank God for these moments we have spent together and for any insights I have been given concerning the text.

Sunday February 7
Fifth Sunday in Ordinary Time
Mark 1:29–39

As soon as they left the synagogue, they entered the house of Simon and Andrew, with James and John. Now Simon's mother-in-law was in bed with a fever, and they told him about her at once. He came and took her by the hand and lifted her up. Then the fever left her, and she began to serve them.

That evening, at sunset, they brought to him all who were sick or possessed with demons. And the whole city was gathered around the door. And he cured many who were sick with various diseases, and cast out many demons; and he would not permit the demons to speak, because they knew him.

In the morning, while it was still very dark, he got up and went out to a deserted place, and there he prayed. And Simon and his companions hunted for him. When they found him, they said to him, "Everyone is searching for you." He answered, "Let us go on to the neighboring towns, so that I may proclaim the message there also; for that is what I came out to do." And he went throughout Galilee, proclaiming the message in their synagogues and casting out demons.

- There is a moment of truth in the cure of Simon's mother-in-law. When we are cured from a sickness by whatever means, it is tempting to sit back and accept people's good wishes and congratulations. This sick woman felt her temperature drop and energy return to her limbs "and she began to serve them."

- Lord, thank you for my health, not something to luxuriate in but the means by which I can serve others.

Monday February 8
Mark 6:53–56

When they had crossed over, they came to land at Gennesaret and moored the boat. When they got out of the boat, people at once recognized him, and rushed about that whole region and began to bring the sick on mats to wherever they heard he was. And wherever he went, into villages or cities or farms, they laid the sick in the market-places, and begged him that they might touch even the fringe of his cloak; and all who touched it were healed.

- Do I catch the excitement of the people as Jesus, always so approachable, steps ashore from the boat?
- I bring my friends in need to him in prayer.
- "Ask and you shall receive," he says. He is open to persuasion, even enjoys being pestered; but I must remember to thank him.

Tuesday February 9
Mark 7:1–13

Now when the Pharisees and some of the scribes who had come from Jerusalem gathered around him, they noticed that some of his disciples were eating with defiled hands, that is, without washing them. (For the Pharisees, and all the Jews, do not eat unless they thoroughly wash their hands, thus observing the tradition of the elders; and they do not eat anything from the market unless they wash it; and there are also many other traditions that they observe, the washing of cups, pots, and bronze kettles.) So the Pharisees and the scribes asked him, "Why do your disciples not live according to the tradition of the elders, but eat with defiled hands?" He said to them, "Isaiah prophesied rightly about you hypocrites, as it is written,

'This people honors me with their lips,
but their hearts are far from me;
in vain do they worship me,
teaching human precepts as doctrines.'

You abandon the commandment of God and hold to human tradition."

Then he said to them, "You have a fine way of rejecting the commandment of God in order to keep your tradition! For Moses said, 'Honor your father and your mother'; and, 'Whoever speaks evil of father or mother must surely die.' But you say that if anyone tells father or mother, 'Whatever support you might have had from me is Corban' (that is, an offering to God)—then you no longer permit doing anything for a father or mother, thus making void the word of God through your tradition that you have handed on. And you do many things like this."

- Lord, don't let me laugh at the Pharisees and their silly customs. Let me look to myself: Do I make my choices the way the advertisers want me to? Do I let the spin-doctors decide what I think? Am I predictable, caught in a rut, dull of soul?

- The kingdom of God is always unexpected; it catches me by surprise and demands responses from me that jolt me out of my mediocrity. Its values are countercultural. There the poor come first; despised people are important; wealth is for sharing; hatred is out; forgiveness is in; love is all that matters in the end. Wow!

Wednesday February 10
Mark 7:14–23

Then he called the crowd again and said to them, "Listen to me, all of you, and understand: there is nothing outside a person that by going in can defile, but the things that come out are what defile."

When he had left the crowd and entered the house, his disciples asked him about the parable. He said to them, "Then do you also fail to understand? Do you not see that whatever goes into a person from outside cannot defile, since it enters, not the heart but the stomach, and goes out into the sewer?" (Thus he declared all foods clean.) And he said, "It is what comes out of a person that defiles. For it is from within, from the human heart, that evil intentions come: fornication, theft, murder, adultery, avarice, wickedness, deceit, licentiousness, envy, slander, pride, folly. All these evil things come from within, and they defile a person."

- Jewish tradition held that some foods were clean and others unclean. Jesus says that all foods are clean. What matters, he says, is the heart! By "the heart" he meant what is inside us: moods, thoughts, plans, attitudes, choices, conscience, knowledge, and love. All these must be kept clean.

- Lord, you see into my heart. A pure heart create in me. Take away my heart of stone, and give me a heart of flesh, so that I may become as compassionate as you are.

Thursday February 11
Mark 7:24–30

From there he set out and went away to the region of Tyre. He entered a house and did not want anyone to know he was there. Yet he could not escape notice, but a woman whose little daughter had an unclean spirit immediately heard about him, and she came and bowed down at his feet. Now the woman was a Gentile, of Syrophoenician origin. She begged him to cast the demon out of her daughter. He said to her, "Let the children be fed first, for it is not fair to take the children's food and throw it to the dogs." But she answered him, "Sir, even the dogs under the table eat the children's crumbs." Then he said to her, "For saying that, you may go—the demon has left your daughter." So she went home, found the child lying on the bed, and the demon gone.

- Here is one of the great women of the Gospels. She is focused intensely on Jesus and on what she needs from him. She has no concern about herself but only for her little daughter. Jesus is no match for her: she won't go away, she beats him in the argument, she breaks down his resistance. And she trusts him.

- Take a few moments to walk home with her: how is she feeling as she nears her house? Watch her as she rushes to the child's bedside—and finds the demon gone. This story has a lot to teach us about real prayer.

Friday February 12
Mark 7:31–37

Then he returned from the region of Tyre, and went by way of Sidon toward the Sea of Galilee, in the region of the Decapolis. They brought to him a deaf man who had an impediment in his speech; and they begged him to lay his hand on him. He took him aside in private, away from the crowd, and put his fingers into his ears, and he spat and touched his tongue. Then looking up to heaven, he sighed and said to him, "Ephphatha," that is, "Be opened." And immediately his ears were opened, his tongue was released, and he spoke plainly. Then Jesus ordered them to tell no one; but the more he ordered them, the more zealously they proclaimed it. They were astounded beyond measure, saying, "He has done everything well; he even makes the deaf to hear and the mute to speak."

- Jesus shows great care and sensitivity in his encounter with this deaf man. Deaf people often say they feel cut off from life and that they are forced to live in a world of their own. Jesus opens out his world again.

- I also can sometimes be deaf—deaf to the things of God. I can be cut off from the life that really matters—the life of God. I can hear the word of God but not put it into practice; I can receive the Eucharist but not be nourished by it. So I take this time with Jesus and ask him to touch the ears of my heart and loosen my tongue so that I may hear his life-giving words and speak clearly about how God is working in my life.

Saturday February 13
Mark 8:1–10

In those days when there was again a great crowd without anything to eat, he called his disciples and said to them, "I have compassion for the crowd, because they have been with me now for three days and have nothing to eat. If I send them away hungry to their homes, they will faint on the way—and some of them have come from a great distance." His disciples replied, "How can one feed these people with bread here in the desert?" He asked them, "How many loaves do you have?" They said, "Seven." Then he ordered the crowd to sit down on the ground; and he took the seven loaves, and after giving thanks he broke them and gave them to his disciples to distribute; and they distributed them to the crowd. They had also a few small fish; and after blessing them, he ordered that these too should be distributed. They ate and were filled; and they took up the broken pieces left over, seven baskets full. Now there were about four thousand people. And he sent them away. And immediately he got into the boat with his disciples and went to the district of Dalmanutha.

- "I have compassion," says Jesus. I need to have it too. Compassion means that when faced with misery, you are moved "to the very guts" and you try to help. Have I ever experienced deep compassion from someone: a parent, a friend, a nurse, a teacher? Do I have a sense of the compassion of God toward me? Of course, if I do not acknowledge my needs, the compassion of others will be irrelevant.

- "How can one feed these people?" The disciples have not yet understood that nothing is impossible for God. Jesus does not scold them: instead he provides bread in abundance. Our God is a lavish God. Later, in the Passion, it will be he himself who, like the bread, is taken, blessed, broken, and given. The pattern of my life is to be the same. I am to be taken, blessed, broken, and given, until, like Jesus, I am emptied out, and yet mysteriously filled with love.

February 14–20, 2021

Something to think and pray about each day this week:

The Good Shepherd invites us to rest awhile among the grassy meadows and flowing streams. He wants us to relax in his presence—to be nourished, strengthened, and renewed. In this place, we may turn from a closed fist of denial, frustration, and turmoil to an open hand of acceptance, relaxation, and serenity. After the rest, we may be invited to walk more closely with him, to be freer and more confident and to be better able to navigate the often-hazy paths of our lives. It is true that we all need to work on maintaining balance in our lives, but we are not alone. We can learn so much from modern and contemplative wisdom to live life with great richness, and when all is said and done, we can rejoice that we are infinitely loved.

Ad majorem Dei gloriam
("To the greater glory of God")

Too many of us learn to "love" distress and anxiety: we say it is the way of work and the world. Just five minutes of silence seems pointless. But we get in touch with the "inner teacher" when we find times to be still in our day, connecting us with deep peace and balance. It is available to be tapped into as we live in the moment: talking to people, working on tasks, walking with a fresh breeze on our faces, even running. I am so grateful that I listened to the invitation of the wise man at the retreat center. It has stirred me to stop fixing my eyes on the ground and see the beautiful ordinary.

—Gavin Thomas Murphy, *Bursting Out in Praise:*
Spirituality & Mental Health

The Presence of God

The more we call on God, the more we can feel God's presence. Day by day we are drawn closer to the loving heart of God.

Freedom

I am free. When I look at these words in writing, they seem to create in me a feeling of awe. Yes, a wonderful feeling of freedom. Thank you, God.

Consciousness

Help me, Lord, become more conscious of your presence. Teach me to recognize your presence in others. Fill my heart with gratitude for the times your love has been shown to me through the care of others.

The Word

The word of God comes down to us through the Scriptures. May the Holy Spirit enlighten my mind and my heart to respond to the Gospel teachings. (*Please turn to the Scripture on the following pages. Inspiration points are there, should you need them. When you are ready, return here to continue.*)

Conversation

Conversation requires talking and listening.
As I talk to Jesus, may I also learn to pause and listen.
I picture the gentleness in his eyes and the love in his smile.
I can be totally honest with Jesus as I tell him my worries and cares.
I will open my heart to Jesus as I tell him my fears and doubts.
I will ask him to help me place myself fully in his care, knowing that he always desires good for me.

Conclusion

Glory be to the Father, and to the Son, and to the Holy Spirit,
As it was in the beginning, is now, and ever shall be,
World without end. Amen.

Sunday February 14
Sixth Sunday in Ordinary Time
Mark 1:40–45

A leper came to him begging him, and kneeling he said to him, "If you choose, you can make me clean." Moved with pity, Jesus stretched out his hand and touched him, and said to him, "I do choose. Be made clean!" Immediately the leprosy left him, and he was made clean. After sternly warning him he sent him away at once, saying to him, "See that you say nothing to anyone; but go, show yourself to the priest, and offer for your cleansing what Moses commanded, as a testimony to them." But he went out and began to proclaim it freely, and to spread the word, so that Jesus could no longer go into a town openly, but stayed out in the country; and people came to him from every quarter.

• Again in this Gospel we find Jesus moved with pity. Leprosy was a living death: the sufferer was isolated from family and community and had to cry out "Unclean, unclean!" when anyone approached. Touching the leper made Jesus ritually unclean also. There are no lengths to which Jesus will not go to help this man. He touches him, speaks to him, and gives him his freedom to be fully human again.

• I spend a few moments with the leper before his cure, and then meet him afterward. What might he say to me about faith in Jesus? About my pity for others in need? Whom do I touch?

Monday February 15
Mark 8:11–13

The Pharisees came and began to argue with him, asking him for a sign from heaven, to test him. And he sighed deeply in his spirit and said, "Why does this generation ask for a sign? Truly I tell you, no sign will be given to this generation." And he left them, and getting into the boat again, he went across to the other side.

• Arguing can be acceptable, but the Pharisees are hostile: they have decided that Jesus is their enemy. From now on in the Gospel they will be testing Jesus, trying to find his weaknesses, so they can do away with him. Nothing he does will satisfy them: their hearts are closed. God often tests us, but it is in order to bring out the best in us, to make our faith and love grow deeper.

- Do I sometimes make Jesus "sigh deeply"? Am I waiting for him to do something spectacular for me? Is it not enough for him to have given his life to save the world? Am I a wavering disciple who cannot be depended on? I pray: "Jesus, don't leave me behind! Drag me along with you as you cross over to a place I cannot reach without you, the kingdom of God."

Tuesday February 16
Mark 8:14–21

Now the disciples had forgotten to bring any bread; and they had only one loaf with them in the boat. And he cautioned them, saying, "Watch out—beware of the yeast of the Pharisees and the yeast of Herod." They said to one another, "It is because we have no bread." And becoming aware of it, Jesus said to them, "Why are you talking about having no bread? Do you still not perceive or understand? Are your hearts hardened? Do you have eyes, and fail to see? Do you have ears, and fail to hear? And do you not remember? When I broke the five loaves for the five thousand, how many baskets full of broken pieces did you collect?" They said to him, "Twelve." "And the seven for the four thousand, how many baskets full of broken pieces did you collect?" And they said to him, "Seven." Then he said to them, "Do you not yet understand?"

- Jesus is angry at the disciples' inability to grasp who he really is. They cannot understand what he is capable of doing for them. He fires ten pointed questions at them, yet we can imagine them asking at the end, "What is it that we do not yet understand?" They can't break out of their all-too-human view of Jesus. And, even after 2,000 years of Christianity, can I?

- Lord, break down the walls that press in on my small heart: let me believe that you are the Son of God and that in company with you I truly live. Help me see that you yourself are the bread I need to stay alive. Help me to hang all my hope on you.

Wednesday February 17
Ash Wednesday
Matthew 6:1–6, 16–18

"Beware of practicing your piety before others in order to be seen by them; for then you have no reward from your Father in heaven.

"So whenever you give alms, do not sound a trumpet before you, as the hypocrites do in the synagogues and in the streets, so that they may be praised by others. Truly I tell you, they have received their reward. But when you give alms, do not let your left hand know what your right hand is doing, so that your alms may be done in secret; and your Father who sees in secret will reward you. . . .

"And whenever you pray, do not be like the hypocrites; for they love to stand and pray in the synagogues and at the street corners, so that they may be seen by others. Truly I tell you, they have received their reward. But whenever you pray, go into your room and shut the door and pray to your Father who is in secret; and your Father who sees in secret will reward you.

"And whenever you fast, do not look dismal, like the hypocrites, for they disfigure their faces so as to show others that they are fasting. Truly I tell you, they have received their reward. But when you fast, put oil on your head and wash your face, so that your fasting may be seen not by others but by your Father who is in secret; and your Father who sees in secret will reward you."

• Jesus seems to call for great courage, asking us to draw deeply on our reserves. He is really asking us to depend on him, to let his spirit come to life.

• What Jesus suggests would upset the balance of the world; it contradicts the neat arrangements of tidy minds. Help me, Lord, to receive courage and strength to act in unexpected and life-giving ways.

Thursday February 18
Luke 9:22–25

"The Son of Man must undergo great suffering, and be rejected by the elders, chief priests, and scribes, and be killed, and on the third day be raised."

Then he said to them all, "If any want to become my followers, let them deny themselves and take up their cross daily and follow me. For those who want to save their life will lose it, and those who lose their life for my sake will save it. What does it profit them if they gain the whole world, but lose or forfeit themselves?"

- Taking up one's cross is not a matter of simply putting up with the headaches and ordinary troubles of life, but of not being ashamed of Jesus, and being prepared to be true followers with all the dangers, even possible martyrdom, that that implies. Trying to save one's own skin by denying Jesus will only result in the loss of eternal life, of intimate union with God.

Friday February 19
Matthew 9:14–15

Then the disciples of John came to him, saying, "Why do we and the Pharisees fast often, but your disciples do not fast?" And Jesus said to them, "The wedding-guests cannot mourn as long as the bridegroom is with them, can they? The days will come when the bridegroom is taken away from them, and then they will fast."

- The disciples of John compared their religious observation to that of Jesus and his followers. Do I sometimes contrast my practice with that of others? Am I drawn either to pride or to despair? Lent calls me to walk humbly with God in company with and in prayer for others.

- If I put some things aside or give up some things for Lent, it is so that I can be more clearly in the presence of the bridegroom who rejoices in my company.

Saturday February 20
Luke 5:27–32

After this he went out and saw a tax-collector named Levi, sitting at the tax booth; and he said to him, "Follow me." And he got up, left everything, and followed him.

Then Levi gave a great banquet for him in his house; and there was a large crowd of tax-collectors and others sitting at the table with them. The Pharisees and their scribes were complaining to his disciples, saying,

"Why do you eat and drink with tax-collectors and sinners?" Jesus answered, "Those who are well have no need of a physician, but those who are sick; I have come to call not the righteous but sinners to repentance."

- Who today would be in Matthew's position? Who are the Levis in our world, hated and despised by the public? Not the tax collectors: it is quite respectable now to work for the IRS. The tabloid newspapers have different hate-objects today: in some cases drug addicts, and in others rapists and pedophiles. You would sit with them all, Lord. They all need your grace.

The First Week of Lent
February 21–27, 2021

Something to think and pray about each day this week:

"The Lord asks everything of us, and in return he offers us true life, the happiness for which we were created" (*Gaudete et Exsultate*, 1).

Lent does not normally begin with happiness. We are more accustomed to hearing how hard it will be. The theme of conversion, which the season of Lent begins with, is often understood in terms of sacrifice, struggle, and even suffering. An overly moralistic approach to Lent means, however, that Christians can sometimes look, in a line from the Pope's previous exhortation, *Evangelii Gaudium* (The Joy of the Gospel), "like someone who has just come back from a funeral" (*EG*, 10). The challenge of the Gospel is to consider the call to repentance in the light of what we receive from God. This means holding the darkness of our lives up against the light of God's love, seeing the contrast between the sin of the world and the salvation offered in the kingdom of God.

Pope Francis is clear that Lenten and lifelong conversion "asks everything of us." Conversion asks for a change of mind, heart, and even body, perhaps even to the extent of losing our lives. However, Pope Francis is equally clear that conversion will not cost happiness, will not cheat us of human fulfillment. Happiness hinges on holiness. True human happiness needs the healing and hope that holiness holds out; holiness helps us become fully human. Offering everything is not one option among others but an opening of our minds, hearts, and bodies to truth, love, and wholeness. The goal of conversion is communion with God and others. Repentance is turning toward holiness, returning to receive "the happiness for which we were created." Holiness is the hallmark of authentic happiness.

—Kevin O'Gorman, *Journeying in Joy and Gladness:
Lent and Holy Week with* Gaudete et Exsultate

The Presence of God
Lord, help me be fully alive to your holy presence. Enfold me in your love.
Let my heart become one with yours.
My soul longs for your presence, Lord. When I turn my thoughts to you,
I find peace and contentment.

Freedom
Your death on the cross has set me free. I can live joyously and freely
without fear of death. Your mercy knows no bounds.

Consciousness
At this moment, Lord, I turn my thoughts to you.
I will leave aside my chores and preoccupations.
I will take rest and refreshment in your presence.

The Word
The word of God comes down to us through the Scriptures.
May the Holy Spirit enlighten my mind and my heart
to respond to the Gospel teachings:
to love my neighbor as myself,
to care for my sisters and brothers in Christ.
(*Please turn to the Scripture on the following pages. Inspiration points are
there, should you need them. When you are ready, return here to continue.*)

Conversation
Begin to talk to Jesus about the Scripture you have just read. What part
of it strikes a chord in you? Perhaps the words of a friend—or some story
you have heard recently—will slowly rise to the surface of your consciousness. If so, does the story throw light on what the Scripture passage may
be saying to you?

Conclusion
I thank God for these moments we have spent together and for any insights I have been given concerning the text.

Sunday February 21
First Sunday of Lent
Mark 1:12–15

And the Spirit immediately drove him out into the wilderness. He was in the wilderness for forty days, tempted by Satan; and he was with the wild beasts; and the angels waited on him.

Now after John was arrested, Jesus came to Galilee, proclaiming the good news of God, and saying, "The time is fulfilled, and the kingdom of God has come near; repent, and believe in the good news."

- Only God could be so human as to endure temptation. Mark's Gospel depicts Jesus as divine but also deeply human. He enters the wilderness for one purpose only: to find God, to seek God and belong to him totally. Only then does he come into Galilee and proclaim good news.

- Lord, come with me into my wilderness. Speak to my preoccupied heart. Reveal to me where addiction to power, possession, and gratification choke my path. Only when I am free from these can I be good news to others. Only then do I become part of the solution to the world's problems.

Monday February 22
St. Peter's Chair
Matthew 16:13–19

Now when Jesus came into the district of Caesarea Philippi, he asked his disciples, "Who do people say that the Son of Man is?" And they said, "Some say John the Baptist, but others Elijah, and still others Jeremiah or one of the prophets." He said to them, "But who do you say that I am?" Simon Peter answered, "You are the Messiah, the Son of the living God." And Jesus answered him, "Blessed are you, Simon son of Jonah! For flesh and blood has not revealed this to you, but my Father in heaven. And I tell you, you are Peter, and on this rock I will build my church, and the gates of Hades will not prevail against it. I will give you the keys of the kingdom of heaven, and whatever you bind on earth will be bound in heaven, and whatever you loose on earth will be loosed in heaven."

- When Peter is moved to identify Jesus as the Messiah, Jesus congratulates him, so to speak, on having allowed himself to be inspired in his answer by the heavenly Father: at last his thinking has been raised onto the properly spiritual plane.

- Jesus reveals that he is founding a church—a community of faith and worship—which the powers of hell will not be able to overcome. But community always needs leadership, and to Peter (whose name resembles the word for "rock"—depending on the language being spoken) is entrusted the authority of binding and loosing—always associated with a people with whom the Lord has entered into a covenant bond.

Tuesday February 23
Matthew 6:7–15

"When you are praying, do not heap up empty phrases as the Gentiles do; for they think that they will be heard because of their many words. Do not be like them, for your Father knows what you need before you ask him.

"Pray then in this way:
Our Father in heaven,
hallowed be your name.
Your kingdom come.
Your will be done,
on earth as it is in heaven.
Give us this day our daily bread.
And forgive us our debts,
as we also have forgiven our debtors.
And do not bring us to the time of trial,
but rescue us from the evil one.

For if you forgive others their trespasses, your heavenly Father will also forgive you; but if you do not forgive others, neither will your Father forgive your trespasses."

- The phrases of the Our Father may be very familiar to me. I might let just one of them offer itself now; I take time to let it sink in again and take it with me through the day.
- Debts, evil, and trespasses are all brought before God and assume their proper place. I am drawn to God, being made holy, nourished and forgiven.

Wednesday February 24
Luke 11:29–32

When the crowds were increasing, he began to say, "This generation is an evil generation; it asks for a sign, but no sign will be given to it except the sign of Jonah. For just as Jonah became a sign to the people of Nineveh, so the Son of Man will be to this generation. The queen of the South will rise at the judgment with the people of this generation and condemn them, because she came from the ends of the earth to listen to the wisdom of Solomon, and see, something greater than Solomon is here! The people of Nineveh will rise up at the judgment with this generation and condemn it, because they repented at the proclamation of Jonah, and see, something greater than Jonah is here!"

• Jonah converted the great city of Nineveh by his godliness and his preaching, not by miracles. Holiness is a greater marvel than special effects, but less easily recognized. The spectacular is what draws the crowds. Lord, your hand is more evident in saintliness than in extraordinary signs. Open my eyes to your work in my sisters and brothers.

Thursday February 25
Matthew 7:7–12

"Ask, and it will be given to you; search, and you will find; knock, and the door will be opened for you. For everyone who asks receives, and everyone who searches finds, and for everyone who knocks, the door will be opened. Is there anyone among you who, if your child asks for bread, will give a stone? Or if the child asks for a fish, will give a snake? If you then, who are evil, know how to give good gifts to your children, how much more will your Father in heaven give good things to those who ask him!

"In everything do to others as you would have them do to you; for this is the law and the prophets."

• Prayer is never wasted. Good things come in prayer, maybe not what someone asks for. Prayer opens the heart for good things from God. Be grateful at the end of prayer for time spent with the God of all goodness. Prayer time is always productive time in making us people of more love.

Friday February 26
Matthew 5:20–26

"For I tell you, unless your righteousness exceeds that of the scribes and Pharisees, you will never enter the kingdom of heaven.

"You have heard that it was said to those of ancient times, 'You shall not murder'; and 'whoever murders shall be liable to judgment.' But I say to you that if you are angry with a brother or sister, you will be liable to judgment; and if you insult a brother or sister, you will be liable to the council; and if you say, 'You fool,' you will be liable to the hell of fire. So when you are offering your gift at the altar, if you remember that your brother or sister has something against you, leave your gift there before the altar and go; first be reconciled to your brother or sister, and then come and offer your gift. Come to terms quickly with your accuser while you are on the way to court with him, or your accuser may hand you over to the judge, and the judge to the guard, and you will be thrown into prison. Truly I tell you, you will never get out until you have paid the last penny."

- How challenging the Gospel is! I am called not only to do love but also to think love! Can I invite Jesus into my heart to create that sort of loving, respectful heart for me?

- The Spirit is calling me to be changed, to become a more loving, kinder, more merciful, and more just person: to be transformed. Do I notice the difference in myself when I am loving and when I am unloving? Do I talk to Jesus about this?

Saturday February 27
Matthew 5:43–48

"You have heard that it was said, 'You shall love your neighbor and hate your enemy.' But I say to you, Love your enemies and pray for those who persecute you, so that you may be children of your Father in heaven; for he makes his sun rise on the evil and on the good, and sends rain on the righteous and on the unrighteous. For if you love those who love you, what reward do you have? Do not even the tax-collectors do the same? And if you greet only your brothers and sisters, what more are you doing than others? Do not even the Gentiles do the same? Be perfect, therefore, as your heavenly Father is perfect."

- There are times, Lord, when you lift us beyond what we thought possible. Here you ask me to be perfect: meaning that in my heart I should bless even those who hate me and wrong me. The love of God can be poured out in our hearts through the Holy Spirit who is given to us. Even when I feel far from blessed myself, even when old age makes me feel that there is little I can do for others, I can still give my approval and blessing to those I meet; that will lift them.

- As I think of those whose love I return, I thank God for them and for the blessings we share.

- As I pray for those who bring blessings to me, I pray that I may include others in a widening circle of compassion.

February 28—March 6, 2021

Something to think and pray about each day this week:

Many years ago, when we were told about the hazards of alcoholism in secondary school, we were given the image of a timid, shy, person who had to consume alcohol to gain courage to socialize. Years later, I've come to understand the damage that is done to the person who has to hide behind addiction. The task of recovery involves meeting the person you felt was unworthy of attention and loving them back into wholeness and worthiness again.

Conversations with students have made me realize that the addictions today are more subtle. Students tell me that they are more and more under pressure to project an image of themselves that is socially acceptable and, like the alcoholic, they often find themselves suppressing their real self.

In this regard, one truth that students find revealing when I share it with them is the one that tells of the impact of modern devices. They are engendering a new narcissism that creates personalities that are more and more fragile. The insecurity of this fragility means that people are seeking more and more affirmation from shallow agents that can only prop us up until we need more from them.

It's hard for God to get a look in, as He is really only interested in the person that we are. Over and over again in the Gospel, through His Son, the Father calls people from falsehood to truth. He's a lot easier on the real person who struggles; He finds oceans of forgiveness and understanding for them. It's the false people he can't work with. Let's get over creating the tacky image of ourselves that we create so we can be an acceptable "image" to those who don't really matter. As my mother says, "it's all very false, son." It's our deepest real and true selves that matter and it is deeply lovable.

—Alan Hilliard, *Dipping into Lent*

The Presence of God

I remind myself that, as I sit here now,
God is gazing on me with love and holding me in being.
I pause for a moment and think of this.

Freedom

"There are very few people who realize what God would make of them if they abandoned themselves into his hands, and let themselves be formed by his grace" (St. Ignatius). I ask for the grace to trust myself totally to God's love.

Consciousness

Where do I sense hope, encouragement, and growth in my life? By looking back over the past few months, I might see what produced rich fruit, and determine to give those areas time and space in the future.

The Word

Lord Jesus, you became human to communicate with me.
You walked and worked on this earth.
You endured the heat and struggled with the cold.
All your time on this earth was spent in caring for humanity.
You healed the sick, you raised the dead.
Most important of all, you saved me from death.
(*Please turn to the Scripture on the following pages. Inspiration points are there, should you need them. When you are ready, return here to continue.*)

Conversation

What is stirring in me as I pray? Am I consoled, troubled, left cold? I imagine Jesus at my side, and I share my feelings with him.

Conclusion

Glory be to the Father, and to the Son, and to the Holy Spirit,
As it was in the beginning, is now, and ever shall be,
World without end. Amen.

Sunday February 28: Second Sunday of Lent
Mark 9:2–10

Six days later, Jesus took with him Peter and James and John, and led them up a high mountain apart, by themselves. And he was transfigured before them, and his clothes became dazzling white, such as no one on earth could bleach them. And there appeared to them Elijah with Moses, who were talking with Jesus. Then Peter said to Jesus, "Rabbi, it is good for us to be here; let us make three dwellings, one for you, one for Moses, and one for Elijah." He did not know what to say, for they were terrified. Then a cloud overshadowed them, and from the cloud there came a voice, "This is my Son, the Beloved; listen to him!" Suddenly when they looked around, they saw no one with them any more, but only Jesus.

As they were coming down the mountain, he ordered them to tell no one about what they had seen, until after the Son of Man had risen from the dead. So they kept the matter to themselves, questioning what this rising from the dead could mean.

• Peter cries out in delight and wonder, "Master, it is good for us to be here!" This is how we are surely meant to experience the presence of God—in wonder and delight, the created glorying in the Creator's presence. Too often, we glide along the surface of the spinning earth, never listening to its heartbeat. We look into the depths of the universe and never hear the singing of the stars.

• When did I last sing and make melody to the Lord with all my heart or clap my hands or shout for joy to him?

Monday March 1
Luke 6:36–38

"Be merciful, just as your Father is merciful. Do not judge, and you will not be judged; do not condemn, and you will not be condemned. Forgive, and you will be forgiven; give, and it will be given to you. A good measure, pressed down, shaken together, running over, will be put into your lap; for the measure you give will be the measure you get back."

• Jesus invites us to be as God is—nothing less! He does not intend to overwhelm us or cause us to feel frustrated by such an enormous invitation but wants us to wonder at the immensity of God's capacity to love. In our humanity, we are not infinite, but we are called to great love and hope. The invitation reaches out to us as we are, calling us into the life of God.

- Judgment, condemnation, and lack of forgiveness inhibit good and bind up the spirit. Lord help me to be generous, not by forcing anything from myself but by sharing fully what you give to me.

Tuesday March 2
Matthew 23:1–12

Then Jesus said to the crowds and to his disciples, "The scribes and the Pharisees sit on Moses' seat; therefore, do whatever they teach you and follow it; but do not do as they do, for they do not practice what they teach. They tie up heavy burdens, hard to bear, and lay them on the shoulders of others; but they themselves are unwilling to lift a finger to move them. They do all their deeds to be seen by others; for they make their phylacteries broad and their fringes long. They love to have the place of honor at banquets and the best seats in the synagogues, and to be greeted with respect in the market-places, and to have people call them rabbi. But you are not to be called rabbi, for you have one teacher, and you are all students. And call no one your father on earth, for you have one Father—the one in heaven. Nor are you to be called instructors, for you have one instructor, the Messiah. The greatest among you will be your servant. All who exalt themselves will be humbled, and all who humble themselves will be exalted."

- Although the content of this passage reflects conflicts in the early Church between the Christians and the Jews led by the Pharisees, there is no doubt the fierce denunciations of the Pharisees go back to Jesus. His denunciation is an indication that they were corrosive of true religion by not giving priority to the good and the needs of the person.

- Jesus' disciples are not to make a big display of religion, nor are they to seek honorable titles like "father" and "teacher" and "rabbi." Our teacher is God, and the true disciple learns only from God. I think of what it would be like for me to assume the lowest place, to really take to heart what Jesus says about humility. I begin my prayer by asking God for the help I need, humbly and sincerely.

Wednesday March 3
Matthew 20:17–28

While Jesus was going up to Jerusalem, he took the twelve disciples aside by themselves, and said to them on the way, "See, we are going up to Jerusalem, and the Son of Man will be handed over to the chief priests and scribes, and they will condemn him to death; then they will hand him over to the Gentiles to be mocked and flogged and crucified; and on the third day he will be raised."

Then the mother of the sons of Zebedee came to him with her sons, and kneeling before him, she asked a favor of him. And he said to her, "What do you want?" She said to him, "Declare that these two sons of mine will sit, one at your right hand and one at your left, in your kingdom." But Jesus answered, "You do not know what you are asking. Are you able to drink the cup that I am about to drink?" They said to him, "We are able." He said to them, "You will indeed drink my cup, but to sit at my right hand and at my left, this is not mine to grant, but it is for those for whom it has been prepared by my Father."

When the ten heard it, they were angry with the two brothers. But Jesus called them to him and said, "You know that the rulers of the Gentiles lord it over them, and their great ones are tyrants over them. It will not be so among you; but whoever wishes to be great among you must be your servant, and whoever wishes to be first among you must be your slave; just as the Son of Man came not to be served but to serve, and to give his life as a ransom for many."

- Our prayer often finds us asking for what we want. As we grow in awareness of the presence of God, we realize how God wants something greater for us. It may appear that we are asked to let go of our requests, but we soon realize that nothing we really want is lost in God.

- Jesus was clear about his relationship with God; he knew who he was and what was his to give. Lord, help me know more clearly what is mine to do and what I might best leave to you.

Thursday March 4
Luke 16:19–31

There was a rich man who was dressed in purple and fine linen and who feasted sumptuously every day. And at his gate lay a poor man named

Lazarus, covered with sores, who longed to satisfy his hunger with what fell from the rich man's table; even the dogs would come and lick his sores. The poor man died and was carried away by the angels to be with Abraham. The rich man also died and was buried. In Hades, where he was being tormented, he looked up and saw Abraham far away with Lazarus by his side. He called out, "Father Abraham, have mercy on me, and send Lazarus to dip the tip of his finger in water and cool my tongue; for I am in agony in these flames." But Abraham said, "Child, remember that during your lifetime you received your good things, and Lazarus in like manner evil things; but now he is comforted here, and you are in agony. Besides all this, between you and us a great chasm has been fixed, so that those who might want to pass from here to you cannot do so, and no one can cross from there to us." He said, "Then, father, I beg you to send him to my father's house—for I have five brothers—that he may warn them, so that they will not also come into this place of torment." Abraham replied, "They have Moses and the prophets; they should listen to them." He said, "No, father Abraham; but if someone goes to them from the dead, they will repent." He said to him, "If they do not listen to Moses and the prophets, neither will they be convinced even if someone rises from the dead."

- Jesus is asking his listeners to open their eyes to what is around them, and to open their ears to the simple command of the Gospel: love your neighbor.

- Praying on this story can challenge us to care for the needy in whatever way we can to improve the lives of poor people.

- All, whether rich or poor, must die. "When we look at the wise, they die . . . and leave their wealth to others" (Psalm 49:10). Death is inevitable for us all, and there is no escape from it. We prepare our future dwelling place now by charity and patient endurance.

Friday March 5
Matthew 21:33–43, 45–46

"Listen to another parable. There was a landowner who planted a vineyard, put a fence around it, dug a wine press in it, and built a watch-tower. Then he leased it to tenants and went to another country. When the harvest time had come, he sent his slaves to the tenants to collect his produce. But the tenants seized his slaves and beat one, killed another and stoned another. Again he sent other slaves, more than the first; and they treated them in the same way. Finally he sent his son to them, saying, 'They will respect my son.' But when the tenants saw the son, they said to themselves, 'This is the heir; come, let us kill him and get his inheritance.' So they seized him, threw him out of the vineyard, and killed him. Now when the owner of the vineyard comes, what will he do to those tenants?" They said to him, "He will put those wretches to a miserable death, and lease the vineyard to other tenants who will give him the produce at the harvest time."

> Jesus said to them, "Have you never read in the scriptures:
> 'The stone that the builders rejected
> has become the cornerstone;
> this was the Lord's doing,
> and it is amazing in our eyes'?

Therefore I tell you, the kingdom of God will be taken away from you and given to a people that produces the fruits of the kingdom.". . .

When the chief priests and the Pharisees heard his parables, they realized that he was speaking about them. They wanted to arrest him, but they feared the crowds, because they regarded him as a prophet.

- One of the saddest statements in the Gospels is this innocent comment of the father: "They will respect my son." I am frightened to think what would happen if Jesus came into our world today. His message about the kingdom of God would put him in direct opposition to so many other kingdoms. He would become an enemy to be got rid of.

- Jesus, you were thrown out and killed. But you took no revenge. Instead you excused your torturers, and by your love you reconciled everyone with God. You showed what divine love is like. You love me totally, no matter what I do. May I always wish others well and pray for them instead of taking revenge on them when they hurt me.

Saturday March 6
Luke 15:1–3, 11–32

Now all the tax-collectors and sinners were coming near to listen to him. And the Pharisees and the scribes were grumbling and saying, "This fellow welcomes sinners and eats with them."

So he told them this parable: "There was a man who had two sons. The younger of them said to his father, 'Father, give me the share of the property that will belong to me.' So he divided his property between them. A few days later the younger son gathered all he had and traveled to a distant country, and there he squandered his property in dissolute living. When he had spent everything, a severe famine took place throughout that country, and he began to be in need. So he went and hired himself out to one of the citizens of that country, who sent him to his fields to feed the pigs. He would gladly have filled himself with the pods that the pigs were eating; and no one gave him anything. But when he came to himself he said, 'How many of my father's hired hands have bread enough and to spare, but here I am dying of hunger! I will get up and go to my father, and I will say to him, "Father, I have sinned against heaven and before you; I am no longer worthy to be called your son; treat me like one of your hired hands."' So he set off and went to his father. But while he was still far off, his father saw him and was filled with compassion; he ran and put his arms around him and kissed him. Then the son said to him, 'Father, I have sinned against heaven and before you; I am no longer worthy to be called your son.' But the father said to his slaves, 'Quickly, bring out a robe—the best one—and put it on him; put a ring on his finger and sandals on his feet. And get the fatted calf and kill it, and let us eat and celebrate; for this son of mine was dead and is alive again; he was lost and is found!' And they began to celebrate.

"Now his elder son was in the field; and when he came and approached the house, he heard music and dancing. He called one of the slaves and asked what was going on. He replied, 'Your brother has come, and your father has killed the fatted calf, because he has got him back safe and sound.' Then he became angry and refused to go in. His father came out and began to plead with him. But he answered his father, 'Listen! For all these years I have been working like a slave for you, and I have never disobeyed your command; yet you have never given me even a young goat so that I might celebrate with my friends. But when this son of yours came back, who has devoured your property with prostitutes, you killed the fatted calf for him!' Then the father said to him, 'Son, you are always with me, and all that is mine is yours. But we had to celebrate and rejoice, because this brother of yours was dead and has come to life; he was lost and has been found.'"

- The parable of the Prodigal Son gives me a picture of the steadfast love of God. There, Lord, you show how your heavenly father would appear in human form. When he welcomes back his lost son with tears of delight, kills the fatted calf, brings out the best robe, and throws a great party, it is not to please other people but to give expression to his own overwhelming pleasure that his child has come home. You delight in me.

- Time and again God promises me goodness. I pray that my eyes may be opened to appreciate where God is working in my life.

The Third Week of Lent
March 7–13, 2021

Something to think and pray about each day this week:

The temptations of Jesus are not at all temptations to this or that sin but, rather, fundamental options that matter for the direction of his life. Jesus was tempted in the course of his ministry to choose other ways of being God's prophet, the Messiah or anointed one. In a less obvious way, we too can be attracted by choices that can shape the way our life unfolds. We ask, What do I live on? What's my true goal? Where is my nourishment? The human, no less than the kingdom, is more than food and drink. Only the word of God truly nourishes and illuminates.

Every so often, we catch a glimpse of the "something more" that God has in store for us. These fleeting experiences are to be treasured: the birth of my first child, falling in love, a sense of being held by God's presence. Such experiences may help us approach the Transfiguration. Like all transcendent experiences, it is fleeting, yet it etches a memory and leaves a longing. What should we do? Practice listening to him. Be not afraid. We cannot always be "on the mountain," yet what happens on the heights can help us on the lowlands of the everyday.

—Kieran J. O'Mahony, OSA, *Hearers of the Word: Praying and Exploring the Readings for Lent & Holy Week, Year A*

The Presence of God
I remind myself that I am in the presence of God, who is my strength in times of weakness and my comforter in times of sorrow.

Freedom
St. Ignatius thought that a thick and shapeless tree trunk would never believe that it could become a statue, admired as a miracle of sculpture, and would never submit itself to the chisel of the sculptor, who sees by her genius what she can make of it. I ask for the grace to let myself be shaped by my loving Creator.

Consciousness
Dear Lord, help me remember that you gave me life. Teach me to slow down, to be still and enjoy the pleasures created for me, to be aware of the beauty that surrounds me: the marvel of mountains, the calmness of lakes, the fragility of a flower petal. I need to remember that all these things come from you.

The Word
In this expectant state of mind, please turn to the text for the day with confidence. Believe that the Holy Spirit is present and may reveal whatever the passage has to say to you. Read reflectively, listening with a third ear to what may be going on in your heart. (*Please turn to the Scripture on the following pages. Inspiration points are there, should you need them. When you are ready, return here to continue.*)

Conversation
What feelings are rising in me as I pray and reflect on God's word? I imagine Jesus himself sitting or standing near me, and I open my heart to him.

Conclusion
I thank God for these moments we have spent together and for any insights I have been given concerning the text.

Sunday March 7
Third Sunday of Lent
John 2:13–25

The Passover of the Jews was near, and Jesus went up to Jerusalem. In the temple he found people selling cattle, sheep and doves, and the money-changers seated at their tables. Making a whip of cords, he drove all of them out of the temple, both the sheep and the cattle. He also poured out the coins of the money-changers and overturned their tables. He told those who were selling the doves, "Take these things out of here! Stop making my Father's house a market-place!" His disciples remembered that it was written, "Zeal for your house will consume me." The Jews then said to him, "What sign can you show us for doing this?" Jesus answered them, "Destroy this temple, and in three days I will raise it up." The Jews then said, "This temple has been under construction for forty-six years, and will you raise it up in three days?" But he was speaking of the temple of his body. After he was raised from the dead, his disciples remembered that he had said this; and they believed the scripture and the word that Jesus had spoken.

When he was in Jerusalem during the Passover festival, many believed in his name because they saw the signs that he was doing. But Jesus on his part would not entrust himself to them, because he knew all people and needed no one to testify about anyone; for he himself knew what was in everyone.

- I imagine myself visiting the temple when Jesus enters. I am accustomed to the money-changers and to the hucksters who convenience worshippers by selling cattle, sheep, and doves for the ritual sacrifices. The fury of Jesus startles and upsets me, makes me think. Surely these guys are making a few honest bucks?

- But this is the house of God. When money creeps in, it tends to take over. Is there any of the Christian sacraments untouched by commercialism? Christening parties, First Communion money, Confirmation dances, wedding feasts . . . They are meant to be the touch of God at key moments in our lives; but can God get a hearing amid the clatter of coins?

Monday March 8

John 4:5–42

So he came to a Samaritan city called Sychar, near the plot of ground that Jacob had given to his son Joseph. Jacob's well was there, and Jesus, tired out by his journey, was sitting by the well. It was about noon.

A Samaritan woman came to draw water, and Jesus said to her, "Give me a drink." (His disciples had gone to the city to buy food.) The Samaritan woman said to him, "How is it that you, a Jew, ask a drink of me, a woman of Samaria?" (Jews do not share things in common with Samaritans.) Jesus answered her, "If you knew the gift of God, and who it is that is saying to you, 'Give me a drink,' you would have asked him, and he would have given you living water." The woman said to him, "Sir, you have no bucket, and the well is deep. Where do you get that living water? Are you greater than our ancestor Jacob, who gave us the well, and with his sons and his flocks drank from it?" Jesus said to her, "Everyone who drinks of this water will be thirsty again, but those who drink of the water that I will give them will never be thirsty. The water that I will give will become in them a spring of water gushing up to eternal life." The woman said to him, "Sir, give me this water, so that I may never be thirsty or have to keep coming here to draw water."

Jesus said to her, "Go, call your husband, and come back." The woman answered him, "I have no husband." Jesus said to her, "You are right in saying, 'I have no husband'; for you have had five husbands, and the one you have now is not your husband. What you have said is true!" The woman said to him, "Sir, I see that you are a prophet. Our ancestors worshipped on this mountain, but you say that the place where people must worship is in Jerusalem." Jesus said to her, "Woman, believe me, the hour is coming when you will worship the Father neither on this mountain nor in Jerusalem. You worship what you do not know; we worship what we know, for salvation is from the Jews. But the hour is coming, and is now here, when the true worshippers will worship the Father in spirit and truth, for the Father seeks such as these to worship him. God is spirit, and those who worship him must worship in spirit and truth." The woman said to him, "I know that the Messiah is coming" (who is called Christ). "When he comes, he will proclaim all things to us." Jesus said to her, "I am he, the one who is speaking to you."

Just then his disciples came. They were astonished that he was speaking with a woman, but no one said, "What do you want?" or, "Why are you speaking with her?" Then the woman left her water-jar and went back to the city. She said to the people, "Come and see a man who told me everything I have ever done! He cannot be the Messiah, can he?" They left the city and were on their way to him.

Meanwhile the disciples were urging him, "Rabbi, eat something." But he said to them, "I have food to eat that you do not know about." So the disciples said to one another, "Surely no one has brought him something to eat?" Jesus said to them, "My food is to do the will of him who sent me and to complete his work. Do you not say, 'Four months more, then comes the harvest'? But I tell you, look around you, and see how the fields are ripe for harvesting. The reaper is already receiving wages and is gathering fruit for eternal life, so that sower and reaper may rejoice together. For here the saying holds true, 'One sows and another reaps.' I sent you to reap that for which you did not labor. Others have labored, and you have entered into their labor."

Many Samaritans from that city believed in him because of the woman's testimony, "He told me everything I have ever done." So when the Samaritans came to him, they asked him to stay with them; and he stayed there for two days. And many more believed because of his word. They said to the woman, "It is no longer because of what you said that we believe, for we have heard for ourselves, and we know that this is truly the Savior of the world."

- Lord, I am going about my business like the Samaritan woman, and I'm taken aback when you accost me at the well. You interrupt my business, my getting and spending, and the routines of my day. Let me savor this encounter, imagine you probing my desires, showing you know the waywardness of my heart. At the end, like her, I am moved with such joy at meeting you that I cannot keep it to myself. Lord, you tell me to lift up me eyes and see how the fields are already white for harvest.

Tuesday March 9
Matthew 18:21–35

Then Peter came and said to him, "Lord, if another member of the church sins against me, how often should I forgive? As many as seven times?" Jesus said to him, "Not seven times, but, I tell you, seventy-seven times.

"For this reason the kingdom of heaven may be compared to a king who wished to settle accounts with his slaves. When he began the reckoning, one who owed him ten thousand talents was brought to him; and, as he could not pay, his lord ordered him to be sold, together with his wife and children and all his possessions, and payment to be made. So the slave fell on his knees before him, saying, 'Have patience with me, and I will pay you everything.' And out of pity for him, the lord of that slave released him and forgave him the debt. But that same slave, as he went out, came upon one of his fellow-slaves who owed him a hundred denarii; and seizing him by the throat, he said, 'Pay what you owe.' Then his fellow-slave fell down and pleaded with him, 'Have patience with me, and I will pay you.' But he refused; then he went and threw him into prison until he should pay the debt. When his fellow-slaves saw what had happened, they were greatly distressed, and they went and reported to their lord all that had taken place. Then his lord summoned him and said to him, 'You wicked slave! I forgave you all that debt because you pleaded with me. Should you not have had mercy on your fellow-slave, as I had mercy on you?' And in anger his lord handed him over to be tortured until he should pay his entire debt. So my heavenly Father will also do to every one of you, if you do not forgive your brother or sister from your heart."

- Forgiveness is very creative and goes beyond the existing facts. It recognizes the deeper goodness in people, despite what they have done.

- As theologian Romano Guardini pointed out, there is no forgiveness if one wants punishment. Forgiveness means pardoning and letting go completely, creating and making the offender new again. It requires great grace to forgive.

- Justice can be the enemy of love. It indicates the normal legal way of proceeding. We often hear people say: "We want justice done." But mercy or forgiveness is far nobler and says, "I want the person to be fully well and alive again."

Wednesday March 10
Matthew 5:17–19

"Do not think that I have come to abolish the law or the prophets; I have come not to abolish but to fulfill. For truly I tell you, until heaven and earth pass away, not one letter, not one stroke of a letter, will pass from the law until all is accomplished. Therefore, whoever breaks one of the least of these commandments, and teaches others to do the same, will be called least in the kingdom of heaven; but whoever does them and teaches them will be called great in the kingdom of heaven."

- Jesus teaches by word and action, by saying and doing. His example of life is our guide and our encouragement. There is a link between what we say and what we do, and when this link is strong, we are strong in the kingdom of God. We are to "walk it as we talk it." We are called to sincerity and integrity of life.

- I consider how my way of living influences others. I pray in thanksgiving for those areas in which I can imagine that I have a good influence. I ask God's help in the areas where my example and inspiration might be better.

Thursday March 11
Luke 11:14–23

Now he was casting out a demon that was mute; when the demon had gone out, the one who had been mute spoke, and the crowds were amazed. But some of them said, "He casts out demons by Beelzebul, the ruler of the demons." Others, to test him, kept demanding from him a sign from heaven. But he knew what they were thinking and said to them, "Every kingdom divided against itself becomes a desert, and house falls on house. If Satan also is divided against himself, how will his kingdom stand?—for you say that I cast out the demons by Beelzebul. Now if I cast out the demons by Beelzebul, by whom do your exorcists cast them out? Therefore they will be your judges. But if it is by the finger of God that I cast out the demons, then the kingdom of God has come to you. When a strong man, fully armed, guards his castle, his property is safe. But when one stronger than he attacks him and overpowers him, he takes away his armor in which he trusted and divides his plunder. Whoever is not with me is against me, and whoever does not gather with me scatters.

- When you have to speak in public, it helps if those listening are on your side, or at least give you a fair hearing. For Jesus it is often the opposite—men arguing against him, trying to catch him out. In today's Scripture passage it is even worse. He is accused of being in league with Satan, the devil.

- How does he feel? Jesus, the Son of God, who willingly gave his life that we might have life. "I came that they may have life and have it abundantly" (John 10:10).

- You know how painful it is if your motives are misunderstood, if a twisted interpretation is put on your good intentions. Such experiences help you identify with Jesus and feel with him. Be there with him; share your experiences with him.

Friday March 12
Mark 12:28–34

One of the scribes came near and heard them disputing with one another, and seeing that he answered them well, he asked him, "Which commandment is the first of all?" Jesus answered, "The first is, 'Hear, O Israel: the Lord our God, the Lord is one; you shall love the Lord your God with all your heart, and with all your soul, and with all your mind, and with all your strength.' The second is this, 'You shall love your neighbor as yourself.' There is no other commandment greater than these." Then the scribe said to him, "You are right, Teacher; you have truly said that 'he is one, and besides him there is no other'; and 'to love him with all the heart, and with all the understanding, and with all the strength,' and 'to love one's neighbor as oneself'—this is much more important than all whole burnt-offerings and sacrifices." When Jesus saw that he answered wisely, he said to him, "You are not far from the kingdom of God." After that no one dared to ask him any question.

- Lord, why should I love you with all my heart? Because if a group of good people set up a beautiful house and gardens for me to live in, I would love them. If they worked against all that might hurt me, I would love them. If one of them were to die a horrible death to save me from disaster, I would love them. If they, Lord, promised me eternal joy, I would love them.

- Lord, enlarge my heart. Make me more and more sensitive to the quality of your love, especially as Holy Week comes near. There you show me so dramatically how much you love me. Make me a grateful person.

Saturday March 13
Luke 18:9–14

He also told this parable to some who trusted in themselves that they were righteous and regarded others with contempt: "Two men went up to the temple to pray, one a Pharisee and the other a tax-collector. The Pharisee, standing by himself, was praying thus, 'God, I thank you that I am not like other people: thieves, rogues, adulterers, or even like this tax-collector. I fast twice a week; I give a tenth of all my income.' But the tax-collector, standing far off, would not even look up to heaven, but was beating his breast and saying, 'God, be merciful to me, a sinner!' I tell you, this man went down to his home justified rather than the other; for all who exalt themselves will be humbled, but all who humble themselves will be exalted."

- The Pharisee is not actually condemned by Jesus. In fact, many of the things he does are good. However, his prayer is less acceptable to God because he trusts in his own righteousness, whereas the tax collector throws himself wholly on God's mercy. One is centered on God; the other is centered on himself.

- The Pharisee derives his satisfaction from the fact that he does not commit the sins that other people do. But what matters is not avoiding this and doing that, but rather handing oneself over to God's mercy.

March 14–20, 2021

Something to think and pray about each day this week:

We are all pilgrims in the world and only passing through, but it is easy to get attached to things and believe the illusion of the material world. It goes without saying that you have to let go of a lot to be a pilgrim; walking the Camino de Santiago is the modern equivalent. As on the Camino and as in life, we have to travel light and adapt to whatever comes our way, whether it is the weather, health issues, unexpected obstacles, or inner wounds or blocks. The point is that many of these things are beyond our control, and leaving control aside and trusting in providence is the only way to really live. However, it's not so easy as it sounds because expectations get in the way like those for good food, rest, hygiene, and luxury. Modern life presupposes control of our environment, and lots of technology surrounds and cushions us. The liberation involved in letting go of comfort, ease, and security is hard won.

Being a pilgrim on the Camino gives freedom from trivial "things" to concentrate on more important ones: walking, talking, praying, appreciating, living. You actually need very little to get by, and all the things we think we need (technology, comfort, riches, style) have no value on the road. A rucksack that would contain everything you think you need would be impossible to carry. This is a great liberation and the recuperation of what it means to be human: a pilgrim on the road, dependent on providence and on others. The joy attached to this is palpable and infectious.

St. Ignatius calls this spiritual freedom: the ability to be free of small things for greater things. The opposite of freedom is attachment. I have to have certain things, I impose limits. I won't accept the basic simplicity of the Camino. This is the tragedy, of course: that such great joy exists so close, and yet we are kept from it by smaller things.

—Brendan McManus SJ, *Contemplating the Camino:*
An Ignatian Guide

The Presence of God
I pause for a moment
and reflect on God's life-giving presence
in every part of my body,
in everything around me,
in the whole of my life.

Freedom
Many countries are at this moment suffering the agonies of war. I bow my head in thanksgiving for my freedom. I pray for all prisoners and captives.

Consciousness
Knowing that God loves me unconditionally, I look honestly over the past day, its events, and my feelings. Do I have something to be grateful for? Then I give thanks. Is there something I am sorry for? Then I ask forgiveness.

The Word
Now I turn to the Scripture set out for me this day. I read slowly over the words and see if any sentence or sentiment appeals to me. (*Please turn to the Scripture on the following pages. Inspiration points are there, should you need them. When you are ready, return here to continue.*)

Conversation
I know with certainty that there were times when you carried me, Lord. There were times when it was through your strength that I got through the dark times in my life.

Conclusion
Glory be to the Father, and to the Son, and to the Holy Spirit,
As it was in the beginning, is now, and ever shall be,
World without end. Amen.

Sunday March 14
Fourth Sunday of Lent
John 3:14–21

"And just as Moses lifted up the serpent in the wilderness, so must the Son of Man be lifted up, that whoever believes in him may have eternal life.

"For God so loved the world that he gave his only Son, so that everyone who believes in him may not perish but may have eternal life.

"Indeed, God did not send the Son into the world to condemn the world, but in order that the world might be saved through him. Those who believe in him are not condemned; but those who do not believe are condemned already, because they have not believed in the name of the only Son of God. And this is the judgment, that the light has come into the world, and people loved darkness rather than light because their deeds were evil. For all who do evil hate the light and do not come to the light, so that their deeds may not be exposed. But those who do what is true come to the light, so that it may be clearly seen that their deeds have been done in God."

- God loved the world. This is my faith, Lord. Sometimes it seems to go against the evidence, when floods, earthquakes, droughts, and tsunamis devastate poor people. Central to my faith is the figure of Jesus, lifted on the cross, knowing what it was to be devastated and a failure, but offering himself in love for us.

Monday March 15
John 9:1–41

As he walked along, he saw a man blind from birth. His disciples asked him, "Rabbi, who sinned, this man or his parents, that he was born blind?" Jesus answered, "Neither this man nor his parents sinned; he was born blind so that God's works might be revealed in him. We must work the works of him who sent me while it is day; night is coming when no one can work. As long as I am in the world, I am the light of the world." When he had said this, he spat on the ground and made mud with the saliva and spread the mud on the man's eyes, saying to him, "Go, wash in the pool of Siloam" (which means Sent). Then he went and washed and came back able to see. The neighbors and those who had seen him before as a beggar began to ask, "Is this not the man who used to sit and beg?" Some were saying, "It is he." Others were saying, "No, but it is someone like him." He kept saying, "I am the man." But they kept asking him, "Then how were your eyes opened?" He answered, "The man called Jesus made mud, spread it on my eyes, and said to me, 'Go to Siloam and wash.' Then I went and washed and received my sight." They said to him, "Where is he?" He said, "I do not know."

They brought to the Pharisees the man who had formerly been blind. Now it was a sabbath day when Jesus made the mud and opened his eyes. Then the Pharisees also began to ask him how he had received his sight. He said to them, "He put mud on my eyes. Then I washed, and now I see." Some of the Pharisees said, "This man is not from God, for he does not observe the sabbath." But others said, "How can a man who is a sinner perform such signs?" And they were divided. So they said again to the blind man, "What do you say about him? It was your eyes he opened." He said, "He is a prophet."

The Jews did not believe that he had been blind and had received his sight until they called the parents of the man who had received his sight and asked them, "Is this your son, who you say was born blind? How then does he now see?" His parents answered, "We know that this is our son, and that he was born blind; but we do not know how it is that now he sees, nor do we know who opened his eyes. Ask him; he is of age. He will speak for himself." His parents said this because they were afraid of the Jews; for the Jews had already agreed that anyone who confessed Jesus to be the Messiah would be put out of the synagogue. Therefore his parents said, "He is of age; ask him."

So for the second time they called the man who had been blind, and they said to him, "Give glory to God! We know that this man is a sinner." He answered, "I do not know whether he is a sinner. One thing I do know, that though I was blind, now I see." They said to him, "What did he do to you? How did he open your eyes?" He answered them, "I have told you already, and you would not listen. Why do you want to hear it again? Do you also want to become his disciples?" Then they reviled him, saying, "You are his disciple, but we are disciples of Moses. We know that God has spoken to Moses, but as for this man, we do not know where he comes from." The man answered, "Here is an astonishing thing! You do not know where he comes from, and yet he opened my eyes. We know that God does not listen to sinners, but he does listen to one who worships him and obeys his will. Never since the world began has it been heard that anyone opened the eyes of a person born blind. If this man were not from God, he could do nothing." They answered him, "You were born entirely in sin, and are you trying to teach us?" And they drove him out.

Jesus heard that they had driven him out, and when he found him, he said, "Do you believe in the Son of Man?" He answered, "And who is he, sir? Tell me, so that I may believe in him." Jesus said to him, "You have seen him, and the one speaking with you is he." He said, "Lord, I believe." And he worshipped him. Jesus said, "I came into this world for judgment so that those who do not see may see, and those who do see may become blind." Some of the Pharisees near him heard this and said to him, "Surely we are not blind, are we?" Jesus said to them, "If you were blind, you would not have sin. But now that you say, 'We see,' your sin remains."

- The blind man receives not only his sight but also the courage to acknowledge what Jesus has done for him. "I am the man." In the full story in John 9:1–38, when the Pharisees argue with him about how Jesus is a sinner breaking the law by healing on the Sabbath, he fearlessly replies, "He is a prophet." Finally when he is driven out of the temple and Jesus goes looking for him, we hear him say, "Lord, I believe." He now sees with the eyes of faith as well.

- Spend time thanking the Lord for what he has done for you. Thanking God and others opens our eyes!

Tuesday March 16
John 5:1–16

After this there was a festival of the Jews, and Jesus went up to Jerusalem.

Now in Jerusalem by the Sheep Gate there is a pool, called in Hebrew Beth-zatha, which has five porticoes. In these lay many invalids—blind, lame and paralyzed. One man was there who had been ill for thirty-eight years. When Jesus saw him lying there and knew that he had been there a long time, he said to him, "Do you want to be made well?" The sick man answered him, "Sir, I have no one to put me into the pool when the water is stirred up; and while I am making my way, someone else steps down ahead of me." Jesus said to him, "Stand up, take your mat and walk." At once the man was made well, and he took up his mat and began to walk.

Now that day was a sabbath. So the Jews said to the man who had been cured, "It is the sabbath; it is not lawful for you to carry your mat." But he answered them, "The man who made me well said to me, 'Take up your mat and walk.'" They asked him, "Who is the man who said to you, 'Take it up and walk'?" Now the man who had been healed did not know who it was, for Jesus had disappeared in the crowd that was there. Later Jesus found him in the temple and said to him, "See, you have been made well! Do not sin any more, so that nothing worse happens to you." The man went away and told the Jews that it was Jesus who had made him well. Therefore the Jews started persecuting Jesus, because he was doing such things on the sabbath.

- Jesus saw the man, who had been ill for many years, lying at the pool. He knew the longings that were deep in the sick man's heart. He took the initiative and said to him, "Do you want to be made well?"

- This chronically ill person expected nothing new. There was no one to help him get first into the water that cured. But God can always surprise us. There is no end to his creative ability.

- The three commands of Jesus changed his life completely: "'Stand up, take your mat and walk." Or, in other words, become active again. Only when spoken by Jesus do these words have such force.

- If we allow Christ to speak these same words to us, we will achieve much.

Wednesday March 17
St. Patrick, Bishop and Patron of Ireland
John 5:17–30

But Jesus answered them, "My Father is still working, and I also am working." For this reason the Jews were seeking all the more to kill him, because he was not only breaking the sabbath, but was also calling God his own Father, thereby making himself equal to God. Jesus said to them, "Very truly, I tell you, the Son can do nothing on his own, but only what he sees the Father doing; for whatever the Father does, the Son does likewise. The Father loves the Son and shows him all that he himself is doing; and he will show him greater works than these, so that you will be astonished. Indeed, just as the Father raises the dead and gives them life, so also the Son gives life to whomsoever he wishes. The Father judges no one but has given all judgment to the Son, so that all may honor the Son just as they honor the Father. Anyone who does not honor the Son does not honor the Father who sent him. Very truly, I tell you, anyone who hears my word and believes him who sent me has eternal life, and does not come under judgment, but has passed from death to life. "Very truly, I tell you, the hour is coming, and is now here, when the dead will hear the voice of the Son of God, and those who hear will live. For just as the Father has life in himself, so he has granted the Son also to have life in himself; and he has given him authority to execute judgment, because he is the Son of Man. Do not be astonished at this; for the hour is coming when all who are in their graves will hear his voice and will come out— those who have done good, to the resurrection of life, and those who have done evil, to the resurrection of condemnation. I can do nothing on my own. As I hear, I judge; and my judgment is just, because I seek to do not my own will but the will of him who sent me."

- It's not so easy to pray this Gospel story! Read it a few times, stopping wherever a phrase catches your attention. Talk it over with the Lord.

- "My Father is still working, and I also am working." St. Ignatius Loyola used to say that the Lord is ever laboring on our behalf: an unexpected outcome; you are in the right place at the right time. Signs of God's providence at work. Thank the Lord for these moments.

- "My aim is to do not my own will, but the will of him who sent me." We get a glimpse of Jesus' heart in unison with his Father. Jesus does nothing without praying to his Father. End by slowly praying "Father" a number of times.

Thursday March 18
John 5:31–47

"If I testify about myself, my testimony is not true. There is another who testifies on my behalf, and I know that his testimony to me is true. You sent messengers to John, and he testified to the truth. Not that I accept such human testimony, but I say these things so that you may be saved. He was a burning and shining lamp, and you were willing to rejoice for a while in his light. But I have a testimony greater than John's. The works that the Father has given me to complete, the very works that I am doing, testify on my behalf that the Father has sent me. And the Father who sent me has himself testified on my behalf. You have never heard his voice or seen his form, and you do not have his word abiding in you, because you do not believe him whom he has sent.

"You search the scriptures because you think that in them you have eternal life; and it is they that testify on my behalf. Yet you refuse to come to me to have life. I do not accept glory from human beings. But I know that you do not have the love of God in you. I have come in my Father's name, and you do not accept me; if another comes in his own name, you will accept him. How can you believe when you accept glory from one another and do not seek the glory that comes from the one who alone is God? Do not think that I will accuse you before the Father; your accuser is Moses, on whom you have set your hope. If you believed Moses, you would believe me, for he wrote about me. But if you do not believe what he wrote, how will you believe what I say?"

- The biblical rule of evidence required two witnesses. Jesus calls on John the Baptist and Moses to testify to his identity and his mission. What would a person of integrity say about me?

- John the Baptist fulfilled Isaiah's prophecy, that a voice would cry, "In the wilderness prepare the way of the Lord; make straight in the desert a highway for our God." As we make our Lenten journey, let us reflect on what we are doing to make our own crooked ways straight.

Friday March 19
St. Joseph, Spouse of the Blessed Virgin Mary
Luke 2:41–51a

Now every year his parents went to Jerusalem for the festival of the Passover. And when he was twelve years old, they went up as usual for the festival. When the festival was ended and they started to return, the boy Jesus stayed behind in Jerusalem, but his parents did not know it. Assuming that he was in the group of travelers, they went a day's journey. Then they started to look for him among their relatives and friends. When they did not find him, they returned to Jerusalem to search for him. After three days they found him in the temple, sitting among the teachers, listening to them and asking them questions. And all who heard him were amazed at his understanding and his answers. When his parents saw him they were astonished; and his mother said to him, "Child, why have you treated us like this? Look, your father and I have been searching for you in great anxiety." He said to them, "Why were you searching for me? Did you not know that I must be in my Father's house?" But they did not understand what he said to them. Then he went down with them and came to Nazareth, and was obedient to them. His mother treasured all these things in her heart.

- The parents of Jesus were observant Jews. This vignette is the last we will hear of Jesus' early years. Jesus is coming of age. He is entering his teens. We see already the gradual, slow but steady growing into his sense of identity and mission.

- Lord, today I remember all the missing children of our world through slavery, bonded labor, and trafficking. I pray for their distraught parents who frantically seek for the child entrusted to them.

Saturday March 20
John 7:40–53

When they heard these words, some in the crowd said, "This is really the prophet." Others said, "This is the Messiah." But some asked, "Surely the Messiah does not come from Galilee, does he? Has not the scripture said that the Messiah is descended from David and comes from Bethlehem, the village where David lived?" So there was a division in the crowd because of him. Some of them wanted to arrest him, but no one laid hands on him.

Then the temple police went back to the chief priests and Pharisees, who asked them, "Why did you not arrest him?" The police answered, "Never has anyone spoken like this!" Then the Pharisees replied, "Surely you have not been deceived too, have you? Has any one of the authorities or of the Pharisees believed in him? But this crowd, which does not know the law—they are accursed." Nicodemus, who had gone to Jesus before, and who was one of them, asked, "Our law does not judge people without first giving them a hearing to find out what they are doing, does it?" They replied, "Surely you are not also from Galilee, are you? Search and you will see that no prophet is to arise from Galilee."

- There is a wide range of views among the Jewish people as to who Jesus really is. Notice the constant appeal to the Old Testament. We may be more convinced by what the temple police report: "Never has anyone spoken like this!" Jesus speaks with integrity, with wisdom, and with authority. This impresses these unsophisticated men. They are able to recognize the goodness of Jesus, which was hidden from the religious leaders.

- Pope Francis teaches that we must listen to the poor and the marginalized because they have a special insight into the reality of the world and of God.

The Fifth Week of Lent
March 21–27, 2021

Something to think and pray about each day this week:

Again, the angel answered her core concern: "The Holy Spirit will come upon you, and the power of the Most High will overshadow you" (Luke 1:35). The angel made it clear that Joseph, the man to whom Mary was engaged, would have no part to play in the conception of this child. All Mary needed to do was give her assent, and then God's own creative power would bring this child into existence. Because this child would be the gift of God, and not of any man, the angel Gabriel emphasized that "the child to be born will be holy; he will be called the Son of God" (Luke 1:35). Son of God because the Son of the Heavenly Father, and not of any earthly father. Mary's unique relationship with God would not be compromised.

We are so familiar with the story of the Annunciation that it can be easy to take Mary's faith for granted. It's easy to forget that Gabriel's message opened up a vast new horizon for Mary. He didn't give Mary any human guarantees, he didn't offer her a familiar or secure way forward. He took her completely beyond any comfort zone. Everything about this singular episode demanded a huge leap of faith: it was already hard enough to accept that an angel was speaking to her, it was even more difficult to believe that a virgin could conceive. But who could imagine that any woman could possibly become God's own mother! Gabriel was painting a picture that bordered on the preposterous. Mary didn't stop to think about the sheer unlikelihood of what was being announced. If she had, she most likely would have refused to believe. Mary's focus was on God. She believed enough in God's power and love to accept the message that Gabriel communicated to her. She plunged wholeheartedly into the limitless ocean of God as she said: "Behold the servant of the Lord, let it be done unto me according to your word" (Luke 1:38).

—Thomas Casey, SJ, *Smile of Joy: Mary of Nazareth*

The Presence of God
I pause for a moment and think of the love and the grace that God showers on me. I am created in the image and likeness of God; I am God's dwelling place.

Freedom
Lord, you granted me the great gift of freedom. In these times, O Lord, grant that I may be free from any form of racism or intolerance. Remind me that we are all equal in your loving eyes.

Consciousness
Knowing that God loves me unconditionally,
I can afford to be honest about how I am.
How has the day been, and how do I feel now?
I share my feelings openly with the Lord.

The Word
I take my time to read the word of God slowly, a few times, allowing myself to dwell on anything that strikes me. (*Please turn to the Scripture on the following pages. Inspiration points are there, should you need them. When you are ready, return here to continue.*)

Conversation
Sometimes I wonder what I might say if I were to meet you in person, Lord.
I think I might say, "Thank you" because you are always there for me.

Conclusion
I thank God for these moments we have spent together and for any insights I have been given concerning the text.

Sunday March 21
Fifth Sunday of Lent
John 12:20–33

Now among those who went up to worship at the festival were some Greeks. They came to Philip, who was from Bethsaida in Galilee, and said to him, "Sir, we wish to see Jesus." Philip went and told Andrew; then Andrew and Philip went and told Jesus. Jesus answered them, "The hour has come for the Son of Man to be glorified. Very truly, I tell you, unless a grain of wheat falls into the earth and dies, it remains just a single grain; but if it dies, it bears much fruit. Those who love their life lose it, and those who hate their life in this world will keep it for eternal life. Whoever serves me must follow me, and where I am, there will my servant be also. Whoever serves me, the Father will honor.

"Now my soul is troubled. And what should I say—'Father, save me from this hour'? No, it is for this reason that I have come to this hour. Father, glorify your name." Then a voice came from heaven, "I have glorified it, and I will glorify it again." The crowd standing there heard it and said that it was thunder. Others said, "An angel has spoken to him." Jesus answered, "This voice has come for your sake, not for mine. Now is the judgment of this world; now the ruler of this world will be driven out. And I, when I am lifted up from the earth, will draw all people to myself." He said this to indicate the kind of death he was to die.

- In every death, there is life—this is the big message of Lent and of Easter. The grain of wheat will die and will through death nourish us with food. In the death of relationships, of health, of faith, and all that may be dear to us there is always the invitation to deeper life. In our final death is the call to everlasting life.

Monday March 22
John 11:1–45

Now a certain man was ill, Lazarus of Bethany, the village of Mary and her sister Martha. Mary was the one who anointed the Lord with perfume and wiped his feet with her hair; her brother Lazarus was ill. So the sisters sent a message to Jesus, "Lord, he whom you love is ill." But when Jesus heard it, he said, "This illness does not lead to death; rather it is for God's glory, so that the Son of God may be glorified through it." Accordingly, though Jesus loved Martha and her sister and Lazarus, after having heard that Lazarus was ill, he stayed two days longer in the place where he was.

Then after this he said to the disciples, "Let us go to Judea again." The disciples said to him, "Rabbi, the Jews were just now trying to stone you, and are you going there again?" Jesus answered, "Are there not twelve hours of daylight? Those who walk during the day do not stumble, because they see the light of this world. But those who walk at night stumble, because the light is not in them." After saying this, he told them, "Our friend Lazarus has fallen asleep, but I am going there to awaken him." The disciples said to him, "Lord, if he has fallen asleep, he will be all right." Jesus, however, had been speaking about his death, but they thought that he was referring merely to sleep. Then Jesus told them plainly, "Lazarus is dead. For your sake I am glad I was not there, so that you may believe. But let us go to him." Thomas, who was called the Twin, said to his fellow-disciples, "Let us also go, that we may die with him."

When Jesus arrived, he found that Lazarus had already been in the tomb for four days. Now Bethany was near Jerusalem, some two miles away, and many of the Jews had come to Martha and Mary to console them about their brother. When Martha heard that Jesus was coming, she went and met him, while Mary stayed at home. Martha said to Jesus, "Lord, if you had been here, my brother would not have died. But even now I know that God will give you whatever you ask of him." Jesus said to her, "Your brother will rise again." Martha said to him, "I know that he will rise again in the resurrection on the last day." Jesus said to her, "I am the resurrection and the life. Those who believe in me, even though they die, will live, and everyone who lives and believes in me will never die. Do you believe this?" She said to him, "Yes, Lord, I believe that you are the Messiah, the Son of God, the one coming into the world."

When she had said this, she went back and called her sister Mary, and told her privately, "The Teacher is here and is calling for you." And when she heard it, she got up quickly and went to him. Now Jesus had not yet come to the village, but was still at the place where Martha had met him. The Jews who were with her in the house, consoling her, saw Mary get up quickly and go out. They followed her because they thought that she was going to the tomb to weep there. When Mary came where Jesus was and saw him, she knelt at his feet and said to him, "Lord, if you had been here, my brother would not have died." When Jesus saw her weeping, and the Jews who came with her also weeping, he was greatly disturbed in spirit and deeply moved. He said, "Where have you laid him?" They said to him, "Lord, come and see." Jesus began to weep. So the Jews said, "See how he loved him!" But some of them said, "Could not he who opened the eyes of the blind man have kept this man from dying?"

Then Jesus, again greatly disturbed, came to the tomb. It was a cave, and a stone was lying against it. Jesus said, "Take away the stone." Martha, the sister of the dead man, said to him, "Lord, already there is a stench because he has been dead for four days." Jesus said to her, "Did I not tell you that if you believed, you would see the glory of God?" So they took away the stone. And Jesus looked upward and said, "Father, I thank you for having heard me. I knew that you always hear me, but I have said this for the sake of the crowd standing here, so that they may believe that you sent me." When he had said this, he cried with a loud voice, "Lazarus, come out!" The dead man came out, his hands and feet bound with strips of cloth, and his face wrapped in a cloth. Jesus said to them, "Unbind him, and let him go."

Many of the Jews therefore, who had come with Mary and had seen what Jesus did, believed in him.

- I hear you asking me the same question, Lord: "Do you believe that I am the resurrection and the life?" In the long run, nothing is more important than my answer to this. I cannot grasp your words in my imagination, Lord, but I believe. Help my unbelief.

Tuesday March 23
John 8:21–30

Again he said to them, "I am going away, and you will search for me, but you will die in your sin. Where I am going, you cannot come." Then the Jews said, "Is he going to kill himself? Is that what he means by saying, 'Where I am going, you cannot come'?" He said to them, "You are from below, I am from above; you are of this world, I am not of this world. I told you that you would die in your sins, for you will die in your sins unless you believe that I am he." They said to him, "Who are you?" Jesus said to them, "Why do I speak to you at all? I have much to say about you and much to condemn; but the one who sent me is true, and I declare to the world what I have heard from him." They did not understand that he was speaking to them about the Father. So Jesus said, "When you have lifted up the Son of Man, then you will realize that I am he, and that I do nothing on my own, but I speak these things as the Father instructed me. And the one who sent me is with me; he has not left me alone, for I always do what is pleasing to him." As he was saying these things, many believed in him.

- St. John wants the early Christians to realize that Jesus is totally unique: he belongs to the world of the divine. He reveals the mystery of what God is like. When I knock on God's door, Jesus opens it and invites me in to meet his Father!

- "I always do what is pleasing to the Father." This reveals the heart of Jesus' spirituality. I pray that it may become the truth of my life too, because God is so good to me.

Wednesday March 24
John 8:31–42

Then Jesus said to the Jews who had believed in him, "If you continue in my word, you are truly my disciples; and you will know the truth, and the truth will make you free." They answered him, "We are descendants of Abraham and have never been slaves to anyone. What do you mean by saying, 'You will be made free'?"

Jesus answered them, "Very truly, I tell you, everyone who commits sin is a slave to sin. The slave does not have a permanent place in the household; the son has a place there for ever. So if the Son makes you free, you will be free indeed. I know that you are descendants of Abraham; yet you look for an opportunity to kill me, because there is no place in you for my word. I declare what I have seen in the Father's presence; as for you, you should do what you have heard from the Father."

They answered him, "Abraham is our father." Jesus said to them, "If you were Abraham's children, you would be doing what Abraham did, but now you are trying to kill me, a man who has told you the truth that I heard from God. This is not what Abraham did. You are indeed doing what your father does." They said to him, "We are not illegitimate children; we have one father, God himself." Jesus said to them, "If God were your Father, you would love me, for I came from God and now I am here. I did not come on my own, but he sent me."

- Jesus' promise is that the truth will make us free. Lord, I do want to be free, so let me listen to those who tell me the truth about myself. Let me listen also to your word, which tries to reach into my heart and liberate me. Let me start with the great truth of which you try to convince me: that I am endlessly loved by you.

- When have I had an experience that made me truly see Jesus as the one sent by God?

Thursday March 25
The Annunciation of the Lord
Luke 1:26–38

In the sixth month the angel Gabriel was sent by God to a town in Galilee called Nazareth, to a virgin engaged to a man whose name was Joseph, of the house of David. The virgin's name was Mary. And he came to her and said, "Greetings, favored one! The Lord is with you." But she was much perplexed by his words and pondered what sort of greeting this might be. The angel said to her, "Do not be afraid, Mary, for you have found favor with God. And now, you will conceive in your womb and bear a son, and you will name him Jesus. He will be great, and will be called the Son of the Most High, and the Lord God will give to him the throne of his ancestor David. He will reign over the house of Jacob for ever, and of his kingdom there will be no end." Mary said to the angel, "How can this be, since I am a virgin?" The angel said to her, "The Holy Spirit will come upon you, and the power of the Most High will overshadow you; therefore the child to be born will be holy; he will be called Son of God. And now, your relative Elizabeth in her old age has also conceived a son; and this is the sixth month for her who was said to be barren. For nothing will be impossible with God." Then Mary said, "Here am I, the servant of the Lord; let it be with me according to your word." Then the angel departed from her.

- For Mary the angel's message is a blessing; but very much a blessing in disguise. It is placing her in a very difficult position socially, culturally, religiously, and personally. She has to trust this interior movement in her heart and "go with it." And she does.

- In our lives too there are turning points where we may experience an invitation to embrace something difficult rather than discard it.

Something that wrecks our dream for ourselves or for our loved ones. There's a need to discern the spirits.

- Is there release from something into another way of being more open, more generous, more humble, deeper in service of Christ Jesus?
- If it is disconcerting that does not mean that it is bad. What response would your better self give?

Friday March 26
John 10:31–42

The Jews took up stones again to stone him. Jesus replied, "I have shown you many good works from the Father. For which of these are you going to stone me?" The Jews answered, "It is not for a good work that we are going to stone you, but for blasphemy, because you, though only a human being, are making yourself God." Jesus answered, "Is it not written in your law, 'I said, you are gods'? If those to whom the word of God came were called 'gods'—and the scripture cannot be annulled—can you say that the one whom the Father has sanctified and sent into the world is blaspheming because I said, 'I am God's Son'? If I am not doing the works of my Father, then do not believe me. But if I do them, even though you do not believe me, believe the works, so that you may know and understand that the Father is in me and I am in the Father." Then they tried to arrest him again, but he escaped from their hands.

He went away again across the Jordan to the place where John had been baptizing earlier, and he remained there. Many came to him, and they were saying, "John performed no sign, but everything that John said about this man was true." And many believed in him there.

- The works of Jesus are the works of love. This is the love we know of him—love unto death. What we see in Jesus, we can see of the Father. What the Father sees in Jesus, he sees and loves in us. We pray that our hearts may be made like the heart of Jesus.

Saturday March 27
John 11:45–56

Many of the Jews, therefore, who had come with Mary and had seen what Jesus did, believed in him. But some of them went to the Pharisees and told them what he had done. So the chief priests and the Pharisees called a meeting of the council, and said, "What are we to do? This man is performing many signs. If we let him go on like this, everyone will believe in him, and the Romans will come and destroy both our holy place and our nation." But one of them, Caiaphas, who was high priest that year, said to them, "You know nothing at all! You do not understand that it is better for you to have one man die for the people than to have the whole nation destroyed." He did not say this on his own, but being high priest that year he prophesied that Jesus was about to die for the nation, and not for the nation only, but to gather into one the dispersed children of God. So from that day on they planned to put him to death.

Jesus therefore no longer walked about openly among the Jews, but went from there to a town called Ephraim in the region near the wilderness; and he remained there with the disciples.

Now the Passover of the Jews was near, and many went up from the country to Jerusalem before the Passover to purify themselves. They were looking for Jesus and were asking one another as they stood in the temple, "What do you think? Surely he will not come to the festival, will he?"

- The chief priests and the scribes—among the most learned people in Israel—did not recognize Jesus. Blinded by prejudice, they decided to put him to death. Do I ever harbor death wishes for another, even subconsciously?

Holy Week
March 28—April 3, 2021

Something to think and pray about each day this week:

Is Holy Week a strange name for the week of Jesus' passion? It seems a week of torture, pain, imprisonment, denial, and betrayal, ending in death for Jesus. It was a week of enormous crisis for the followers of Jesus, and a week of intense pain for Mary, his mother. Why call it holy? Why call Good Friday "good" when it seems to be one of the worst days of human history? A key would be in the letter of Pope Francis on Holiness, *Gaudete et Exsultate* (2017). His view of holiness is of a life marked by, among other things, perseverance, patience, and gentleness (112–21), boldness and passion (129–39), and constant prayer (147–57).

In Holy Week Jesus did not give up, and he prayed often. This is why the week is holy: Jesus is totally committed to God in this week in ordinary and extraordinary ways.

Palm Sunday reminds us of the victory of Jesus over death; the washing of the feet reminds us of the call to all of service; the cross of Friday of the huge love of Jesus for us, and Holy Saturday of patient waiting for the victory of Jesus. This is a holy week.

For us Holy Week is not just a memory. It is a week to remember all that Jesus did to save us, a week to grow in holiness ourselves, and a week that leads into the joy of the resurrection, which is the beginning of the new life of Jesus.

It is the high point of the Church year; we can mark it by taking part in the ceremonies of the last three days (the triduum), by praying with www.sacredspace.ie or www.prayasyougo.org, or spending time with readings in quiet prayer before attending the ceremonies; we can go to a Lenten confession, to Mass during the week, and keep an eye out for how we can be of loving service to those near to us, and far away. Then it will be a holy week for ourselves, and a sharing in the holiness of God.

—Donal Neary, SJ, *The Sacred Heart Messenger*,
April 2020

The Presence of God

I pause for a moment and think of the love and the grace that God showers on me. I am created in the image and likeness of God; I am God's dwelling place.

Freedom

I am free. When I look at these words in writing, they seem to create in me a feeling of awe. Yes, a wonderful feeling of freedom. Thank you, God.

Consciousness

In the presence of my loving Creator, I look honestly at my feelings over the past day: the highs, the lows, and the level ground. Can I see where the Lord has been present?

The Word

I read the word of God slowly, a few times over, and I listen to what God is saying to me. (*Please turn to the Scripture on the following pages. Inspiration points are there, should you need them. When you are ready, return here to continue.*)

Conversation

Remembering that I am still in God's presence,
I imagine Jesus standing or sitting beside me,
and I say whatever is on my mind, whatever is in my heart,
speaking as one friend to another.

Conclusion

Glory be to the Father, and to the Son, and to the Holy Spirit,
As it was in the beginning, is now, and ever shall be,
World without end. Amen.

Sunday March 28
Palm Sunday of the Passion of the Lord
Mark 14:1–15:47

It was two days before the Passover and the festival of Unleavened Bread. The chief priests and the scribes were looking for a way to arrest Jesus by stealth and kill him; for they said, "Not during the festival, or there may be a riot among the people."

While he was at Bethany in the house of Simon the leper, as he sat at the table, a woman came with an alabaster jar of very costly ointment of nard, and she broke open the jar and poured the ointment on his head. But some were there who said to one another in anger, "Why was the ointment wasted in this way? For this ointment could have been sold for more than three hundred denarii, and the money given to the poor." And they scolded her. But Jesus said, "Let her alone; why do you trouble her? She has performed a good service for me. For you always have the poor with you, and you can show kindness to them whenever you wish; but you will not always have me. She has done what she could; she has anointed my body beforehand for its burial. Truly I tell you, wherever the good news is proclaimed in the whole world, what she has done will be told in remembrance of her."

Then Judas Iscariot, who was one of the twelve, went to the chief priests in order to betray him to them. When they heard it, they were greatly pleased, and promised to give him money. So he began to look for an opportunity to betray him.

On the first day of Unleavened Bread, when the Passover lamb is sacrificed, his disciples said to him, "Where do you want us to go and make the preparations for you to eat the Passover?" So he sent two of his disciples, saying to them, "Go into the city, and a man carrying a jar of water will meet you; follow him, and wherever he enters, say to the owner of the house, 'The Teacher asks, Where is my guest room where I may eat the Passover with my disciples?' He will show you a large room upstairs, furnished and ready. Make preparations for us there." So the disciples set out and went to the city, and found everything as he had told them; and they prepared the Passover meal.

When it was evening, he came with the twelve. And when they had taken their places and were eating, Jesus said, "Truly I tell you, one of you will betray me, one who is eating with me." They began to be distressed and to say to him one after another, "Surely, not I?" He said to them, "It is one of the twelve, one who is dipping bread into the bowl with me. For the Son of Man goes as it is written of him, but woe to that one by whom the Son of Man is betrayed! It would have been better for that one not to have been born."

While they were eating, he took a loaf of bread, and after blessing it he broke it, gave it to them, and said, "Take; this is my body." Then he took a cup, and after giving thanks he gave it to them, and all of them drank from it. He said to them, "This is my blood of the covenant, which is poured out for many. Truly I tell you, I will never again drink of the fruit of the vine until that day when I drink it new in the kingdom of God."

When they had sung the hymn, they went out to the Mount of Olives. And Jesus said to them, "You will all become deserters; for it is written,

'I will strike the shepherd,
and the sheep will be scattered.'

But after I am raised up, I will go before you to Galilee." Peter said to him, "Even though all become deserters, I will not." Jesus said to him, "Truly I tell you, this day, this very night, before the cock crows twice, you will deny me three times." But he said vehemently, "Even though I must die with you, I will not deny you." And all of them said the same.

They went to a place called Gethsemane; and he said to his disciples, "Sit here while I pray." He took with him Peter and James and John, and began to be distressed and agitated. And he said to them, "I am deeply grieved, even to death; remain here, and keep awake." And going a little farther, he threw himself on the ground and prayed that, if it were possible, the hour might pass from him. He said, "Abba, Father, for you all things are possible; remove this cup from me; yet, not what I want, but what you want." He came and found them sleeping; and he said to Peter, "Simon, are you asleep? Could you not keep awake one hour? Keep awake and pray that you may not come into the time of trial; the spirit indeed is willing, but the flesh is weak." And again he went away and prayed, saying the same words. And once more he came and found them sleeping, for their eyes were very heavy; and they did not know what to say to him. He came a third time and said to them, "Are you still sleeping and taking your rest? Enough! The hour has come; the Son of Man is betrayed into the hands of sinners. Get up, let us be going. See, my betrayer is at hand."

Immediately, while he was still speaking, Judas, one of the twelve, arrived; and with him there was a crowd with swords and clubs, from the chief priests, the scribes, and the elders. Now the betrayer had given them a sign, saying, "The one I will kiss is the man; arrest him and lead him away under guard." So when he came, he went up to him at once and said, "Rabbi!" and kissed him. Then they laid hands on him and arrested him. But one of those who stood near drew his sword and struck the slave of the high priest, cutting off his ear. Then Jesus said to them, "Have you come out with swords and clubs to arrest me as though I were a bandit? Day after day I was with you in the temple teaching, and you did not arrest me. But let the scriptures be fulfilled." All of them deserted him and fled.

A certain young man was following him, wearing nothing but a linen cloth. They caught hold of him, but he left the linen cloth and ran off naked.

They took Jesus to the high priest; and all the chief priests, the elders and the scribes were assembled. Peter had followed him at a distance, right into the courtyard of the high priest; and he was sitting with the guards, warming himself at the fire. Now the chief priests and the whole council were looking for testimony against Jesus to put him to death; but they found none. For many gave false testimony against him, and their testimony did not agree. Some stood up and gave false testimony against him, saying, "We heard him say, 'I will destroy this temple that is made with hands, and in three days I will build another, not made with hands.'" But even on this point their testimony did not agree. Then the high priest stood up before them and asked Jesus, "Have you no answer? What is it that they testify against you?" But he was silent and did not answer. Again the high priest asked him, "Are you the Messiah, the Son of the Blessed One?" Jesus said, "I am; and

> 'you will see the Son of Man
> seated at the right hand of the Power,'
> and 'coming with the clouds of heaven.'"

Then the high priest tore his clothes and said, "Why do we still need witnesses? You have heard his blasphemy! What is your decision?" All of them condemned him as deserving death. Some began to spit on him, to blindfold him, and to strike him, saying to him, "Prophesy!" The guards also took him over and beat him.

While Peter was below in the courtyard, one of the servant-girls of the high priest came by. When she saw Peter warming himself, she stared at him and said, "You also were with Jesus, the man from Nazareth." But he denied it, saying, "I do not know or understand what you are talking about." And he went out into the forecourt. Then the cock crowed. And the servant-girl, on seeing him, began again to say to the bystanders, "This man is one of them." But again he denied it. Then after a little while the bystanders again said to Peter, "Certainly you are one of them; for you are a Galilean." But he began to curse, and he swore an oath, "I do not know this man you are talking about." At that moment the cock crowed for the second time. Then Peter remembered that Jesus had said to him, "Before the cock crows twice, you will deny me three times." And he broke down and wept.

As soon as it was morning, the chief priests held a consultation with the elders and scribes and the whole council. They bound Jesus, led him away, and handed him over to Pilate. Pilate asked him, "Are you the King of the Jews?" He answered him, "You say so." Then the chief priests accused him of many things. Pilate asked him again, "Have you no answer? See how many charges they bring against you." But Jesus made no further reply, so that Pilate was amazed.

Now at the festival he used to release a prisoner for them, anyone for whom they asked. Now a man called Barabbas was in prison with the rebels who had committed murder during the insurrection. So the crowd came and began to ask Pilate to do for them according to his custom. Then he answered them, "Do you want me to release for you the King of the Jews?" For he realized that it was out of jealousy that the chief priests had handed him over. But the chief priests stirred up the crowd to have him release Barabbas for them instead. Pilate spoke to them again, "Then what do you wish me to do with the man you call the King of the Jews?" They shouted back, "Crucify him!" Pilate asked them, "Why, what evil has he done?" But they shouted all the more, "Crucify him!" So Pilate, wishing to satisfy the crowd, released Barabbas for them; and after flogging Jesus, he handed him over to be crucified.

Then the soldiers led him into the courtyard of the palace (that is, the governor's headquarters); and they called together the whole cohort. And they clothed him in a purple cloak; and after twisting some thorns into a crown, they put it on him. And they began saluting him, "Hail, King of the Jews!" They struck his head with a reed, spat upon him, and knelt down in homage to him. After mocking him, they stripped him of the purple cloak and put his own clothes on him. Then they led him out to crucify him.

They compelled a passer-by, who was coming in from the country, to carry his cross; it was Simon of Cyrene, the father of Alexander and Rufus. Then they brought Jesus to the place called Golgotha (which means the place of a skull). And they offered him wine mixed with myrrh; but he did not take it. And they crucified him, and divided his clothes among them, casting lots to decide what each should take.

It was nine o'clock in the morning when they crucified him. The inscription of the charge against him read, "The King of the Jews." And with him they crucified two bandits, one on his right and one on his left. Those who passed by derided him, shaking their heads and saying, "Aha! You who would destroy the temple and build it in three days, save yourself, and come down from the cross!" In the same way the chief priests, along with the scribes, were also mocking him among themselves and saying, "He saved others; he cannot save himself. Let the Messiah, the King of Israel, come down from the cross now, so that we may see and believe." Those who were crucified with him also taunted him.

When it was noon, darkness came over the whole land until three in the afternoon. At three o'clock Jesus cried out with a loud voice, "*Eloi, Eloi, lama sabachthani?*" which means, "My God, my God, why have you forsaken me?" When some of the bystanders heard it, they said, "Listen, he is calling for Elijah." And someone ran, filled a sponge with sour wine, put it on a stick, and gave it to him to drink, saying, "Wait, let us see whether Elijah will come to take him down." Then Jesus gave a loud cry and breathed his last. And the curtain of the temple was torn in two, from top to bottom. Now when the centurion, who stood facing him, saw that in this way he breathed his last, he said, "Truly this man was God's Son!"

There were also women looking on from a distance; among them were Mary Magdalene, and Mary the mother of James the younger and of Joses, and Salome. These used to follow him and provided for him when he was in Galilee; and there were many other women who had come up with him to Jerusalem.

When evening had come, and since it was the day of Preparation, that is, the day before the sabbath, Joseph of Arimathea, a respected member of the council, who was also himself waiting expectantly for the kingdom of God, went boldly to Pilate and asked for the body of Jesus. Then Pilate wondered if he were already dead; and summoning the centurion, he asked him whether he had been dead for some time. When he learned from the centurion that he was dead, he granted the body to Joseph. Then Joseph bought a linen cloth, and taking down the body, wrapped it in the linen cloth, and laid it in a tomb that had been hewn out of the rock. He then rolled a stone against the door of the tomb. Mary Magdalene and Mary the mother of Joses saw where the body was laid.

- As I read these seminal verses, I pray to have the faith of Peter, who was the rock on whom the early Christians leaned. I look at Jesus and seek words to express what he means to me, and open my heart to God's revelation.

- She came to comfort the man in danger. A woman who put her own reputation and safety on the line to comfort the one she loved in thanks for his compassion for her. Her action would be remembered forever, and the scent of her ointment is the scent of resurrection: this nard would soothe the spirits of those who would always miss Jesus.

- Part of our prayer is missing Jesus when he seems so absent and prayerful feelings seem so distant. The scent of the Lord in our lives keeps us going.

Monday March 29
Luke 4:16–21

When he came to Nazareth, where he had been brought up, he went to the synagogue on the sabbath day, as was his custom. He stood up to read, and the scroll of the prophet Isaiah was given to him. He unrolled the scroll and found the place where it was written:

> "The Spirit of the Lord is upon me,
> because he has anointed me
> to bring good news to the poor.
> He has sent me to proclaim release to the captives
> and recovery of sight to the blind,
> to let the oppressed go free,
> to proclaim the year of the Lord's favor."

And he rolled up the scroll, gave it back to the attendant, and sat down. The eyes of all in the synagogue were fixed on him. Then he began to say to them, "Today this scripture has been fulfilled in your hearing."

- Lord, this is a scene I would love to have witnessed. Let me unroll it slowly.

- Jesus' good news is that we are all loved unconditionally by God—no ifs, no buts. When I accept that, truly believe and live by it, I gain freedom of heart and mind and a new insight into the ways God works in our lives.

Tuesday March 30
John 13:21–33, 36–38

After saying this Jesus was troubled in spirit, and declared, "Very truly, I tell you, one of you will betray me." The disciples looked at one another, uncertain of whom he was speaking. One of his disciples—the one whom Jesus loved—was reclining next to him; Simon Peter therefore motioned to him to ask Jesus of whom he was speaking. So, while reclining next to Jesus, he asked him, "Lord, who is it?" Jesus answered, "It is the one to whom I give this piece of bread when I have dipped it in the dish." So when he had dipped the piece of bread, he gave it to Judas son of Simon Iscariot. After he received the piece of bread, Satan entered into him. Jesus said to him, "Do quickly what you are going to do." Now no one at the table knew why he said this to him. Some thought that, because Judas had the common purse, Jesus was telling him, "Buy what we need for the festival"; or, that he should give something to the poor. So, after receiving the piece of bread, he immediately went out. And it was night.

When he had gone out, Jesus said, "Now the Son of Man has been glorified, and God has been glorified in him. If God has been glorified in him, God will also glorify him in himself and will glorify him at once. Little children, I am with you only a little longer. You will look for me; and as I said to the Jews so now I say to you, 'Where I am going, you cannot come.'" . . .

Simon Peter said to him, "Lord, where are you going?" Jesus answered, "Where I am going, you cannot follow me now; but you will follow afterward." Peter said to him, "Lord, why can I not follow you now? I will lay down my life for you." Jesus answered, "Will you lay down your life for me? Very truly, I tell you, before the cock crows, you will have denied me three times."

- Peter hit deep points of his life in this scene. His sureness of following Jesus was challenged by Jesus himself. He would later find himself weak and failing in this following. But this would not be the last word; even when Peter said later that he didn't know Jesus, there would be time for taking it back and speaking it with his life. We oscillate in our following of the Lord; these days let us know in the certainty of Jesus' love that there is always another day, another chance, another joy in our following of Jesus.

Wednesday March 31
Matthew 26:14–25

Then one of the twelve, who was called Judas Iscariot, went to the chief priests and said, "What will you give me if I betray him to you?" They paid him thirty pieces of silver. And from that moment he began to look for an opportunity to betray him.

On the first day of Unleavened Bread the disciples came to Jesus, saying, "Where do you want us to make the preparations for you to eat the Passover?" He said, "Go into the city to a certain man, and say to him, 'The Teacher says, My time is near; I will keep the Passover at your house with my disciples.'" So the disciples did as Jesus had directed them, and they prepared the Passover meal.

When it was evening, he took his place with the twelve; and while they were eating, he said, "Truly I tell you, one of you will betray me." And they became greatly distressed and began to say to him one after another, "Surely not I, Lord?" He answered, "The one who has dipped his hand into the bowl with me will betray me. The Son of Man goes as it is written of him, but woe to that one by whom the Son of Man is betrayed! It would have been better for that one not to have been born." Judas, who betrayed him, said, "Surely not I, Rabbi?" He replied, "You have said so."

- Holy Week is an invitation to walk closely with Jesus: we fix our gaze on him and accompany him in his suffering; we let him look closely at us and see us as we really are. We do not have to present a brave face to him but can tell him about where we have been disappointed, let down—perhaps even betrayed. We avoid getting stuck in our own misfortune by seeing as he sees, by learning from his heart.

- Help me to see, Jesus, how you do not condemn. You invite each of us to recognize the truth of our own discipleship. You invite us to follow you willingly, freely, forgiven.

Thursday April 1
Holy Thursday
John 13:1–15

Now before the festival of the Passover, Jesus knew that his hour had come to depart from this world and go to the Father. Having loved his own who were in the world, he loved them to the end. The devil had already put it into the heart of Judas son of Simon Iscariot to betray him. And during supper Jesus, knowing that the Father had given all things into his hands, and that he had come from God and was going to God, got up from the table, took off his outer robe, and tied a towel around himself. Then he poured water into a basin and began to wash the disciples' feet and to wipe them with the towel that was tied around him. He came to Simon Peter, who said to him, "Lord, are you going to wash my feet?" Jesus answered, "You do not know now what I am doing, but later you will understand." Peter said to him, "You will never wash my feet." Jesus answered, "Unless I wash you, you have no share with me." Simon Peter said to him, "Lord, not my feet only but also my hands and my head!" Jesus said to him, "One who has bathed does not need to wash, except for the feet, but is entirely clean. And you are clean, though not all of you." For he knew who was to betray him; for this reason he said, "Not all of you are clean."

After he had washed their feet, had put on his robe, and had returned to the table, he said to them, "Do you know what I have done to you? You call me Teacher and Lord—and you are right, for that is what I am. So if I, your Lord and Teacher, have washed your feet, you also ought to wash one another's feet. For I have set you an example, that you also should do as I have done to you."

- It may be important for us to think of what we want to do for Jesus, to let him know and to seek his approval. Jesus smiles and invites us to listen first—to notice, to be. He asks if we can allow him to serve us. "See what I do," he seems to say. "Accept who I am. Then be who you are!"

- Jesus says, "Later you will understand." Sometimes that's not enough for me! I want to understand now. Help me, Jesus, to live as you did even when I don't fully comprehend what you are asking of me.

Friday April 2
Good Friday
John 18:1–19:42

After Jesus had spoken these words, he went out with his disciples across the Kidron valley to a place where there was a garden, which he and his disciples entered. Now Judas, who betrayed him, also knew the place, because Jesus often met there with his disciples. So Judas brought a detachment of soldiers together with police from the chief priests and the Pharisees, and they came there with lanterns and torches and weapons. Then Jesus, knowing all that was to happen to him, came forward and asked them, "For whom are you looking?" They answered, "Jesus of Nazareth." Jesus replied, "I am he." Judas, who betrayed him, was standing with them. When Jesus said to them, "I am he," they stepped back and fell to the ground. Again he asked them, "For whom are you looking?" And they said, "Jesus of Nazareth." Jesus answered, "I told you that I am he. So if you are looking for me, let these men go." This was to fulfil the word that he had spoken, "I did not lose a single one of those whom you gave me." Then Simon Peter, who had a sword, drew it, struck the high priest's slave, and cut off his right ear. The slave's name was Malchus. Jesus said to Peter, "Put your sword back into its sheath. Am I not to drink the cup that the Father has given me?"

So the soldiers, their officer, and the Jewish police arrested Jesus and bound him. First they took him to Annas, who was the father-in-law of Caiaphas, the high priest that year. Caiaphas was the one who had advised the Jews that it was better to have one person die for the people.

Simon Peter and another disciple followed Jesus. Since that disciple was known to the high priest, he went with Jesus into the courtyard of the high priest, but Peter was standing outside at the gate. So the other disciple, who was known to the high priest, went out, spoke to the woman who guarded the gate, and brought Peter in. The woman said to

Peter, "You are not also one of this man's disciples, are you?" He said, "I am not." Now the slaves and the police had made a charcoal fire because it was cold, and they were standing around it and warming themselves. Peter also was standing with them and warming himself.

Then the high priest questioned Jesus about his disciples and about his teaching. Jesus answered, "I have spoken openly to the world; I have always taught in synagogues and in the temple, where all the Jews come together. I have said nothing in secret. Why do you ask me? Ask those who heard what I said to them; they know what I said." When he had said this, one of the police standing nearby struck Jesus on the face, saying, "Is that how you answer the high priest?" Jesus answered, "If I have spoken wrongly, testify to the wrong. But if I have spoken rightly, why do you strike me?" Then Annas sent him bound to Caiaphas the high priest.

Now Simon Peter was standing and warming himself. They asked him, "You are not also one of his disciples, are you?" He denied it and said, "I am not." One of the slaves of the high priest, a relative of the man whose ear Peter had cut off, asked, "Did I not see you in the garden with him?" Again Peter denied it, and at that moment the cock crowed.

Then they took Jesus from Caiaphas to Pilate's headquarters. It was early in the morning. They themselves did not enter the headquarters, so as to avoid ritual defilement and to be able to eat the Passover. So Pilate went out to them and said, "What accusation do you bring against this man?" They answered, "If this man were not a criminal, we would not have handed him over to you." Pilate said to them, "Take him yourselves and judge him according to your law." The Jews replied, "We are not permitted to put anyone to death." (This was to fulfill what Jesus had said when he indicated the kind of death he was to die.)

Then Pilate entered the headquarters again, summoned Jesus, and asked him, "Are you the King of the Jews?" Jesus answered, "Do you ask this on your own, or did others tell you about me?" Pilate replied, "I am not a Jew, am I? Your own nation and the chief priests have handed you over to me. What have you done?" Jesus answered, "My kingdom is not from this world. If my kingdom were from this world, my followers would be fighting to keep me from being handed over to the Jews. But as it is, my kingdom is not from here." Pilate asked him, "So you are a king?" Jesus answered, "You say that I am a king. For this I was born, and for this I came into the world, to testify to the truth. Everyone who belongs to the truth listens to my voice." Pilate asked him, "What is truth?"

After he had said this, he went out to the Jews again and told them, "I find no case against him. But you have a custom that I release someone for you at the Passover. Do you want me to release for you the King of the Jews?" They shouted in reply, "Not this man, but Barabbas!" Now Barabbas was a bandit.

Then Pilate took Jesus and had him flogged. And the soldiers wove a crown of thorns and put it on his head, and they dressed him in a purple robe. They kept coming up to him, saying, "Hail, King of the Jews!" and striking him on the face. Pilate went out again and said to them, "Look, I am bringing him out to you to let you know that I find no case against him." So Jesus came out, wearing the crown of thorns and the purple robe. Pilate said to them, "Here is the man!" When the chief priests and the police saw him, they shouted, "Crucify him! Crucify him!" Pilate said to them, "Take him yourselves and crucify him; I find no case against him." The Jews answered him, "We have a law, and according to that law he ought to die because he has claimed to be the Son of God."

Now when Pilate heard this, he was more afraid than ever. He entered his headquarters again and asked Jesus, "Where are you from?" But Jesus gave him no answer. Pilate therefore said to him, "Do you refuse to speak to me? Do you not know that I have power to release you, and power to crucify you?" Jesus answered him, "You would have no power over me unless it had been given you from above; therefore the one who handed me over to you is guilty of a greater sin." From then on Pilate tried to release him, but the Jews cried out, "If you release this man, you are no friend of the emperor. Everyone who claims to be a king sets himself against the emperor."

When Pilate heard these words, he brought Jesus outside and sat on the judge's bench at a place called The Stone Pavement, or in Hebrew Gabbatha. Now it was the day of Preparation for the Passover; and it was about noon. He said to the Jews, "Here is your King!" They cried out, "Away with him! Away with him! Crucify him!" Pilate asked them, "Shall I crucify your King?" The chief priests answered, "We have no king but the emperor." Then he handed him over to them to be crucified.

So they took Jesus; and carrying the cross by himself, he went out to what is called The Place of the Skull, which in Hebrew is called Golgotha.

There they crucified him, and with him two others, one on either side, with Jesus between them. Pilate also had an inscription written and put on the cross. It read, "Jesus of Nazareth, the King of the Jews." Many of the Jews read this inscription, because the place where Jesus was crucified was near the city; and it was written in Hebrew, in Latin, and in Greek. Then the chief priests of the Jews said to Pilate, "Do not write, 'The King of the Jews,' but, 'This man said, I am King of the Jews.'" Pilate answered, "What I have written I have written." When the soldiers had crucified Jesus, they took his clothes and divided them into four parts, one for each soldier. They also took his tunic; now the tunic was seamless, woven in one piece from the top. So they said to one another, "Let us not tear it, but cast lots for it to see who will get it." This was to fulfill what the scripture says,

"They divided my clothes among themselves,
and for my clothing they cast lots."

And that is what the soldiers did.

Meanwhile, standing near the cross of Jesus were his mother, and his mother's sister, Mary the wife of Clopas, and Mary Magdalene. When Jesus saw his mother and the disciple whom he loved standing beside her, he said to his mother, "Woman, here is your son." Then he said to the disciple, "Here is your mother." And from that hour the disciple took her into his own home.

After this, when Jesus knew that all was now finished, he said (in order to fulfill the scripture), "I am thirsty." A jar full of sour wine was standing there. So they put a sponge full of the wine on a branch of hyssop and held it to his mouth. When Jesus had received the wine, he said, "It is finished." Then he bowed his head and gave up his spirit.

Since it was the day of Preparation, the Jews did not want the bodies left on the cross during the sabbath, especially because that sabbath was a day of great solemnity. So they asked Pilate to have the legs of the crucified men broken and the bodies removed. Then the soldiers came and broke the legs of the first and of the other who had been crucified with him. But when they came to Jesus and saw that he was already dead, they did not break his legs. Instead, one of the soldiers pierced his side with a spear, and at once blood and water came out. (He who saw this has testified so that you also may believe. His testimony is true, and he knows that he tells the truth.) These things occurred so that the scripture might be fulfilled, "None of his bones shall be broken." And again another passage of scripture says, "They will look on the one whom they have pierced."

After these things, Joseph of Arimathea, who was a disciple of Jesus, though a secret one because of his fear of the Jews, asked Pilate to let him take away the body of Jesus. Pilate gave him permission; so he came and removed his body. Nicodemus, who had at first come to Jesus by night, also came, bringing a mixture of myrrh and aloes, weighing about a hundred pounds. They took the body of Jesus and wrapped it with the spices in linen cloths, according to the burial custom of the Jews. Now there was a garden in the place where he was crucified, and in the garden there was a new tomb in which no one had ever been laid. And so, because it was the Jewish day of Preparation, and the tomb was nearby, they laid Jesus there.

- Who is really on trial in the exchange with Pilate? Who has the real authority? Jesus is the Truth, Pilate does not know what truth is. Am I a person of truth?

- I watch him subjected to disgraceful injustice and unspeakable torture and humiliation as he moves through his passion. He does not protest or cry out. How do I respond to injustice, ill-treatment, and humiliation in my own life? What can I learn from him?

- "I thirst." Jesus once promised the Samaritan woman the water of eternal life with the Father, the life to which he is now going and for which he longs. He offers that water to us.

Saturday April 3
Holy Saturday
Mark 16:1–7

When the sabbath was over, Mary Magdalene, and Mary the mother of James, and Salome bought spices, so that they might go and anoint him. And very early on the first day of the week, when the sun had risen, they went to the tomb. They had been saying to one another, "Who will roll away the stone for us from the entrance to the tomb?" When they looked up, they saw that the stone, which was very large, had already been rolled back. As they entered the tomb, they saw a young man, dressed in a white robe, sitting on the right side; and they were alarmed. But he said to them, "Do not be alarmed; you are looking for Jesus of Nazareth, who was crucified. He has been raised; he is not here. Look, there is the place they laid him. But go, tell his disciples and Peter that he is going ahead of you to Galilee; there you will see him, just as he told you."

- The disciples are slow to believe in Jesus' resurrection. They are stubborn, mourning, and weeping, stuck in a gray world. Perhaps I often feel that way? But Jesus does not despair of his followers. He gives them the extraordinary commission to bring good news to the whole of creation! Pope Francis echoes that call: every Christian is to be an evangelizer, to bring good news to those around them. This leaves no space for sulking or self-absorption or doubting!

April 4–10, 2021

Something to think and pray about each day this week:

The Gospels do not describe Jesus' resurrection at Easter anywhere. What you can read is that he became alive again after his death. It is not known exactly how this happened. The grave is empty, the witnesses say. They also say that they have seen, heard, and touched him. Some even ate with him. Their encounters are real; Jesus is not a ghost that lights up. Yet there is a lot of mystery around it. The risen Jesus comes in while the doors are closed. Another time he disappears inexplicably. More than once he comes to his disciples, but "they don't recognize him" (Luke 24:16).

The resurrection of Jesus means that he has entered the world of God, a world that is still unimaginable for us. Jesus' resurrection does not mean that his dead body began to breathe and move again. He has not become an ordinary living and therefore mortal man again. The risen Jesus is immortal. He is different and yet the same.

It is not easy to believe in the resurrection. It is no coincidence that in almost all apparitions there is unbelief and doubt, also among the people who knew Jesus very well. At the same time these hesitant witnesses are going to proclaim his resurrection.

Perhaps this is the strongest proof of the reality of the resurrection. The disciples of Jesus were traumatized by the shameful failure that Jesus' (and their own) life's work had turned out to be. They had fled in all directions. Shortly after that the same people are going to proclaim with unimaginable passion that their hero is the Savior of the people. They no longer conceal his death on the cross. They will now proclaim it almost with pride. Between both moments they must have experienced something even more shocking and dramatic than the catastrophe of Jesus' crucifixion: his resurrection.

—Nikolaas Sintobin, SJ, *Did Jesus Really Exist?*
and 51 Other Questions

The Presence of God

God is with me, but more,
God is within me, giving me existence.
Let me dwell for a moment on God's life-giving presence
in my body, my mind, my heart,
and in the whole of my life.

Freedom

Lord, you created me to live in freedom. May your Holy Spirit guide me
to follow you freely. Instill in my heart a desire to know and love you
more each day.

Consciousness

In God's loving presence I unwind the past day,
starting from now and looking back, moment by moment.
I gather in all the goodness and light, in gratitude.
I attend to the shadows and what they say to me,
seeking healing, courage, forgiveness.

The Word

God speaks to each of us individually. I listen attentively to hear what he
is saying to me. Read the text a few times, then listen. (*Please turn to the
Scripture on the following pages. Inspiration points are there, should you need
them. When you are ready, return here to continue.*)

Conversation

Jesus, you always welcomed little children when you walked on this earth.
Teach me to have a childlike trust in you. Teach me to live in the knowledge that you will never abandon me.

Conclusion

I thank God for these moments we have spent together and for any insights I have been given concerning the text.

Sunday April 4
Easter Sunday of the Resurrection of Our Lord
John 20:1–9

Early on the first day of the week, while it was still dark, Mary Magdalene came to the tomb and saw that the stone had been removed from the tomb. So she ran and went to Simon Peter and the other disciple, the one whom Jesus loved, and said to them, "They have taken the Lord out of the tomb, and we do not know where they have laid him." Then Peter and the other disciple set out and went toward the tomb. The two were running together, but the other disciple outran Peter and reached the tomb first. He bent down to look in and saw the linen wrappings lying there, but he did not go in. Then Simon Peter came, following him, and went into the tomb. He saw the linen wrappings lying there, and the cloth that had been on Jesus' head, not lying with the linen wrappings but rolled up in a place by itself. Then the other disciple, who reached the tomb first, also went in, and he saw and believed; for as yet they did not understand the scripture, that he must rise from the dead.

• As described by Benedict XVI, the resurrection was like an explosion of light, a cosmic event linking heaven and earth. Above all, it was an explosion of love. It ushered in a new dimension of being, through which a new world emerges. It is a leap in the history of evolution and of life in general toward a new future life, toward a new world which, starting from Christ, already continuously permeates this world of ours, transforms it, and draws it to itself. The resurrection unites us with God and others. If we live in this way, we will transform the world.

Monday April 5
Matthew 28:8–15

So they left the tomb quickly with fear and great joy, and ran to tell his disciples. Suddenly Jesus met them and said, "Greetings!" And they came to him, took hold of his feet, and worshipped him. Then Jesus said to them, "Do not be afraid; go and tell my brothers to go to Galilee; there they will see me."

While they were going, some of the guard went into the city and told the chief priests everything that had happened. After the priests had assembled with the elders, they devised a plan to give a large sum of money to the soldiers, telling them, "You must say, 'His disciples came by night and stole him away while we were asleep.' If this comes to the governor's ears, we will satisfy him and keep you out of trouble." So they took the money and did as they were directed. And this story is still told among the Jews to this day.

- The women left the tomb with joy, interpreting the emptiness positively; having gone to care for the dead, they realized their task was to announce the living. So it was that they were able to meet Jesus and to receive from him a new mission.

- The invitation of Jesus is to go to Galilee and there "they will see me." It's the same invitation that he gives to us. "Galilee" can be the neighborhood, the family, the prayer space, the poor, and the many moments we find ourselves aware of Jesus' presence. Prayer is one of them; prayer will heighten our awareness of times we met the Lord.

- Go back in your own memory to when God was close, and be grateful. Allow God in prayer to tell you to "go and see."

Tuesday April 6
John 20:11–18

Mary stood weeping outside the tomb. As she wept, she bent over to look into the tomb; and she saw two angels in white, sitting where the body of Jesus had been lying, one at the head and the other at the feet. They said to her, "Woman, why are you weeping?" She said to them, "They have taken away my Lord, and I do not know where they have laid him." When she had said this, she turned round and saw Jesus standing there, but she did not know that it was Jesus. Jesus said to her, "Woman, why are you weeping? For whom are you looking?" Supposing him to be the gardener, she said to him, "Sir, if you have carried him away, tell me where you have laid him, and I will take him away." Jesus said to her, "Mary!" She turned and said to him in Hebrew, "Rabbouni!" (which means Teacher). Jesus said to her, "Do not hold on to me, because I have not yet ascended to the Father. But go to my brothers and say to them, 'I am ascending to my Father and your Father, to my God and your God.'" Mary Magdalene went and announced to the disciples, "I have seen the Lord"; and she told them that he had said these things to her.

- Lord, you offer me a parable of your dealings with me. Like Mary I am looking for you, following the call of love, but not recognizing you because I am too caught up in my own emotions. But all the time you are looking at me, and it is when you call me by my name and reach me with some intimately personal experience that I recognize you with joy as my Rabbouni.

Wednesday April 7
Luke 24:13–35

Now on that same day two of them were going to a village called Emmaus, about seven miles from Jerusalem, and talking with each other about all these things that had happened. While they were talking and discussing, Jesus himself came near and went with them, but their eyes were kept from recognizing him. And he said to them, "What are you discussing with each other while you walk along?" They stood still, looking sad. Then one of them, whose name was Cleopas, answered him, "Are you the only stranger in Jerusalem who does not know the things that have taken place there in these days?" He asked them, "What things?" They replied, "The things about Jesus of Nazareth, who was a prophet mighty in deed and word before God and all the people, and how our chief priests and leaders handed him over to be condemned to death and crucified him. But we had hoped that he was the one to redeem Israel. Yes, and besides all this, it is now the third day since these things took place. Moreover, some women of our group astounded us. They were at the tomb early this morning, and when they did not find his body there, they came back and told us that they had indeed seen a vision of angels who said that he was alive. Some of those who were with us went to the tomb and found it just as the women had said; but they did not see him." Then he said to them, "Oh, how foolish you are, and how slow of heart to believe all that the prophets have declared! Was it not necessary that the Messiah should suffer these things and then enter into his glory?" Then beginning with Moses and all the prophets, he interpreted to them the things about himself in all the Scriptures.

As they came near the village to which they were going, he walked ahead as if he were going on. But they urged him strongly, saying, "Stay with us, because it is almost evening and the day is now nearly over." So he went in to stay with them. When he was at the table with them, he took bread, blessed and broke it, and gave it to them. Then their eyes were opened, and they recognized him; and he vanished from their sight. They said to each other, "Were not our hearts burning within us while he was talking to us on the road, while he was opening the scriptures to us?" That same hour they got up and returned to Jerusalem; and they found the eleven and their companions gathered together. They were saying, "The Lord has risen indeed, and he has appeared to Simon!" Then they told what had happened on the road, and how he had been made known to them in the breaking of the bread.

- This story offers a rich image of prayer. You start out on your own, perhaps quite hopeless, if life has been going badly. Jesus comes by unobtrusively; you welcome him and tell your story. He listens intently, then gently throws light on what has been bothering you.

- Friendship grows, and by the end of the prayer you don't want him to leave, but you know he will always be watching out for you and will meet you again tomorrow. You can pray: "Stay with me, Lord, because it is nearly evening and the day is almost over."

Thursday April 8
Luke 24:35–48

Then they told what had happened on the road, and how he had been made known to them in the breaking of the bread.

While they were talking about this, Jesus himself stood among them and said to them, "Peace be with you." They were startled and terrified, and thought that they were seeing a ghost. He said to them, "Why are you frightened, and why do doubts arise in your hearts? Look at my hands and my feet; see that it is I myself. Touch me and see; for a ghost does not have flesh and bones as you see that I have." And when he had said this, he showed them his hands and his feet. While in their joy they were disbelieving and still wondering, he said to them, "Have you anything here to eat?" They gave him a piece of broiled fish, and he took it and ate in their presence.

Then he said to them, "These are my words that I spoke to you while I was still with you—that everything written about me in the law of Moses, the prophets and the psalms must be fulfilled." Then he opened their minds to understand the Scriptures, and he said to them, "Thus it is written, that the Messiah is to suffer and to rise from the dead on the third day, and that repentance and forgiveness of sins is to be proclaimed in his name to all nations, beginning from Jerusalem. You are witnesses of these things."

• We see the disciples, feel their fear, and observe their fear being changed into joy as they realize that the Lord is indeed in their midst and has a solid body. Share the emotions of the disciples. Can you sense the emotion of the Lord?

• Jesus reiterates the "law of the cross" as he did to the disciples on the way to Emmaus. He then commissions them to continue his mission. As you listen to the disciples receiving their mission, what are your feelings?

Friday April 9
John 21:1–14

After these things Jesus showed himself again to the disciples by the Sea of Tiberias; and he showed himself in this way. Gathered there together were Simon Peter, Thomas called the Twin, Nathanael of Cana in Galilee, the sons of Zebedee, and two others of his disciples. Simon Peter said to them, "I am going fishing." They said to him, "We will go with you." They went out and got into the boat, but that night they caught nothing.

Just after daybreak, Jesus stood on the beach; but the disciples did not know that it was Jesus. Jesus said to them, "Children, you have no fish, have you?" They answered him, "No." He said to them, "Cast the net to the right side of the boat, and you will find some." So they cast it, and now they were not able to haul it in because there were so many fish. That disciple whom Jesus loved said to Peter, "It is the Lord!" When Simon Peter heard that it was the Lord, he put on some clothes, for he was naked, and jumped into the lake. But the other disciples came in the boat, dragging the net full of fish, for they were not far from the land, only about a hundred yards off.

When they had gone ashore, they saw a charcoal fire there, with fish on it, and bread. Jesus said to them, "Bring some of the fish that you have just caught." So Simon Peter went aboard and hauled the net ashore, full of large fish, a hundred and fifty-three of them; and though there were so many, the net was not torn. Jesus said to them, "Come and have breakfast." Now none of the disciples dared to ask him, "Who are you?" because they knew it was the Lord. Jesus came and took the bread and gave it to them, and did the same with the fish. This was now the third time that Jesus appeared to the disciples after he was raised from the dead.

- A night of futile fishing leaves empty nets and empty hearts. Jesus takes the initiative and meets them in the early morning light. He invites them to eat: "Come and have breakfast." There is an abundant table ready—of fish, food, love, warmth, and great joy. Here, fractured relationships are healed.

- Jesus, you meet me at the water's edge of my ordinary life. You accept me lovingly, you encourage me, you invite me to abundance. Nourished by the food of your word, warmed by the fire of your unfailing love, may I in turn nourish, heal, and love those I meet today.

Saturday April 10
Mark 16:9–15

Now after he rose early on the first day of the week, he appeared first to Mary Magdalene, from whom he had cast out seven demons. She went out and told those who had been with him, while they were mourning and weeping. But when they heard that he was alive and had been seen by her, they would not believe it.

After this he appeared in another form to two of them, as they were walking into the country. And they went back and told the rest, but they did not believe them.

Later he appeared to the eleven themselves as they were sitting at the table; and he upbraided them for their lack of faith and stubbornness, because they had not believed those who saw him after he had risen. And he said to them, "Go into all the world and proclaim the good news to the whole creation."

- To be disciples and share the good news is the invitation of Jesus to all of us. We do so in silence, or with words, and with our way of life. Hear him speaking these words to you and ask, "What can I do this day to spread God's good news?"

April 11–17, 2021

Something to think and pray about each day this week:

Prayer is a beautiful mystery. Many years ago, my first primary teacher spoke to the students about this mystery. I do not remember her exact words now, but I do recall very clearly the impact some of her words had on me. She certainly helped me set out on that special journey with God which is prayer. Our teacher told us we could pray anywhere—that I do remember—and I know that I found that information most helpful and beneficial. One did not always have to pray with others. One could pray alone and in private (as Jesus did).

Through the years my prayer has been inspired by church music, by some aspects of nature, by Scripture passages, and beautiful churches. I have been moved to prayer, too, by holy priests and by the spectacle of human suffering. Whatever raises the heart and mind to God is surely a source of prayer. Thus, St. Thérèse of Lisieux writes of "the surge of the heart, a simple look toward Heaven, a cry of recognition and love" in moments of prayer.

I especially associate great organ music with the call to prayer. I was gifted, at a young age, to hear such music in the Carmelite church on Whitefriar Street in Dublin where my father often took me to Mass. Nature, a walk by the sea or by a quiet riverside—all these can lift us above the mundane realities of life and can lead to new insights through prayer.

—Aideen Madden, *The Sacred Heart Messenger*

The Presence of God

Dear Lord, as I come to you today, fill my heart, my whole being, with the wonder of your presence. Help me remain receptive to you as I put aside the cares of this world. Fill my mind with your peace.

Freedom

Lord, grant me the grace to be free from the excesses of this life. Let me not get caught up with the desire for wealth. Keep my heart and mind free to love and serve you.

Consciousness

I exist in a web of relationships: links to nature, people, God.
I trace out these links,
giving thanks for the life that flows through them.
Some links are twisted or broken; I may feel regret, anger, disappointment.
I pray for the gift of acceptance and forgiveness.

The Word

God speaks to each of us individually. I listen attentively to hear what he is saying to me. Read the text a few times, then listen. (*Please turn to the Scripture on the following pages. Inspiration points are there, should you need them. When you are ready, return here to continue.*)

Conversation

Jesus, you speak to me through the words of the Gospels. May I respond to your call today. Teach me to recognize your hand at work in my daily living.

Conclusion

I thank God for these moments we have spent together and for any insights I have been given concerning the text.

Sunday April 11
Second Sunday of Easter (Divine Mercy Sunday)
John 20:19–31

When it was evening on that day, the first day of the week, and the doors of the house where the disciples had met were locked for fear of the Jews, Jesus came and stood among them and said, "Peace be with you." After he said this, he showed them his hands and his side. Then the disciples rejoiced when they saw the Lord. Jesus said to them again, "Peace be with you. As the Father has sent me, so I send you." When he had said this, he breathed on them and said to them, "Receive the Holy Spirit. If you forgive the sins of any, they are forgiven them; if you retain the sins of any, they are retained."

But Thomas (who was called the Twin), one of the twelve, was not with them when Jesus came. So the other disciples told him, "We have seen the Lord." But he said to them, "Unless I see the mark of the nails in his hands, and put my finger in the mark of the nails and my hand in his side, I will not believe."

A week later his disciples were again in the house, and Thomas was with them. Although the doors were shut, Jesus came and stood among them and said, "Peace be with you." Then he said to Thomas, "Put your finger here and see my hands. Reach out your hand and put it in my side. Do not doubt but believe." Thomas answered him, "My Lord and my God!" Jesus said to him, "Have you believed because you have seen me? Blessed are those who have not seen and yet have come to believe."

Now Jesus did many other signs in the presence of his disciples, which are not written in this book. But these are written so that you may come to believe that Jesus is the Messiah, the Son of God, and that through believing you may have life in his name.

- Thomas places his hands in the wounds of Jesus, and the experience draws from him the first, ringing affirmation of Christ's divinity: "My Lord and my God!" Fully human, and fully divine. Eternally human, eternally divine. His human nature is glorified, just as his divinity is humanized. Our human nature will be forever in him; his divinity dwells within us and will remain with us even to the consummation of the world.

Monday April 12
John 3:1–8

Now there was a Pharisee named Nicodemus, a leader of the Jews. He came to Jesus by night and said to him, "Rabbi, we know that you are a teacher who has come from God; for no one can do these signs that you do apart from the presence of God." Jesus answered him, "Very truly, I tell you, no one can see the kingdom of God without being born from above." Nicodemus said to him, "How can anyone be born after having grown old? Can one enter a second time into the mother's womb and be born?" Jesus answered, "Very truly, I tell you, no one can enter the kingdom of God without being born of water and the Spirit. What is born of the flesh is flesh, and what is born of the Spirit is spirit. Do not be astonished that I said to you, 'You must be born from above.' The wind blows where it chooses, and you hear the sound of it, but you do not know where it comes from or where it goes. So it is with everyone who is born of the Spirit."

- Nicodemus is a teacher. When Jesus tries to teach him, Nicodemus does not seem to learn. It is God's part to give, ours to receive. How receptive am I as a learner? Is my heart open? What are my limits and conditions?

Tuesday April 13
John 3:7–15

"Do not be astonished that I said to you, 'You must be born from above.' The wind blows where it chooses, and you hear the sound of it, but you do not know where it comes from or where it goes. So it is with everyone who is born of the Spirit." Nicodemus said to him, "How can these things be?" Jesus answered him, "Are you a teacher of Israel, and yet you do not understand these things?

"Very truly, I tell you, we speak of what we know and testify to what we have seen; yet you do not receive our testimony. If I have told you about earthly things and you do not believe, how can you believe if I tell you about heavenly things? No one has ascended into heaven except the one who descended from heaven, the Son of Man. And just as Moses lifted up the serpent in the wilderness, so must the Son of Man be lifted up, that whoever believes in him may have eternal life."

- Like Nicodemus I am puzzled about "being born again." I ask Jesus to explain. He tells me that he wants me to present myself in the world in a new way: I am to start over. He wants me to live out a Spirit-filled life. I am to attend to the promptings of the Spirit in making my choices. He tells me that in this way I become "the light of the world"! What a promise!

Wednesday April 14
John 3:16–21

"For God so loved the world that he gave his only Son, so that everyone who believes in him may not perish but may have eternal life.

"Indeed, God did not send the Son into the world to condemn the world, but in order that the world might be saved through him. Those who believe in him are not condemned; but those who do not believe are condemned already, because they have not believed in the name of the only Son of God. And this is the judgment, that the light has come into the world, and people loved darkness rather than light because their deeds were evil. For all who do evil hate the light and do not come to the light, so that their deeds may not be exposed. But those who do what is true come to the light, so that it may be clearly seen that their deeds have been done in God."

- God loves the world, loves each one of us, loves me. This is the whole message of Jesus, expressed in his words and embodied, directly or indirectly, in the whole of his life. Am I convinced of this myself?

- We live in the new world of God when we love; when we love others and love God. Prayer is relaxing into the mystery of being loved by God. Prayer moments such as praying with Sacred Space bring us into the "beyond," the world of love, of mystery, and of endurance.

Thursday April 15
John 3:31–36

"The one who comes from above is above all; the one who is of the earth belongs to the earth and speaks about earthly things. The one who comes from heaven is above all. He testifies to what he has seen and heard, yet no one accepts his testimony. Whoever has accepted his testimony has certified this, that God is true. He whom God has sent speaks the words of God, for he gives the Spirit without measure. The Father loves the Son and has placed all things in his hands. Whoever believes in the Son has eternal life; whoever disobeys the Son will not see life, but must endure God's wrath."

- Lord, when I look at you, I feel so earthbound. I am stuck in the mud, busy about my little anxieties and desires. Raise me up: keep reminding me that you want me to be with you in that divine dimension that you inhabit. All things are in your hands, including me, so help me believe more deeply in you and your promise of eternal life. Let me be like you and speak "the words of God" to others.

Friday April 16
John 6:1–15

After this Jesus went to the other side of the Sea of Galilee, also called the Sea of Tiberias. A large crowd kept following him, because they saw the signs that he was doing for the sick. Jesus went up the mountain and sat down there with his disciples. Now the Passover, the festival of the Jews, was near. When he looked up and saw a large crowd coming toward him, Jesus said to Philip, "Where are we to buy bread for these people to eat?" He said this to test him, for he himself knew what he was going to do. Philip answered him, "Six months' wages would not buy enough bread for each of them to get a little." One of his disciples, Andrew, Simon Peter's brother, said to him, "There is a boy here who has five barley loaves and two fish. But what are they among so many people?" Jesus said, "Make the people sit down." Now there was a great deal of grass in the place; so they sat down, about five thousand in all. Then Jesus took the loaves, and when he had given thanks, he distributed them to those who were seated; so also the fish, as much as they wanted. When they were satisfied, he told his disciples, "Gather up the fragments left over, so that nothing may be lost." So they gathered them up, and from the fragments of the five barley loaves, left by those who had eaten, they filled twelve baskets. When the people saw the sign that he had done, they began to say, "This is indeed the prophet who is to come into the world."

When Jesus realized that they were about to come and take him by force to make him king, he withdrew again to the mountain by himself.

- In today's Gospel, Jesus performs the miracle of the multiplication of the loaves and fishes. It is, of course, a symbol of the Eucharist; there are deliberate signals that this is so. This incident is memorable, but it pales in significance when compared to the wonder of the Eucharist. Try to devote some time to seeing the occasion, speaking to the participants, and drawing fruit for yourself and your life.

- The small offering of the young man fed the people. God can make much of what we offer. Our attempts to live in his love and follow him are nothing without him. We never know where our efforts to love, to help, and to support others may bear fruit.

Saturday April 17
John 6:16–21

When evening came, his disciples went down to the lake, got into a boat, and started across the lake to Capernaum. It was now dark, and Jesus had not yet come to them. The lake became rough because a strong wind was blowing. When they had rowed about three or four miles, they saw Jesus walking on the lake and coming near the boat, and they were terrified. But he said to them, "It is I; do not be afraid." Then they wanted to take him into the boat, and immediately the boat reached the land toward which they were going.

- This scene provides a revelation of the sort of person God is! Our resources are never enough, but God has limitless resources, enough for us to do what God wants done.

- Jesus reveals the God of abundance, but notice that the focus is on the poor and the needy, not on making rich people richer. Jesus needs my help in caring for those at the bottom of the human pyramid. This is the theme of Pope Francis's encyclical, *Laudato Si'*.

The Third Week of Easter
April 18–24, 2021

Something to think and pray about each day this week:

The current global action to protect and restore Planet Earth is being prompted and enabled by the Spirit of God, the Giver of Life: "the Holy Ghost over the bent / World broods with warm breast and with ah! bright wings" (G. M. Hopkins). Humankind is not alone, fighting a helpless cause. Prophetic voices from all sides are supporting our unique historical moment of grace and challenge. We are discovering that what seems lost and beyond recovery can come to life again, as with species being rescued from extinction and with the planting of a great green wall of trees across African deserts. The boundless wisdom and dynamics of the universe that have shaped things thus far are available to us: we are not adrift in cosmic isolation but immersed in a sea of divine energy beyond all comprehension. We must do all we can, and pray deeply, and be willing to suffer much, knowing that divine power is at work within us to carry out God's purposes beyond our hopes and dreams (Ephesians 3:20). In our global crisis we are also witnessing the surprising growth, even if fragile, of the community of humankind. People of all faiths and none are joining hands in the common cause, and this meets God's underlying desire that we all may be one in universal harmony (John 17:11).

The divine plan for Creation remains steady, and with God all things are possible, including its restoration: see Acts 3:21. In Genesis, God utters a word and the world is made. With a divine word the world can be re-fashioned. Our God is a saving, creating, and restoring God, a God of limitless love who has compassion on all things. Love has always been the key element in God's decisions on the next step for our Planet: this love cannot come to an end but will be revealed when God will be "all in all" (1 Corinthians 15:28; Colossians 3:11).

As Bishop Desmond Tutu says, "Only God knows what's next!"

—Brian Grogan, SJ, *Creation Walk: The Amazing Story of a Small Blue Planet*

The Presence of God

Dear Jesus, today I call on you, but not to ask for anything. I'd like only to dwell in your presence. May my heart respond to your love.

Freedom

God my creator, you gave me life and the gift of freedom. Through your love I exist in this world. May I never take the gift of life for granted. May I always respect others' right to life.

Consciousness

I ask how I am today. Am I particularly tired, stressed, or anxious? If any of these characteristics apply, can I try to let go of the concerns that disturb me?

The Word

The word of God comes down to us through the Scriptures. May the Holy Spirit enlighten my mind and my heart to respond to the Gospel teachings. (*Please turn to the Scripture on the following pages. Inspiration points are there, should you need them. When you are ready, return here to continue.*)

Conversation

I begin to talk with Jesus about the Scripture I have just read. What part of it strikes a chord in me? Perhaps the words of a friend—or some story I have heard recently—will rise to the surface in my consciousness. If so, does the story throw light on what the Scripture passage may be saying to me?

Conclusion

Glory be to the Father, and to the Son, and to the Holy Spirit,
As it was in the beginning, is now, and ever shall be,
World without end. Amen.

Sunday April 18
Third Sunday of Easter
Luke 24:35–48

Then they told what had happened on the road, and how he had been made known to them in the breaking of the bread.

While they were talking about this, Jesus himself stood among them and said to them, "Peace be with you." They were startled and terrified, and thought that they were seeing a ghost. He said to them, "Why are you frightened, and why do doubts arise in your hearts? Look at my hands and my feet; see that it is I myself. Touch me and see; for a ghost does not have flesh and bones as you see that I have." And when he had said this, he showed them his hands and his feet. While in their joy they were disbelieving and still wondering, he said to them, "Have you anything here to eat?" They gave him a piece of broiled fish, and he took it and ate in their presence.

Then he said to them, "These are my words that I spoke to you while I was still with you—that everything written about me in the law of Moses, the prophets, and the psalms must be fulfilled." Then he opened their minds to understand the scriptures, and he said to them, "Thus it is written, that the Messiah is to suffer and to rise from the dead on the third day, and that repentance and forgiveness of sins is to be proclaimed in his name to all nations, beginning from Jerusalem. You are witnesses of these things."

- We see the disciples, feel their fear, and observe their fear being changed into joy as they realize that the Lord is indeed in their midst and has a solid body. Share the emotions of the disciples. Can you sense the emotion of the Lord?

- Jesus reiterates the "law of the cross" as he did to the disciples on the way to Emmaus. He then commissions them to continue his mission. As you listen to the disciples receiving their mission, what are your feelings?

Monday April 19
John 6:22–29

The next day the crowd that had stayed on the other side of the lake saw that there had been only one boat there. They also saw that Jesus had not got into the boat with his disciples, but that his disciples had gone away alone. Then some boats from Tiberias came near the place where they had eaten the bread after the Lord had given thanks. So when the crowd saw that neither Jesus nor his disciples were there, they themselves got into the boats and went to Capernaum looking for Jesus.

When they found him on the other side of the lake, they said to him, "Rabbi, when did you come here?" Jesus answered them, "Very truly, I tell you, you are looking for me, not because you saw signs, but because you ate your fill of the loaves. Do not work for the food that perishes, but for the food that endures for eternal life, which the Son of Man will give you. For it is on him that God the Father has set his seal." Then they said to him, "What must we do to perform the works of God?" Jesus answered them, "This is the work of God, that you believe in him whom he has sent."

- The crowds followed Jesus, not because they had grasped the significance of the multiplication of the loaves and fishes, but because they had their fill. They did not have the faith he demands because they did not see beyond the sign and so did not grasp the significance of the miracle.

- Can you identify with the attitude of those who followed Jesus across the lake in their desire to see signs? Putting yourself into the scene, how do you think you might have reacted?

Tuesday April 20
John 6:30–35

So they said to him, "What sign are you going to give us then, so that we may see it and believe you? What work are you performing? Our ancestors ate the manna in the wilderness; as it is written, 'He gave them bread from heaven to eat.'" Then Jesus said to them, "Very truly, I tell you, it was not Moses who gave you the bread from heaven, but it is my Father who gives you the true bread from heaven. For the bread of God is that which comes down from heaven and gives life to the world." They said to him, "Sir, give us this bread always."

Jesus said to them, "I am the bread of life. Whoever comes to me will never be hungry, and whoever believes in me will never be thirsty."

- The people were sure about what they wanted, clear about how God had worked in the past; they had a template, and they wanted to see whether Jesus fit it. We sometimes approach Jesus in the same way, asking for what we need, expecting a particular answer. Jesus wants to open our hearts to receive what God is offering; we need to open our eyes to recognize it.

- Help us, Lord, when we are limited by our past. When we know how we have been blessed, help us stay before you in trust, aware of how little we deserve but ready to receive your grace in new ways.

Wednesday April 21
John 6:35–40

Jesus said to them, "I am the bread of life. Whoever comes to me will never be hungry, and whoever believes in me will never be thirsty. But I said to you that you have seen me and yet do not believe. Everything that the Father gives me will come to me, and anyone who comes to me I will never drive away; for I have come down from heaven, not to do my own will, but the will of him who sent me. And this is the will of him who sent me, that I should lose nothing of all that he has given me, but raise it up on the last day. This is indeed the will of my Father, that all who see the Son and believe in him may have eternal life; and I will raise them up on the last day."

- It is the will of God that nothing should be lost; may I look on everything that is good as a gift from God and an invitation to embrace the life that God offers.

- So much is offered to God each day! I pray that all people who are blessed may realize that their identity and destiny lie in God.

Thursday April 22
John 6:44–51

"No one can come to me unless drawn by the Father who sent me; and I will raise that person up on the last day. It is written in the prophets, 'And they shall all be taught by God.' Everyone who has heard and learned from the Father comes to me. Not that anyone has seen the Father except the one who is from God; he has seen the Father. Very truly, I tell you, whoever believes has eternal life. I am the bread of life. Your ancestors ate the manna in the wilderness, and they died. This is the bread that comes down from heaven, so that one may eat of it and not die. I am the living bread that came down from heaven. Whoever eats of this bread will live for ever; and the bread that I will give for the life of the world is my flesh."

- In today's Gospel passage, Jesus teaches that his Father draws one to believe and that those who believe in him (Jesus) have everlasting life. He reiterates the point that he is the bread of life from heaven, and that those who eat this bread (listen to and accept his word) will not die. How do you understand this?

- Our prayer is not our own initiative but is itself a response to God who draws us. God draws me to what is true, to what is life-giving, to what is loving.

Friday April 23
John 6:52–59

The Jews then disputed among themselves, saying, "How can this man give us his flesh to eat?" So Jesus said to them, "Very truly, I tell you, unless you eat the flesh of the Son of Man and drink his blood, you have no life in you. Those who eat my flesh and drink my blood have eternal life, and I will raise them up on the last day; for my flesh is true food and my blood is true drink. Those who eat my flesh and drink my blood abide in me, and I in them. Just as the living Father sent me, and I live because of the Father, so whoever eats me will live because of me. This is the bread that came down from heaven, not like that which your ancestors ate, and they died. But the one who eats this bread will live for ever." He said these things while he was teaching in the synagogue at Capernaum.

- "He who eats my flesh and drinks my blood lives in me, and I live in him." When we eat ordinary food, provided we are well, we digest it naturally without our noticing. The receiving of the Lord in the Eucharist requires our attentiveness, our welcome, our silence, our prayers of intercession to the Lord we have just received. Thank you, Lord Jesus, I bring before you my day and all the concerns of my heart.

Saturday April 24

John 6:60–69

When many of his disciples heard it, they said, "This teaching is difficult; who can accept it?" But Jesus, being aware that his disciples were complaining about it, said to them, "Does this offend you? Then what if you were to see the Son of Man ascending to where he was before? It is the spirit that gives life; the flesh is useless. The words that I have spoken to you are spirit and life. But among you there are some who do not believe." For Jesus knew from the first who were the ones that did not believe, and who was the one that would betray him. And he said, "For this reason I have told you that no one can come to me unless it is granted by the Father."

Because of this many of his disciples turned back and no longer went about with him. So Jesus asked the twelve, "Do you also wish to go away?" Simon Peter answered him, "Lord, to whom can we go? You have the words of eternal life. We have come to believe and know that you are the Holy One of God."

- We need the gifts of "spirit and life," or we will be like those disciples who no longer went about with Jesus. He was there in front of them, but they could not recognize who he really was. We must not think that only some people are given the gift of faith: no, the Spirit is poured out on everyone, and Jesus' abiding desire is give everyone life to the full.

- Lord, draw me close to you, and be spirit and life for me.

The Fourth Week of Easter
April 25—May 1, 2021

Something to think and pray about each day this week:

The apostle Paul speaks bluntly. In one of his letters he writes, "If Christ has not risen, then all we say is nonsense. Then the whole faith is meaningless" (1 Corinthians 15:14). Without resurrection there is no question of Christianity. Without faith in the resurrection of Jesus there is no Christian faith. If Jesus has not been resurrected, then at best his life is an impressive story with a tragic ending: his execution.

Jesus did not raise himself from the dead. It was God who did so. At the end of the life and death of Jesus, this is the personal signature of God. By doing so, he confirms and approves what Jesus thought was important. Through the resurrection it becomes clear that the story of Jesus, the Son of God, is the story of God.

Because of the resurrection it is clear to Christians that Jesus' Good News really comes from God. Jesus is the example that every person can follow. His way of love is the God-approved way that leads people to life as God intended.

—Nikolaas Sintobin, SJ, *Did Jesus Really Exist?*
and 51 Other Questions

The Presence of God

Dear Jesus, I come to you today longing for your presence. I desire to love you as you love me. May nothing ever separate me from you.

Freedom

Lord, grant me the grace to have freedom of the Spirit. Cleanse my heart and soul so that I may live joyously in your love.

Consciousness

Where am I with God? With others?
Do I have something to be grateful for? Then I give thanks.
Is there something I am sorry for? Then I ask forgiveness.

The Word

The word of God comes down to us through the Scriptures. May the Holy Spirit enlighten my mind and my heart to respond to the Gospel teachings. (*Please turn to the Scripture on the following pages. Inspiration points are there, should you need them. When you are ready, return here to continue.*)

Conversation

How has God's word moved me? Has it left me cold?
Has it consoled me or moved me to act in a new way?
I imagine Jesus standing or sitting beside me;
I turn and share my feelings with him.

Conclusion

I thank God for these moments we have spent together and for any insights I have been given concerning the text.

Sunday April 25
Fourth Sunday of Easter
John 10:11–18

"I am the good shepherd. The good shepherd lays down his life for the sheep. The hired hand, who is not the shepherd and does not own the sheep, sees the wolf coming and leaves the sheep and runs away—and the wolf snatches them and scatters them. The hired hand runs away because a hired hand does not care for the sheep. I am the good shepherd. I know my own and my own know me, just as the Father knows me and I know the Father. And I lay down my life for the sheep. I have other sheep that do not belong to this fold. I must bring them also, and they will listen to my voice. So there will be one flock, one shepherd. For this reason the Father loves me, because I lay down my life in order to take it up again. No one takes it from me, but I lay it down of my own accord. I have power to lay it down, and I have power to take it up again. I have received this command from my Father."

- Sunday reminds us that we do not come to God alone; our worship draws us into community and identifies us as sheep of the Good Shepherd. Being thought of as a sheep is not to demean us but to rescue us from thinking too much of ourselves. Jesus calls us to humility and trust, cautioning us against those who work only for what they get and warning against whatever might snatch or scatter us.

- The shepherd keeps the sheep in view, regarding them and seeing beyond them. I ask God for the humility I need, that I might listen for the voice of the Good Shepherd, allowing him to lead me and trusting that he is leading others too—even if in ways I don't understand.

Monday April 26
John 10:1–10

"Very truly, I tell you, anyone who does not enter the sheepfold by the gate but climbs in by another way is a thief and a bandit. The one who enters by the gate is the shepherd of the sheep. The gatekeeper opens the gate for him, and the sheep hear his voice. He calls his own sheep by name and leads them out. When he has brought out all his own, he goes ahead of them, and the sheep follow him because they know his voice.

They will not follow a stranger, but they will run from him because they do not know the voice of strangers." Jesus used this figure of speech with them, but they did not understand what he was saying to them.

So again Jesus said to them, "Very truly, I tell you, I am the gate for the sheep. All who came before me are thieves and bandits; but the sheep did not listen to them. I am the gate. Whoever enters by me will be saved, and will come in and go out and find pasture. The thief comes only to steal and kill and destroy. I came that they may have life, and have it abundantly."

- The lovely phrase, found only in John's Gospel, that Jesus "has come so that we might have life, and have it abundantly," is very attractive. We have here a picture of total freedom, together with total security; really, a New Testament version of Psalm 23, where the sheep wants for absolutely nothing and who is followed, for its whole life, by goodness and mercy.

Tuesday April 27
John 10:22–30

At that time the festival of the Dedication took place in Jerusalem. It was winter, and Jesus was walking in the temple, in the portico of Solomon. So the Jews gathered around him and said to him, "How long will you keep us in suspense? If you are the Messiah, tell us plainly." Jesus answered, "I have told you, and you do not believe. The works that I do in my Father's name testify to me; but you do not believe, because you do not belong to my sheep. My sheep hear my voice. I know them, and they follow me. I give them eternal life, and they will never perish. No one will snatch them out of my hand. What my Father has given me is greater than all else, and no one can snatch it out of the Father's hand. The Father and I are one."

- If my prayer and my Christian life are dull and lifeless, is it because I do not believe all that Jesus has told me about his love for me? We Christians should be the happiest of people, no matter what our problems. Why? Because our future is fully secure and totally attractive. There are no terms and conditions.

Wednesday April 28
John 12:44–50

Then Jesus cried aloud: "Whoever believes in me believes not in me but in him who sent me. And whoever sees me sees him who sent me. I have come as light into the world, so that everyone who believes in me should not remain in the darkness. I do not judge anyone who hears my words and does not keep them, for I came not to judge the world, but to save the world. The one who rejects me and does not receive my word has a judge; on the last day the word that I have spoken will serve as judge, for I have not spoken on my own, but the Father who sent me has himself given me a commandment about what to say and what to speak. And I know that his commandment is eternal life. What I speak, therefore, I speak just as the Father has told me."

- Jesus is always pointing us to his Father. Their relationship is good beyond our imagining. They are ecstatic about one another, they share everything and work perfectly together. They think the world of one another. Imagine the most harmonious relationship you have, expand it a thousand times, and then you have a dim sense of how Father and Son get along!

- But the great revelation is that all of us are invited into the family life of God. We will be swept off our feet and made radiantly happy when we meet God directly. If I want this to begin even now, I can open myself more and more to God in my daily prayer.

Thursday April 29
St. Catherine of Siena, Virgin and Doctor of the Church
John 13:16–20

"Very truly, I tell you, servants are not greater than their master, nor are messengers greater than the one who sent them. If you know these things, you are blessed if you do them. I am not speaking of all of you; I know whom I have chosen. But it is to fulfill the scripture, 'The one who ate my bread has lifted his heel against me.' I tell you this now, before it occurs, so that when it does occur, you may believe that I am he. Very truly, I tell you, whoever receives one whom I send receives me; and whoever receives me receives him who sent me."

- This passage follows the washing of the feet of Jesus' disciples. It is notable that John substitutes the washing of the feet for the institution of the Eucharist at the Last Supper. Jesus wanted his followers to remember this lesson as a central part of his teaching, and he places it at the Lord's solemn farewell meal.

- Followers of Jesus are called to serve. He is himself the model of service. Consider what it means to be a follower of Jesus. Do I sometimes take my relationship with him for granted?

Friday April 30
John 14:1–6

"Do not let your hearts be troubled. Believe in God, believe also in me. In my Father's house there are many dwelling-places. If it were not so, would I have told you that I go to prepare a place for you? And if I go and prepare a place for you, I will come again and will take you to myself, so that where I am, there you may be also. And you know the way to the place where I am going." Thomas said to him, "Lord, we do not know where you are going. How can we know the way?" Jesus said to him, "I am the way, and the truth, and the life. No one comes to the Father except through me."

- Jesuit mystic Teilhard de Chardin was fond of reminding us, "We are spiritual beings having a human experience, not human beings having a spiritual experience." The spiritual embraces and transcends the human dimension of our lives. Do you have a sense that your life includes and is more than your span of life on earth?

Saturday May 1
Matthew 13:54–58

He came to his home town and began to teach the people in their synagogue, so that they were astounded and said, "Where did this man get this wisdom and these deeds of power? Is not this the carpenter's son? Is not his mother called Mary? And are not his brothers James and Joseph and Simon and Judas? And are not all his sisters with us? Where then did this man get all this?" And they took offense at him. But Jesus said to them, "Prophets are not without honor except in their own country and in their own house." And he did not do many deeds of power there, because of their unbelief.

- We can easily ignore or despise what is familiar. How was it for Jesus when his own people "took offense at him" just because they knew him? Speak with Jesus about this, recalling what it's like for you when people are rude to you.

- Ask Jesus for the grace to realize that every time you meet him in your prayer you are meeting God. Allow his disturbing freshness to captivate you. Like Mary, allow Jesus to do "deeds of power" through you for the good of the world.

The Fifth Week of Easter
May 2–8, 2021

Something to think and pray about each day this week:

While recuperating from his wounds, Ignatius Loyola spent a good deal of time in bed. He had a lot of free time and was looking for entertainment. Initially, he wanted to read popular works of fiction to satisfy his active imagination. He was disappointed to find that the books he wanted were not available, and he had to make do with holy books instead. Reading these books left him time to think about Jesus and the lives of the saints. At first, he preferred to imagine more worldly things, but progressively he found greater pleasure in daydreaming about Jesus and the lives of the saints.

By making space for something new, Ignatius began to contemplate things beyond his standard frame of reference. He began to consider the possibility that God loved him and wanted to be in a relationship with him. By opening his mind to this, Ignatius was able to make sense of things and see that he was called to a greater form of service than he had previously envisioned. The more Ignatius moved into contemplation, the less relevant his previous enjoyments came to be. In their place he discovered real fulfillment and contentment.

—Patrick Corkery, SJ, *The Sacred Heart Messenger*

The Presence of God

Dear Jesus, as I call on you today, I realize that often I come asking for favors. Today I'd like just to be in your presence. Draw my heart in response to your love.

Freedom

Grant, O Lord, that I may be free
from greed and selfishness.

Consciousness

How am I really feeling? Lighthearted? Heavyhearted? I may be very much at peace, happy to be here.
Equally, I may be frustrated, worried, or angry.
I acknowledge how I really am. It is the real me whom the Lord loves.

The Word

Lord Jesus, you became human to communicate with me.
You walked and worked on this earth.
You endured the heat and struggled with the cold.
All your time on this earth was spent in caring for humanity.
You healed the sick, you raised the dead.
Most important of all, you saved me from death.
(*Please turn to the Scripture on the following pages. Inspiration points are there, should you need them. When you are ready, return here to continue.*)

Conversation

Do I notice myself reacting as I pray with the word of God? Do I feel challenged, comforted, angry? Imagining Jesus sitting or standing by me, I speak out my feelings, as one trusted friend to another.

Conclusion

Glory be to the Father, and to the Son, and to the Holy Spirit,
As it was in the beginning, is now, and ever shall be,
World without end. Amen.

Sunday May 2
Fifth Sunday of Easter
John 15:1–8

"I am the true vine, and my Father is the vine-grower. He removes every branch in me that bears no fruit. Every branch that bears fruit he prunes to make it bear more fruit. You have already been cleansed by the word that I have spoken to you. Abide in me as I abide in you. Just as the branch cannot bear fruit by itself unless it abides in the vine, neither can you unless you abide in me. I am the vine, you are the branches. Those who abide in me and I in them bear much fruit, because apart from me you can do nothing. Whoever does not abide in me is thrown away like a branch and withers; such branches are gathered, thrown into the fire, and burned. If you abide in me, and my words abide in you, ask for whatever you wish, and it will be done for you. My Father is glorified by this, that you bear much fruit and become my disciples."

- "Apart from me you can do nothing." We could call to mind our total dependence on Christ for life and love. Recall his many gifts over the years and ask for more.

- The Father is pruning us, working deep in our hearts to draw us closer to himself in Christ. Am I resisting his efforts? Let us ask for the gift of openness to his pruning work.

Monday May 3
Ss. Philip and James, Apostles
John 14:6–14

Jesus said to him, "I am the way, and the truth, and the life. No one comes to the Father except through me. If you know me, you will know my Father also. From now on you do know him and have seen him."

Philip said to him, "Lord, show us the Father, and we will be satisfied." Jesus said to him, "Have I been with you all this time, Philip, and you still do not know me? Whoever has seen me has seen the Father. How can you say, 'Show us the Father'? Do you not believe that I am in the Father and the Father is in me? The words that I say to you I do not speak on my own; but the Father who dwells in me does his works. Believe me that I am in the Father and the Father is in me; but if you do not, then believe me because of the works themselves. Very truly, I tell you, the one who believes in me will also do the works that I do and, in fact, will do greater works than these, because I am going to the Father. I will do whatever you ask in my name, so that the Father may be glorified in the Son. If in my name you ask me for anything, I will do it."

- Following Jesus is a call to be in relationship. Jesus invites me into the very heart of life, the source of goodness; to be with him "in the Father."

- We learn from the Gospels that it was the close relationship he had with his Father that led Jesus to behave in the ways he did. The movement of God's spirit within me draws me into the life of Jesus and the Father. I take a few moments to recognize and appreciate where God is working in and around me.

Tuesday May 4
John 14:27–31a

"Peace I leave with you; my peace I give to you. I do not give to you as the world gives. Do not let your hearts be troubled, and do not let them be afraid. You heard me say to you, 'I am going away, and I am coming to you.' If you loved me, you would rejoice that I am going to the Father, because the Father is greater than I. And now I have told you this before it occurs, so that when it does occur, you may believe. I will no longer talk much with you, for the ruler of this world is coming. He has no power over me; but I do as the Father has commanded me, so that the world may know that I love the Father."

- "You heard me say to you, 'I am going away, and I am coming to you.'" We are reminded of the lovely image of Jesus, the servant, going ahead of us to prepare our rooms, and returning to bring us when they are ready.

- "The ruler of the world" is on his way; the darkness that seeks to extinguish the Light. But the Light is stronger: "He has no power over me."

Wednesday May 5
John 15:1–8

"I am the true vine, and my Father is the vine-grower. He removes every branch in me that bears no fruit. Every branch that bears fruit he prunes to make it bear more fruit. You have already been cleansed by the word that I have spoken to you. Abide in me as I abide in you. Just as the branch cannot bear fruit by itself unless it abides in the vine, neither can you unless you abide in me. I am the vine, you are the branches. Those who abide in me and I in them bear much fruit, because apart from me you can do nothing. Whoever does not abide in me is thrown away like a branch and withers; such branches are gathered, thrown into the fire, and burned. If you abide in me, and my words abide in you, ask for whatever you wish, and it will be done for you. My Father is glorified by this, that you bear much fruit and become my disciples."

- The term "to abide" was music to the Hebrews who had been nomads and exiles. They longed for a place in which they could rest permanently. Jesus offers, not a country, but his very self, for this abiding. Relationship, not place, is what matters. I thank God that even though my life is always changing, Jesus is my home, my permanent resting place.

- When I feel that my life is barren and fruitless, I may come to see that this is because I am "apart" from Jesus and so can "do nothing." Shocked, I may resolve to catch up with God in prayer again. Then I find that I begin "to bear much fruit."

Thursday May 6
John 15:9–11

"As the Father has loved me, so I have loved you; abide in my love. If you keep my commandments, you will abide in my love, just as I have kept my Father's commandments and abide in his love. I have said these things to you so that my joy may be in you, and that your joy may be complete."

- Jesus tells us that we must keep "his" commandments. Think of one of them: "Love your enemies," "Turn the other cheek," "Take up your cross every day."

- He reminds us how he has kept his Father's commandments, doing his will in all things. Following Jesus' example of obedience to the will of God is foundational in the Christian life.

Friday May 7
John 15:12–17

"This is my commandment, that you love one another as I have loved you. No one has greater love than this, to lay down one's life for one's friends. You are my friends if you do what I command you. I do not call you servants any longer, because the servant does not know what the master is doing; but I have called you friends, because I have made known to you everything that I have heard from my Father. You did not choose me but I chose you. And I appointed you to go and bear fruit, fruit that will last, so that the Father will give you whatever you ask him in my name. I am giving you these commands so that you may love one another."

- Jesus chose me. He created me and he called me because he loves me. I so want to respond generously to his call. "Dearest Lord, teach me to be generous!"

Saturday May 8
John 15:18–21

"If the world hates you, be aware that it hated me before it hated you. If you belonged to the world, the world would love you as its own. Because you do not belong to the world, but I have chosen you out of the world—therefore the world hates you. Remember the word that I said to you, 'Servants are not greater than their master.' If they persecuted me, they will persecute you; if they kept my word, they will keep yours also. But they will do all these things to you on account of my name, because they do not know him who sent me."

- Lord, could I bear to be "hated"? Perhaps, but only if I keep in mind that then I am not alone; you are with me.

- Witnessing to love means standing for justice, and the unjust will not like it. Standing for truth will infuriate those who live by lies. I won't look for trouble, but if it comes, let me not run away. Your kingdom is a kingdom of justice and truth. At the end of my life I will be glad to have contributed what I could to its growth, and those I stood by will intercede for me.

The Sixth Week of Easter
May 9–15, 2021

Something to think and pray about each day this week:

"Where will it all end up?" is a question often posed today by people who value the role of the Church in their lives, their community, and their society. To say that there is a lot of confusion tending toward despair about the future of the Church in Ireland and indeed Europe is commonplace.

The future lies more in creating great human beings and less in great institutions. Those who have made it to the top of the ecclesiastical structure were often people who made the institutions look great, and their humanness was often not a priority. In a world that has enormous possibilities and increasingly diverse influences, Christianity is desperate for more ambassadors and fewer bureaucrats.

The Gospel reminds us that people want to meet other people whose humanity points toward something worth striving for. "All spoke well of him." "How can this be," they asked, "Isn't this Joseph's son?" (Luke 4:22). "And they were amazed, and asked, 'What kind of man is this?'" (Matthew 8:27). "The centurion, seeing what had happened, praised God and said, 'Surely this was a righteous man'" (Luke 23:47).

Furthermore, over the last two thousand years, the rituals of faith, the words of tradition, the noblest of people who allowed grace to influence their humanity are a great reservoir of hope and a resource of incalculable value as we foster a faith appropriate to our age.

—Alan Hilliard, *Dipping into Lent*

The Presence of God

At any time of the day or night we can call on Jesus.
He is always waiting, listening for our call.
What a wonderful blessing.
No phone needed, no e-mails, just a whisper.

Freedom

If God were trying to tell me something, would I know?
If God were reassuring me or challenging me, would I notice?
I ask for the grace to be free of my own preoccupations
and open to what God may be saying to me.

Consciousness

Help me, Lord, become more conscious of your presence. Teach me to recognize your presence in others. Fill my heart with gratitude for the times your love has been shown to me through the care of others.

The Word

In this expectant state of mind, please turn to the text for the day with confidence. Believe that the Holy Spirit is present and may reveal whatever the passage has to say to you. Read reflectively, listening with a third ear to what may be going on in your heart. (*Please turn to the Scripture on the following pages. Inspiration points are there, should you need them. When you are ready, return here to continue.*)

Conversation

Conversation requires talking and listening.
As I talk to Jesus, may I also learn to pause and listen.
I will ask him to help me place myself fully in his care, knowing that he always desires good for me.

Conclusion

I thank God for these moments we have spent together and for any insights I have been given concerning the text.

Sunday May 9
John 17:11b–19

"And now I am no longer in the world, but they are in the world, and I am coming to you. Holy Father, protect them in your name that you have given me, so that they may be one, as we are one. While I was with them, I protected them in your name that you have given me. I guarded them, and not one of them was lost except the one destined to be lost, so that the scripture might be fulfilled. But now I am coming to you, and I speak these things in the world so that they may have my joy made complete in themselves. I have given them your word, and the world has hated them because they do not belong to the world, just as I do not belong to the world. I am not asking you to take them out of the world, but I ask you to protect them from the evil one. They do not belong to the world, just as I do not belong to the world. Sanctify them in the truth; your word is truth. As you have sent me into the world, so I have sent them into the world. And for their sakes I sanctify myself, so that they also may be sanctified in truth."

- Divisions among Christians are a betrayal of the very unity that Jesus died for. Divisions are a scandal that prevents people from accepting the gospel. What small step can I take to reach out to other Christians?

- The words for "joy" occur 335 times in the Bible! It is God's gift to us. God does not want us to be sorrowful. Is Jesus' joy complete in me?

Monday May 10
John 15:26–16:4a

"When the Advocate comes, whom I will send to you from the Father, the Spirit of truth who comes from the Father, he will testify on my behalf. You also are to testify because you have been with me from the beginning.

"I have said these things to you to keep you from stumbling. They will put you out of the synagogues. Indeed, an hour is coming when those who kill you will think that by doing so they are offering worship to God. And they will do this because they have not known the Father or me. But I have said these things to you so that when their hour comes you may remember that I told you about them.

"I did not say these things to you from the beginning, because I was with you."

- The disciples were able to testify to Jesus because they had lived and worked alongside him. In this passage, Jesus promises to send them the Holy Spirit, the "Advocate," after he has gone. The work of the Holy Spirit affirms the life and love of Jesus, giving witness to what is true.

- To testify and bear witness to something, I must have personal experience so that I can say: "This is true, and I know it." Lord, I have not been with you from the beginning. I am one of those who did not see and yet believed. Show me yourself, strengthen your Spirit in me, so that my life and my words may testify to you.

Tuesday May 11
John 16:5–11

"But now I am going to him who sent me; yet none of you asks me, 'Where are you going?' But because I have said these things to you, sorrow has filled your hearts. Nevertheless, I tell you the truth: it is to your advantage that I go away, for if I do not go away, the Advocate will not come to you; but if I go, I will send him to you. And when he comes, he will prove the world wrong about sin and righteousness and judgment: about sin, because they do not believe in me; about righteousness, because I am going to the Father and you will see me no longer; about judgment, because the ruler of this world has been condemned."

- It seemed like abandonment to the disciples, but Jesus says he goes away for our good, so that the Advocate, the Holy Spirit, might come to us. Because of the gift of the Holy Spirit, we don't have to rely on our own resources to reach God. Our call is to become better attuned to the wavelength of the Holy Spirit so that our lives are shaped by the Holy Spirit.

- Sometimes when I read a piece of Scripture, I do not understand what it is saying to me. In that case, let my not understanding be my prayer; I can chat to Jesus or ask the Holy Spirit to enlighten me about the difficulty I have with the passage. Remember, Jesus loves me just as I am, right here and now.

- The Holy Spirit inspires us, that is, breathes into us and breathes in us. I sit with that image and allow the Holy Spirit to breathe into me.

Wednesday May 12
John 16:12–15

"I still have many things to say to you, but you cannot bear them now. When the Spirit of truth comes, he will guide you into all the truth; for he will not speak on his own, but will speak whatever he hears, and he will declare to you the things that are to come. He will glorify me, because he will take what is mine and declare it to you. All that the Father has is mine. For this reason I said that he will take what is mine and declare it to you."

• Here is Jesus, nearing his own death, and he is pouring out the depth of his love for his followers. He spoke these words at the Last Supper, as he gathered with his disciples, sharing life with them. His words and actions comforted and strengthened them in ways that only the Holy Spirit might help them understand.

• If you have had the experience of being with someone you loved as they are close to death, then you know the significance of final words spoken to loved ones. Perhaps you will remember their words, how they said them, and some of the emotions you experienced in that precious time.

• The love that God the Father has for Jesus is the love Jesus has for each of us! Can I ask for this grace, of knowing and experiencing, deep down, this tremendous love?

Thursday May 13
John 16:16–20

[Jesus said to his disciples,] "A little while, and you will no longer see me, and again a little while, and you will see me." Then some of his disciples said to one another, "What does he mean by saying to us, 'A little while, and you will no longer see me, and again a little while, and you will see me'; and 'Because I am going to the Father'?" They said, "What does he mean by this 'a little while'? We do not know what he is talking about." Jesus knew that they wanted to ask him, so he said to them, "Are you discussing among yourselves what I meant when I said, 'A little while, and you will no longer see me, and again a little while, and you will see me'? Very truly, I tell you, you will weep and mourn, but the world will rejoice; you will have pain, but your pain will turn into joy."

- Jesus told the disciples about his death and resurrection. He would be taken from them in death and would come back after his resurrection. Their sorrow would turn to joy.

- Our sorrow also will turn to joy. We interpret the troubles of our lives in this way, in the light of the cross. Sorrow is an opportunity to enter the experience of the cross as the way to eternal life with Christ.

Friday May 14
St. Matthias, Apostle
John 15:9–17

"As the Father has loved me, so I have loved you; abide in my love. If you keep my commandments, you will abide in my love, just as I have kept my Father's commandments and abide in his love. I have said these things to you so that my joy may be in you, and that your joy may be complete.

"This is my commandment, that you love one another as I have loved you. No one has greater love than this, to lay down one's life for one's friends. You are my friends if you do what I command you. I do not call you servants any longer, because the servant does not know what the master is doing; but I have called you friends, because I have made known to you everything that I have heard from my Father. You did not choose me but I chose you. And I appointed you to go and bear fruit, fruit that will last, so that the Father will give you whatever you ask him in my name. I am giving you these commands so that you may love one another."

- My love for others must not be conditioned by how they respond. Jesus loves me totally, whether I am good or bad or indifferent. My love must have that quality too. This is costly love; it could demand my very life!

- This costly love will bear rich fruit, whether I see it or not. Just so, Jesus' love bears fruit only after his death. I must not be discouraged when my love seems to be wasted. True love never comes to an end (1 Corinthians 13:8). Loving actions are the building blocks of eternal life.

Saturday May 15

John 16:23b–28

"Very truly, I tell you, if you ask anything of the Father in my name, he will give it to you. Until now you have not asked for anything in my name. Ask and you will receive, so that your joy may be complete.

"I have said these things to you in figures of speech. The hour is coming when I will no longer speak to you in figures, but will tell you plainly of the Father. On that day you will ask in my name. I do not say to you that I will ask the Father on your behalf; for the Father himself loves you, because you have loved me and have believed that I came from God. I came from the Father and have come into the world; again, I am leaving the world and am going to the Father."

- Jesus says, "Ask and you will receive." We may lose the conviction that it is worthwhile asking for what we want in prayer. Jesus awaits our asking. Full-hearted asking of God always brings a gift in return; it may be a specific grace or petition we ask for, or it may be simply the deep support from God that enables us to cope and to grow even when life is difficult.

- Jesus speaks of joy. What is the source of my joy? I recall the times I have been joyful and allow my joy to be more complete by recognizing, appreciating, and giving thanks for these times.

The Seventh Week of Easter
May 16–22, 2021

Something to think and pray about each day this week:

Laudato Si' (May You be Praised) has channeled massive energy into care of our Common Home. Pope Francis shares with all humankind the crucified Christ's challenge to St. Francis of Assisi in 1205: "Francis, go and repair my house which as you see is falling into disrepair." Note the divine command, "Go!" *Laudato Si'* is interwoven with a strong thread of hope, as the following encouraging quotations show:

> Hope would have us recognize that there is always a way out (61). All it takes is one good person to restore hope (71). We must speak of the figure of a Father who creates and who alone owns the world (74). The God who created the universe out of nothing can also intervene in this world and overcome every form of evil (75). A spirituality which forgets God as all-powerful and Creator is not acceptable (75).
>
> Jesus has taken to himself this material world (221), and through his Incarnation he has incorporated into his person part of the material world, the seed of definitive transformation (235). The ultimate destiny of the universe is in the fullness of God (83). The world is now journeying toward its final perfection (80, Note 49). The Eucharist is itself an act of cosmic love which penetrates all creation, for in the bread of the Eucharist creation is projected toward divinization, toward its final transfiguration (236). We come together to take charge of this home which has been entrusted to us, knowing that all the good which exists here will be taken up into the heavenly feast. Let us sing as we go. May our struggles and our concern for this planet never take away the joy of our hope (244).

—Brian Grogan, SJ, *Creation Walk: The Amazing Story of a Small Blue Planet*

The Presence of God
As I sit here, the beating of my heart,
the ebb and flow of my breathing, the movements of my mind
are all signs of God's ongoing creation of me.
I pause for a moment and become aware
of this presence of God within me.

Freedom
I will ask God's help
to be free from my own preoccupations,
to be open to God in this time of prayer,
to come to know, love, and serve God more.

Consciousness
At this moment, Lord, I turn my thoughts to you.
I will leave aside my chores and preoccupations.
I will take rest and refreshment in your presence.

The Word
Now I turn to the Scripture set out for me this day. I read slowly over the
words and see if any sentence or sentiment appeals to me. (*Please turn to
the Scripture on the following pages. Inspiration points are there, should you
need them. When you are ready, return here to continue.*)

Conversation
Begin to talk to Jesus about the Scripture you have just read. What part
of it strikes a chord in you? Perhaps the words of a friend—or some story
you have heard recently—will slowly rise to the surface of your consciousness. If so, does the story throw light on what the Scripture passage may
be saying to you?

Conclusion
Glory be to the Father, and to the Son, and to the Holy Spirit,
As it was in the beginning, is now, and ever shall be,
World without end. Amen.

Sunday May 16
The Ascension of the Lord
Mark 16:15–20

And he said to them, "Go into all the world and proclaim the good news to the whole creation. The one who believes and is baptized will be saved; but the one who does not believe will be condemned. And these signs will accompany those who believe: by using my name they will cast out demons; they will speak in new tongues; they will pick up snakes in their hands, and if they drink any deadly thing, it will not hurt them; they will lay their hands on the sick, and they will recover."

So then the Lord Jesus, after he had spoken to them, was taken up into heaven and sat down at the right hand of God. And they went out and proclaimed the good news everywhere, while the Lord worked with them and confirmed the message by the signs that accompanied it.

- Pope Francis is calling us today to obey the Lord's command given 2,000 years ago. We are to work out together how to share the Good News. We cannot bury or hoard the gift we have been given because everyone needs to hear the good news that they are loved. We are to be "the good news in the present tense."

- God is determined to bring us all into the final community of love which is gathering day by day. So, Lord, let me listen to you as you say "Go!" and let me find creative ways to be good news to those around me.

Monday May 17
John 16:29–33

His disciples said, "Yes, now you are speaking plainly, not in any figure of speech! Now we know that you know all things, and do not need to have anyone question you; by this we believe that you came from God." Jesus answered them, "Do you now believe? The hour is coming, indeed it has come, when you will be scattered, each one to his home, and you will leave me alone. Yet I am not alone because the Father is with me. I have said this to you, so that in me you may have peace. In the world you face persecution. But take courage; I have conquered the world!"

- Is faith a challenge for me? In what way? Do I feel in good company among the disciples who are "slow learners"? Is there a sense in which faith is always "beyond"? Beyond what I know, what I can imagine or even hope for?

- Do I have a sense of not being alone? Can I ask God to not leave me alone, to always be with me? Have I ever experienced that peace John speaks of? Can I ask for it?

Tuesday May 18
John 17:1–11a

After Jesus had spoken these words, he looked up to heaven and said, "Father, the hour has come; glorify your Son so that the Son may glorify you, since you have given him authority over all people, to give eternal life to all whom you have given him. And this is eternal life, that they may know you, the only true God, and Jesus Christ whom you have sent. I glorified you on earth by finishing the work that you gave me to do. So now, Father, glorify me in your own presence with the glory that I had in your presence before the world existed.

"I have made your name known to those whom you gave me from the world. They were yours, and you gave them to me, and they have kept your word. Now they know that everything you have given me is from you; for the words that you gave to me I have given to them, and they have received them and know in truth that I came from you; and they have believed that you sent me. I am asking on their behalf; I am not asking on behalf of the world, but on behalf of those whom you gave me, because they are yours. All mine are yours, and yours are mine; and I have been glorified in them. And now I am no longer in the world, but they are in the world, and I am coming to you. Holy Father, protect them in your name that you have given me, so that they may be one, as we are one."

- The mission of Jesus is about to be accomplished. St. John sees the passion and death of Jesus as the moment in which he is most glorious because his mission is to reveal, in human form, the infinite love and mercy of God, in all circumstances, for the whole of humanity.

- Love and mercy are most evident when Jesus responds with love and mercy to his being betrayed, rejected, mocked, scourged, and crucified. The message is that nothing can separate us from his love and mercy. He makes clear the inner nature of God. The evil of the whole human race is transformed in the heart of Jesus crucified.

- Gaze at the Cross of Jesus and ponder what he endures to convey the infinite mercy and love of God. "By his wounds you have been healed" (1 Peter 2:24).

Wednesday May 19
John 17:11b–19

"And now I am no longer in the world, but they are in the world, and I am coming to you. Holy Father, protect them in your name that you have given me, so that they may be one, as we are one. While I was with them, I protected them in your name that you have given me. I guarded them, and not one of them was lost except the one destined to be lost, so that the scripture might be fulfilled. But now I am coming to you, and I speak these things in the world so that they may have my joy made complete in themselves. I have given them your word, and the world has hated them because they do not belong to the world, just as I do not belong to the world. I am not asking you to take them out of the world, but I ask you to protect them from the evil one. They do not belong to the world, just as I do not belong to the world. Sanctify them in the truth; your word is truth. As you have sent me into the world, so I have sent them into the world. And for their sakes I sanctify myself, so that they also may be sanctified in truth."

- This chapter of John's Gospel presents Jesus as the giver of divine life. He possesses the fullness of Godly life. This is what he leaves to us in his flesh and blood, the Eucharist. Prayer unites us to the sacrifice of Jesus who, all through his life, not just at Calvary, gave himself to us as teacher, healer, protector—always as loving friend. What is your favorite title for Jesus? Repeat that in prayer and bring it through the day like a lingering line of a song or a tune.

Thursday May 20
John 17:20–26

"I ask not only on behalf of these, but also on behalf of those who will be-lieve in me through their word, that they may all be one. As you, Father, are in me and I am in you, may they also be in us, so that the world may believe that you have sent me. The glory that you have given me I have given them, so that they may be one, as we are one, I in them and you in me, that they may become completely one, so that the world may know that you have sent me and have loved them even as you have loved me. Father, I desire that those also, whom you have given me, may be with me where I am, to see my glory, which you have given me because you loved me before the foundation of the world.

"Righteous Father, the world does not know you, but I know you; and these know that you have sent me. I made your name known to them, and I will make it known, so that the love with which you have loved me may be in them, and I in them."

- Jesus' prayer that "all may be one" can be misinterpreted. This oneness is much greater and deeper than uniformity, than people professing the same faith and observing the same religious practices. This is a oneness in which love is given and received, a love which embraces difference. Jesus and the Father, while being one, remain distinct from each other. The disciples, while being one with Jesus, retain their own identity and individuality.

- Lord, help me understand that in love there is difference, but not division.

Friday May 21
John 21:15–19

When they had finished breakfast, Jesus said to Simon Peter, "Simon son of John, do you love me more than these?" He said to him, "Yes, Lord; you know that I love you." Jesus said to him, "Feed my lambs." A second time he said to him, "Simon son of John, do you love me?" He said to him, "Yes, Lord; you know that I love you." Jesus said to him, "Tend my sheep." He said to him the third time, "Simon son of John, do you love me?" Peter felt hurt because he said to him the third time, "Do you love me?" And he said to him, "Lord, you know everything; you know that I love you." Jesus said to him, "Feed my sheep. Very truly, I tell you, when you were younger, you used to fasten your own belt and to go wherever you wished. But when you grow old, you will stretch out your hands, and someone else will fasten a belt around you and take you where you do not wish to go." (He said this to indicate the kind of death by which he would glorify God.) After this he said to him, "Follow me."

- "Do you love me?" Peter is asked this question; I am asked this question too. Do I see the goodness in me that Jesus sees?

- As Peter stands before Jesus, it is reasonable to presume that he is all too aware of his failure to stand by and with his beloved master during the Passion. Jesus focuses on his capacity to love, not on his failure. He does not admonish Peter for his betrayals. Because he loves, Peter is reinstated and given a great responsibility to care for the early Christian community.

- Is this an issue for me, focusing on my failures and unwilling or unable to accept that the Lord loves me as I am—and still has work for me to do?

Saturday May 22
John 21:20–25

Peter turned and saw the disciple whom Jesus loved following them; he was the one who had reclined next to Jesus at the supper and had said, "Lord, who is it that is going to betray you?" When Peter saw him, he said to Jesus, "Lord, what about him?" Jesus said to him, "If it is my will that he remain until I come, what is that to you? Follow me!" So the rumor spread in the community that this disciple would not die. Yet Jesus did not say to him that he would not die, but, "If it is my will that he remain until I come, what is that to you?"

This is the disciple who is testifying to these things and has written them, and we know that his testimony is true. But there are also many other things that Jesus did; if every one of them were written down, I suppose that the world itself could not contain the books that would be written.

- The blank page at the end of a Bible is for us to write our own gospel! All the books in the world cannot contain responses to the Christian story. Our gospel story begins at birth through the times in life we have, like the apostles, "met the Lord." Maybe today you can give thanks to the Lord for the ways you have found him close in life: in times good and bad. In the journal of a life is the love and the action of God. And in the Journal of God, our names are written "in the book of life."

May 23–29, 2021

Something to think and pray about each day this week:

Life can occur to us as an uncomfortable journey. We can even feel lost at times. In these times, it isn't so much about what we do to regain our direction that counts, but what we are willing to let God do. We can get so caught up that we miss the little moments of beauty and relief that we are given along the way. Life can seem all wilderness. But that is never the whole story. Bad times end. This is not to patronize you or minimize the difficulties you face. It is simply a statement of reality and hope. The bad times end.

What journey in your life are you on right now? Name it. Where do you experience feeling lost? Name it. Breathe in and say, "Lord, I feel lost." Breathe out and say, "Lord, I let you find me." *Repeat for a few minutes.*

Jeremiah 29:11: "For surely I know the plans I have for you, says the Lord, plans for your welfare and not for harm, to give you a future with hope."

—Brendan McManus, SJ, and Jim Deeds, *Deeper into the Mess:*
Praying Through Tough Times

The Presence of God

"Be still, and know that I am God!" Lord, your words lead us to the calmness and greatness of your presence.

Freedom

God is not foreign to my freedom. The Spirit breathes life into my most intimate desires, gently nudging me toward all that is good. I ask for the grace to let myself be enfolded by the Spirit.

Consciousness

Where do I sense hope, encouragement, and growth in my life? By looking back over the past few months, I may be able to see which activities and occasions have produced rich fruit. If I do notice such areas, I will determine to give those areas both time and space in the future.

The Word

The word of God comes down to us through the Scriptures. May the Holy Spirit enlighten my mind and my heart to respond to the Gospel teachings. (*Please turn to the Scripture on the following pages. Inspiration points are there, should you need them. When you are ready, return here to continue.*)

Conversation

What is stirring in me as I pray? Am I consoled, troubled, left cold? I imagine Jesus standing or sitting at my side, and I share my feelings with him.

Conclusion

Glory be to the Father, and to the Son, and to the Holy Spirit,
As it was in the beginning, is now, and ever shall be,
World without end. Amen.

Sunday May 23
Pentecost Sunday
John 20:19–23

When it was evening on that day, the first day of the week, and the doors of the house where the disciples had met were locked for fear of the Jews, Jesus came and stood among them and said, "Peace be with you." After he said this, he showed them his hands and his side. Then the disciples rejoiced when they saw the Lord. Jesus said to them again, "Peace be with you. As the Father has sent me, so I send you." When he had said this, he breathed on them and said to them, "Receive the Holy Spirit. If you forgive the sins of any, they are forgiven them; if you retain the sins of any, they are retained."

• Jesus' disciples were afraid. What causes me to be afraid?

• Is faith a source of peace for me? Have I ever found myself in that room with the disciples? And then what happened?

• He "breathed" on them! Reminiscent of Genesis and God breathing on the chaos. Can I ask him to breathe on my chaos?

• Can I ask for the gift of his Spirit to fill me with his peace and his light?

Monday May 24
Mark 10:17–27

As he was setting out on a journey, a man ran up and knelt before him, and asked him, "Good Teacher, what must I do to inherit eternal life?" Jesus said to him, "Why do you call me good? No one is good but God alone. You know the commandments: 'You shall not murder; You shall not commit adultery; You shall not steal; You shall not bear false witness; You shall not defraud; Honor your father and mother.'" He said to him, "Teacher, I have kept all these since my youth." Jesus, looking at him, loved him and said, "You lack one thing; go, sell what you own, and give the money to the poor, and you will have treasure in heaven; then come, follow me." When he heard this, he was shocked and went away grieving, for he had many possessions.

Then Jesus looked around and said to his disciples, "How hard it will be for those who have wealth to enter the kingdom of God!" And the disciples were perplexed at these words. But Jesus said to them again,

"Children, how hard it is to enter the kingdom of God! It is easier for a camel to go through the eye of a needle than for someone who is rich to enter the kingdom of God." They were greatly astounded and said to one another, "Then who can be saved?" Jesus looked at them and said, "For mortals it is impossible, but not for God; for God all things are possible."

• Have you ever been sad because you didn't do something good that you could have done? The visit to a sick or lonely person postponed, the help not given to someone in great financial need, the prayer time not given, the failure to listen to your children or people close to you—many ways in which you could, without too much difficulty, have said a "yes" to love. This is something like the feeling of the rich man when he walked away with his wealth and his sadness. Let that be part of prayer today.

Tuesday May 25
Mark 10:28–31

Peter began to say to him, "Look, we have left everything and followed you." Jesus said, "Truly I tell you, there is no one who has left house or brothers or sisters or mother or father or children or fields, for my sake and for the sake of the good news, who will not receive a hundredfold now in this age—houses, brothers and sisters, mothers and children, and fields, with persecutions—and in the age to come eternal life. But many who are first will be last, and the last will be first."

• Peter's experience as a fisherman had taught him that taking stock was necessary from time to time. Although he was often enthusiastic and spontaneous, now he seems to panic as he suddenly realizes that he may be left with nothing. I pray for a deeper trust and faith in the message of Jesus, in his presence to me. Aware of anything that causes me to be too cautious or calculating, I ask God's help.

Wednesday May 26
Mark 10:32–45

They were on the road, going up to Jerusalem, and Jesus was walking ahead of them; they were amazed, and those who followed were afraid. He took the twelve aside again and began to tell them what was to happen to him, saying, "See, we are going up to Jerusalem, and the Son of

Man will be handed over to the chief priests and the scribes, and they will condemn him to death; then they will hand him over to the Gentiles; they will mock him, and spit upon him, and flog him, and kill him; and after three days he will rise again."

James and John, the sons of Zebedee, came forward to him and said to him, "Teacher, we want you to do for us whatever we ask of you." And he said to them, "What is it you want me to do for you?" And they said to him, "Grant us to sit, one at your right hand and one at your left, in your glory." But Jesus said to them, "You do not know what you are asking. Are you able to drink the cup that I drink, or be baptized with the baptism that I am baptized with?" They replied, "We are able." Then Jesus said to them, "The cup that I drink you will drink; and with the baptism with which I am baptized, you will be baptized; but to sit at my right hand or at my left is not mine to grant, but it is for those for whom it has been prepared."

When the ten heard this, they began to be angry with James and John. So Jesus called them and said to them, "You know that among the Gentiles those whom they recognize as their rulers lord it over them, and their great ones are tyrants over them. But it is not so among you; but whoever wishes to become great among you must be your servant, and whoever wishes to be first among you must be slave of all. For the Son of Man came not to be served but to serve, and to give his life a ransom for many."

- Anyone who follows Jesus must be not a slave of Jesus but "a slave of all." A slave usually does the bidding of one single owner. By saying that his followers must become the "slaves of all," Jesus is emphasizing the ideal of indiscriminate love and service. That will be my Passion.

Thursday May 27
Mark 10:46–52

They came to Jericho. As he and his disciples and a large crowd were leaving Jericho, Bartimaeus son of Timaeus, a blind beggar, was sitting by the roadside. When he heard that it was Jesus of Nazareth, he began to shout out and say, "Jesus, Son of David, have mercy on me!" Many sternly ordered him to be quiet, but he cried out even more loudly, "Son of David, have mercy on me!" Jesus stood still and said, "Call him here."

And they called the blind man, saying to him, "Take heart; get up, he is calling you." So throwing off his cloak, he sprang up and came to Jesus. Then Jesus said to him, "What do you want me to do for you?" The blind man said to him, "My teacher, let me see again." Jesus said to him, "Go; your faith has made you well." Immediately he regained his sight and followed him on the way.

• Lord, I sometimes open my eyes in the morning and do not notice the sunshine, the green of trees, the colors in my room, the warmth or sorrow in the faces around me. If I had been blind, like Bartimaeus in today's Gospel, I would long to open my eyes and see all that is to be seen. I could not have enough of this light-filled world around me.

• Give me a relish, Lord, for all that my eyes can take in: not the preselected shots of the TV screen, but the endlessly varied landscape and peoplescape that surrounds me. I pray with Bartimaeus: "Master, let me receive my sight."

Friday May 28
Mark 11:11–26

Then he entered Jerusalem and went into the temple; and when he had looked around at everything, as it was already late, he went out to Bethany with the twelve.

On the following day, when they came from Bethany, he was hungry. Seeing in the distance a fig tree in leaf, he went to see whether perhaps he would find anything on it. When he came to it, he found nothing but leaves, for it was not the season for figs. He said to it, "May no one ever eat fruit from you again." And his disciples heard it.

Then they came to Jerusalem. And he entered the temple and began to drive out those who were selling and those who were buying in the temple, and he overturned the tables of the money-changers and the seats of those who sold doves; and he would not allow anyone to carry anything through the temple. He was teaching and saying, "Is it not written,

'My house shall be called a house of prayer for all the nations'?
But you have made it a den of robbers."

And when the chief priests and the scribes heard it, they kept looking for a way to kill him; for they were afraid of him, because the whole crowd was spellbound by his teaching. And when evening came, Jesus and his disciples went out of the city.

In the morning as they passed by, they saw the fig tree withered away to its roots. Then Peter remembered and said to him, "Rabbi, look! The fig tree that you cursed has withered." Jesus answered them, "Have faith in God. Truly I tell you, if you say to this mountain, 'Be taken up and thrown into the sea,' and if you do not doubt in your heart, but believe that what you say will come to pass, it will be done for you. So I tell you, whatever you ask for in prayer, believe that you have received it, and it will be yours.

"Whenever you stand praying, forgive, if you have anything against anyone; so that your Father in heaven may also forgive you your trespasses."

- What aroused anger in Jesus was that commerce and caste had ousted reverence. The money-changers and sellers of doves used their privilege and license to extort high prices from poor pilgrims. Men had created barriers and divisions between the courts, to exclude Gentiles and women from some areas.

- Do I always respect what a church should be? A house of prayer, not of commerce—for all nations, without compartments—and a place where all can seek God.

Saturday May 29
Mark 11:27–33

Again they came to Jerusalem. As he was walking in the temple, the chief priests, the scribes, and the elders came to him and said, "By what authority are you doing these things? Who gave you this authority to do them?" Jesus said to them, "I will ask you one question; answer me, and I will tell you by what authority I do these things. Did the baptism of John come from heaven, or was it of human origin? Answer me." They argued with one another, "If we say, 'From heaven' he will say, 'Why then did you not believe him?' But shall we say, 'Of human origin'?"—they were afraid of the crowd, for all regarded John as truly a prophet. So they answered Jesus, "We do not know." And Jesus said to them, "Neither will I tell you by what authority I am doing these things."

- The opponents of Jesus question the source of his authority. They fear it may undermine their own power. Jesus prefers the company

of sinners and tax collectors, who made no claim to any authority of
their own.

- True authority is not a personal possession. It comes from God and is
to be used always with an eye on God. Whatever authority we have—
as parents, teachers, priests, and others—we must use sensitively so
that God would be pleased.

The Ninth Week in Ordinary Time
May 30—June 5, 2021

Something to think and pray about each day this week:

The sacred space of an icon is in its message and its invitation to enter the divine presence . . . One can gaze through the icon, as it were, and see or experience the divine as though present to the viewer, focusing on the mystery there depicted. One can also gaze as though at a mirror, so that we see ourselves as God sees us. There is no attempt at reality in an icon; there are no shadows to create an illusion of space, and the icon simply gazes at us and invites our gaze in return.

It is best to stand or sit before an icon, being aware of the sacred nature of the space, having familiarized oneself with the Gospel story it depicts (John 4:1–42). We then wait for the icon to reveal itself to us, allowing the eye to rove across it until it rests on the natural focus.

In the case of the icon of the woman at the well, we can listen and try to hear this harmony with inner senses of the heart. We can hear the words of Jesus as he speaks to the woman, asking for a drink. We can experience his thirst. We can listen to the tone of the woman's first response.

In order to help us in this, the iconographer uses light and color to express the mystery. Symbols are also employed to nudge us toward the profound theology expressed in the image. As the dialogue unfolds, the theology of Jesus' divine nature is revealed to the woman; not in the way that the transfiguration was revealed to the disciples Peter, James, and John—who were taken into an experience of the divinity of Jesus—but in the context of what appears to be a chance encounter with a stranger. There are no visions and there is no voice from the cloud, but the revelation is specific and deep. Living water is promised and the numinous nature of God is clothed in weariness and thirst.

—Magdalen Lawler, SND, *Well of Living Water*

The Presence of God

"I am standing at the door, knocking," says the Lord. What a wonderful privilege that the Lord of all creation desires to come to me. I welcome his presence.

Freedom

Everything has the potential to draw forth from me a fuller love and life. Yet my desires are often fixed, caught, on illusions of fulfillment. I ask that God, through my freedom, may orchestrate my desires in a vibrant loving melody rich in harmony.

Consciousness

To be conscious about something is to be aware of it.
Dear Lord, help me remember that you gave me life.
Thank you for the gift of life.
Teach me to slow down, to be still and enjoy the pleasures created for me. To be aware of the beauty that surrounds me: the marvel of mountains, the calmness of lakes, the fragility of a flower petal. I need to remember that all these things come from you.

The Word

I read the word of God slowly, a few times over, and I listen to what God is saying to me. (*Please turn to the Scripture on the following pages. Inspiration points are there, should you need them. When you are ready, return here to continue.*)

Conversation

What feelings are rising in me as I pray and reflect on God's word? I imagine Jesus himself sitting or standing near me, and I open my heart to him.

Conclusion

I thank God for these moments we have spent together and for any insights I have been given concerning the text.

Sunday May 30
The Most Holy Trinity
Matthew 28:16–20

Now the eleven disciples went to Galilee, to the mountain to which Jesus had directed them. When they saw him, they worshiped him; but some doubted. And Jesus came and said to them, "All authority in heaven and on earth has been given to me. Go therefore and make disciples of all nations, baptizing them in the name of the Father and of the Son and of the Holy Spirit, and teaching them to obey everything that I have commanded you. And remember, I am with you always, to the end of the age."

- Lord, you terrify me with this command, "Go and teach all nations." You were talking to eleven men without education, money, or influence, in a despised province of the Roman Empire. But they obeyed you because they knew you were with them. And today Christians are the largest body of believers on this planet. Today's preaching is different. We are educated, sometimes too well. It is harder than ever to make our voice heard. Yet in Sacred Space your word goes out potentially to all nations, and you are still with us.

Monday May 31
The Visitation of the Blessed Virgin Mary
Luke 1:39–56

In those days Mary set out and went with haste to a Judean town in the hill country, where she entered the house of Zechariah and greeted Elizabeth. When Elizabeth heard Mary's greeting, the child leaped in her womb. And Elizabeth was filled with the Holy Spirit and exclaimed with a loud cry, "Blessed are you among women, and blessed is the fruit of your womb. And why has this happened to me, that the mother of my Lord comes to me? For as soon as I heard the sound of your greeting, the child in my womb leaped for joy. And blessed is she who believed that there would be a fulfillment of what was spoken to her by the Lord."

And Mary said,

"My soul magnifies the Lord,
    and my spirit rejoices in God my Savior,
for he has looked with favor on the lowliness of his servant.

Surely, from now on all generations will call me blessed;
for the Mighty One has done great things for me,
    and holy is his name.
His mercy is for those who fear him
    from generation to generation.
He has shown strength with his arm;
    he has scattered the proud in the thoughts of their hearts.
He has brought down the powerful from their thrones,
    and lifted up the lowly;
he has filled the hungry with good things,
    and sent the rich away empty.
He has helped his servant Israel,
    in remembrance of his mercy,
according to the promise he made to our ancestors,
    to Abraham and to his descendants for ever."

And Mary remained with her for about three months and then returned
to her home.

- Two pregnant women take center stage here, and you are privileged to
listen in on their conversation. They chat about the mysterious workings of God, to which their own lives bear eloquent witness. Allow
them to invite you to participate. Perhaps one of them asks you what
you are doing to bear witness to the values of God, which run counter
to those of your culture.

- Mary rejoices in God's activity in her life: does that find an echo in
your own heart? She comes across as very much alive, with a revolutionary spirit: she is passionate about justice and the reign of God. Ask
her to fire you with the same passion!

Tuesday June 1
Mark 12:13–17

Then they sent to him some Pharisees and some Herodians to trap him
in what he said. And they came and said to him, "Teacher, we know that
you are sincere, and show deference to no one; for you do not regard people with partiality, but teach the way of God in accordance with truth.
Is it lawful to pay taxes to the emperor, or not? Should we pay them, or
should we not?" But knowing their hypocrisy, he said to them, "Why are

you putting me to the test? Bring me a denarius and let me see it." And they brought one. Then he said to them, "Whose head is this, and whose title?" They answered, "The emperor's." Jesus said to them, "Give to the emperor the things that are the emperor's, and to God the things that are God's." And they were utterly amazed at him.

- Often Jewish traders used Roman coinage to do profitable business. Some were more interested in trapping Jesus than in getting an honest answer. Jesus' advice is relevant today because our lives are complex, We are to be good Christians and also good citizens. St. Peter tries to express Jesus' mind: "Accept the authority of every human institution, whether of the emperor or of governors. [But] as servants of God, live as free people. Honor everyone. Love the family of believers" (1 Peter 2:13–17).

- Yes and no answers will not always suffice today. We are citizens of the state and members of the Church. State laws and programs may be at variance with basic Christian beliefs. We ask ourselves what values guide our lives and decisions. Do we have the courage to stand by our convictions?

Wednesday June 2
Mark 12:18–27

Some Sadducees, who say there is no resurrection, came to him and asked him a question, saying, "Teacher, Moses wrote for us that if a man's brother dies, leaving a wife but no child, the man shall marry the widow and raise up children for his brother. There were seven brothers; the first married and, when he died, left no children; and the second married her and died, leaving no children; and the third likewise; none of the seven left children. Last of all the woman herself died. In the resurrection whose wife will she be? For the seven had married her."

Jesus said to them, "Is not this the reason you are wrong, that you know neither the scriptures nor the power of God? For when they rise from the dead, they neither marry nor are given in marriage, but are like angels in heaven. And as for the dead being raised, have you not read in the book of Moses, in the story about the bush, how God said to him, 'I am the God of Abraham, the God of Isaac, and the God of Jacob'? He is God not of the dead, but of the living; you are quite wrong."

- God is not of the dead but of the living. Our world is so concerned with competition and the violence it generates that it does need to hear this wonderful message. Yet religious people seem to waste so much time arguing about details, while the life-giving message is neglected. Pope Francis said that when they speak about the gospel, some Christians sound more like they are just coming out of a funeral than they are proclaiming the joy of the Good News of God's love for the world. May my life show that God has come to give us life, and life in abundance.

- Do I sometimes find myself closing my heart to others in God's name because I am a Christian? Lord Jesus, save me from such blasphemy.

Thursday June 3
Mark 12:28–34

One of the scribes came near and heard them disputing with one another, and seeing that he answered them well, he asked him, "Which commandment is the first of all?" Jesus answered, "The first is, 'Hear, O Israel: the Lord our God, the Lord is one; you shall love the Lord your God with all your heart, and with all your soul, and with all your mind, and with all your strength.' The second is this, 'You shall love your neighbor as yourself.' There is no other commandment greater than these." Then the scribe said to him, "You are right, Teacher; you have truly said that 'he is one, and besides him there is no other'; and 'to love him with all the heart, and with all the understanding, and with all the strength', and 'to love one's neighbor as oneself'—this is much more important than all whole burnt-offerings and sacrifices." When Jesus saw that he answered wisely, he said to him, "You are not far from the kingdom of God." After that no one dared to ask him any question.

- As we struggle with so many commitments and responsibilities, we ask the same question as the scribe, "Which of the commandments is the first of all?" What should be first in my list of priorities, what is my most important duty? Jesus' reply is disarming in its simplicity; no wonder they did not dare ask him any more questions. I let his reply echo in my heart, asking for the grace to understand what it means to put love as my highest priority.

- I also ask myself, in the presence of Jesus, what it means to love God with all my heart, all my soul, and with all my mind, and with all my strength. I ask for this single-mindedness, and for seeing all my life embraced in this commitment.

Friday June 4
Mark 12:35–37

While Jesus was teaching in the temple, he said, "How can the scribes say that the Messiah is the son of David? David himself, by the Holy Spirit, declared,

> 'The Lord said to my Lord,
> "Sit at my right hand,
> until I put your enemies under your feet."'

David himself calls him Lord; so how can he be his son?" And the large crowd was listening to him with delight.

- Jesus provoked people to think about who he really was. He did not have an identity crisis himself! God who was revealed in mysterious ways in the past is now being made known by the incarnate Word. Jesus reveals to us what God is truly like.
- Who is Jesus for me? How would I introduce him to someone else? All titles are inadequate for him. Above all, he is the Son of God. Spending time with him is a means to knowing him more fully. There is an on-going invitation to form a deeper relationship with him.

Saturday June 5
Mark 12:38–44

As he taught, he said, "Beware of the scribes, who like to walk around in long robes, and to be greeted with respect in the market-places, and to have the best seats in the synagogues and places of honor at banquets! They devour widows' houses and for the sake of appearance say long prayers. They will receive the greater condemnation."

He sat down opposite the treasury, and watched the crowd putting money into the treasury. Many rich people put in large sums. A poor widow came and put in two small copper coins, which are worth a penny.

Then he called his disciples and said to them, "Truly I tell you, this poor widow has put in more than all those who are contributing to the treasury. For all of them have contributed out of their abundance; but she out of her poverty has put in everything she had, all she had to live on."

- Scribes played an important role in Jewish society as lawyers and theologians. Jesus does not condemn all scribes but only those who live ostentatiously, seek social privileges, defraud the vulnerable (widows), and are hypocritical in their religious observance.

- This behavior contrasts with the portrait of the poor widow in the second half of the reading. Out of sincere faith and remarkable generosity she contributes all she owns (two small copper coins) to the upkeep of the temple. But is Jesus holding her up as a model to be imitated or as a victim of religious exploitation? Is he speaking words of praise or of lamentation?

The Tenth Week in Ordinary Time
June 6–12, 2021

Something to think and pray about each day this week:

At twelve years of age, following a visit to Jerusalem and on the return journey, Joseph and Mary realize that Jesus is missing. Searching for him first among their own relations, they realize he is not with them. Terror sets in and they return to Jerusalem in search of their son. The search is frantic and their hearts are broken. Eventually they find Jesus in the temple, sitting among the doctors of the Law and the learned people who are amazed at the wisdom spoken by this young child. Mary rushes to Jesus, grabs him, and leaves him in no doubt that what he has done is wrong and that he has caused great worry to her and Joseph. Jesus tells them there was no need to worry and adds: "Did you not know that I must be about my father's business?" (Luke 2:49). It's a moment of recognition perhaps, for Mary and Joseph, that their son is marked out for something special and something that will, in time, take Jesus away from them in a way they could not imagine.

In an age where we hear so much about children going missing, we might pray here for parents who must face that awful reality and whose lives are torn asunder. We might too remember children who though not physically lost, can often go through lengthy periods of being spiritually missing and sometimes are not found. This too can be a source of heartbreak for parents. The fact that Jesus was found in the temple could be a focus for our prayer as well, reminding us that we stand a better chance of finding Jesus in a place of worship and surrounded by worshipping people. The mystery is again an opportunity to pray for our parents and family circle—remembering that Mary and Joseph's relations were also involved in the search and in the care of Jesus.

—Vincent Sherlock, *Telling the Rosary*

The Presence of God
"Come to me, all you who are weary and are carrying heavy burdens, and I will give you rest." Here I am, Lord. I come to seek your presence. I long for your healing power.

Freedom
By God's grace I was born to live in freedom. Free to enjoy the pleasures he created for me. Dear Lord, grant that I may live as you intended, with complete confidence in your loving care.

Consciousness
Knowing that God loves me unconditionally, I look honestly over the past day, its events, and my feelings. Do I have something to be grateful for? Then I give thanks. Is there something I am sorry for? Then I ask forgiveness.

The Word
God speaks to each of us individually. I listen attentively to hear what he is saying to me. Read the text a few times, then listen. (*Please turn to the Scripture on the following pages. Inspiration points are there, should you need them. When you are ready, return here to continue.*)

Conversation
I know with certainty that there were times when you carried me, Lord. There were times when it was through your strength that I got through the dark times.

Conclusion
Glory be to the Father, and to the Son, and to the Holy Spirit,
As it was in the beginning, is now, and ever shall be,
World without end. Amen.

Sunday June 6
The Most Holy Body and Blood of Christ
Mark 14:12–16, 22–26

On the first day of Unleavened Bread, when the Passover lamb is sacrificed, his disciples said to him, "Where do you want us to go and make the preparations for you to eat the Passover?" So he sent two of his disciples, saying to them, "Go into the city, and a man carrying a jar of water will meet you; follow him, and wherever he enters, say to the owner of the house, 'The Teacher asks, Where is my guest room where I may eat the Passover with my disciples?' He will show you a large room upstairs, furnished and ready. Make preparations for us there." So the disciples set out and went to the city, and found everything as he had told them; and they prepared the Passover meal. . . .

While they were eating, he took a loaf of bread, and after blessing it he broke it, gave it to them, and said, "Take; this is my body." Then he took a cup, and after giving thanks he gave it to them, and all of them drank from it. He said to them, "This is my blood of the covenant, which is poured out for many. Truly I tell you, I will never again drink of the fruit of the vine until that day when I drink it new in the kingdom of God."

When they had sung the hymn, they went out to the Mount of Olives.

• Today's feast of Corpus Christi is a revisiting of the liturgy of Holy Thursday with an emphasis on the institution of the Eucharist. We are reminded of the Jewish context of the Last supper (Passover meal, sacrificial lamb). The terms "my body" and "my blood of the covenant" both express the total self-giving of Jesus for us. The Last Supper is the prologue to the Passion.

• Do I appreciate the "bread from heaven" that Jesus offers us?

Monday June 7
Matthew 5:1–12

When Jesus saw the crowds, he went up the mountain; and after he sat down, his disciples came to him. Then he began to speak, and taught them, saying:

"Blessed are the poor in spirit, for theirs is the kingdom of heaven.
"Blessed are those who mourn, for they will be comforted.

"Blessed are the meek, for they will inherit the earth.

"Blessed are those who hunger and thirst for righteousness, for they
will be filled.

"Blessed are the merciful, for they will receive mercy.

"Blessed are the pure in heart, for they will see God.

"Blessed are the peacemakers, for they will be called children of
God.

"Blessed are those who are persecuted for righteousness' sake, for
theirs is the kingdom of heaven.

"Blessed are you when people revile you and persecute you and utter
all kinds of evil against you falsely on my account. Rejoice and
be glad, for your reward is great in heaven, for in the same way
they persecuted the prophets who were before you.

- What the world sees as tragic or empty, Jesus sees as blessed: humility, mourning, gentleness, peacefulness, and other virtues. Jesus lived
by these qualities himself, and we can notice them in his words and
actions during his life with us on earth. He could encourage us to live
in the spirit of the Beatitudes because he himself lived them and knew
that a life of integrity and honesty is indeed a blessed life.

- It's easy to recite these "blesseds" as a sort of mantra. They are the vision statement of Jesus. He lived what he said: that all of life is blessed,
even the experiences we might never ask for. All who live according to
his way of life are—and will be—richly blessed.

Tuesday June 8
Matthew 5:13–16

"You are the salt of the earth; but if salt has lost its taste, how can its
saltiness be restored? It is no longer good for anything, but is thrown out
and trampled under foot.

"You are the light of the world. A city built on a hill cannot be hidden.
No one after lighting a lamp puts it under the bushel basket, but on the
lampstand, and it gives light to all in the house. In the same way, let your
light shine before others, so that they may see your good works and give
glory to your Father in heaven."

- Riches, power, and control are valued highly in our world. But Jesus
draws on little things to teach deeper values. Salt preserves food: in the

hands of a skilled cook it adds flavor. But its work is hidden. As salt of the earth we can be effective in bringing more taste to life for others.

- Light does not change a room: it enables us to see what is in it. It helps us appreciate what is good and beautiful, just as it facilitates avoiding pitfalls. We are children of the light: our lives are illumined by Jesus, the light of the world (John 8:12). This light helps us see the hidden hope of glory that is in us. So we can rejoice even in the darkness of the world.

Wednesday June 9
Matthew 5:17–19

"Do not think that I have come to abolish the law or the prophets; I have come not to abolish but to fulfill. For truly I tell you, until heaven and earth pass away, not one letter, not one stroke of a letter, will pass from the law until all is accomplished. Therefore, whoever breaks one of the least of these commandments, and teaches others to do the same, will be called least in the kingdom of heaven; but whoever does them and teaches them will be called great in the kingdom of heaven."

- Jesus is no destroyer of people's devotions and faith. He does not abolish the faith practice of a people or a person. All the goodness of our religion and our faith is precious to him. His grace is given to each personally; each of us prays differently or with a variety of times, places, and moods. "Pray as you can, not as you can't" is one of the oldest and wisest recommendations for prayer. Prayer is entering and relaxing into the mystery of God's love, each in our own way.

Thursday June 10
Matthew 5:20–26

"For I tell you, unless your righteousness exceeds that of the scribes and Pharisees, you will never enter the kingdom of heaven.

"You have heard that it was said to those of ancient times, 'You shall not murder'; and 'whoever murders shall be liable to judgment.' But I say to you that if you are angry with a brother or sister, you will be liable to judgment; and if you insult a brother or sister, you will be liable to the council; and if you say, 'You fool,' you will be liable to the hell of fire. So when you are offering your gift at the altar, if you remember that your brother or sister has something against you, leave your gift there before the altar and go; first be reconciled to your brother or sister, and then come and offer your gift. Come to terms quickly with your accuser while you are on the way to court with him, or your accuser may hand you over to the judge, and the judge to the guard, and you will be thrown into prison. Truly I tell you, you will never get out until you have paid the last penny."

- Jesus often uses exaggeration to teach a really important point: don't take the exaggeration as literal truth but pay attention to the point he's trying to teach.

- Being angry, insulting one another, or calling names is not a way that Jesus wants us to behave.

- Pay attention to the way we deal with one another; seek reconciliation above all.

Friday June 11
The Most Sacred Heart of Jesus
John 19:31–37

Since it was the day of Preparation, the Jews did not want the bodies left on the cross during the sabbath, especially because that sabbath was a day of great solemnity. So they asked Pilate to have the legs of the crucified men broken and the bodies removed. Then the soldiers came and broke the legs of the first and of the other who had been crucified with him. But when they came to Jesus and saw that he was already dead, they did not break his legs. Instead, one of the soldiers pierced his side with a spear, and at once blood and water came out. (He who saw this has testified so that you also may believe. His testimony is true, and he knows that he tells the truth.) These things occurred so that the scripture might be fulfilled, "None of his bones shall be broken." And again another passage of scripture says, "They will look on the one whom they have pierced."

- It is necessary to recognize the scriptural roots of devotion to the Sacred Heart. Otherwise an unhelpful sentimentality can creep in. The symbolism of the piercing of Jesus' side is a sound basis for the devotion. Enter this familiar scene on Calvary and "look on the one they have pierced." See the blood and water flowing from his pierced side. Some interpret this as representing the Eucharist and Baptism. What does it represent for me?

- How is the Sacred Heart communicating his love for me today? Have I any response?

Saturday June 12
Luke 2:41–51

Now every year his parents went to Jerusalem for the festival of the Passover. And when he was twelve years old, they went up as usual for the festival. When the festival was ended and they started to return, the boy Jesus stayed behind in Jerusalem, but his parents did not know it. Assuming that he was in the group of travelers, they went a day's journey. Then they started to look for him among their relatives and friends. When they did not find him, they returned to Jerusalem to search for him. After three days they found him in the temple, sitting among the teachers, listening to them and asking them questions. And all who heard him were amazed at his understanding and his answers. When his parents saw him they were astonished; and his mother said to him, "Child, why have you treated us like this? Look, your father and I have been searching for you in great anxiety." He said to them, "Why were you searching for me? Did you not know that I must be in my Father's house?" But they did not understand what he said to them. Then he went down with them and came to Nazareth, and was obedient to them. His mother treasured all these things in her heart.

- "In my Father's house." Do I believe that the Father's house may be found within myself? If I do, I can perhaps open myself to an even greater wonder: "Those who love me will keep my word, and my Father will love them, and we will come to them and make our home with them" (John 14:23).

- Mary and Joseph made a distraught visit to the temple in Jerusalem, seeking him whom they had lost. Unlike them, when I go to the temple of the Holy Spirit within me, I go with the certainty of finding God there.

The Eleventh Week in Ordinary Time
June 13–19, 2021

Something to think and pray about each day this week:

In his letters, Paul often speaks out of a sense of having been greatly graced by God. Although "less than the least of all the saints" (the baptized), he has been entrusted with a "special grace." The grace Paul speaks about is the Gospel, which unveils the mystery of Christ. Paul is overawed by "the depths that I see in the mystery of Christ." He is very aware that this grace that has been entrusted to him carries with it a responsibility. He is called to be a servant of this Gospel with which he has been graced, responsible for proclaiming it to those who have never heard it, and sees himself as a "steward" who has been given much by his master and who now needs to show that he is worthy of what has been entrusted to him. We have all been graced in various ways by the Lord. We have been baptized into Christ; we have been given a share in his Spirit; we have been entrusted with the Gospel; we are members of Christ's body, the Church; we receive his coming as bread of life in the Eucharist; we are touched by his merciful presence in the Sacrament of Reconciliation. Like trustworthy stewards, we have been entrusted with a great deal by the Lord. As "faithful and wise" stewards, we need to keep treasuring the many graces we have received from God and live out of what has been entrusted to us. We have been graced by the Lord so that we can grace others with what we have received.

—Martin Hogan, *The Word of God Is Living and Active*

The Presence of God

"Be still, and know that I am God!" Lord, your words lead us to the calmness and greatness of your presence.

Freedom

Leave me here freely all alone. / In cell where never sunlight shone. / Should no one ever speak to me. / This golden silence makes me free!

—Part of a poem by Bl. Titus Brandsma, written while he was a prisoner at Dachau concentration camp

Consciousness

Knowing that God loves me unconditionally, I can afford to be honest about how I am.

How has the day been, and how do I feel now? I share my feelings openly with the Lord.

The Word

I take my time to read the word of God slowly, a few times, allowing myself to dwell on anything that strikes me. (*Please turn to the Scripture on the following pages. Inspiration points are there, should you need them. When you are ready, return here to continue.*)

Conversation

Sometimes I wonder what I might say if I were to meet you in person, Lord.

I think I might say, "Thank you" because you are always there for me.

Conclusion

I thank God for these moments we have spent together and for any insights I have been given concerning the text.

Sunday June 13
Eleventh Sunday in Ordinary Time
Mark 4:26–34

He also said, "The kingdom of God is as if someone would scatter seed on the ground, and would sleep and rise night and day, and the seed would sprout and grow, he does not know how. The earth produces of itself, first the stalk, then the head, then the full grain in the head. But when the grain is ripe, at once he goes in with his sickle, because the harvest has come."

He also said, "With what can we compare the kingdom of God, or what parable will we use for it? It is like a mustard seed, which, when sown upon the ground, is the smallest of all the seeds on earth; yet when it is sown it grows up and becomes the greatest of all shrubs, and puts forth large branches, so that the birds of the air can make nests in its shade."

With many such parables he spoke the word to them, as they were able to hear it; he did not speak to them except in parables, but he explained everything in private to his disciples.

- Simple things we say or do can have a big influence. One person can affect many, even without knowing it. Like good seed growing underground the kingdom of God grows of its own impetus in the world, and nobody can stop it. God is the God of here, there, and everywhere. Seeds may sprout anywhere in the field, and the kingdom can find its way into the lives of individuals and communities in ways that may surprise us. The mustard seed becomes a tree for all; the kingdom of God is for every man, woman, and child. Have you ever brought something of the kingdom of God—of love and peace, prayer and faith, justice and hope—when you didn't recognize it? Let that fill your mind and heart with gratitude as you pray.

Monday June 14
Matthew 5:38–42

"You have heard that it was said, 'An eye for an eye and a tooth for a tooth.' But I say to you, Do not resist an evildoer. But if anyone strikes you on the right cheek, turn the other also; and if anyone wants to sue you and take your coat, give your cloak as well; and if anyone forces you to go one mile, go also the second mile. Give to everyone who begs from you, and do not refuse anyone who wants to borrow from you."

- Jesus calls us to look beyond the limit of the law. We need to be generous and imaginative if we are to rise beyond the restrictions that life presents.

- I think of how I might be free from the constraints I find by acting from a generous spirit. I ask God to inspire and help me.

- The law and duty will provide basic guidelines but won't be enough for a disciple and certainly not enough for one who wants to be a friend of Jesus. Where do I need more generosity or freedom to respond to the vision that Jesus puts before me?

Tuesday June 15
Matthew 5:43–48

"You have heard that it was said, 'You shall love your neighbor and hate your enemy.' But I say to you, Love your enemies and pray for those who persecute you, so that you may be children of your Father in heaven; for he makes his sun rise on the evil and on the good, and sends rain on the righteous and on the unrighteous. For if you love those who love you, what reward do you have? Do not even the tax-collectors do the same? And if you greet only your brothers and sisters, what more are you doing than others? Do not even the Gentiles do the same? Be perfect, therefore, as your heavenly Father is perfect."

- Jesus seems to call for great courage, asking us to draw deeply on our reserves. He is really asking us to depend on him, to let his spirit come to life.

- What Jesus suggests would upset the balance of the world; it contradicts the neat arrangements of tidy minds. Help me, Lord, to receive courage and strength to act in unexpected and life-giving ways.

Wednesday June 16
Matthew 6:1–6, 16–18

"Beware of practicing your piety before others in order to be seen by them; for then you have no reward from your Father in heaven.

"So whenever you give alms, do not sound a trumpet before you, as the hypocrites do in the synagogues and in the streets, so that they may be praised by others. Truly I tell you, they have received their reward. But when you give alms, do not let your left hand know what your right hand is doing, so that your alms may be done in secret; and your Father who sees in secret will reward you.

"And whenever you pray, do not be like the hypocrites; for they love to stand and pray in the synagogues and at the street corners, so that they may be seen by others. Truly I tell you, they have received their reward. But whenever you pray, go into your room and shut the door and pray to your Father who is in secret; and your Father who sees in secret will reward you.

"And whenever you fast, do not look dismal, like the hypocrites, for they disfigure their faces so as to show others that they are fasting. Truly I tell you, they have received their reward. But when you fast, put oil on your head and wash your face, so that your fasting may be seen not by others but by your Father who is in secret; and your Father who sees in secret will reward you."

- How does this passage touch me? Do I recognize myself as hypocrite or Pharisee?

- Do I experience a tension between this passage and the call to be salt, to be light, to bear witness to my faith?

- Am I able to enter into that "private room" to be with my Father God? Does this presume that I am able to accept that I am greatly loved and cherished? Or open to becoming such?

Thursday June 17
Matthew 6:7–15

[Jesus said,] "When you are praying, do not heap up empty phrases as the Gentiles do; for they think that they will be heard because of their many words. Do not be like them, for your Father knows what you need before you ask him.

"Pray then in this way:
Our Father in heaven,
hallowed be your name.
Your kingdom come.
Your will be done,
on earth as it is in heaven.

Give us this day our daily bread.
And forgive us our debts,
as we also have forgiven our debtors.
And do not bring us to the time of trial,
but rescue us from the evil one.

For if you forgive others their trespasses, your heavenly Father will also forgive you; but if you do not forgive others, neither will your Father forgive your trespasses."

- Prayer techniques can be learned and simple habits and skills developed. But sometimes an honest cry to the Father says as much as is needed.

- An honest cry says that I believe and trust that God is there for us and is loving me.

- Next, an honest cry knows that if God is there for me, then God is there for us all and is loving and caring to us all.

- So, my prayer has to open me to the people I hurt and by whom I am hurt.

Friday June 18
Matthew 6:19–23

"Do not store up for yourselves treasures on earth, where moth and rust consume and where thieves break in and steal; but store up for yourselves treasures in heaven, where neither moth nor rust consumes and where thieves do not break in and steal. For where your treasure is, there your heart will be also.

"The eye is the lamp of the body. So, if your eye is healthy, your whole body will be full of light; but if your eye is unhealthy, your whole body will be full of darkness. If then the light in you is darkness, how great is the darkness!"

- Jesus once again reminds us that God looks at the heart, and he challenges us to ask ourselves where our real priorities lie. Where is my heart? My treasure? Is it something that is durable, that cannot be corrupted by moth or by rust, or is it merely material or ethereal, like money or success or popularity?

- When I look at my heart, I may find that it is divided, undecided, torn between different or conflicting loyalties, whose light is weak and does not illuminate my path in life. I look with gratitude on those persons I admire for their integrity, and I pray for the grace of an undivided heart.

- If my heart is in darkness, then I thank Jesus for his word, which is prodding me to walk toward the light.

Saturday June 19
Matthew 6:24–34

"No one can serve two masters; for a slave will either hate the one and love the other, or be devoted to the one and despise the other. You cannot serve God and wealth.

"Therefore I tell you, do not worry about your life, what you will eat or what you will drink, or about your body, what you will wear. Is not life more than food, and the body more than clothing? Look at the birds of the air; they neither sow nor reap nor gather into barns, and yet your heavenly Father feeds them. Are you not of more value than they? And can any of you by worrying add a single hour to your span of life? And why do you worry about clothing? Consider the lilies of the field, how they grow; they neither toil nor spin, yet I tell you, even Solomon in all his glory was not clothed like one of these. But if God so clothes the grass of the field, which is alive today and tomorrow is thrown into the oven, will he not much more clothe you—you of little faith? Therefore do not worry, saying, 'What will we eat?' or 'What will we drink?' or 'What will we wear?' For it is the Gentiles who strive for all these things; and indeed your heavenly Father knows that you need all these things. But strive first for the kingdom of God and his righteousness, and all these things will be given to you as well.

"So do not worry about tomorrow, for tomorrow will bring worries of its own. Today's trouble is enough for today."

- I listen to Jesus' words not just as advice; I consider how he lived them out. I think of the difference his living freely made in the lives of others and continues to make in mine. I talk to him about my worries and listen to his response as he takes on my cares.

- Jesus shows us that worry undermines faith. I bring my worries before God and ask for help to bring them into a truer perspective.

The Twelfth Week in Ordinary Time
June 20–26, 2021

Something to think and pray about each day this week:

There was something special about John the Baptist. The Gospel reading suggests that his being given the name "John" was itself special or unusual. Neighbors and relations objected to this name. "No one in your family has that name," they said. Yet John's parents understood that God wanted their child to be called "John." In Hebrew the name "John" means "the Lord has shown favor." God was inaugurating a new era of favor through this child. After the resistance of the neighbors and relations to this unconventional name had been overcome, they went on to ask, "What will this child turn out to be?" That question of the neighbors and relations could be asked of any of us at every stage of our lives, "What will we turn out to be?" or to put the question in other terms, "Who is God calling us to be?" Our calling is to surrender to what today's second reading calls God's "whole purpose" for our lives, as John did. God's purpose for John's life and God's purpose for all our lives have a great deal in common. God wants all of us to do what John did, to point out the Savior, to make way for Jesus, to lead others to him by what we say and do. John the Baptist has something to teach us about how we might keep faithful to this God-given calling. He was a man of the desert, a man of prayer. We all need to find our own desert place of prayer if we are to remain true to our calling, if we are to turn out as God wants us to.

—Martin Hogan, *The Word of God Is Living and Active*

The Presence of God

"Come to me, all you who are weary and are carrying heavy burdens, and I will give you rest." Here I am, Lord. I come to seek your presence. I long for your healing power.

Freedom

By God's grace I was born to live in freedom. Free to enjoy the pleasures he created for me. Dear Lord, grant that I may live as you intended, with complete confidence in your loving care.

Consciousness

Knowing that God loves me unconditionally, I look honestly over the past day, its events and my feelings. Do I have something to be grateful for? Then I give thanks. Is there something I am sorry for? Then I ask forgiveness.

The Word

God speaks to each of us individually. I listen attentively to hear what he is saying to me. Read the text a few times, then listen. (*Please turn to the Scripture on the following pages. Inspiration points are there, should you need them. When you are ready, return here to continue.*)

Conversation

I know with certainty that there were times when you carried me, Lord. There were times when it was through your strength that I got through the dark times in my life.

Conclusion

Glory be to the Father, and to the Son, and to the Holy Spirit,
As it was in the beginning, is now and ever shall be,
World without end. Amen.

Sunday June 20
Twelfth Sunday in Ordinary Time
Mark 4:35–41

On that day, when evening had come, Jesus said to them, "Let us go across to the other side." And leaving the crowd behind, they took him with them in the boat, just as he was. Other boats were with him. A great gale arose, and the waves beat into the boat, so that the boat was already being swamped. But he was in the stern, asleep on the cushion; and they woke him up and said to him, "Teacher, do you not care that we are perishing?" He woke up and rebuked the wind, and said to the sea, "Peace! Be still!" Then the wind ceased, and there was a dead calm. He said to them, "Why are you afraid? Have you still no faith?" And they were filled with great awe and said to one another, "Who then is this, that even the wind and the sea obey him?"

- Put yourself imaginatively into the boat with the disciples. Allow yourself to experience the happy anticipation at the start of the voyage and then the terror as the gale sweeps in. Your life is in danger. You look to Jesus to save you, but he is asleep—as if he doesn't care. Then feel the relief as he speaks with authority and calms the wind and sea. Are you embarrassed when he questions your faith? Is there anything you want to say to him after this adventure?

Monday June 21
Matthew 7:1–5

"Do not judge, so that you may not be judged. For with the judgment you make you will be judged, and the measure you give will be the measure you get. Why do you see the speck in your neighbor's eye, but do not notice the log in your own eye? Or how can you say to your neighbor, 'Let me take the speck out of your eye,' while the log is in your own eye? You hypocrite, first take the log out of your own eye, and then you will see clearly to take the speck out of your neighbor's eye."

- "Who am I to judge?" must rank as one of the best-known phrases of Pope Francis. Perhaps that is because it touches a very sensitive point in our pluralistic cultures. How can we ever judge the behavior of others? This can sometimes degenerate into a passive, uncaring attitude toward others: I will not judge you, for you are responsible for your own choices; now do not expect me to help you in any way, for I am not responsible for you at all. Jesus is saying something quite different: be careful not to judge others more harshly than you judge yourself. Try to be free of prejudice, for this can cloud your judgment.

Tuesday June 22
Matthew 7:6, 12–14

"Do not give what is holy to dogs; and do not throw your pearls before swine, or they will trample them under foot and turn and maul you. . . .

"In everything do to others as you would have them do to you; for this is the law and the prophets.

"Enter through the narrow gate; for the gate is wide and the road is easy that leads to destruction, and there are many who take it. For the gate is narrow and the road is hard that leads to life, and there are few who find it."

- What could "the narrow gate" mean for you?
- Is there a discipline in life that eludes you at present? An austerity, a way of living and loving that costs but yields its fruit during adversity?
- And remember, Christian discipline such as fasting and prayer aims at freeing us for greater fruits.

Wednesday June 23
Matthew 7:15–20

"Beware of false prophets, who come to you in sheep's clothing but inwardly are ravenous wolves. You will know them by their fruits. Are grapes gathered from thorns, or figs from thistles? In the same way, every good tree bears good fruit, but the bad tree bears bad fruit. A good tree cannot bear bad fruit, nor can a bad tree bear good fruit. Every tree that does not bear good fruit is cut down and thrown into the fire. Thus you will know them by their fruits."

- Jesus warns us to beware of false prophets, and he gives us a very concrete and practical guideline for our discernment: knowing them by their fruits. Our world sometimes can be confusing, making so many promises of happiness and well-being yet being so full of suffering and loneliness. We need to discern, to realize that there are not only false prophets, who bear fruit that is not good, but also good prophets, whose message is true because it produces good fruit. I pray for the grace of insight and wisdom.

- In this series of passages, I might be struck by Jesus' words about a future judgment: the tree that does not bear good fruit will be cut down and thrown into the fire. I too am called to bear good fruit, with a certain urgency.

Thursday June 24
The Nativity of John the Baptist
Luke 1:57–66, 80

Now the time came for Elizabeth to give birth, and she bore a son. Her neighbors and relatives heard that the Lord had shown his great mercy to her, and they rejoiced with her.

On the eighth day they came to circumcise the child, and they were going to name him Zechariah after his father. But his mother said, "No; he is to be called John." They said to her, "None of your relatives has this name." Then they began motioning to his father to find out what name he wanted to give him. He asked for a writing-tablet and wrote, "His name is John." And all of them were amazed. Immediately his mouth was opened and his tongue freed, and he began to speak, praising God. Fear came over all their neighbors, and all these things were talked about throughout the entire hill country of Judea. All who heard them pondered them and said, "What then will this child become?" For, indeed, the hand of the Lord was with him.

The child grew and became strong in spirit, and he was in the wilderness until the day he appeared publicly to Israel.

- Parents are co-creators of new life! If I am a parent I recall the "joy" of a new birth. If I am not a parent, I recall events in my life when I gave "new life" to someone through my actions, and I give thanks.

- Do I have any significant memories surrounding my name? Surrounding the names of my children?

- Have I ever had an experience of the Lord speaking my name in love and calling me? I will ponder "my dreams" for my children and my parents' dreams for me.

Friday June 25
Matthew 8:1–4

When Jesus had come down from the mountain, great crowds followed him; and there was a leper who came to him and knelt before him, saying, "Lord, if you choose, you can make me clean." He stretched out his hand and touched him, saying, "I do choose. Be made clean!" Immediately his leprosy was cleansed. Then Jesus said to him, "See that you say nothing to anyone; but go, show yourself to the priest, and offer the gift that Moses commanded, as a testimony to them."

- Lord, let me taste the drama of this eager leper. He was breaking the law, which forbade him to come closer than fifty feet to a non-leper or to exchange greetings with others. When this man's faith broke through legal limitations, Jesus not merely spoke with him but touched him. Jesus cannot bear to see us isolated from him.

- When Irish President Mary McAleese was visiting a leper colony in Uganda, she was placed, for her speech, at a safe distance from the ring of lepers. Like Jesus, she broke protocol, walked across, and, with her husband, shook each of them by the hand—or in some cases by the stump where the hand had been. Overcome by her gesture, they broke into a spontaneous ululation of joy: a moment of grace.

Saturday June 26
Matthew 8:5–17

When he entered Capernaum, a centurion came to him, appealing to him and saying, "Lord, my servant is lying at home paralyzed, in terrible distress." And he said to him, "I will come and cure him." The centurion answered, "Lord, I am not worthy to have you come under my roof; but only speak the word, and my servant will be healed. For I also am a man under authority, with soldiers under me; and I say to one, 'Go,' and he goes, and to another, 'Come,' and he comes, and to my slave, 'Do this,' and the slave does it." When Jesus heard him, he was amazed and said to those who followed him, "Truly I tell you, in no one in Israel have I found such faith. I tell you, many will come from east and west and will eat with Abraham and Isaac and Jacob in the kingdom of heaven, while the heirs of the kingdom will be thrown into the outer darkness, where there will be weeping and gnashing of teeth." And to the centurion Jesus said, "Go; let it be done for you according to your faith." And the servant was healed in that hour.

When Jesus entered Peter's house, he saw his mother-in-law lying in bed with a fever; he touched her hand, and the fever left her, and she got up and began to serve him. That evening they brought to him many who were possessed by demons; and he cast out the spirits with a word, and cured all who were sick. This was to fulfill what had been spoken through the prophet Isaiah, "He took our infirmities and bore our diseases."

- "Lord, I am not worthy to have you come under my roof; but only speak the word, and my servant will be healed." These words expressed the centurion's full trust in Jesus and led to a unique commendation of this pagan man's faith. Let me spend some time pondering these words.

- "[Jesus] took our infirmities and bore our diseases." People felt they could take their sick and their own sickness to Jesus to be healed. Let me do so too, bringing to Jesus my sick dear ones and all that needs healing in me.

The Thirteenth Week in Ordinary Time
June 27—July 3, 2021

Something to think and pray about each day this week:

In the course of his letters, Paul often speaks about his prayer. He tells us the content of his prayer, what he gives thanks to God for, what he petitions God for, the people he prays for. We have a wonderful example of Paul's prayer in today's first reading, which is one of my favorite passages from Paul's letters. Paul's prayer in this passage is both a prayer of petition and a prayer of praise. In both of these prayers, Paul refers to the power of God or the power of the Spirit. He petitions God to give the members of the church in Ephesus the power through the Spirit for their hidden self to grow strong, so that Christ may live in their hearts. He goes on to give praise to God whose power working in us can do infinitely more than all we can ask or imagine. Paul declares that through the power of God, the power of the Spirit at work in our hearts, Christ comes to live in us and, when that happens, our hidden self, our true self, grows strong. There is a very beautiful Trinitarian vision of the Christian life contained in that prayer. God the Father sends the Holy Spirit into our lives so that Christ, his Son, can live in us, and, thereby, our true self, our Christ-self, grows strong. It is through his Son, in particular his Son's death, resurrection, and ascension, that God the Father sends the Holy Spirit into our lives. In the Gospel reading, Jesus makes reference to his role of sending us the Holy Spirit from the Father. "I have come to bring fire to the earth," he says, the fire of the Spirit, the fire of God's love. Each day, we are called to open our hearts afresh to this gift of the Holy Spirit who comes to us from the Father through the Son, so that God's Son may be formed in us and we become our true selves, in the words of that first reading, "filled with the utter fullness of God."

—Martin Hogan, *The Word of God Is Living and Active*

The Presence of God
"Be still, and know that I am God!" Lord, your words lead us to the calmness and greatness of your presence.

Freedom
God is not foreign to my freedom. The Spirit breathes life into my most intimate desires, gently nudging me toward all that is good. I ask for the grace to let myself be enfolded by the Spirit.

Consciousness
Where do I sense hope, encouragement, and growth in my life? By looking back over the past few months, I may be able to see which activities and occasions have produced rich fruit. If I do notice such areas, I will determine to give them time and space in the future.

The Word
The word of God comes down to us through the Scriptures. May the Holy Spirit enlighten my mind and my heart to respond to the Gospel teachings. (*Please turn to the Scripture on the following pages. Inspiration points are there, should you need them. When you are ready, return here to continue.*)

Conversation
What is stirring in me as I pray? Am I consoled, troubled, left cold? I imagine Jesus standing or sitting at my side, and I share my feelings with him.

Conclusion
Glory be to the Father, and to the Son, and to the Holy Spirit,
As it was in the beginning, is now, and ever shall be,
World without end. Amen.

Sunday June 27
Thirteenth Sunday in Ordinary Time
Mark 5:21–43

When Jesus had crossed again in the boat to the other side, a great crowd gathered round him; and he was by the lake. Then one of the leaders of the synagogue named Jairus came and, when he saw him, fell at his feet and begged him repeatedly, "My little daughter is at the point of death. Come and lay your hands on her, so that she may be made well, and live." So he went with him.

And a large crowd followed him and pressed in on him. Now there was a woman who had been suffering from hemorrhages for twelve years. She had endured much under many physicians, and had spent all that she had; and she was no better, but rather grew worse. She had heard about Jesus, and came up behind him in the crowd and touched his cloak, for she said, "If I but touch his clothes, I will be made well." Immediately her hemorrhage stopped; and she felt in her body that she was healed of her disease. Immediately aware that power had gone forth from him, Jesus turned about in the crowd and said, "Who touched my clothes?" And his disciples said to him, "You see the crowd pressing in on you; how can you say, 'Who touched me?'" He looked all round to see who had done it. But the woman, knowing what had happened to her, came in fear and trembling, fell down before him, and told him the whole truth. He said to her, "Daughter, your faith has made you well; go in peace, and be healed of your disease."

While he was still speaking, some people came from the leader's house to say, "Your daughter is dead. Why trouble the teacher any further?" But overhearing what they said, Jesus said to the leader of the synagogue, "Do not fear, only believe." He allowed no one to follow him except Peter, James, and John, the brother of James. When they came to the house of the leader of the synagogue, he saw a commotion, people weeping and wailing loudly. When he had entered, he said to them, "Why do you make a commotion and weep? The child is not dead but sleeping." And they laughed at him. Then he put them all outside, and took the child's father and mother and those who were with him, and went in where the child was. He took her by the hand and said to her, "Talitha cum," which means, "Little girl, get up!" And immediately the girl got up and began to walk about (she was twelve years of age). At this they were overcome with amazement. He strictly ordered them that no one should know this, and told them to give her something to eat.

- Perhaps you are suffering right now: burning with anger at someone who has hurt you, or unable to forgive an old hurt, or you are a bit depressed. Talk with the woman who had been in pain for twelve years. Listen to her telling you to touch Jesus' cloak. Imagine doing that. This is not magic but a meeting with Jesus, asking for his help: touching God carries its own healing power. Prayer can often feel like touching only the hem of Jesus' garment, but it is authentic when, like the woman, you tell the Lord "the whole truth." In ways that may surprise you "the truth sets you free" (John 8:32).

Monday June 28
Matthew 8:18–22

Now when Jesus saw great crowds around him, he gave orders to go over to the other side. A scribe then approached and said, "Teacher, I will follow you wherever you go." And Jesus said to him, "Foxes have holes, and birds of the air have nests; but the Son of Man has nowhere to lay his head." Another of his disciples said to him, "Lord, first let me go and bury my father." But Jesus said to him, "Follow me, and let the dead bury their own dead."

- Jesus uses the starkest possible words to stress the radicality of his calling. Unlike us, he is not so interested in numbers but in the quality of the commitment of the disciple, in the readiness to follow in the footsteps of the Master.

- "The Son of Man has nowhere to lay his head." Jesus was born in a manger and died on the cross, outside the city walls. No wonder that we discover that following him means some renunciation of material goods and comforts for everyone, though to different degrees.

Tuesday June 29
Ss. Peter and Paul, Apostles
Matthew 16:13–19

Now when Jesus came into the district of Caesarea Philippi, he asked his disciples, "Who do people say that the Son of Man is?" And they said,

"Some say John the Baptist, but others Elijah, and still others Jeremiah or one of the prophets." He said to them, "But who do you say that I am?" Simon Peter answered, "You are the Messiah, the Son of the living God." And Jesus answered him, "Blessed are you, Simon son of Jonah! For flesh and blood has not revealed this to you, but my Father in heaven. And I tell you, you are Peter, and on this rock I will build my church, and the gates of Hades will not prevail against it. I will give you the keys of the kingdom of heaven, and whatever you bind on earth will be bound in heaven, and whatever you loose on earth will be loosed in heaven."

- Suppose that Jesus suddenly put his question to me in my prayer today. What would I answer?

- Let me be honest with him, no matter if I feel ashamed of what I come up with. Jesus reads my heart long before I speak. Perhaps he then invites me to chat with Peter, who got the formula right in this scene. In a little while Peter will deny that he even knows Jesus!

- Lord, let me see that Peter's weakness is the making of him: he finally learns not to trust in himself but in you alone. After the resurrection, when you question him again, he is honest in saying, "You know I love you." And that is enough. Let him teach me to encounter your forgiving love through my weaknesses, and let me love you ever more deeply.

Wednesday June 30
Matthew 8:28–34

When he came to the other side, to the country of the Gadarenes, two demoniacs coming out of the tombs met him. They were so fierce that no one could pass that way. Suddenly they shouted, "What have you to do with us, Son of God? Have you come here to torment us before the time?" Now a large herd of swine was feeding at some distance from them. The demons begged him, "If you cast us out, send us into the herd of swine." And he said to them, "Go!" So they came out and entered the swine; and suddenly, the whole herd rushed down the steep bank into the lake and perished in the water. The swineherds ran off, and on going into the town, they told the whole story about what had happened to the demoniacs. Then the whole town came out to meet Jesus; and when they saw him, they begged him to leave their neighborhood.

- Because the townspeople cannot cope with divine power, they ask Jesus to leave. But Jesus has won a fundamental victory over evil and has established the reign of God.

- This incident in the Gospels is a revelation of the compassion of Jesus for people like us and shows that he will do anything he can to free us from the demons such as fear, anxiety, or resentment that we have allowed to enslave us. By staying close to Jesus, we have nothing to fear from the devil or the world.

Thursday July 1
Matthew 9:1–8

And after getting into a boat he crossed the water and came to his own town.

And just then some people were carrying a paralyzed man lying on a bed. When Jesus saw their faith, he said to the paralytic, "Take heart, son; your sins are forgiven." Then some of the scribes said to themselves, "This man is blaspheming." But Jesus, perceiving their thoughts, said, "Why do you think evil in your hearts? For which is easier, to say, 'Your sins are forgiven,' or to say, 'Stand up and walk'? But so that you may know that the Son of Man has authority on earth to forgive sins"—he then said to the paralytic—"Stand up, take your bed and go to your home." And he stood up and went to his home. When the crowds saw it, they were filled with awe, and they glorified God, who had given such authority to human beings.

- This passage focuses on something that is central to Jesus' way of relating with us. He sees how all of us are in need of forgiveness, of having our limited and sinful human nature accepted. Rather than be angry, guilty, or aggressive with ourselves and others, he suggests that we assume a gentle, forgiving, or accepting attitude to this limited side of ourselves.

Friday July 2
Matthew 9:9–13

As Jesus was walking along, he saw a man called Matthew sitting at the tax booth; and he said to him, "Follow me." And he got up and followed him.

And as he sat at dinner in the house, many tax-collectors and sinners came and were sitting with him and his disciples. When the Pharisees saw this, they said to his disciples, "Why does your teacher eat with tax-collectors and sinners?" But when he heard this, he said, "Those who are well have no need of a physician, but those who are sick. Go and learn what this means, 'I desire mercy, not sacrifice.' For I have come to call not the righteous but sinners."

- Jesus is inclusive—even tax-collectors and sinners are welcomed. They represent those whose professions and social status are not respectable. But Jesus shows that he has come for all people, without exception, and especially the weak and the vulnerable, the sick and the sinner.

- How inclusive and compassionate Jesus is in his ministry! I ask myself if I am prejudiced against any individuals or groups? Lord, help me become more like you in thought, word, and deed. Make me large-hearted.

Saturday July 3
John 20:24–29

But Thomas (who was called the Twin), one of the twelve, was not with them when Jesus came. So the other disciples told him, "We have seen the Lord." But he said to them, "Unless I see the mark of the nails in his hands, and put my finger in the mark of the nails and my hand in his side, I will not believe."

A week later his disciples were again in the house, and Thomas was with them. Although the doors were shut, Jesus came and stood among them and said, "Peace be with you." Then he said to Thomas, "Put your finger here and see my hands. Reach out your hand and put it in my side. Do not doubt but believe." Thomas answered him, "My Lord and my God!" Jesus said to him, "Have you believed because you have seen me? Blessed are those who have not seen and yet have come to believe."

- In this reading Jesus is saying, in effect, to Thomas, "I am in the process of leaving you and ascending to my Father. This means that you will have to find me present in a new way or through your faith in my love for you." This is like when someone you love and who loves you goes away for a long time. Since he or she is no longer physically or emotionally present, you have to rely on what you have learned to believe about this person's love for you.

- Jesus leaves you with the Gospel stories and invites you to listen to what they are saying to you about how he looks at and loves you now. He does this so that you might believe what each Gospel story is saying to you about his love for you.

The Fourteenth Week in Ordinary Time
July 4–10, 2021

Something to think and pray about each day this week:

One of the hardest things I've ever had to do is play guitar, in church, in Guyana, in South America, in the dark. What would often happen is that just as we were playing nicely along with a hymn, suddenly, with no warning, all the lights would go out and we would be plunged into absolute darkness. The blackout came without warning or prediction, apparently at the time of its own malevolent choosing. Perhaps it was just my imagination, but it always seemed to come at the least convenient moments, and it would last sometimes minutes, sometimes hours, sometimes days. There was no way of knowing when it would come and go.

The really embarrassing thing for me was that when it happened as I was playing guitar in church, being unable to see the music, I would immediately stop playing, but everyone else would just keep calm and carry on. The whole Mass would keep calm and carry on, and at the end everyone would laugh at me because I was a guitarist who could only play when he could see the music. They, of course, had lived in Guyana all their lives and were used to sudden blackouts and had learned not to depend on being able to see the music all the time. I asked them how they did it and they said, "Oh we just remember how it goes and carry on."

At the time, it seemed just a matter of technical skill, to automatically memorize the main theme of any music ever put in front of you so as to be able to carry on playing if and when the blackout came. After a while, I even got quite good at it myself, and for a time I thought that was all there was to it.

It was only later that I came to realize that this was not just a well-practiced musical skill: it was a comprehensive attitude to life, and faith.

—Paul O'Reilly, SJ, *Finding Hope in All Things*

The Presence of God

As I sit here, the beating of my heart,
the ebb and flow of my breathing, the movements of my mind
are all signs of God's ongoing creation of me.
I pause for a moment and become aware
of this presence of God within me.

Freedom

I will ask God's help
to be free from my own preoccupations,
to be open to God in this time of prayer,
to come to know, love, and serve God more.

Consciousness

At this moment, Lord, I turn my thoughts to you.
I will leave aside my chores and preoccupations.
I will take rest and refreshment in your presence.

The Word

Now I turn to the Scripture set out for me this day. I read slowly over the
words and see if any sentence or sentiment appeals to me. (*Please turn to
the Scripture on the following pages. Inspiration points are there, should you
need them. When you are ready, return here to continue.*)

Conversation

Begin to talk to Jesus about the Scripture you have just read. What part
of it strikes a chord in you? Perhaps the words of a friend—or some story
you have heard recently—will slowly rise to the surface of your consciousness. If so, does the story throw light on what the Scripture passage may
be saying to you?

Conclusion

Glory be to the Father, and to the Son, and to the Holy Spirit,
As it was in the beginning, is now, and ever shall be,
World without end. Amen.

Sunday July 4
Fourteenth Sunday in Ordinary Time
Mark 6:1–6

He left that place and came to his home town, and his disciples followed him. On the sabbath he began to teach in the synagogue, and many who heard him were astounded. They said, "Where did this man get all this? What is this wisdom that has been given to him? What deeds of power are being done by his hands! Is not this the carpenter, the son of Mary and brother of James and Joses and Judas and Simon, and are not his sisters here with us?" And they took offense at him. Then Jesus said to them, "Prophets are not without honor, except in their home town, and among their own kin, and in their own house." And he could do no deed of power there, except that he laid his hands on a few sick people and cured them. And he was amazed at their unbelief.

Then he went about among the villages teaching.

- What kind of reception does Jesus expect when he returns to his home town? Instead of mixing with strangers or newly found disciples, he will now be surrounded by people who have known him all his life, who saw him grow from childhood to adulthood, who regard him as one of their own. Does he expect to be feted as a success story, one who has brought honor to his place of origin? Or does he foresee that he will be disowned, treated as an upstart who has risen above his station?

- The citizens of Nazareth recognize the wisdom of Jesus' teaching and accept that he has performed "deeds of power"—yet they reject him! Why? Have you ever seen this dynamic of negativity and cynicism operating in other communities? In church life? In politics? Have you ever been sucked into it yourself?

Monday July 5
Matthew 9:18–26

While he was saying these things to them, suddenly a leader of the synagogue came in and knelt before him, saying, "My daughter has just died; but come and lay your hand on her, and she will live." And Jesus got up and followed him, with his disciples. Then suddenly a woman who had been suffering from hemorrhages for twelve years came up behind him and touched the fringe of his cloak, for she said to herself, "If I only touch his cloak, I will be made well." Jesus turned, and seeing her he said, "Take heart, daughter; your faith has made you well." And instantly the woman was made well. When Jesus came to the leader's house and saw the flute-players and the crowd making a commotion, he said, "Go away; for the girl is not dead but sleeping." And they laughed at him. But when the crowd had been put outside, he went in and took her by the hand, and the girl got up. And the report of this spread throughout that district.

- Jesus relates wonderfully to people who have faith. Faith establishes a strong relationship between Jesus and ourselves, and so his power flows to us.

- In your prayer you might focus on how you touch Jesus and how he touches or moves you. This is effected by your faith, as a knowledge born of love, or of Jesus' love for you and yours for him. You might focus on his desire to be in a one-to-one relationship with you so that you get a sense of your personal significance or worth for him. Jesus has a deep desire to touch you in this way and for you to feel touched by him.

Tuesday July 6
Matthew 9:32–38

After they had gone away, a demoniac who was mute was brought to him. And when the demon had been cast out, the one who had been mute spoke; and the crowds were amazed and said, "Never has anything like this been seen in Israel." But the Pharisees said, "By the ruler of the demons he casts out the demons."

Then Jesus went about all the cities and villages, teaching in their synagogues, and proclaiming the good news of the kingdom, and curing every disease and every sickness. When he saw the crowds, he had compassion for them, because they were harassed and helpless, like sheep without a shepherd. Then he said to his disciples, "The harvest is plentiful, but the laborers are few; therefore ask the Lord of the harvest to send out laborers into his harvest."

- Jesus has deep compassion for the needs of all people. He sees when they are harassed and dejected, wandering and aimless like sheep without a guiding shepherd. At the same time, he has to contend with the Pharisees who are not open to listening, seeing, or indeed speaking of his goodness.

- Jesus needs many helpers today. The harvest is as big as ever; people are as lost and rudderless as they have ever been. Where are the laborers? They are not just the bishops, priests, or religious. Every baptized person is called, in some way, to share the good news of Jesus Christ. Each of us has a vocation, a call to serve and to build the kingdom of God. Let us pray today to know our unique vocation.

Wednesday July 7
Matthew 10:1–7

Then Jesus summoned his twelve disciples and gave them authority over unclean spirits, to cast them out, and to cure every disease and every sickness. These are the names of the twelve apostles: first, Simon, also known as Peter, and his brother Andrew; James son of Zebedee, and his brother John; Philip and Bartholomew; Thomas and Matthew the tax-collector; James son of Alphaeus, and Thaddaeus; Simon the Cananaean, and Judas Iscariot, the one who betrayed him.

These twelve Jesus sent out with the following instructions: "Go nowhere among the Gentiles, and enter no town of the Samaritans, but go rather to the lost sheep of the house of Israel. As you go, proclaim the good news, 'The kingdom of heaven has come near.'"

- In this scene from the Gospel, Jesus calls twelve people he wants to be with and then shares what he is passionate about doing with them. Though his call to believe the Good News is common to all, it comes to each of us in a unique way.

- Listen, as Jesus calls you to be with him and then sends you out to share the Good News in a way that only you can. He also wants you to realize that he calls you to work alongside him in a way that no one else can.

Thursday July 8
Matthew 10:7–15

"As you go, proclaim the good news, 'the kingdom of heaven has come near.' Cure the sick, raise the dead, cleanse the lepers, cast out demons. You received without payment; give without payment. Take no gold, or silver, or copper in your belts, no bag for your journey, or two tunics, or sandals, or a staff; for laborers deserve their food. Whatever town or village you enter, find out who in it is worthy, and stay there until you leave. As you enter the house, greet it. If the house is worthy, let your peace come upon it; but if it is not worthy, let your peace return to you. If anyone will not welcome you or listen to your words, shake off the dust from your feet as you leave that house or town. Truly I tell you, it will be more tolerable for the land of Sodom and Gomorrah on the day of judgment than for that town."

- Jesus imparts a radical message to his disciples as he sends them out on mission. They are to cast out demons and cleanse lepers just as he did and take nothing for the journey, not even a spare tunic or sandals for their feet. It is a rallying call by Jesus to his closest followers to trust completely in the providence and love of God.

- I pray, Lord, that I may cling less to material things and more to your providential presence in my life, which is alive and active in every moment of my day and every decision I make. Help me place all my hope and trust in you—for your love and generosity are never outdone.

Friday July 9
Matthew 10:16–23

"See, I am sending you out like sheep into the midst of wolves; so be wise as serpents and innocent as doves. Beware of them, for they will hand you over to councils and flog you in their synagogues; and you will be dragged before governors and kings because of me, as a testimony to them and the Gentiles. When they hand you over, do not worry about how you are to speak or what you are to say; for what you are to say will be given to you at that time; for it is not you who speak, but the Spirit of your Father speaking through you. Brother will betray brother to death, and a father his child, and children will rise against parents and have them put to death; and you will be hated by all because of my name. But the one who endures to the end will be saved. When they persecute you in one town, flee to the next; for truly I tell you, you will not have gone through all the towns of Israel before the Son of Man comes."

- The circumstances in which Jesus invites us to share the Good News and the obstacles we experience in doing this are very different today than they were in Jesus' time.

- To be with this reading in a prayerful way, name some of the difficulties you experience in being the best person you can be and speak to Jesus about them. Notice how gentle, appreciative, and grateful he is for your doing the best you can. Tell him how you feel about him being like this; it is likely that a part of you will relish it but that another part will resist it.

Saturday July 10
Matthew 10:24–33

"A disciple is not above the teacher, nor a slave above the master; it is enough for the disciple to be like the teacher, and the slave like the master. If they have called the master of the house Beelzebul, how much more will they malign those of his household!

"So have no fear of them; for nothing is covered up that will not be uncovered, and nothing secret that will not become known. What I say to you in the dark, tell in the light; and what you hear whispered, proclaim from the housetops. Do not fear those who kill the body but cannot kill the soul; rather fear him who can destroy both soul and body in hell. Are not two sparrows sold for a penny? Yet not one of them will fall to the ground unperceived by your Father. And even the hairs of your head are all counted. So do not be afraid; you are of more value than many sparrows."

- In this Gospel reading, Jesus continues to elaborate on the price we will pay for being his followers. He also opens up for us the reality of his Father's provident concern for us, of which he gives us two striking images. One is of the Father's care for everything in creation, even for small birds that are almost valueless in most people's estimation. The second image is of the hairs of your head that the Father "counts" or gives his full attention to and cares for.

- In an age when we incline to see everything in material, monetary, and functional terms it is good to talk to Jesus about how nothing "falls to the ground unperceived," much less you who "are of more value than many sparrows."

July 11–17, 2021

Something to think and pray about each day this week:

How does one deal with the inner world? I feel that too little attention is paid to this realm of interiority, spirituality, and the soul, and that's a shame. To put it plainly, one cannot be a Christian without paying heed to God's voice speaking inwardly. These last words are not my words; the Second Vatican Council wrote: "Conscience is the most intimate center and sanctuary of a person, in which he or she is alone with God whose voice echoes within them." It is not sufficient, therefore, to stick to the Church's doctrinal or moral teachings. Church leaders have the task "to form consciences, not to replace them," as Pope Francis declared in his encyclical *Amoris Laetitia*. In order to form consciences, it is necessary to know the movements in the soul, their multiplicity, their beauty, and their deceptiveness. The Christian is inhabited and moved by spirits (figuratively speaking) of peace, joy, goodness, patience—the Holy Spirit. But equally moved by spirits of cold duty, angry frustration for the shortcomings of others, or cynicism (for example, cynicism about society, or the bishop, or other leaders). To take the example of a Eucharistic celebration: it requires not only the right content, texts, and charity, but also the right inner movements and spirituality. I have the impression that the same applies to other Christian churches. Yet tragically, in ecclesiastical contexts, spirituality and interiority sometimes seem to be viewed as threats. That fear may be caused by mottos such as "believing without belonging" or "spirituality, yes, Church, no" and the popularity of magazines and programs promoting superficial "feel-good" spirituality. I do not consider the popularity of spirituality as a threat to the churches but as a critical mirror that compels us to question whether in our zeal for orthodoxy and orthopraxy, we may be forgetting something? Have we forgotten the soul, interiority, spirituality?

—Jos Moons, SJ, *The Art of Spiritual Direction:*
A Guide to Ignatian Practice

Presence of God
Dear Jesus, I come to you today longing for your presence. I desire to love you as you love me. May nothing ever separate me from you.

Freedom
Lord, grant me the grace to have freedom of the spirit. Cleanse my heart and soul so that I may live joyously in your love.

Consciousness
Where am I with God? With others?
Do I have something to be grateful for? Then I give thanks.
Is there something I am sorry for? Then I ask forgiveness.

The Word
The word of God comes down to us through the Scriptures. May the Holy Spirit enlighten my mind and my heart to respond to the Gospel teachings. (*Please turn to the Scripture on the following pages. Inspiration points are there, should you need them. When you are ready, return here to continue.*)

Conversation
How has God's word moved me? Has it left me cold?
Has it consoled me or moved me to act in a new way?
I imagine Jesus standing or sitting beside me;
I turn and share my feelings with him.

Conclusion
I thank God for these moments we have spent together and for any insights I have been given concerning the text.

Sunday July 11
Fifteenth Sunday in Ordinary Time
Mark 6:7–13

He called the twelve and began to send them out two by two, and gave them authority over the unclean spirits. He ordered them to take nothing for their journey except a staff; no bread, no bag, no money in their belts; but to wear sandals and not to put on two tunics. He said to them, "Wherever you enter a house, stay there until you leave the place. If any place will not welcome you and they refuse to hear you, as you leave, shake off the dust that is on your feet as a testimony against them." So they went out and proclaimed that all should repent. They cast out many demons, and anointed with oil many who were sick and cured them.

- Jesus promised to be with his disciples to the end of time. The Church he founded has lived through all sorts of challenging times. Many of its members have brought little credit to their great baptismal calling. This should not come as so great a surprise. As the prolific English author Gilbert Keith Chesterton once put it, Jesus did not found a Church for good men. He founded a Church for all men. So we should not be surprised to find many in it who are anything but good.

- In sending out his disciples two by two, as the Gospel records, Jesus knew exactly what he was doing. The vast majority of those he has sent out have been married couples. His plan of salvation depends on them, and it will still be so until the end of time.

Monday July 12
Matthew 10:34–11:1

"Do not think that I have come to bring peace to the earth; I have not come to bring peace, but a sword.

> For I have come to set a man against his father,
> and a daughter against her mother,
> and a daughter-in-law against her mother-in-law;
> and one's foes will be members of one's own household.

"Whoever loves father or mother more than me is not worthy of me; and whoever loves son or daughter more than me is not worthy of me; and whoever does not take up the cross and follow me is not worthy of me.

Those who find their life will lose it, and those who lose their life for my sake will find it.

"Whoever welcomes you welcomes me, and whoever welcomes me welcomes the one who sent me. Whoever welcomes a prophet in the name of a prophet will receive a prophet's reward; and whoever welcomes a righteous person in the name of a righteous person will receive the reward of the righteous; and whoever gives even a cup of cold water to one of these little ones in the name of a disciple—truly I tell you, none of these will lose their reward."

Now when Jesus had finished instructing his twelve disciples, he went on from there to teach and proclaim his message in their cities.

- This Gospel passage consists of a number of sayings by Jesus on discipleship. He does not directly intend these tensions and divisions in family life, but he wants us to put God first and accept the consequences. The different ways in which the Gospel is welcomed or rejected bring their own pain.

- " . . . whoever gives even a cup of cold water to one of these little ones" has eternal significance. This truth highlights the dignity of each and every human being, no matter how lowly or insignificant. Lord, help me see your face in my neighbor, and especially the poor and the needy, and to respond accordingly.

Tuesday July 13
Matthew 11:20–24

Then he began to reproach the cities in which most of his deeds of power had been done, because they did not repent. "Woe to you, Chorazin! Woe to you, Bethsaida! For if the deeds of power done in you had been done in Tyre and Sidon, they would have repented long ago in sackcloth and ashes. But I tell you, on the day of judgment it will be more tolerable for Tyre and Sidon than for you. And you, Capernaum, will you be exalted to heaven? No, you will be brought down to Hades. For if the deeds of power done in you had been done in Sodom, it would have remained until this day. But I tell you that on the day of judgment it will be more tolerable for the land of Sodom than for you."

- These verses hint at the mass of unrecorded history that the Gospels omit: the deeds of power performed by Jesus in the towns at the northern end of the Sea of Tiberias. Here were communities that listened to Jesus, and saw his miracles, but shrugged their shoulders and sent him on his way.

• Lord, open my eyes and my heart to the signs of your grace around me. Help me hear your message, even if it upsets my habits.

Wednesday July 14
Matthew 11:25–27

At that time Jesus said, "I thank you, Father, Lord of heaven and earth, because you have hidden these things from the wise and the intelligent and have revealed them to infants; yes, Father, for such was your gracious will. All things have been handed over to me by my Father; and no one knows the Son except the Father, and no one knows the Father except the Son and anyone to whom the Son chooses to reveal him."

• In this reading we meet again the passionate Jesus, and he clarifies for us what he is passionate about. We see that he is consumed by a desire to reveal his Father's "gracious will" to all, and that each of us needs to have the openness of a little child to it.

• Be with Jesus and listen to his deepest desire for you. Perhaps this desire is that you would appreciate more who you already are than who you might yet become.

Thursday July 15
Matthew 11:28–30

"Come to me, all you that are weary and are carrying heavy burdens, and I will give you rest. Take my yoke upon you, and learn from me; for I am gentle and humble in heart, and you will find rest for your souls. For my yoke is easy, and my burden is light."

• A yoke has traditionally been used between a pair of animals, usually oxen, to help them pull together on a load. Who is joined to me in this yoke? Surely it is Jesus himself!

• Jesus is not suggesting that we live free from any yoke. "And what is this yoke of yours that does not weary but gives rest?" asked the Jesuit saint Robert Bellarmine. "It is, of course, that first and greatest commandment: 'You shall love the Lord your God with all your heart.'"

Friday July 16
Matthew 12:1–8

At that time Jesus went through the cornfields on the sabbath; his disciples were hungry, and they began to pluck heads of grain and to eat. When the Pharisees saw it, they said to him, "Look, your disciples are doing what is not lawful to do on the sabbath." He said to them, "Have you not read what David did when he and his companions were hungry? He entered the house of God and ate the bread of the Presence, which it was not lawful for him or his companions to eat, but only for the priests. Or have you not read in the law that on the sabbath the priests in the temple break the sabbath and yet are guiltless? I tell you, something greater than the temple is here. But if you had known what this means, 'I desire mercy and not sacrifice,' you would not have condemned the guiltless. For the Son of Man is lord of the sabbath."

- In this reading we meet Jesus as one who believes that all law must serve the law of love. He calls this his commandment, and in it he highlights his love for us as what must shape the way we see ourselves and others, the way we relate to God and to all creation. The law finds its fullness in Jesus, "Do not think that I have come to abolish the law or the prophets; I have come not to abolish but to fulfill" (Matthew 5:17).

- Be with Jesus for a short while and with his essential call to believe the Good News of his love for you. This is Jesus' call to love yourself and others as he has loved you in the many ways you have witnessed him doing this. Is this how I live—putting love before all else?

Saturday July 17
Matthew 12:14–21

But the Pharisees went out and conspired against him, how to destroy him.

When Jesus became aware of this, he departed. Many crowds followed him, and he cured all of them, and he ordered them not to make him known. This was to fulfill what had been spoken through the prophet Isaiah:

> "Here is my servant, whom I have chosen,
> my beloved, with whom my soul is well pleased.

I will put my Spirit upon him,
and he will proclaim justice to the Gentiles.
He will not wrangle or cry aloud,
nor will anyone hear his voice in the streets.
He will not break a bruised reed
or quench a smoldering wick
until he brings justice to victory.
And in his name the Gentiles will hope."

- How can I walk in Jesus' footsteps and imitate him? Perhaps by helping refugees, by working for justice, by taking action to protect the earth. This will demand costly love, but it will help me witness to him by being a person for others.

- Above all, I need to welcome into my life the marginalized and the excluded. Jesus accepted them all, so I must also.

July 18–24, 2021

Something to think and pray about each day this week:

Yes to your promptings, your movement within,
Yes to your inner light, your sunny sensualities.
Yes to her hands filled with openness,
Sing Hallelujah to her magnificent lowliness.

Yes to your gaze, your soft sensitivities,
Yes to your blissfulness, your heavenly mindfulness.
Yes to her eyes filled with pureness.
Sing Hallelujah to her magnificent blessedness.

Yes to your open road, your warm invitations,
Yes to your genuineness, your grounded worldliness,
Yes to her embrace filled with wholeness,
Sing Hallelujah to her magnificent fruitfulness.

Yes to your lion-heart, your brave inspirations,
Yes to your expansiveness, your meditative spaciousness.
Oh Yes, Forever yes, My Goodness!

—"The Magnificent Magnificat of Mary," Gavin Thomas Murphy,
Bursting Out in Praise: Spirituality & Mental Health

The Presence of God
Dear Lord, as I come to you today, fill my heart, my whole being, with the wonder of your presence. Help me remain receptive to you as I put aside the cares of this world. Fill my mind with your peace.

Freedom
Lord, grant me the grace to be free from the excesses of this life. Let me not get caught up with the desire for wealth. Keep my heart and mind free to love and serve you.

Consciousness
I exist in a web of relationships: links to nature, people, God.
I trace out these links,
giving thanks for the life that flows through them.
Some links are twisted or broken; I may feel regret, anger, disappointment.
I pray for the gift of acceptance and forgiveness.

The Word
God speaks to each of us individually. I listen attentively to hear what he is saying to me. Read the text a few times, then listen. (*Please turn to the Scripture on the following pages. Inspiration points are there, should you need them. When you are ready, return here to continue.*)

Conversation
Jesus, you speak to me through the words of the Gospels. May I respond to your call today. Teach me to recognize your hand at work in my daily living.

Conclusion
I thank God for these moments we have spent together and for any insights I have been given concerning the text.

Sunday July 18
Sixteenth Sunday in Ordinary Time
Mark 6:30–34

The apostles gathered around Jesus, and told him all that they had done and taught. He said to them, "Come away to a deserted place all by yourselves and rest a while." For many were coming and going, and they had no leisure even to eat. And they went away in the boat to a deserted place by themselves. Now many saw them going and recognized them, and they hurried there on foot from all the towns and arrived ahead of them. As he went ashore, he saw a great crowd; and he had compassion for them, because they were like sheep without a shepherd; and he began to teach them many things.

- Lord, there are times when I want to get away from the crowds, when I feel oppressed by company. There are other times when I just wish that somebody knew that I exist; I can have too much of aloneness. If I can reach you in prayer, and know that you are more central to me than my own thoughts, I feel at peace, as the apostles must have felt.

Monday July 19
Matthew 12:38–42

Then some of the scribes and Pharisees said to him, "Teacher, we wish to see a sign from you." But he answered them, "An evil and adulterous generation asks for a sign, but no sign will be given to it except the sign of the prophet Jonah. For just as Jonah was for three days and three nights in the belly of the sea monster, so for three days and three nights the Son of Man will be in the heart of the earth. The people of Nineveh will rise up at the judgment with this generation and condemn it, because they repented at the proclamation of Jonah, and see, something greater than Jonah is here! The queen of the South will rise up at the judgment with this generation and condemn it, because she came from the ends of the earth to listen to the wisdom of Solomon, and see, something greater than Solomon is here!"

- I need a spiritual transformation in my life so that I become alive to God. That will be a resurrection for me. Then I can become a helpful sign to this generation.

- True Christians are signs that the world can see, and so come to know Jesus. People see Jesus through you and me. As Christians, as the Church, we are always to be witnesses to God's saving mercy.

Tuesday July 20
Matthew 12:46–50

While he was still speaking to the crowds, his mother and his brothers were standing outside, wanting to speak to him. Someone told him, "Look, your mother and your brothers are standing outside, wanting to speak to you." But to the one who had told him this, Jesus replied, "Who is my mother, and who are my brothers?" And pointing to his disciples, he said, "Here are my mother and my brothers! For whoever does the will of my Father in heaven is my brother and sister and mother."

- Jesus invites me here to become a disciple. This does not mean plodding along after him but becoming a cherished member of his family. Mary is the model disciple: she is fully open to God's will and supports Jesus in his ministry. She is our gentle mother and helps all of God's children become brothers and sisters in the Lord.

- "The family is the fundamental locus of the covenant between the Church and God's creation." (Pope Francis)

Wednesday July 21
Matthew 13:1–9

That same day Jesus went out of the house and sat beside the lake. Such great crowds gathered around him that he got into a boat and sat there, while the whole crowd stood on the beach. And he told them many things in parables, saying: "Listen! A sower went out to sow. And as he sowed, some seeds fell on the path, and the birds came and ate them up. Other seeds fell on rocky ground, where they did not have much soil, and they sprang up quickly, since they had no depth of soil. But when the sun rose, they were scorched; and since they had no root, they withered away. Other seeds fell among thorns, and the thorns grew up and choked them. Other seeds fell on good soil and brought forth grain, some a hundredfold, some sixty, some thirty. Let anyone with ears listen!"

- This is the parable of Christian optimism: even if the sower was only moderately good, most of the seed would fall on good ground, bringing forth abundant fruit, at least thirtyfold. Let anyone with ears listen!

Thursday July 22
John 20:1–2, 11–18

Early on the first day of the week, while it was still dark, Mary Magdalene came to the tomb and saw that the stone had been removed from the tomb. So she ran and went to Simon Peter and the other disciple, the one whom Jesus loved, and said to them, "They have taken the Lord out of the tomb, and we do not know where they have laid him.". . .

But Mary stood weeping outside the tomb. As she wept, she bent over to look into the tomb; and she saw two angels in white, sitting where the body of Jesus had been lying, one at the head and the other at the feet. They said to her, "Woman, why are you weeping?" She said to them, "They have taken away my Lord, and I do not know where they have laid him." When she had said this, she turned round and saw Jesus standing there, but she did not know that it was Jesus. Jesus said to her, "Woman, why are you weeping? For whom are you looking?" Supposing him to be the gardener, she said to him, "Sir, if you have carried him away, tell me where you have laid him, and I will take him away." Jesus said to her, "Mary!" She turned and said to him in Hebrew, "Rabbouni!" (which means Teacher). Jesus said to her, "Do not hold on to me, because I have not yet ascended to the Father. But go to my brothers and say to them, 'I am ascending to my Father and your Father, to my God and your God.'" Mary Magdalene went and announced to the disciples, "I have seen the Lord"; and she told them that he had said these things to her.

- Mary of Magdala is nowadays accorded the rank of "apostle": announcer, messenger, herald. Her belief has become strong enough for her to be commissioned by the risen Jesus to go and impart this belief to his disciples.

- There would seem to have been two stages by which Mary's belief in the Risen Lord was purified. The second stage is when she tries to grasp this new reality by trying to cling to or clasp the figure of Jesus. (In another Gospel, two women make the same attempt.) This would be to privilege the experience of the senses in an exaggerated way.

- The earlier stage is when Mary might seem a little slow at picking up the hints of his presence that Jesus is offering (mistaking him for the gardener).

- Our Christian faith requires us to avoid both errors: not trying too hard to "grasp at miracles"—and at the same time being open to the cumulative force of the hints and traces of himself which Jesus has left available to us.

Friday July 23
Matthew 13:18–23

"Hear then the parable of the sower. When anyone hears the word of the kingdom and does not understand it, the evil one comes and snatches away what is sown in the heart; this is what was sown on the path. As for what was sown on rocky ground, this is the one who hears the word and immediately receives it with joy; yet such a person has no root, but endures only for a while, and when trouble or persecution arises on account of the word, that person immediately falls away. As for what was sown among thorns, this is the one who hears the word, but the cares of the world and the lure of wealth choke the word, and it yields nothing. But as for what was sown on good soil, this is the one who hears the word and understands it, who indeed bears fruit and yields, in one case a hundredfold, in another sixty, and in another thirty."

- We get so used to hearing Jesus' parables that we may fail to appreciate how full of wisdom they are, a wisdom that is beautifully expressed in language anyone can understand. In an earlier passage in Matthew, we heard Jesus talk about how "the queen of the South will rise up at the judgment with this generation and condemn it, because she came from the ends of the earth to listen to the wisdom of Solomon, and see, something greater than Solomon is here!" (Matthew 12:42)

- As you read today's Gospel, let yourself dwell on Jesus' wisdom as one of his most attractive characteristics.

Saturday July 24
Matthew 13:24–30

He put before them another parable: "The kingdom of heaven may be compared to someone who sowed good seed in his field; but while everybody was asleep, an enemy came and sowed weeds among the wheat, and then went away. So when the plants came up and bore grain, then the weeds appeared as well. And the slaves of the householder came and said to him, 'Master, did you not sow good seed in your field? Where, then, did these weeds come from?' He answered, 'An enemy has done this.' The slaves said to him, 'Then do you want us to go and gather them?' But he replied, 'No; for in gathering the weeds you would uproot the wheat along with them. Let both of them grow together until the harvest; and at harvest time I will tell the reapers, Collect the weeds first and bind them in bundles to be burned, but gather the wheat into my barn.'"

- Sometimes we may think that perfection is acquired by becoming aware of our faults and working to root these out. However, when we become more familiar with Jesus' attitude to the limited and sinful side of ourselves, we learn to accept our limited and sinful self just as Jesus did with Zacchaeus (Luke 19:1–10). If we don't accept this side of ourselves, we tend to become fixated on it and fail to appreciate the fullness of life Jesus has already given us.

- Be with Jesus and let him teach you to let the weeds grow with the wheat, lest seeking to uproot them you might fail to appreciate all that is good and even beautiful about your life.

The Seventeenth Week in Ordinary Time
July 25–31, 2021

Something to think and pray about each day this week:

In Dick Farrelly's iconic song, "The Isle of Innisfree," an emigrant reflects on his memories of home, missing so much all that was familiar to him and remains embedded in his memory. Among his most cherished memories is that of family prayer, and his description is wonderful:

> "And then into a humble shack I wander
> my dear old home, and tenderly behold
> the folks I love around the turf fire gathered
> on bended knees their rosary is told."

It is said that Farrelly got the idea for this song when traveling by bus from Meath to Dublin. I have an image of him scribbling down the lines lest he forget them. I wonder if these words were included in his original thoughts, but whether they were or not, I am so pleased they found their way into the song he released.

"On bended knee their rosary is told." He could have said the Rosary was "said," "recited," "prayed," but no, the verb he used is the past tense of the verb "to tell." The Rosary then, as he sees it, is the telling of a story, and so it is.

What is that story? It's the story of Christ—told from Gabriel's visit to Mary in the first joyful mystery of the Annunciation right through to the second Glorious mystery of the Ascension, followed by the fulfillment of the Lord's promise that he would send to us "an Advocate," as prayed in the third Glorious Mystery, "the descent of The Holy Spirit."

In the pages to follow, maybe we could look at that story, as "told" in the Rosary. Maybe a phrase or two to wrap around the Our Father, ten Hail Marys and Glory Be. A thought or two to accompany you as you take the beads in hand.

—Vincent Sherlock, *Telling the Rosary.* "The Isle of Inisfree,"
by Dick Farrelly, used with kind permission of his family.

The Presence of God
God is with me, but even more astounding, God is within me.
Let me dwell for a moment on God's life-giving presence
in my body, in my mind, in my heart,
as I sit here, right now.

Freedom
Lord, may I never take the gift of freedom for granted. You gave me the
great blessing of freedom of spirit. Fill my spirit with your peace and joy.

Consciousness
I remind myself that I am in the presence of God, who is my strength in
times of weakness and my comforter in times of sorrow.

The Word
I take my time to read the word of God slowly, a few times, allowing myself to dwell on anything that strikes me. (*Please turn to the Scripture on
the following pages. Inspiration points are there, should you need them. When
you are ready, return here to continue.*)

Conversation
Jesus, you always welcomed little children when you walked on this earth.
Teach me to have a childlike trust in you. Teach me to live in the knowl-
edge that you will never abandon me.

Conclusion
Glory be to the Father, and to the Son, and to the Holy Spirit,
As it was in the beginning, is now, and ever shall be,
World without end. Amen.

Sunday July 25
Seventeenth Sunday in Ordinary Time
John 6:1–15

After this Jesus went to the other side of the Sea of Galilee, also called the Sea of Tiberias. A large crowd kept following him, because they saw the signs that he was doing for the sick. Jesus went up the mountain and sat down there with his disciples. Now the Passover, the festival of the Jews, was near. When he looked up and saw a large crowd coming toward him, Jesus said to Philip, "Where are we to buy bread for these people to eat?" He said this to test him, for he himself knew what he was going to do. Philip answered him, "Six months' wages would not buy enough bread for each of them to get a little." One of his disciples, Andrew, Simon Peter's brother, said to him, "There is a boy here who has five barley loaves and two fish. But what are they among so many people?" Jesus said, "Make the people sit down." Now there was a great deal of grass in the place; so they sat down, about five thousand in all. Then Jesus took the loaves, and when he had given thanks, he distributed them to those who were seated; so also the fish, as much as they wanted. When they were satisfied, he told his disciples, "Gather up the fragments left over, so that nothing may be lost." So they gathered them up, and from the fragments of the five barley loaves, left by those who had eaten, they filled twelve baskets. When the people saw the sign that he had done, they began to say, "This is indeed the prophet who is to come into the world."

When Jesus realized that they were about to come and take him by force to make him king, he withdrew again to the mountain by himself.

- In today's Gospel, Jesus performs the miracle of the multiplication of the loaves and fishes. It is, of course, a symbol of the Eucharist; there are deliberate signals that this is so. This incident is memorable, but it pales in significance when compared to the wonder of the Eucharist. Try to devote some time to seeing the occasion, speaking to the participants, and drawing fruit for yourself and your life.

- The small offering of the young man fed the people. God can make much of what we offer. Our attempts to live in his love and follow him are nothing without him. We never know where our efforts to love, to help, and to support others may bear fruit.

Monday July 26
Matthew 13:31–35

He put before them another parable: "The kingdom of heaven is like a mustard seed that someone took and sowed in his field; it is the smallest of all the seeds, but when it has grown it is the greatest of shrubs and becomes a tree, so that the birds of the air come and make nests in its branches."

He told them another parable: "The kingdom of heaven is like yeast that a woman took and mixed in with three measures of flour until all of it was leavened."

Jesus told the crowds all these things in parables; without a parable he told them nothing. This was to fulfill what had been spoken through the prophet:

"I will open my mouth to speak in parables;
I will proclaim what has been hidden from the foundation of the world."

- From the parables Jesus told we can see how much he valued stories as a way of revealing "what has been hidden from the foundation of the world." In the two parables he tells in today's reading, he speaks about the wonderful workings of the Good News of God's love and providence in the life of those who believe in him. The way Jesus leads us into his love will always be slow and gentle, for it depends on how ready and willing we are to accept or believe in it.

- Be with Jesus who, like the excellent teacher he is, is always sensitive to, respectful of, and deferential toward you concerning how much of his love and plan you are willing and ripe to adopt.

Tuesday July 27
Matthew 13:36–43

Then he left the crowds and went into the house. And his disciples approached him, saying, "Explain to us the parable of the weeds of the field." He answered, "The one who sows the good seed is the Son of Man; the field is the world, and the good seeds are the children of the kingdom; the weeds are the children of the evil one, and the enemy who sowed them is the devil; the harvest is the end of the age, and the reapers are angels. Just as the weeds are collected and burned up with fire, so will it be at the end of the age. The Son of Man will send his angels, and they will collect out of his kingdom all causes of sin and all evildoers, and they will throw them into the furnace of fire, where there will be weeping and gnashing of teeth. Then the righteous will shine like the sun in the kingdom of their Father. Let anyone with ears listen!"

- The force of this parable, of the wheat and the weeds, hits us every day. It is about having patience with the persistence of evil in the world. We may face malicious vandalism, like the enemy who sowed weeds in his neighbor's field. In their early stages the weeds looked like wheat, and you could not root up weeds without taking some wheat as well. So too some of the evils we face are dressed up to look respectable. We have to fight evil, but we need not give ourselves ulcers if we find that society remains far from perfect. The final judgment lies with God.

Wednesday July 28
Matthew 13:44–46

"The kingdom of heaven is like treasure hidden in a field, which someone found and hid; then in his joy he goes and sells all that he has and buys that field.

"Again, the kingdom of heaven is like a merchant in search of fine pearls; on finding one pearl of great value, he went and sold all that he had and bought it."

- What is my pearl, the thing I value most? What is that buried treasure for which I would be willing to sacrifice everything?

- What would the world be like if the pearl I seek were to be serving the poor and marginalized and working for peace and justice? Jesus says the world would then be like the kingdom of heaven!

Thursday July 29
Luke 10:38–42

Now as they went on their way, he entered a certain village, where a woman named Martha welcomed him into her home. She had a sister named Mary, who sat at the Lord's feet and listened to what he was saying. But Martha was distracted by her many tasks; so she came to him and asked, "Lord, do you not care that my sister has left me to do all the work by myself? Tell her then to help me." But the Lord answered her, "Martha, Martha, you are worried and distracted by many things; there is need of only one thing. Mary has chosen the better part, which will not be taken away from her."

- The friendship between Jesus and the family at Bethany—Martha, Mary, and Lazarus—is beautifully described in the eleventh chapter of the Gospel of John. It is a household where Jesus is warmly, even intimately, welcomed. This is less evident in today's reading from Luke, which speaks rather of the tension in the household, as a result of the unfair division of labor between the two sisters. All of us can recognize this scenario! It is important not to lose sight of the domestic ordinariness; delightful, even if this is a moment of tension.

Friday July 30
Matthew 13:54–58

He came to his home town and began to teach the people in their synagogue, so that they were astounded and said, "Where did this man get this wisdom and these deeds of power? Is not this the carpenter's son? Is not his mother called Mary? And are not his brothers James and Joseph and Simon and Judas? And are not all his sisters with us? Where then did this man get all this?" And they took offense at him. But Jesus said to them, "Prophets are not without honor except in their own country and in their own house." And he did not do many deeds of power there, because of their unbelief.

- We can easily ignore or despise what is familiar. How was it for Jesus when his own people "took offense at him" just because they knew him? Speak with Jesus about this, recalling what it's like for you when people are rude to you.

- Ask Jesus for the grace to realize that every time you meet him in your prayer you are meeting God. Allow his disturbing freshness to captivate you. Like Mary, allow Jesus to do "deeds of power" through you for the good of the world.

Saturday July 31

Matthew 14:1–12

At that time Herod the ruler heard reports about Jesus; and he said to his servants, "This is John the Baptist; he has been raised from the dead, and for this reason these powers are at work in him." For Herod had arrested John, bound him, and put him in prison on account of Herodias, his brother Philip's wife, because John had been telling him, "It is not lawful for you to have her." Though Herod wanted to put him to death, he feared the crowd, because they regarded him as a prophet. But when Herod's birthday came, the daughter of Herodias danced before the company, and she pleased Herod so much that he promised on oath to grant her whatever she might ask. Prompted by her mother, she said, "Give me the head of John the Baptist here on a platter." The king was grieved, yet out of regard for his oaths and for the guests, he commanded it to be given; he sent and had John beheaded in the prison. The head was brought on a platter and given to the girl, who brought it to her mother. His disciples came and took the body and buried it; then they went and told Jesus.

- John the Baptist is held in the highest regard by the Gospels, even by Jesus himself. He is often presented as very similar to Jesus: Herod thinks Jesus is John risen from the dead. Yet the Gospels insist that John was also very different from Jesus, especially in what he claimed to be. His style, too, is very different from that of Jesus, who was an itinerant preacher, while people flocked to the desert to hear John. Yet both ended up giving up their lives for the truth. Sometimes we are uncomfortable with different styles in the Church, we would prefer all to be the same, as if the Church were an army or a political party. I pray for openness and freedom to welcome the different manifestations of the one Spirit.

- Speaking truth to power is never easy, it always exacts a price. For John the price was a steep one indeed, yet he was ready to pay it, even though it must have seemed a lost cause even to him. I pray for the courage and wisdom I need to to say what I believe to be true, to be always a person of integrity.

The Eighteenth Week in Ordinary Time
August 1–7, 2021

Something to think and pray about each day this week:

Anybody who has walked through barren, arid terrain in the heat of the day will appreciate how essential it is to find wells along the way in order to slake their thirst. A combination of exercise and intense heat soon leads to dehydration. Many pilgrims on their way to Santiago de Compostela in Spain understand the challenges, especially as they walk through the arid landscape between Burgos and Leon. In a similar way, as we make our way through life, there are moments when our life is like a desert and we need to stop at the first oasis to fill up on water.

Many of us are concerned about work-life balance in a socioeconomic environment where many of us are run off our feet, working every hour that God sends, and at the end of it all still find it challenging to put a roof over our heads. It often feels overwhelming. Relationships can be put under strain. The quality of family life can suffer. It can be more attractive to engage with virtual acquaintances than the people around us, especially in a culture where instant and frequent affirmation is the norm and where we don't want to miss out. We experience the pressure but are often not sure what to do. Within a family there may be a variety of schedules: children at school, study, choir, and games, while parents may work irregular hours, have a long and tiring commute, or work night shifts. The idea of a common meal such as dinner may be unsustainable, even though it may be the most important event of the day for facilitating quality family life. Constant exposure to a variety of stimuli is simply not good for us. Social media boundaries are important. Slowing-down time is essential for destressing and recovering our mental equilibrium.

—Jim Maher, SJ, *What's It All About?*

The Presence of God

Dear Jesus, today I call on you, but not to ask for anything. I'd like only to dwell in your presence. May my heart respond to your love.

Freedom

God my creator, you gave me life and the gift of freedom. Through your love I exist in this world. May I never take the gift of life for granted. May I always respect others' right to life.

Consciousness

I ask how I am today. Am I particularly tired, stressed or anxious? If any of these characteristics apply, can I try to let go of the concerns that disturb me?

The Word

The word of God comes down to us through the Scriptures. May the Holy Spirit enlighten my mind and my heart to respond to the Gospel teachings. (*Please turn to the Scripture on the following pages. Inspiration points are there, should you need them. When you are ready, return here to continue.*)

Conversation

I begin to talk with Jesus about the Scripture I have just read. What part of it strikes a chord in me? Perhaps the words of a friend—or some story I have heard recently—will rise to the surface in my consciousness. If so, does the story throw light on what the Scripture passage may be saying to me?

Conclusion

Glory be to the Father, and to the Son, and to the Holy Spirit,
As it was in the beginning, is now, and ever shall be,
World without end. Amen.

Sunday August 1
Eighteenth Sunday in Ordinary Time
John 6:24–35

So when the crowd saw that neither Jesus nor his disciples were there, they themselves got into the boats and went to Capernaum looking for Jesus.

When they found him on the other side of the lake, they said to him, "Rabbi, when did you come here?" Jesus answered them, "Very truly, I tell you, you are looking for me, not because you saw signs, but because you ate your fill of the loaves. Do not work for the food that perishes, but for the food that endures for eternal life, which the Son of Man will give you. For it is on him that God the Father has set his seal." Then they said to him, "What must we do to perform the works of God?" Jesus answered them, "This is the work of God, that you believe in him whom he has sent." So they said to him, "What sign are you going to give us then, so that we may see it and believe you? What work are you performing? Our ancestors ate the manna in the wilderness; as it is written, 'He gave them bread from heaven to eat.'" Then Jesus said to them, "Very truly, I tell you, it was not Moses who gave you the bread from heaven, but it is my Father who gives you the true bread from heaven. For the bread of God is that which comes down from heaven and gives life to the world." They said to him, "Sir, give us this bread always."

Jesus said to them, "I am the bread of life. Whoever comes to me will never be hungry, and whoever believes in me will never be thirsty."

- If you came today to a startling awareness of the goodness and generosity of God toward the world, how would you share it with others? This was the challenge that Jesus faced from childhood, because he had a unique appreciation of what God is like!

- Here Jesus uses the simplest of images to help us understand: he talks of bread. In his day, when diets were simple, bread kept people alive; it satisfied their hunger and gave them strength to keep going. Here Jesus is saying that he is "the bread of life" for them: by accepting his friendship they will be nourished, fed, and strengthened, and will become more alive.

- I pray: "Lord, help me always to draw life from your friendship with me."

Monday August 2
Matthew 14:13–21

Now when Jesus heard this, he withdrew from there in a boat to a deserted place by himself. But when the crowds heard it, they followed him on foot from the towns. When he went ashore, he saw a great crowd; and he had compassion for them and cured their sick. When it was evening, the disciples came to him and said, "This is a deserted place, and the hour is now late; send the crowds away so that they may go into the villages and buy food for themselves." Jesus said to them, "They need not go away; you give them something to eat." They replied, "We have nothing here but five loaves and two fish." And he said, "Bring them here to me." Then he ordered the crowds to sit down on the grass. Taking the five loaves and the two fish, he looked up to heaven, and blessed and broke the loaves, and gave them to the disciples, and the disciples gave them to the crowds. And all ate and were filled; and they took up what was left over of the broken pieces, twelve baskets full. And those who ate were about five thousand men, besides women and children.

- Mother Teresa said about Jesus, "He uses us to be his love and compassion in the world in spite of our weaknesses and frailties." In this miracle Jesus does not produce food out of nowhere. He takes the little that the apostles have, and he multiplies it a thousandfold.

- In the miracle of the multiplication of the loaves and fishes, I am reminded that Jesus can provide spiritual nourishment beyond my imagining. There is a mysterious disproportion between what I give and what the Lord makes of it.

Tuesday August 3
Matthew 14:22–36

Immediately he made the disciples get into the boat and go on ahead to the other side, while he dismissed the crowds. And after he had dismissed the crowds, he went up the mountain by himself to pray. When evening came, he was there alone, but by this time the boat, battered by the waves, was far from the land, for the wind was against them. And early in the morning he came walking toward them on the lake. But when the disciples saw him walking on the lake, they were terrified, saying, "It is a ghost!" And they cried out in fear. But immediately Jesus spoke to them and said, "Take heart, it is I; do not be afraid."

Peter answered him, "Lord, if it is you, command me to come to you on the water." He said, "Come." So Peter got out of the boat, started walking on the water, and came toward Jesus. But when he noticed the strong wind, he became frightened, and beginning to sink, he cried out, "Lord, save me!" Jesus immediately reached out his hand and caught him, saying to him, "You of little faith, why did you doubt?" When they got into the boat, the wind ceased. And those in the boat worshipped him, saying, "Truly you are the Son of God."

When they had crossed over, they came to land at Gennesaret. After the people of that place recognized him, they sent word throughout the region and brought all who were sick to him, and begged him that they might touch even the fringe of his cloak; and all who touched it were healed.

- The apostles, despite living side-by-side with Jesus and seeing the wonders he worked, failed to believe that he could save them from the ferocity of the storm. So many storms batter our own lives—storms of sin and temptation, anxiety, fear, and despair—and yet Jesus is no farther away from us than he was from the disciples in that small boat.

- Lord, when we are afraid, help us realize that you are always at our side. In all the difficult times of our lives, help us hear your encouraging words: "Do not be afraid." With our hand in yours, nothing can be too much for us.

Wednesday August 4
Matthew 15:21–28

Jesus left that place and went away to the district of Tyre and Sidon. Just then a Canaanite woman from that region came out and started shouting, "Have mercy on me, Lord, Son of David; my daughter is tormented by a demon." But he did not answer her at all. And his disciples came and urged him, saying, "Send her away, for she keeps shouting after us." He answered, "I was sent only to the lost sheep of the house of Israel." But she came and knelt before him, saying, "Lord, help me." He answered, "It is not fair to take the children's food and throw it to the dogs." She said, "Yes, Lord, yet even the dogs eat the crumbs that fall from their masters' table." Then Jesus answered her, "Woman, great is your faith! Let it be done for you as you wish." And her daughter was healed instantly.

- This woman was persistent in pursuing what she wanted as she announced her request. Jesus often meets such people and puts the question back to them: how important is it to you? Jesus, rescue me from any habit of prayer that focuses on my action or words instead of listening for your voice. Help me enter conversation with you now and to remain in relationship with you always.

Thursday August 5
Matthew 16:13–23

Now when Jesus came into the district of Caesarea Philippi, he asked his disciples, "Who do people say that the Son of Man is?" And they said, "Some say John the Baptist, but others Elijah, and still others Jeremiah or one of the prophets." He said to them, "But who do you say that I am?" Simon Peter answered, "You are the Messiah, the Son of the living God." And Jesus answered him, "Blessed are you, Simon son of Jonah! For flesh and blood has not revealed this to you, but my Father in heaven. And I tell you, you are Peter, and on this rock I will build my church, and the gates of Hades will not prevail against it. I will give you the keys of the kingdom of heaven, and whatever you bind on earth will be bound in heaven, and whatever you loose on earth will be loosed in heaven." Then he sternly ordered the disciples not to tell anyone that he was the Messiah.

From that time on, Jesus began to show his disciples that he must go to Jerusalem and undergo great suffering at the hands of the elders and chief priests and scribes, and be killed, and on the third day be raised. And Peter took him aside and began to rebuke him, saying, "God forbid it, Lord! This must never happen to you." But he turned and said to Peter, "Get behind me, Satan! You are a stumbling-block to me; for you are setting your mind not on divine things but on human things."

- We live in times of turmoil in the Church, of a deep-seated mistrust in all leaders, including those in the Church. I listen to Jesus giving Peter the mission of being the rock upon which he chose to build his Church. Jesus, who here acknowledges he is the Christ, the promised one, made this choice of building his Church on Peter, when he could well have chosen a different way. I pray to be given the faith that was given to Peter, of professing Jesus as the Son of the living God.

- Yet, immediately after, the Gospel shows us Jesus using the strongest words to reproach Peter for his reaction to the foretelling of Jesus' suffering. The Gospel does not hide the great limitations of Peter and his companions, on the contrary, it shows how difficult they found it to understand the message of Jesus and follow it. I pray for Pope Francis, for my bishop, and for all Church leaders that they may, in their poverty and limitations, lead us toward faith in Jesus.

Friday August 6
The Transfiguration of the Lord
Mark 9:2–10

Six days later, Jesus took with him Peter and James and John, and led them up a high mountain apart, by themselves. And he was transfigured before them, and his clothes became dazzling white, such as no one on earth could bleach them. And there appeared to them Elijah with Moses, who were talking with Jesus. Then Peter said to Jesus, "Rabbi, it is good for us to be here; let us make three dwellings, one for you, one for Moses, and one for Elijah." He did not know what to say, for they were terrified. Then a cloud overshadowed them, and from the cloud there came a voice, "This is my Son, the Beloved; listen to him!" Suddenly when they looked around, they saw no one with them any more, but only Jesus.

As they were coming down the mountain, he ordered them to tell no one about what they had seen, until after the Son of Man had risen from the dead. So they kept the matter to themselves, questioning what this rising from the dead could mean.

- Peter cries out in delight and wonder, "Rabbi, it is good for us to be here!" This is how we are surely meant to experience the presence of God—in wonder and delight, the created glorying in the Creator's presence. Too often, we glide along the surface of the spinning earth, never listening to its heartbeat. We look into the depths of the universe and never hear the singing of the stars.

- When did I last sing and make melody to the Lord with all my heart or clap my hands or shout for joy to him?

Saturday August 7
Matthew 17:14–20

When they came to the crowd, a man came to him, knelt before him, and said, "Lord, have mercy on my son, for he is an epileptic and he suffers terribly; he often falls into the fire and often into the water. And I brought him to your disciples, but they could not cure him." Jesus answered, "You faithless and perverse generation, how much longer must I be with you? How much longer must I put up with you? Bring him here to me." And Jesus rebuked the demon, and it came out of him, and the boy was cured instantly. Then the disciples came to Jesus privately and said, "Why could we not cast it out?" He said to them, "Because of your little faith. For truly I tell you, if you have faith the size of a mustard seed, you will say to this mountain, 'Move from here to there,' and it will move; and nothing will be impossible for you."

• We can understand this story only through contemplation. In prayer, see the people involved, hear what they are saying, and note what they are doing. Enter the scene and question the participants, the Lord included. Listen closely before asking your questions.

• What answers do you get to your questions?

• Jesus has no doubt that if we had enough faith we could move mountains. I pray for an increase in faith and a deeper love of Jesus. "Lord, I believe; help my unbelief" (Mark 9:24).

The Nineteenth Week in Ordinary Time
August 8–14, 2021

Something to think and pray about each day this week:

The model of the community of creation opens up new avenues for understanding liturgy. Unlike the "dominion" and "stewardship" models, it does not place the human at the center or above nature but nests humanity in creation. In a post-modern world it may be romantic to try to simply recover the enchanted realm of the pre-modern world. Yet the "big history" can evoke a new sense of wonder.

We are part of a 13.8 billion-year story. It is not merely a story of inanimate matter, but always in-spirited, graced matter. The intrinsic relations of all there is grounds the imagination that liturgy needs. The divine is not immanent in particular enchanted things, places, people, or cloud-dwelling divinities. Rather, the whole of the cosmos presents the creator to us. We are inextricably linked with all there is. We are composed of the ashes of stars. All the "stuff" that is here and now was present there and then at the very beginning.

In general, liturgies are community events. If humanity is the universe becoming conscious of itself, then liturgies are the universe as a community of creation praising God. Liturgy is not separate from the rest. It is not the action of a celebrant alone or even of the human community alone. It is the voice of the universe praising the one who called it all into being.

—Dermot A. Lane, *Theology and Ecology in Dialogue*

The Presence of God

I pause for a moment and think of the love and the grace that God showers on me. I am created in the image and likeness of God; I am God's dwelling place.

Freedom

Lord, you granted me the great gift of freedom. In these times, O Lord, grant that I may be free from any form of racism or intolerance. Remind me that we are all equal in your loving eyes.

Consciousness

Knowing that God loves me unconditionally,
I can afford to be honest about how I am.
How has the day been, and how do I feel now?
I share my feelings openly with the Lord.

The Word

I take my time to read the word of God slowly, a few times, allowing myself to dwell on anything that strikes me. (*Please turn to the Scripture on the following pages. Inspiration points are there, should you need them. When you are ready, return here to continue.*)

Conversation

Sometimes I wonder what I might say if I were to meet you in person, Lord.
I think I might say, "Thank you" because you are always there for me.

Conclusion

I thank God for these moments we have spent together and for any insights I have been given concerning the text.

Sunday August 8
Nineteenth Sunday in Ordinary Time
John 6:41–51

Then the Jews began to complain about him because he said, "I am the bread that came down from heaven." They were saying, "Is not this Jesus, the son of Joseph, whose father and mother we know? How can he now say, 'I have come down from heaven'?" Jesus answered them, "Do not complain among yourselves. No one can come to me unless drawn by the Father who sent me; and I will raise that person up on the last day. It is written in the prophets, 'And they shall all be taught by God.' Everyone who has heard and learned from the Father comes to me. Not that anyone has seen the Father except the one who is from God; he has seen the Father. Very truly, I tell you, whoever believes has eternal life. I am the bread of life. Your ancestors ate the manna in the wilderness, and they died. This is the bread that comes down from heaven, so that one may eat of it and not die. I am the living bread that came down from heaven. Whoever eats of this bread will live for ever; and the bread that I will give for the life of the world is my flesh."

- Here Jesus is appealing to us to be aware of the divine relationships that underpin our lives. More is going on than we realize: we are being made into the daughters or sons of God! There is more to us than meets the eye, no matter how poorly we are responding!

- The Father is always drawing us into divine life because he loves us limitlessly. He does this through Jesus, who is one like us and who tells us what the Father has in mind for us. So there are divine Persons busy in our lives, enabling us to become like themselves. If we live within these intimate relationships, then we are already sharing in eternal life. How wonderful!

Monday August 9
Matthew 17:22–27

As they were gathering in Galilee, Jesus said to them, "The Son of Man is going to be betrayed into human hands, and they will kill him, and on the third day he will be raised." And they were greatly distressed.

When they reached Capernaum, the collectors of the temple tax came to Peter and said, "Does your teacher not pay the temple tax?" He said,

"Yes, he does." And when he came home, Jesus spoke of it first, asking, "What do you think, Simon? From whom do kings of the earth take toll or tribute? From their children or from others?" When Peter said, "From others," Jesus said to him, "Then the children are free. However, so that we do not give offense to them, go to the lake and cast a hook; take the first fish that comes up; and when you open its mouth, you will find a coin; take that and give it to them for you and me."

- The disciples could not imagine how they might live without Jesus; they had become used to being with him, listening to him, observing him, and reflecting on his words. His talk about change threatened them. The future will threaten me too if I do not hear Jesus' words and receive the assurance of his abiding presence. I pray that I may receive again his words, "Peace be with you," "Take heart," and "Do not be afraid."

Tuesday August 10
John 12:24–26

"Very truly, I tell you, unless a grain of wheat falls into the earth and dies, it remains just a single grain; but if it dies, it bears much fruit. Those who love their life lose it, and those who hate their life in this world will keep it for eternal life. Whoever serves me must follow me, and where I am, there will my servant be also. Whoever serves me, the Father will honor."

- It will not do for the grain of wheat just to die in order to produce fruit. It must "fall into the earth." We will achieve nothing on our own. We need the nourishment that Jesus provides, for he is our life.

- Jesus says here that "serving" and "following" him are the same thing. It is not for us to choose how or where to serve him. We must follow first and let him lead us to where he wants us to serve. A disciple cannot say, "I did it my way!"

Wednesday August 11
Matthew 18:15–20

"If another member of the church sins against you, go and point out the fault when the two of you are alone. If the member listens to you, you have regained that one. But if you are not listened to, take one or two others along with you, so that every word may be confirmed by the evidence of two or three witnesses. If the member refuses to listen to them, tell it to the church; and if the offender refuses to listen even to the church, let such a one be to you as a Gentile and a tax-collector. Truly I tell you, whatever you bind on earth will be bound in heaven, and whatever you loose on earth will be loosed in heaven. Again, truly I tell you, if two of you agree on earth about anything you ask, it will be done for you by my Father in heaven. For where two or three are gathered in my name, I am there among them."

- Jesus is gently reminding us that by being members of the Church community, we are responsible for one another, and one of our tasks of love may be that of correcting our brother or sister who errs. This is never an easy task in our relativistic times, and our advice risks being rejected. Fraternal correction must always be inspired by real charity—it is one of the spiritual works of mercy. I pray to be given this love and the wisdom to find the right way to carry out this task of love.

- Because Jesus shares his own spirit with us, the connection between the community of believers and Jesus is very close: what we bind or loose here is bound or loosed in heaven, and whatever we ask in union will be given to us by the Father. I ask for this insight and for a stronger faith in the presence of Jesus in the midst of the Church.

Thursday August 12
Matthew 18:21–19:1

Then Peter came and said to him, "Lord, if another member of the church sins against me, how often should I forgive? As many as seven times?" Jesus said to him, "Not seven times, but, I tell you, seventy-seven times.

"For this reason the kingdom of heaven may be compared to a king who wished to settle accounts with his slaves. When he began the reckoning, one who owed him ten thousand talents was brought to him; and, as he could not pay, his lord ordered him to be sold, together with his wife and children and all his possessions, and payment to be made. So the slave fell on his knees before him, saying, 'Have patience with me, and I will pay you everything.' And out of pity for him, the lord of that slave released him and forgave him the debt. But that same slave, as he went out, came upon one of his fellow-slaves who owed him a hundred denarii; and seizing him by the throat, he said, 'Pay what you owe.' Then his fellow-slave fell down and pleaded with him, 'Have patience with me, and I will pay you.' But he refused; then he went and threw him into prison until he should pay the debt. When his fellow-slaves saw what had happened, they were greatly distressed, and they went and reported to their lord all that had taken place. Then his lord summoned him and said to him, 'You wicked slave! I forgave you all that debt because you pleaded with me. Should you not have had mercy on your fellow-slave, as I had mercy on you?' And in anger his lord handed him over to be tortured until he should pay his entire debt. So my heavenly Father will also do to every one of you, if you do not forgive your brother or sister from your heart."

When Jesus had finished saying these things, he left Galilee and went to the region of Judea beyond the Jordan.

- Do I think of myself as needing divine forgiveness? If I don't, is it because I am using human standards rather than divine ones? I am meant to love God and my neighbor with my whole heart and soul, but how compassionate am I to those who need my help? Is my life made over to God, or am I a drifter? Am I known as generous and forgiving?

- The world needs me to radiate God's own love and to foster reconciliation and peace. Lord, for my shortcomings in living out the gospel I ask forgiveness and mercy. Enable me, in turn, to show forgiveness to those who do me wrong. In this way I can be more truly the light of the world.

Friday August 13
Matthew 19:3–12

Some Pharisees came to him, and to test him they asked, "Is it lawful for a man to divorce his wife for any cause?" He answered, "Have you not read that the one who made them at the beginning 'made them male and female,' and said, 'For this reason a man shall leave his father and mother and be joined to his wife, and the two shall become one flesh'? So they are no longer two, but one flesh. Therefore what God has joined together, let no one separate." They said to him, "Why then did Moses command us to give a certificate of dismissal and to divorce her?" He said to them, "It was because you were so hard-hearted that Moses allowed you to divorce your wives, but at the beginning it was not so. And I say to you, whoever divorces his wife, except for unchastity, and marries another commits adultery."

His disciples said to him, "If such is the case of a man with his wife, it is better not to marry." But he said to them, "Not everyone can accept this teaching, but only those to whom it is given. For there are eunuchs who have been so from birth, and there are eunuchs who have been made eunuchs by others, and there are eunuchs who have made themselves eunuchs for the sake of the kingdom of heaven. Let anyone accept this who can."

- Pope Francis addresses this demanding text in *Amoris Laetitia*. The Christian community, he states, must always show compassion and integrate those who can't measure up to Jesus' ideal for marriage. "Integration is the key to their pastoral care, a care which would allow them not only to realize that they belong to the Church as the body of Christ, but also to know that they can have a joyful and fruitful experience in it" (299). Condemnation is no help; instead they must be encouraged to discern what they can do. They are, after all, still limitlessly loved and called to become the daughters and sons of God.

- I chat with Jesus about my attitudes toward those who find themselves in irregular unions. Perhaps I find myself in that group: can I trust that God's love for me and my partner never wavers but always invites me onward?

Saturday August 14
Matthew 19:13–15

Then little children were being brought to him in order that he might lay his hands on them and pray. The disciples spoke sternly to those who brought them; but Jesus said, "Let the little children come to me, and do not stop them; for it is to such as these that the kingdom of heaven belongs." And he laid his hands on them and went on his way.

- In this passage, children are taken as representing those whom the world considers unimportant; similarly, the parable of the lost sheep (Matthew 18:12-14) teaches that in the eyes of Jesus the least of all in the eyes of the world is as important as the greatest of all. This reminds us that the weaker people are, the more they require our care and concern.

- Let us pray today that we may deepen our respect for those whom the world holds in low esteem.

The Twentieth Week in Ordinary Time
August 15–21, 2021

Something to think and pray about each day this week:

In what is seen as the just reward for a life truly given to God, Mary is assumed into heaven, body and soul. This tells us that Mary did not go through the gates of death to enter heaven but, rather, as at her conception, was singularly chosen for this honor.

In her assumption, Mary brings with her the needs of the world and continues to intercede for people, witnessing to their needs and responding.

Mary's witness, as recorded in the Knock apparition of 1879, speaks well to the truth of her nature. Standing silently, in the company of Joseph and the beloved disciple John, to whose care she was committed on Calvary, she points toward the altar and, there upon, the Lamb of God. She continues to see herself in the role of "the handmaid of the Lord" and encourages us always to acknowledge God, turn toward him in prayer, and give thanks.

The Assumption, then, is not a farewell or a removal from our midst but a continuation of a relationship that sees Mary noticing people's needs, responding to them, and seeking always to do God's will.

A prayer around gratitude for Mary's "yes" that paved the way for the coming of Christ. We might remember our own mothers too and give thanks for their many acts of selflessness. We could pray for a blessing of family life and for healing where there is division or unhappiness.

—Vincent Sherlock, *Telling the Rosary*

The Presence of God

I pause for a moment
and reflect on God's life-giving presence
in every part of my body,
in everything around me,
in the whole of my life.

Freedom

Many countries are at this moment suffering the agonies of war. I bow my head in thanksgiving for my freedom. I pray for all prisoners and captives.

Consciousness

Knowing that God loves me unconditionally, I look honestly over the past day, its events and my feelings. Do I have something to be grateful for? Then I give thanks. Is there something I am sorry for? Then I ask forgiveness.

The Word

Now I turn to the Scripture set out for me this day. I read slowly over the words and see if any sentence or sentiment appeals to me. (*Please turn to the Scripture on the following pages. Inspiration points are there, should you need them. When you are ready, return here to continue.*)

Conversation

I know with certainty that there were times when you carried me, Lord. There were times when it was through your strength that I got through the dark times.

Conclusion

Glory be to the Father, and to the Son, and to the Holy Spirit,
As it was in the beginning, is now, and ever shall be,
World without end. Amen.

Sunday August 15
The Assumption of the Blessed Virgin Mary
Luke 1:39–56

In those days Mary set out and went with haste to a Judean town in the hill country, where she entered the house of Zechariah and greeted Elizabeth. When Elizabeth heard Mary's greeting, the child leapt in her womb. And Elizabeth was filled with the Holy Spirit and exclaimed with a loud cry, "Blessed are you among women, and blessed is the fruit of your womb. And why has this happened to me, that the mother of my Lord comes to me? For as soon as I heard the sound of your greeting, the child in my womb leapt for joy. And blessed is she who believed that there would be a fulfillment of what was spoken to her by the Lord."

And Mary said,

> "My soul magnifies the Lord,
>   and my spirit rejoices in God my Savior,
> for he has looked with favor on the lowliness of his servant.
>   Surely, from now on all generations will call me blessed;
> for the Mighty One has done great things for me, and holy is
>   his name.
> His mercy is for those who fear him
>   from generation to generation.
> He has shown strength with his arm;
>   he has scattered the proud in the thoughts of their hearts.
> He has brought down the powerful from their thrones,
>   and lifted up the lowly;
> he has filled the hungry with good things,
>   and sent the rich away empty.
> He has helped his servant Israel,
>   in remembrance of his mercy,
> according to the promise he made to our ancestors,
>   to Abraham and to his descendants for ever."

And Mary remained with her for about three months and then returned to her home.

- There is no false humility in Mary's tremendous prayer. There is the true humility of knowing that all that is being accomplished in her is being accomplished by God, "for the Mighty One has done great things for me." Mary makes no effort to minimize this greatness. She accepts it—fully, joyfully, and expectantly. Her great song of praise is a glorious expression of Mary's hope.

- I ask you, Lord, to give me Mary's confidence and generosity of spirit. I ask not just to listen to your voice and do your will but also to do it joyfully and fearlessly. I want to answer your call with an exultant "Yes!" secure in the knowledge that, as I move into the unknown, my journey will be made radiant by your transfiguring presence, and that, as the Psalmist foretold, "your hand shall lead me, and your right hand shall hold me."

Monday August 16
Matthew 19:16–22

Then someone came to him and said, "Teacher, what good deed must I do to have eternal life?" And he said to him, "Why do you ask me about what is good? There is only one who is good. If you wish to enter into life, keep the commandments." He said to him, "Which ones?" And Jesus said, "You shall not murder; You shall not commit adultery; You shall not steal; You shall not bear false witness; Honor your father and mother; also, You shall love your neighbor as yourself." The young man said to him, "I have kept all these; what do I still lack?" Jesus said to him, "If you wish to be perfect, go, sell your possessions, and give the money to the poor, and you will have treasure in heaven; then come, follow me." When the young man heard this word, he went away grieving, for he had many possessions.

- Interestingly, the commandments that Jesus recites to the rich young man do not include the first three, which all relate to our relationship with God. Instead, he lists those that address our relationships with one another. The message is clear: we do not live in isolation. Love for our neighbor is the door to eternal life.

- What attachments in my life are holding me back from a deeper relationship with my neighbor and with God?

Tuesday August 17
Matthew 19:23–30

Then Jesus said to his disciples, "Truly I tell you, it will be hard for a rich person to enter the kingdom of heaven. Again I tell you, it is easier for a camel to go through the eye of a needle than for someone who is rich to enter the kingdom of God." When the disciples heard this, they were greatly astounded and said, "Then who can be saved?" But Jesus looked at them and said, "For mortals it is impossible, but for God all things are possible."

Then Peter said in reply, "Look, we have left everything and followed you. What then will we have?" Jesus said to them, "Truly I tell you, at the renewal of all things, when the Son of Man is seated on the throne of his glory, you who have followed me will also sit on twelve thrones, judging the twelve tribes of Israel. And everyone who has left houses or brothers or sisters or father or mother or children or fields, for my name's sake, will receive a hundredfold, and will inherit eternal life. But many who are first will be last, and the last will be first."

- Jesus is clear that money and riches can be a real obstacle to enter the kingdom. What is my relationship with money? Do I have a balanced attitude, or does it affect the freedom of my choices, as it did to the man who refused to become a disciple because "he was a man of great wealth"? I ask for light and for freedom.

- Sometimes I find myself asking the same questions as Peter in today's reading: "What about us? We have left everything and followed you. What are we to have, then?" I look back at the times when Jesus' promise of a hundredfold return for anything I gave up came true in my life. I let myself be touched by God's generosity and faithfulness.

Wednesday August 18
Matthew 20:1–16

[Jesus said to his disciples,] "For the kingdom of heaven is like a landowner who went out early in the morning to hire laborers for his vineyard. After agreeing with the laborers for the usual daily wage, he sent them into his vineyard. When he went out about nine o'clock, he saw others standing idle in the market-place; and he said to them, 'You also go into the vineyard, and I will pay you whatever is right.' So they went. When he went out again about noon and about three o'clock, he did the same.

And about five o'clock he went out and found others standing around; and he said to them, 'Why are you standing here idle all day?' They said to him, 'Because no one has hired us.' He said to them, 'You also go into the vineyard.' When evening came, the owner of the vineyard said to his manager, 'Call the laborers and give them their pay, beginning with the last and then going to the first.' When those hired about five o'clock came, each of them received the usual daily wage. Now when the first came, they thought they would receive more; but each of them also received the usual daily wage. And when they received it, they grumbled against the landowner, saying, 'These last worked only one hour, and you have made them equal to us who have borne the burden of the day and the scorching heat.' But he replied to one of them, 'Friend, I am doing you no wrong; did you not agree with me for the usual daily wage? Take what belongs to you and go; I choose to give to this last the same as I give to you. Am I not allowed to do what I choose with what belongs to me? Or are you envious because I am generous?' So the last will be first, and the first will be last."

- This parable describes a joyless world of work, where people were engaged for one day, or even for one hour. There is no joy in their work, only heaviness and insecurity, which produce anger and tension. In our world too, more and more people find no joy in their work but only anxiety and hardship.

- The landowner introduces a new style: people work hard, but here work has dignity, and even those who did not manage to find work for the whole day receive enough to safeguard their dignity. The rules of the kingdom are different: they go beyond strict justice and create respect and solidarity. Lord, may your kingdom come in our world so full of injustice and tension.

Thursday August 19
Matthew 22:1–14

Once more Jesus spoke to them in parables, saying: "The kingdom of heaven may be compared to a king who gave a wedding banquet for his son. He sent his slaves to call those who had been invited to the wedding banquet, but they would not come. Again he sent other slaves, saying, 'Tell those who have been invited: Look, I have prepared my dinner, my oxen and my fat calves have been slaughtered, and everything is ready; come to the wedding banquet.' But they made light of it and went away, one to his farm, another to his business, while the rest seized his slaves, maltreated them, and killed them. The king was enraged. He sent his troops, destroyed those murderers, and burned their city. Then he said to his slaves, 'The wedding is ready, but those invited were not worthy. Go therefore into the main streets, and invite everyone you find to the wedding banquet.' Those slaves went out into the streets and gathered all whom they found, both good and bad; so the wedding hall was filled with guests.

"But when the king came in to see the guests, he noticed a man there who was not wearing a wedding robe, and he said to him, 'Friend, how did you get in here without a wedding robe?' And he was speechless. Then the king said to the attendants, 'Bind him hand and foot, and throw him into the outer darkness, where there will be weeping and gnashing of teeth.' For many are called, but few are chosen."

- The parable of the wedding in today's Gospel was spoken when Jesus saw that his own people were moving to reject him. The story is symbolic. But the invitation to us is a real one. It is an invitation to aim at the good life. The invitation to the kingdom of heaven is cast wide, yet we are free to say yes or no. No matter how low a stature I seem to have in life, I am welcome. I will shake off the rags of my injustice, my less good self, and dress in the clothes of a new, more loving person.

- I ask God to help me respond as best I can to this real invitation. Is a quiet voice whispering to me from within?

Friday August 20
Matthew 22:34–40

When the Pharisees heard that he had silenced the Sadducees, they gathered together, and one of them, a lawyer, asked him a question to test him. "Teacher, which commandment in the law is the greatest?" He said to him, "'You shall love the Lord your God with all your heart, and with all your soul, and with all your mind.' This is the greatest and first commandment. And a second is like it: 'You shall love your neighbor as yourself.' On these two commandments hang all the law and the prophets."

- The Gospel today centers the message of Jesus on love; on two loves united in each of us. Love God, love the neighbor—this is the only commandment of Jesus. Without this, all we say we do for him is really done for ourselves. No detail of religious observance is above this law of love. Jesus said this, and lived it. He never allowed the laws of religion to overtake the need for love. The message of Jesus is all-embracing and covers all our relationships, the close relationships of marriage, family, and friendship, as well as the call to love the wider world, particularly where the needs are great.

Saturday August 21
Matthew 23:1–12

Then Jesus said to the crowds and to his disciples, "The scribes and the Pharisees sit on Moses' seat; therefore, do whatever they teach you and follow it; but do not do as they do, for they do not practice what they teach. They tie up heavy burdens, hard to bear, and lay them on the shoulders of others; but they themselves are unwilling to lift a finger to move them. They do all their deeds to be seen by others; for they make their phylacteries broad and their fringes long. They love to have the place of honor at banquets and the best seats in the synagogues, and to be greeted with respect in the market-places, and to have people call them rabbi. But you are not to be called rabbi, for you have one teacher, and you are all students. And call no one your father on earth, for you have one Father—the one in heaven. Nor are you to be called instructors, for you have one instructor, the Messiah. The greatest among you will be your servant. All who exalt themselves will be humbled, and all who humble themselves will be exalted."

- Lord, you pick out the manifestations of vanity and self-importance. "You are all students," you say. In the mysterious way that Scripture works, I am growing daily in knowledge of God's ways. You, Lord, are my teacher.

- The Christian identity is servant, disciple, humble follower. Greatness is seen in love, in being willing to serve the needs of others, as Jesus did. These words can be remembered at the Last Supper, when Jesus washed the feet of the disciples. Many cultures and groups of people honor success, wealth, and the pretense of self-importance. Remember in prayer a moment when you felt humbled as you served somebody or did something really relevant for them. Offer this memory to God in thanks.

The Twenty-First Week in Ordinary time
August 22–28, 2021

Something to think and pray about each day this week:

One of the most interesting and fruitful developments in modern-day theology and spirituality is an appreciation of "story" as a source or carrier of revelation. Whether it be the storytelling of the Old Testament or of the Gospels and the Acts, or those later stories of holy men and women that permeate the Christian tradition, searchers for God in our day find in "story" a readily accessible way of learning about the mysterious interaction of God with God's people.

Stories have the capacity to illuminate and instruct, not by communicating truth in an abstract or purely rational way, but by inviting the searcher to enter imaginatively into another's story. This then draws out the searcher's own story through the recognition of parallels and resemblances, and through the experience of resonances, joyful or painful.

We find, therefore, a growing appreciation of that genre of writing that can be called spiritual autobiography. This is a recognizable and convenient term, yet it runs the risk of associating these writings too closely with the "secular" autobiographies of politicians, sports stars, celebrities, and so on. This can be misleading.

Secular autobiography deals with what a particular person has experienced, achieved, thought, or said. Spiritual autobiography, in contrast, deals more with what God has brought about in the person. It is primarily the record of God's involvement in a human life. God is the main actor. Of course, the narrators will record the events of their lives, will write of their human relationships and how they used their freedom. But all of this will be communicated and interpreted in relation to the initiative of God.

—Brian O'Leary, SJ, *Radical Discipleship:*
Probing the Ignatian Tradition

The Presence of God
I remind myself that, as I sit here now,
God is gazing on me with love and holding me in being.

Freedom
"There are very few people who realize what God would make of them
if they abandoned themselves into his hands, and let themselves be formed
by his grace" (St. Ignatius). I ask for the grace to trust myself totally to
God's love.

Consciousness
Where do I sense hope, encouragement, and growth in my life? If I do notice such areas, I will determine to give them time and space in the future.

The Word
Lord Jesus, you became human to communicate with me.
You walked and worked on this earth.
You endured the heat and struggled with the cold.
All your time on this earth was spent in caring for humanity.
You healed the sick, you raised the dead.
Most important of all, you saved me from death.
(*Please turn to the Scripture on the following pages. Inspiration points are
there, should you need them. When you are ready, return here to continue.*)

Conversation
What is stirring in me as I pray? Am I consoled, troubled, left cold? I
imagine Jesus standing or sitting at my side, and I share my feelings with
him.

Conclusion
Glory be to the Father, and to the Son, and to the Holy Spirit,
As it was in the beginning, is now, and ever shall be,
World without end. Amen.

Sunday August 22
Twenty-First Sunday in Ordinary Time
John 6:60–69

When many of his disciples heard it, they said, "This teaching is difficult; who can accept it?" But Jesus, being aware that his disciples were complaining about it, said to them, "Does this offend you? Then what if you were to see the Son of Man ascending to where he was before? It is the spirit that gives life; the flesh is useless. The words that I have spoken to you are spirit and life. But among you there are some who do not believe." For Jesus knew from the first who were the ones that did not believe, and who was the one that would betray him. And he said, "For this reason I have told you that no one can come to me unless it is granted by the Father."

Because of this many of his disciples turned back and no longer went about with him. So Jesus asked the twelve, "Do you also wish to go away?" Simon Peter answered him, "Lord, to whom can we go? You have the words of eternal life. We have come to believe and know that you are the Holy One of God."

- Lord, how deeply do I desire this transforming relationship you offer me? You want to raise me to the level of "spirit and life." St. Irenaeus said long ago, "The glory of God is the human person fully alive." I know that I'm only half-alive at best, so here and now I ask you to work on me so that I become more like you. You are fully alive as a human being, and this is because you are totally open to God.

- Make that happen to me, whatever it takes! Take me by the hand, hold me tight, and bring me along with you, so I shall become like you.

Monday August 23
Matthew 23:13–22

"But woe to you, scribes and Pharisees, hypocrites! For you lock people out of the kingdom of heaven. For you do not go in yourselves, and when others are going in, you stop them. Woe to you, scribes and Pharisees, hypocrites! For you cross sea and land to make a single convert, and you make the new convert twice as much a child of hell as yourselves.

"Woe to you, blind guides, who say, 'Whoever swears by the sanctuary is bound by nothing, but whoever swears by the gold of the sanctuary is bound by the oath.' You blind fools! For which is greater, the gold or the sanctuary that has made the gold sacred? And you say, 'Whoever swears by the altar is bound by nothing, but whoever swears by the gift that is on the altar is bound by the oath.' How blind you are! For which is greater, the gift or the altar that makes the gift sacred? So whoever swears by the altar, swears by it and by everything on it; and whoever swears by the sanctuary, swears by it and by the one who dwells in it; and whoever swears by heaven, swears by the throne of God and by the one who is seated upon it."

- Jesus keeps the strongest language to condemn those who confuse the externals of religion with what might be at its heart. I let God lead me in my time of prayer, prepared to let go of habits, rituals, and externals—all so that I may better hear the voice of God.

- I pray for the community with which I worship; may we never confuse the beautiful things we have or do with their source, but may we grow together in humble service of God.

Tuesday August 24
St. Bartholomew, Apostle
John 1:45–51

Philip found Nathanael and said to him, "We have found him about whom Moses in the law and also the prophets wrote, Jesus son of Joseph from Nazareth." Nathanael said to him, "Can anything good come out of Nazareth?" Philip said to him, "Come and see." When Jesus saw Nathanael coming toward him, he said of him, "Here is truly an Israelite in whom there is no deceit!" Nathanael asked him, "Where did you come to know me?" Jesus answered, "I saw you under the fig tree before Philip called you." Nathanael replied, "Rabbi, you are the Son of God! You are the King of Israel!" Jesus answered, "Do you believe because I told you that I saw you under the fig tree? You will see greater things than these." And he said to him, "Very truly, I tell you, you will see heaven opened and the angels of God ascending and descending upon the Son of Man."

- Pope Francis has a dream that every Christian may become an "evangelizer." He means for us to share the Good News of God's saving love for all humankind. This can seem a daunting task, but Philip shows very simply how it can be done. His heart has been touched by meeting

Jesus, so off he goes to share his discovery with his friend. He doesn't argue with Nathanael but just says, "Come and see." We come across Philip doing the same thing again, when he found some Greeks who wished to see Jesus.

- You might pray: "Lord, grant me an inner knowledge of yourself that sets me on fire with a desire to share you with others. Even if I can't mention your name, let me always try to be good news to those I meet."

Wednesday August 25
Matthew 23:27–32

"Woe to you, scribes and Pharisees, hypocrites! For you are like white-washed tombs, which on the outside look beautiful, but inside they are full of the bones of the dead and of all kinds of filth. So you also on the outside look righteous to others, but inside you are full of hypocrisy and lawlessness.

"Woe to you, scribes and Pharisees, hypocrites! For you build the tombs of the prophets and decorate the graves of the righteous, and you say, 'If we had lived in the days of our ancestors, we would not have taken part with them in shedding the blood of the prophets.' Thus you testify against yourselves that you are descendants of those who murdered the prophets. Fill up, then, the measure of your ancestors."

- One of the phrases that seems to have captured our imagination is *speaking truth to power*. Even in our democratic times we need brave people who are ready to pay the price for that. I look at Jesus as he takes on the powerful men of his time, the political and religious leaders, and pray for those who are willing to risk speaking truth to power. I pray for those who abuse their power, and for their victims.

- I pray that the eye of my heart be clear, so that I may be aware of the inconsistencies in my thoughts and in my actions. I ask for pardon for all my hypocrisy, and pray for those who suffer because of my weakness.

Thursday August 26
Matthew 24:42–51

Keep awake therefore, for you do not know on what day your Lord is coming. But understand this: if the owner of the house had known in what part of the night the thief was coming, he would have stayed awake and would not have let his house be broken into. Therefore you also must be ready, for the Son of Man is coming at an unexpected hour.

"Who then is the faithful and wise slave, whom his master has put in charge of his household, to give the other slaves their allowance of food at the proper time? Blessed is that slave whom his master will find at work when he arrives. Truly I tell you, he will put that one in charge of all his possessions. But if that wicked slave says to himself, 'My master is delayed,' and he begins to beat his fellow-slaves, and eats and drinks with drunkards, the master of that slave will come on a day when he does not expect him and at an hour that he does not know. He will cut him in pieces and put him with the hypocrites, where there will be weeping and gnashing of teeth."

- The grace and presence of God can hit us at any time. A moment in the countryside, a prayer at Mass, a hug with a loved one, a support in trouble—all can be doors opening to God. Some have recalled the presence of God at a deathbed. Note the moments when the Lord came your way and left an afterglow which has lasted for years.

Friday August 27
Matthew 25:1–13

"Then the kingdom of heaven will be like this. Ten bridesmaids took their lamps and went to meet the bridegroom. Five of them were foolish, and five were wise. When the foolish took their lamps, they took no oil with them; but the wise took flasks of oil with their lamps. As the bridegroom was delayed, all of them became drowsy and slept. But at midnight there was a shout, 'Look! Here is the bridegroom! Come out to meet him.' Then all those bridesmaids got up and trimmed their lamps. The foolish said to the wise, 'Give us some of your oil, for our lamps are going out.' But the wise replied, 'No! there will not be enough for you and for us; you had better go to the dealers and buy some for yourselves.' And while they went to buy it, the bridegroom came, and those who were ready went with him into the wedding banquet; and the door was shut. Later the other bridesmaids came also, saying, 'Lord, lord, open to us.' But he replied, 'Truly I tell you, I do not know you.' Keep awake therefore, for you know neither the day nor the hour."

- This is a parable that can be undone by focusing on what seems like selfishness in the prepared bridesmaids. I need to ask the help of the Holy Spirit who inspired Jesus to speak in this way to help me listen and humbly learn.

- Jesus tells us that there is a right time and also a time when it will be too late. I ask God's help that I may realize what it is I might do now, how I might recognize the approaching bridegroom and welcome him.

Saturday August 28
Matthew 25:14–30

"For it is as if a man, going on a journey, summoned his slaves and entrusted his property to them; to one he gave five talents, to another two, to another one, to each according to his ability. Then he went away. The one who had received the five talents went off at once and traded with them, and made five more talents. In the same way, the one who had the two talents made two more talents. But the one who had received the one talent went off and dug a hole in the ground and hid his master's money. After a long time the master of those slaves came and settled accounts with them. Then the one who had received the five talents came forward, bringing five more talents, saying, 'Master, you handed over to me five talents; see, I have made five more talents.' His master said to him, 'Well done, good and trustworthy slave; you have been trustworthy in a few things, I will put you in charge of many things; enter into the joy of your master.' And the one with the two talents also came forward, saying, 'Master, you handed over to me two talents; see, I have made two more talents.' His master said to him, 'Well done, good and trustworthy slave; you have been trustworthy in a few things, I will put you in charge of many things; enter into the joy of your master.' Then the one who had received the one talent also came forward, saying, 'Master, I knew that you were a harsh man, reaping where you did not sow, and gathering where you did not scatter seed; so I was afraid, and I went and hid your talent in the ground. Here you have what is yours.' But his master replied, 'You wicked and lazy slave! You knew, did you, that I reap where I did not sow, and gather where I did not scatter? Then you ought to have invested my money with the bankers, and on my return I would have received what was my own with interest. So take the talent from him, and give it to the one with the ten talents. For to all those who have, more will be given, and they will have an abundance; but from those who have nothing, even what they have will be taken away. As for this worthless slave, throw him into the outer darkness, where there will be weeping and gnashing of teeth.'"

- My talents: in thanksgiving I dwell on my gifts, firstly looking at them in wonder: my life, my health, my faith, and especially the people who fill my life and who have made me who I am. I then reflect on the gratuity of all this, and ask God for the grace to know how to be grateful by respecting the talents of others.

- I ask myself whether I am like the first two, who worked hard to make their talents bear fruit; or am I like the third one who was more concerned not to lose what he had, and ended up losing everything. Probably I am a bit of both, so I ask for the grace of inner freedom to be able to express my gratitude through the way I live.

August 29—September 4, 2021

Something to think and pray about each day this week:

Jesus asks you to forgive those who have wronged you, and more than a little bit. He asks to forgive "seventy times seven times" (Matthew 18:22). But is forgiveness possible? And if it is at all possible, is it desirable? Isn't forgiveness for the weak? Isn't revenge more powerful?

Forgiveness is not cowardly; on the contrary, it requires that you dare to face up to the evil that the other person has done to you. That's why forgiveness can hurt, but forgiveness is, above all, liberating. Not only for those who are forgiven but especially for the victim who can forgive. Forgiveness means that you can finally let go of anger, resentment, and other negative feelings. Without forgiveness, these feelings threaten to grow deeper and take up more and more space. This is why forgiveness fosters inner healing, makes new life possible, and gives hope. Forgiveness means that you can really turn the page on any evil in your life.

Forgiveness becomes easier when the perpetrator regrets and asks for forgiveness. But fortunately, the victim is not a hostage to the goodwill of the perpetrator. You can also forgive if the perpetrator is unknown, has already died, or does not repent at all. You don't need the offender's permission to cut the chain of the feelings of revenge.

Christians believe that in the end it is God himself who forgives, through them. That's why they find it useful to ask God in prayer to be able to forgive. Even if you want to sometimes, you can't just decide to forgive. Forgiveness of those who have done you harm is given to you. Suddenly you can feel that the time is ripe. That's why Christians call forgiveness a grace. It is a gift from God.

—Nikolaas Sintobin, SJ, *Did Jesus Really Exist?*
and 51 Other Questions

The Presence of God

"Be still, and know that I am God!" Lord, your words lead us to the calmness and greatness of your presence.

Freedom

"In these days, God taught me as a schoolteacher teaches a pupil" (St. Ignatius). I remind myself that there are things God has to teach me yet, and I ask for the grace to hear them and let them change me.

Consciousness

How am I really feeling? Lighthearted? Heavyhearted?
I may be very much at peace, happy to be here.
Equally, I may be frustrated, worried, or angry.
I acknowledge how I really am. It is the real me whom the Lord loves.

The Word

God speaks to each of us individually. I listen attentively to hear what he is saying to me. Read the text a few times, then listen. (*Please turn to the Scripture on the following pages. Inspiration points are there, should you need them. When you are ready, return here to continue.*)

Conversation

Do I notice myself reacting as I pray with the word of God? Do I feel challenged, comforted, angry? Imagining Jesus sitting or standing by me, I speak out my feelings, as one trusted friend to another.

Conclusion

I thank God for these moments we have spent together and for any insights I have been given concerning the text.

Sunday August 29
Twenty-Second Sunday in Ordinary Time
Mark 7:1–8, 14–15, 21–23

Now when the Pharisees and some of the scribes who had come from Jerusalem gathered around him, they noticed that some of his disciples were eating with defiled hands, that is, without washing them. (For the Pharisees, and all the Jews, do not eat unless they thoroughly wash their hands, thus observing the tradition of the elders; and they do not eat anything from the market unless they wash it; and there are also many other traditions that they observe, the washing of cups, pots and bronze kettles.) So the Pharisees and the scribes asked him, "Why do your disciples not live according to the tradition of the elders, but eat with defiled hands?" He said to them, "Isaiah prophesied rightly about you hypocrites, as it is written,

> 'This people honors me with their lips,
> but their hearts are far from me;
> in vain do they worship me,
> teaching human precepts as doctrines.'

You abandon the commandment of God and hold to human tradition.". . . Then he called the crowd again and said to them, "Listen to me, all of you, and understand: there is nothing outside a person that by going in can defile, but the things that come out are what defile. . . . For it is from within, from the human heart, that evil intentions come: fornication, theft, murder, adultery, avarice, wickedness, deceit, licentiousness, envy, slander, pride, folly. All these evil things come from within, and they defile a person."

- God sees the heart and its fluctuations. He judges us on the love of our lives and our efforts to love. In the evening of life, God will see not just what we did but also the heart of goodness by which we lived. A practical way of letting the good flow is to be grateful. On any day we can always think of something to be thankful for. In thanks, the spirit of joy and blessing will flow into us and through us.

Monday August 30
Luke 4:16–30

When he came to Nazareth, where he had been brought up, he went to the synagogue on the sabbath day, as was his custom. He stood up to read, and the scroll of the prophet Isaiah was given to him. He unrolled the scroll and found the place where it was written:

> "The Spirit of the Lord is upon me,
> because he has anointed me
> to bring good news to the poor.
> He has sent me to proclaim release to the captives
> and recovery of sight to the blind,
> to let the oppressed go free,
> to proclaim the year of the Lord's favor."

And he rolled up the scroll, gave it back to the attendant, and sat down. The eyes of all in the synagogue were fixed on him. Then he began to say to them, "Today this scripture has been fulfilled in your hearing." All spoke well of him and were amazed at the gracious words that came from his mouth. They said, "Is not this Joseph's son?" He said to them, "Doubtless you will quote to me this proverb, 'Doctor, cure yourself!' And you will say, 'Do here also in your home town the things that we have heard you did at Capernaum.'" And he said, "Truly I tell you, no prophet is accepted in the prophet's home town. But the truth is, there were many widows in Israel in the time of Elijah, when the heaven was shut up for three years and six months, and there was a severe famine over all the land; yet Elijah was sent to none of them except to a widow at Zarephath in Sidon. There were also many lepers in Israel in the time of the prophet Elisha, and none of them was cleansed except Naaman the Syrian." When they heard this, all in the synagogue were filled with rage. They got up, drove him out of the town, and led him to the brow of the hill on which their town was built, so that they might hurl him off the cliff. But he passed through the midst of them and went on his way.

- Of all the texts available to him, Jesus chose this ringing description of his mission from Isaiah: to bring the good news to the poor, to give sight to the blind, to let the oppressed go free. As I reflect on Jesus' own understanding of his mission, I look at our world as we struggle with so many social issues: the welcome of refugees and migrants to our countries and communities, the growing inequality between those who have and those who have not, the destruction of the environment. What is the Spirit of the Lord sending me to do, as a follower of Jesus? I ask for the grace not to be deaf to his call but to carry it out with great generosity.

Tuesday August 31
Luke 4:31–37

He went down to Capernaum, a city in Galilee, and was teaching them on the sabbath. They were astounded at his teaching, because he spoke with authority. In the synagogue there was a man who had the spirit of an unclean demon, and he cried out with a loud voice, "Let us alone! What have you to do with us, Jesus of Nazareth? Have you come to destroy us? I know who you are, the Holy One of God." But Jesus rebuked him, saying, "Be silent, and come out of him!" When the demon had thrown him down before them, he came out of him without having done him any harm. They were all amazed and kept saying to one another, "What kind of utterance is this? For with authority and power he commands the unclean spirits, and out they come!" And a report about him began to reach every place in the region.

• They say you can get used to anything; could it be that I am so used to Jesus and his ways that I no longer remark on them or consider how they challenge me? The people of Jesus' time were astonished and surprised. His teachings stood in stark contrast not only to the unclean spirits but also to the good and established teachers. Help me, Jesus, to hear your voice and to accept your authority as you seek to lead me to life.

Wednesday September 1
Luke 4:38–44

After leaving the synagogue he entered Simon's house. Now Simon's mother-in-law was suffering from a high fever, and they asked him about her. Then he stood over her and rebuked the fever, and it left her. Immediately she got up and began to serve them.

As the sun was setting, all those who had any who were sick with various kinds of diseases brought them to him; and he laid his hands on each of them and cured them. Demons also came out of many, shouting, "You are the Son of God!" But he rebuked them and would not allow them to speak, because they knew that he was the Messiah.

At daybreak he departed and went into a deserted place. And the crowds were looking for him; and when they reached him, they wanted to prevent him from leaving them. But he said to them, "I must proclaim the good news of the kingdom of God to the other cities also; for I was sent for this purpose." So he continued proclaiming the message in the synagogues of Judea.

- We are always impressed by the amount of space given in the Gospels to the healing ministry of Jesus. Today we see him healing a woman in her home and then continuing to cure all those who were brought to him. The people knew that if you brought a sick person to Jesus, he would be healed. Let me bring some people I know need healing to Jesus, asking him to cure them, to free them from the sickness or the evil that inhabits them.

Thursday September 2
Luke 5:1–11

Once while Jesus was standing beside the lake of Gennesaret, and the crowd was pressing in on him to hear the word of God, he saw two boats there at the shore of the lake; the fishermen had gone out of them and were washing their nets. He got into one of the boats, the one belonging to Simon, and asked him to put out a little way from the shore. Then he sat down and taught the crowds from the boat. When he had finished speaking, he said to Simon, "Put out into the deep water and let down your nets for a catch." Simon answered, "Master, we have worked all night long but have caught nothing. Yet if you say so, I will let down the nets." When they had done this, they caught so many fish that their nets were beginning to break. So they signaled to their partners in the other boat to come and help them. And they came and filled both boats, so that they began to sink. But when Simon Peter saw it, he fell down at Jesus' knees, saying, "Go away from me, Lord, for I am a sinful man!" For he and all who were with him were amazed at the catch of fish that they had taken; and so also were James and John, sons of Zebedee, who were partners with Simon. Then Jesus said to Simon, "Do not be afraid; from now on you will be catching people." When they had brought their boats to shore, they left everything and followed him.

- Peter knows better than Jesus. Are there occasions when I believe that life should be different for myself or others, that God should have arranged things differently? I think of occasions when I was thinking in this way and speak to the Lord about them.

- "Do not be afraid." What do I fear at the moment? I speak to Jesus about these fears.

- "They left everything and followed him." What have I left in order to follow Jesus? What do I find difficult at the moment to leave in order to follow him more closely?

Friday September 3
Luke 5:33–39

Then they said to him, "John's disciples, like the disciples of the Pharisees, frequently fast and pray, but your disciples eat and drink." Jesus said to them, "You cannot make wedding-guests fast while the bridegroom is with them, can you? The days will come when the bridegroom will be taken away from them, and then they will fast in those days." He also told them a parable: "No one tears a piece from a new garment and sews it on an old garment; otherwise the new will be torn, and the piece from the new will not match the old. And no one puts new wine into old wineskins; otherwise the new wine will burst the skins and will be spilled, and the skins will be destroyed. But new wine must be put into fresh wineskins. And no one after drinking old wine desires new wine, but says, 'The old is good.'"

- Many of us lament that that the Jews and Christians, religious cousins, have had such a poor relationship with such dreadful consequences. The old wineskins of the old Testament did not manage to accommodate the new wine of Jesus' message.

- How often do I pray for a reconciliation of the two faiths? Do I take steps to understand and work for greater harmony between them? Do I try to see the situation from the Jewish point of view? I speak to the Lord about this.

Saturday September 4
Luke 6:1–5

One sabbath while Jesus was going through the cornfields, his disciples plucked some heads of grain, rubbed them in their hands, and ate them. But some of the Pharisees said, "Why are you doing what is not lawful on the sabbath?" Jesus answered, "Have you not read what David did when he and his companions were hungry? He entered the house of God and took and ate the bread of the Presence, which it is not lawful for any but the priests to eat, and gave some to his companions?" Then he said to them, "The Son of Man is lord of the sabbath."

- A simple natural action loses its innocence before judgmental scrutiny. Jesus takes a longer view, placing the snacking disciples in the context of their history, inviting the Pharisees to recognize the even longer timeline of God's plan. I pray for the wisdom to know how to place my priorities in the context of God's patient love.

- Jesus invites the Pharisees to recognize that there is more than meets the eye. If I find myself like the Pharisees in judging, I pray that I may be like them too in asking what Jesus thinks.

The Twenty-Third Week in Ordinary Time
September 5–11, 2021

Something to think and pray about each day this week:

Pope St. Paul VI, in an oft-quoted phrase, said that the people of today listen more to witnesses than to teachers, and if they listen to teachers it is because they are witnesses. To expand on this idea, one might say that those who wish to share the Gospel must somehow incarnate the Gospel in their own lives and personalities. They must mirror something of the attractiveness of Christ. What was it that drew people to Jesus of Nazareth? Was it his compassion, his mercy, his understanding, his kindness, his joy, his patience? It was surely all of these and much more besides. Somehow, he communicated love to them, and they sensed in him the presence of the ultimate source of all love, the one whom he addressed as "Abba, Father." Christ-like people who by a combination of the gifts of nature and grace can reproduce something of that in their own lives and in their manner of relation to others will surely make the best evangelizers.

—Aidan Ryan, *Pastoral Ministry in Changing Times*

The Presence of God

What is present to me is what has a hold on my becoming.
I reflect on the presence of God always there in love,
amidst the many things that have a hold on me.
I pause and pray that I may let God
affect my becoming in this precise moment.

Freedom

By God's grace I was born to live in freedom. Free to enjoy the pleasures
he created for me. Dear Lord, grant that I may live as you intended, with
complete confidence in your loving care.

Consciousness

I exist in a web of relationships: links to nature, people, God.
I give thanks for the life that flows through them.
Some links are twisted or broken; I may feel regret, anger, disappointment.
I pray for the gift of acceptance and forgiveness.

The Word

God speaks to each of us individually. I listen attentively to hear what he
is saying to me. Read the text a few times, then listen. (*Please turn to the
Scripture on the following pages. Inspiration points are there, should you need
them. When you are ready, return here to continue.*)

Conversation

I begin to talk with Jesus about the Scripture I have just read. What part
of it strikes a chord in me? Perhaps the words of a friend—or some story
I have heard recently—will rise to the surface in my consciousness. If so,
does the story throw light on what the Scripture passage may be saying
to me?

Conclusion

Glory be to the Father, and to the Son, and to the Holy Spirit,
As it was in the beginning, is now, and ever shall be,
World without end. Amen.

Sunday September 5
Twenty-Third Sunday in Ordinary Time
Mark 7:31–37

Then he returned from the region of Tyre, and went by way of Sidon toward the Sea of Galilee, in the region of the Decapolis. They brought to him a deaf man who had an impediment in his speech; and they begged him to lay his hand on him. He took him aside in private, away from the crowd, and put his fingers into his ears, and he spat and touched his tongue. Then looking up to heaven, he sighed and said to him, "Ephphatha," that is, "Be opened." And immediately his ears were opened, his tongue was released, and he spoke plainly. Then Jesus ordered them to tell no one; but the more he ordered them, the more zealously they proclaimed it. They were astounded beyond measure, saying, "He has done everything well; he even makes the deaf to hear and the mute to speak."

- The prophet Isaiah had forewarned the people that the occurrence of cures and miracles of all kinds would be the sign that the age of Messiah had dawned. "He will come and save you. Then the eyes of the blind shall be opened, and the ears of the deaf unstopped" (Isaiah 35:4–5).

- Jesus tries to bind the onlookers to silence about his identity. The Messiah expected by the Jews was a political/military as well as religious figure, so he was probably unwilling to use such a title, at least without some qualifications, to avoid provoking the Roman authorities.

Monday September 6
Luke 6:6–11

On another sabbath he entered the synagogue and taught, and there was a man there whose right hand was withered. The scribes and the Pharisees watched him to see whether he would cure on the sabbath, so that they might find an accusation against him. Even though he knew what they were thinking, he said to the man who had the withered hand, "Come and stand here." He got up and stood there. Then Jesus said to them, "I ask you, is it lawful to do good or to do harm on the sabbath, to save life or to destroy it?" After looking around at all of them, he said to him, "Stretch out your hand." He did so, and his hand was restored. But they were filled with fury and discussed with one another what they might do to Jesus.

- We are shocked by the reaction of the scribes and Pharisees to Jesus, both before and after the cure of the man with the withered hand. But I am also aware of the danger of closing my own heart to the suffering of others and even to the presence of God in Jesus for similar reasons. I look at Jesus and ask to have his compassionate heart, so sensitive and free when faced with human suffering.

- The authorities were furious at the man's cure and immediately started to discuss how they could stop Jesus. I pray for the pope and for all religious leaders that they may always know how to respond in an evangelical way to whatever is new and may appear shocking.

Tuesday September 7
Luke 6:12–19

Now during those days he went out to the mountain to pray; and he spent the night in prayer to God. And when day came, he called his disciples and chose twelve of them, whom he also named apostles: Simon, whom he named Peter, and his brother Andrew, and James, and John, and Philip, and Bartholomew, and Matthew, and Thomas, and James son of Alphaeus, and Simon, who was called the Zealot, and Judas son of James, and Judas Iscariot, who became a traitor.

He came down with them and stood on a level place, with a great crowd of his disciples and a great multitude of people from all Judea, Jerusalem, and the coast of Tyre and Sidon. They had come to hear him and to be healed of their diseases; and those who were troubled with unclean spirits were cured. And all in the crowd were trying to touch him, for power came out from him and healed all of them.

- In today's Gospel passage, Jesus prayed before he chose his twelve apostles. When you are making decisions, especially important ones that will have a bearing on your life, it's not easy if you feel lonely and unable to make up your mind. Always turn to the Holy Spirit for guidance—that means you will be supported by the three persons in God who will help with your thinking.

- In our prayer we ask for so many things—just like the people in today's Gospel, turning to the love of God shown to them in Jesus. Prayer gives a flavor to your life and a sense of belonging that carries you nearer to God.

Wednesday September 8
The Nativity of the Blessed Virgin Mary
Matthew 1:1–16, 18–23

An account of the genealogy of Jesus the Messiah, the son of David, the son of Abraham.

Abraham was the father of Isaac, and Isaac the father of Jacob, and Jacob the father of Judah and his brothers, and Judah the father of Perez and Zerah by Tamar, and Perez the father of Hezron, and Hezron the father of Aram, and Aram the father of Aminadab, and Aminadab the father of Nahshon, and Nahshon the father of Salmon, and Salmon the father of Boaz by Rahab, and Boaz the father of Obed by Ruth, and Obed the father of Jesse, and Jesse the father of King David.

And David was the father of Solomon by the wife of Uriah, and Solomon the father of Rehoboam, and Rehoboam the father of Abijah, and Abijah the father of Asaph, and Asaph the father of Jehoshaphat, and Jehoshaphat the father of Joram, and Joram the father of Uzziah, and Uzziah the father of Jotham, and Jotham the father of Ahaz, and Ahaz the father of Hezekiah, and Hezekiah the father of Manasseh, and Manasseh the father of Amos, and Amos the father of Josiah, and Josiah the father of Jechoniah and his brothers, at the time of the deportation to Babylon.

And after the deportation to Babylon: Jechoniah was the father of Salathiel, and Salathiel the father of Zerubbabel, and Zerubbabel the father of Abiud, and Abiud the father of Eliakim, and Eliakim the father of Azor, and Azor the father of Zadok, and Zadok the father of Achim, and Achim the father of Eliud, and Eliud the father of Eleazar, and Eleazar the father of Matthan, and Matthan the father of Jacob, and Jacob the father of Joseph the husband of Mary, of whom Jesus was born, who is called the Messiah. . . .

Now the birth of Jesus the Messiah took place in this way. When his mother Mary had been engaged to Joseph, but before they lived together, she was found to be with child from the Holy Spirit. Her husband Joseph, being a righteous man and unwilling to expose her to public disgrace, planned to dismiss her quietly. But just when he had resolved to do this, an angel of the Lord appeared to him in a dream and said, "Joseph, son of David, do not be afraid to take Mary as your wife, for the child conceived in her is from the Holy Spirit. She will bear a son, and you are to name him Jesus, for he will save his people from their sins." All this took place to fulfill what had been spoken by the Lord through the prophet:

"Look, the virgin shall conceive and bear a son,
and they shall name him Emmanuel,"
which means, "God is with us."

• The genealogy of Jesus is sometimes considered a difficult passage of Scripture to comprehend. A question that this passage raises is: Was God less with the Jews in their defeats and subjection than he was in their glory days? Do I believe that God is as close to me when I am in difficulties as when all is seemingly well?

Thursday September 9
Luke 6:27–38

"But I say to you that listen, Love your enemies, do good to those who hate you, bless those who curse you, pray for those who abuse you. If anyone strikes you on the cheek, offer the other also; and from anyone who takes away your coat do not withhold even your shirt. Give to everyone who begs from you; and if anyone takes away your goods, do not ask for them again. Do to others as you would have them do to you.

"If you love those who love you, what credit is that to you? For even sinners love those who love them. If you do good to those who do good to you, what credit is that to you? For even sinners do the same. If you lend to those from whom you hope to receive, what credit is that to you? Even sinners lend to sinners, to receive as much again. But love your enemies, do good, and lend, expecting nothing in return. Your reward will be great, and you will be children of the Most High; for he is kind to the ungrateful and the wicked. Be merciful, just as your Father is merciful.

"Do not judge, and you will not be judged; do not condemn, and you will not be condemned. Forgive, and you will be forgiven; give, and it will be given to you. A good measure, pressed down, shaken together, running over, will be put into your lap; for the measure you give will be the measure you get back."

• This text ranks as one of the most extraordinary passages ever written! It utterly reverses human thinking about enemies and forgiveness. It spells out the way God goes about things, holding nothing against us despite all our failings. This is how Jesus lived; this is how he died for his executioners. His attitude of heart was blessed by his Father and brought him into eternal life.

- My world can be transformed if I take Jesus seriously. My task is to collaborate with him and to live on a higher level of loving than I had imagined possible. I am called to go beyond loving my neighbor as myself, beyond loving only those who love me, beyond loving only nice people. I am to love my enemies, do good to them, pray for them, wish them well! What then shall I pray for now?

Friday September 10
Luke 6:39–42

He also told them a parable: "Can a blind person guide a blind person? Will not both fall into a pit? A disciple is not above the teacher, but everyone who is fully qualified will be like the teacher. Why do you see the speck in your neighbor's eye, but do not notice the log in your own eye? Or how can you say to your neighbor, 'Friend, let me take out the speck in your eye,' when you yourself do not see the log in your own eye? You hypocrite, first take the log out of your own eye, and then you will see clearly to take the speck out of your neighbor's eye."

- If you go about with a plank in your eye, surely it is difficult not to see splinters everywhere! As I review my conversations, I notice where I am critical. I listen again and ask forgiveness as I realize my own weakness.
- What teachers have shaped me most? I give thanks for their influence and effect in my life and wonder how I am like them. If I am aware of those who have led me astray, I pray for them and, in my turn, ask forgiveness.

Saturday September 11
Luke 6:43–49

"No good tree bears bad fruit, nor again does a bad tree bear good fruit; for each tree is known by its own fruit. Figs are not gathered from thorns, nor are grapes picked from a bramble bush. The good person out of the good treasure of the heart produces good, and the evil person out of evil treasure produces evil; for it is out of the abundance of the heart that the mouth speaks.

"Why do you call me 'Lord, Lord,' and do not do what I tell you? I will show you what someone is like who comes to me, hears my words, and acts on them. That one is like a man building a house, who dug deeply and laid the foundation on rock; when a flood arose, the river burst against that house but could not shake it, because it had been well built. But the one who hears and does not act is like a man who built a house on the ground without a foundation. When the river burst against it, immediately it fell, and great was the ruin of that house."

- What is "the good treasure" in my heart? Have I any treasure there at all? I need to look inside and search around: then I will find that my treasure is God, who dwells in my heart always. How do I know that God is there? Because Jesus has promised (John 14:23) that he and his Father will come and make his home with those who try to keep his word. As a member of the Sacred Space community, I try to keep his word.

- Thomas Merton writes: "At the center of our being is a point of nothingness which is untouched by sin and by illusion; a point or spark which belongs entirely to God. It is the pure glory of God in us." This is my good treasure!

Something to think and pray about each day this week:

The Virgin Mary has touched more people than any other woman in history, and for many reasons. She symbolizes maternal love, is an accessible avenue to God, understands suffering. Catherine de Hueck Doherty, a refugee from the Russian Revolution who served the poor of Toronto and New York, expressed it like this: "She possesses the secret of prayer, the secret of wisdom, for she is the Mother of God. Who else can teach you to burn with the fire of love except the Mother of fair love? Who else can teach you to pray except the woman of prayer? Who else can teach you to go through the silence of deserts and nights, the silence of pain and sorrow, the solitude of joy and gladness, except the woman wrapped in silence?"

Although Mary spoke only a handful of times in the New Testament, her personality and character have spoken to countless believers ever since. Mary draws millions of people to shrines across the world. In addition to Guadalupe, Lourdes, and Fatima, there are many other Marian shrines around the world that attract believers of other faiths.

Mary's life was about a yes in reply to a love beyond all her dreams of love, in response to a gift. She received the gift of an encounter with God who drew so near to her that the human flesh of his only-begotten Son was knitted together in her womb. At the heart of Mary's life was this love story with God, a love story that ideally can be at the heart of our lives as well.

Like any good mother, Mary gets us in touch with the affective dimension of our lives and frees us up to be receptive to God. The first step to God is not a matter of theory. Neither is it an exercise in willpower alone. More often it's about opening up the basic flow of our lives so that we are ready to move toward trust, goodness, and love. Encountering the depth of Mary is a humbling invitation to live out of the depths of ourselves.

—Thomas G. Casey, SJ, *Mary in Different Traditions*

The Presence of God

"Come to me, all you who are weary and are carrying heavy burdens, and I will give you rest." Here I am, Lord. I come to seek your presence. I long for your healing power.

Freedom

God is not foreign to my freedom. The Spirit breathes life into my most intimate desires, gently nudging me toward all that is good. I ask for the grace to let myself be enfolded by the Spirit.

Consciousness

I remind myself that I am in the presence of the Lord. I will take refuge in his loving heart. He is my strength in times of weakness. He is my comforter in times of sorrow.

The Word

I take my time to read the word of God slowly, a few times, allowing myself to dwell on anything that strikes me. (*Please turn to the Scripture on the following pages. Inspiration points are there, should you need them. When you are ready, return here to continue.*)

Conversation

Jesus, you always welcomed little children when you walked on this earth. Teach me to have a childlike trust in you. Teach me to live in the knowledge that you will never abandon me.

Conclusion

Glory be to the Father, and to the Son, and to the Holy Spirit,
As it was in the beginning, is now, and ever shall be,
World without end. Amen.

Sunday September 12
Twenty-Fourth Sunday in Ordinary Time
Mark 8:27–35

Jesus went on with his disciples to the villages of Caesarea Philippi; and on the way he asked his disciples, "Who do people say that I am?" And they answered him, "John the Baptist; and others, Elijah; and still others, one of the prophets." He asked them, "But who do you say that I am?" Peter answered him, "You are the Messiah." And he sternly ordered them not to tell anyone about him.

Then he began to teach them that the Son of Man must undergo great suffering, and be rejected by the elders, the chief priests, and the scribes, and be killed, and after three days rise again. He said all this quite openly. And Peter took him aside and began to rebuke him. But turning and looking at his disciples, he rebuked Peter and said, "Get behind me, Satan! For you are setting your mind not on divine things but on human things."

He called the crowd with his disciples, and said to them, "If any want to become my followers, let them deny themselves and take up their cross and follow me. For those who want to save their life will lose it, and those who lose their life for my sake, and for the sake of the gospel, will save it."

- This crucial moment draws the first half of Mark's Gospel to a close. Jesus is not a triumphant but a suffering Messiah. On a surface level, Peter gets Jesus' identity right. But he is reprimanded for his earthbound vision: he seeks to bend Jesus' words and ways to his own all too human thinking. He learns that compromise has no place in Jesus' life.

- Lord, your question to the disciples echoes down the centuries, and I hear it addressed now to me. Strengthen the bonds between us. May our relationship influence my living. Keep me close behind you, as I pick up the crosses and burdens that come from being your disciple.

Monday September 13
Luke 7:1–10

After Jesus had finished all his sayings in the hearing of the people, he entered Capernaum. A centurion there had a slave whom he valued highly, and who was ill and close to death. When he heard about Jesus, he sent some Jewish elders to him, asking him to come and heal his slave. When they came to Jesus, they appealed to him earnestly, saying, "He is worthy of having you do this for him, for he loves our people, and it is he who built our synagogue for us." And Jesus went with them, but when he was not far from the house, the centurion sent friends to say to him, "Lord, do not trouble yourself, for I am not worthy to have you come under my roof; therefore I did not presume to come to you. But only speak the word, and let my servant be healed. For I also am a man set under authority, with soldiers under me; and I say to one, 'Go,' and he goes, and to another, 'Come,' and he comes, and to my slave, 'Do this,' and the slave does it." When Jesus heard this he was amazed at him, and turning to the crowd that followed him, he said, "I tell you, not even in Israel have I found such faith." When those who had been sent returned to the house, they found the slave in good health.

- Jesus is astonished: he is unused to finding such faith and rejoices where he finds freedom. I can pray for the freedom I need to show faith, trust, or humility—even when it is least expected.

- Jesus allows himself to identify with someone who speaks of "our people." Surely he values the generosity and openness of the speaker, glad that it is not used in a narrow or exclusive way. Seeing how Jesus is able to welcome the faith of the stranger and see in it an example, I pray that I may look again at those I consider different and learn from their ways.

Tuesday September 14
The Exaltation of the Holy Cross
John 3:13–17

"No one has ascended into heaven except the one who descended from heaven, the Son of Man. And just as Moses lifted up the serpent in the wilderness, so must the Son of Man be lifted up, that whoever believes in him may have eternal life.

"For God so loved the world that he gave his only Son, so that everyone who believes in him may not perish but may have eternal life.

"Indeed, God did not send the Son into the world to condemn the world, but in order that the world might be saved through him."

- On Good Friday we are caught up with the suffering and death of Jesus and the cost to him of losing his life in such a painful way. Today, the Feast of the Exaltation of the Holy Cross, we celebrate his great love for us as shown in that act of suffering, and we praise him in thanksgiving for thinking of us in this way. Greater love than this no one can have; it is the ultimate expression of love.

- Our thanksgiving is best shown in our attempts to live by the values of Jesus and to appreciate that he is our way, our truth, and our life.

Wednesday September 15
John 19:25–27

Meanwhile, standing near the cross of Jesus were his mother, and his mother's sister, Mary the wife of Clopas, and Mary Magdalene. When Jesus saw his mother and the disciple whom he loved standing beside her, he said to his mother, "Woman, here is your son." Then he said to the disciple, "Here is your mother." And from that hour the disciple took her into his own home.

- Mary was there at the most important moments of Jesus' life, so she had to be under the cross too. I try to imagine her deep confusion at what is going on, her reaction as Jesus asks her for more love and openness to others in this moment of such deep suffering.

- I bring to mind some situations of terrible suffering, situations of interpersonal conflict or of war that have been going on for years. I bring them to the cross, asking Mary to teach me to feel sorrow at such suffering, a sorrow that is illuminated by faithful trust and compassionate love.

Thursday September 16
Luke 7:36–50

One of the Pharisees asked Jesus to eat with him, and he went into the Pharisee's house and took his place at the table. And a woman in the city, who was a sinner, having learned that he was eating in the Pharisee's house, brought an alabaster jar of ointment. She stood behind him at his feet, weeping, and began to bathe his feet with her tears and to dry them with her hair. Then she continued kissing his feet and anointing them with the ointment. Now when the Pharisee who had invited him saw it, he said to himself, "If this man were a prophet, he would have known who and what kind of woman this is who is touching him—that she is a sinner." Jesus spoke up and said to him, "Simon, I have something to say to you." "Teacher," he replied, "speak." "A certain creditor had two debtors; one owed five hundred denarii, and the other fifty. When they could not pay, he canceled the debts for both of them. Now which of them will love him more?" Simon answered, "I suppose the one for whom he canceled the greater debt." And Jesus said to him, "You have judged rightly." Then turning toward the woman, he said to Simon, "Do you see this woman? I entered your house; you gave me no water for my feet, but she has bathed my feet with her tears and dried them with her hair. You gave me no kiss, but from the time I came in she has not stopped kissing my feet. You did not anoint my head with oil, but she has anointed my feet with ointment. Therefore, I tell you, her sins, which were many, have been forgiven; hence she has shown great love. But the one to whom little is forgiven, loves little." Then he said to her, "Your sins are forgiven." But those who were at the table with him began to say among themselves, "Who is this who even forgives sins?" And he said to the woman, "Your faith has saved you; go in peace."

- The extravagant gesture made by this woman is hard for us to understand. Yet it is her way of trying to say thanks for whatever she must have received from Jesus. Simon, on the other hand, not knowing the lovely interior movements of her heart, judges her by the external knowledge that he has of her. Jesus goes to great trouble to tell Simon the deeper meaning of her actions and how much he appreciates her response.

- Have you ever been misjudged for something you did? It's very hurtful. We can always ask the Lord to help us not to judge others too quickly. It gives you an inner spirit of freedom when you are charitable in thought about others.

Friday September 17
Luke 8:1–3

Soon afterwards he went on through cities and villages, proclaiming and bringing the good news of the kingdom of God. The twelve were with him, as well as some women who had been cured of evil spirits and infirmities: Mary, called Magdalene, from whom seven demons had gone out, and Joanna, the wife of Herod's steward Chuza, and Susanna, and many others, who provided for them out of their resources.

- We know little about Susanna and Joanna other than that that they were happy to follow Jesus and were recognized by Luke as disciples. I think of all those quiet disciples whose lives and prayer have contributed to the Church but who have left little evident legacy. I pray for all who support others through their presence—especially women—that they may draw encouragement from knowing how Jesus sees, recognizes, and loves their humble service.

Saturday September 18
Luke 8:4–15

When a great crowd gathered and people from town after town came to him, he said in a parable: "A sower went out to sow his seed; and as he sowed, some fell on the path and was trampled on, and the birds of the air ate it up. Some fell on the rock; and as it grew up, it withered for lack of moisture. Some fell among thorns, and the thorns grew with it and choked it. Some fell into good soil, and when it grew, it produced a hundredfold." As he said this, he called out, "Let anyone with ears to hear listen!"

Then his disciples asked him what this parable meant. He said, "To you it has been given to know the secrets of the kingdom of God; but to others I speak in parables, so that

'looking they may not perceive,
    and listening they may not understand.'

"Now the parable is this: The seed is the word of God. The ones on the path are those who have heard; then the devil comes and takes away the word from their hearts, so that they may not believe and be saved. The ones on the rock are those who, when they hear the word, receive it with joy. But these have no root; they believe only for a while and in a time of testing fall away. As for what fell among the thorns, these are the ones who hear; but as they go on their way, they are choked by the cares and riches and pleasures of life, and their fruit does not mature. But as for that in the good soil, these are the ones who, when they hear the word, hold it fast in an honest and good heart, and bear fruit with patient endurance."

- The first thing here is to spend time looking at the sower, who provides a picture of what God is like. The sower is energetic; he has work to do. He is lavish, non-calculating, generous, extravagant, even—it seems—wasteful. He does not worry that some seed will be lost. We can imagine that he is happy as he goes along. This is what God is like!

- God sows seed in my heart every day through Sacred Space. God does not get annoyed if I ignore the word today: he will go out and sow more words tomorrow if need be. The heart of the Good News is hidden here: it reveals that this is the sort of person God is: tireless, inexhaustible in loving. God never stops giving and does not count the cost. Joy and gratitude well up in me for this, and I thank God for such goodness to me.

The Twenty-Fifth Week in Ordinary Time
September 19–25 2021

Something to think and pray about each day this week:

Ignatius believed, on the basis of his own experience, that when we go beyond all the outward appearances of our lives, and beyond all the various roles we play, we will discover our deepest desires, which coincide with God's hopes for us, in the way that parents have hopes for their child. This is understood as God's will for a person, as opposed to the false idea that God is the puppet master, pulling the strings in conformity with the script. This idea of God implies the absence of human freedom and portrays a God in whom it is impossible to trust or believe. In this understanding of God, my friend who gets knocked down by a car is playing out a pre-ordained role in conformity with God's script. What kind of absurd God is that? Yet, sadly, there are many who believe in such a God! Unfortunately, it's often the case that when a person says they do not believe in God, what they really mean is that they do not believe in misleading images of God that any sensible person would reject.

The novelty of Ignatius is that God speaks to us in the depths of our heart through our desires, thoughts, and feelings. It's as if we are hard-wired to be like God, but for all kinds of increasingly complex reasons, the truth of our existence can evade us. What Ignatius calls disordered desires can get the better of us: pride, greed, fear, perfectionism, the insatiable appetite for instant affirmation generated by social media, over-stimulation, the expectation of 24/7 availability, failure to realize that we are stewards of creation and not its owner, obsession with prestige and status, the "I have more than you" syndrome, and all the other attractions that draw us away from God, ourselves, and others, leaving us in a state of emotional turbulence, excitement, and exhaustion.

My worth as a person is not determined by what I have.

—Jim Maher, SJ, *What's It All About?*

The Presence of God

As I sit here, the beating of my heart,
the ebb and flow of my breathing, the movements of my mind
are all signs of God's ongoing creation of me.
I pause for a moment and become aware
of this presence of God within me.

Freedom

It is so easy to get caught up with the trappings of wealth in this life.
Grant, O Lord, that I may be free from greed and selfishness.
Remind me that the best things in life are free:
Love, laughter, caring, and sharing.

Consciousness

Knowing that God loves me unconditionally,
I can afford to be honest about how I am.
How has the day been, and how do I feel now?
I share my feelings openly with the Lord.

The Word

Lord Jesus, you became human to communicate with me.
You walked and worked on this earth.
You endured the heat and struggled with the cold.
All your time on this earth was spent in caring for humanity.
You healed the sick, you raised the dead.
Most important of all, you saved me from death.
(*Please turn to the Scripture on the following pages. Inspiration points are
there, should you need them. When you are ready, return here to continue.*)

Conversation

I wonder what I might say if I were to meet you in person, Lord.
I think I might say, "Thank you" because you are always there for me.

Conclusion

I thank God for these moments we have spent together and for any insights I have been given concerning the text.

Sunday September 19
Twenty-Fifth Sunday in Ordinary Time
Mark 9:30–37

They went on from there and passed through Galilee. He did not want anyone to know it; for he was teaching his disciples, saying to them, "The Son of Man is to be betrayed into human hands, and they will kill him, and three days after being killed, he will rise again." But they did not understand what he was saying and were afraid to ask him.

Then they came to Capernaum; and when he was in the house he asked them, "What were you arguing about on the way?" But they were silent, for on the way they had argued with one another about who was the greatest. He sat down, called the twelve, and said to them, "Whoever wants to be first must be last of all and servant of all." Then he took a little child and put it among them; and taking it in his arms, he said to them, "Whoever welcomes one such child in my name welcomes me, and whoever welcomes me welcomes not me but the one who sent me."

- Jesus could have eradicated evil from our world; he could have annihilated his enemies. It is a mystery to us that he chose another way. He endured all that the world threw at him and responded to it with great love, and so he helps us cope with our misery. Though that is admirable, however, it is not enough. So in warning his disciples about his passion, note that he always adds in his resurrection. In the Gospels, there is no passion without resurrection. Suffering and death are linked solidly to life after death. The two are opposite sides of the one coin. Evil plays out its role and is finally encompassed by eternal life and joy. God has the last word: divine love conquers all.

Monday September 20
Luke 8:16–18

"No one after lighting a lamp hides it under a jar, or puts it under a bed, but puts it on a lampstand, so that those who enter may see the light. For nothing is hidden that will not be disclosed, nor is anything secret that will not become known and come to light. Then pay attention to how you listen; for to those who have, more will be given; and from those who do not have, even what they seem to have will be taken away."

- Each of the sayings here concerns the role of the disciple. There can be no anonymous discipleship. The gospel calls us to live in light and truth, no matter what the cost. Secret discipleship is a contradiction in terms, for either the secrecy kills the discipleship or the discipleship kills the secrecy.

- Lord, to be a Christian today is challenging. In times of struggle I am tempted to hide my light, to remain anonymous, to be silent out of shame. Lord, when the wick of my lamp flickers and fades, strengthen its beam and let me be again a light-bearer, a beacon of hope to all I daily encounter.

Tuesday September 21
St. Matthew, Apostle and Evangelist
Matthew 9:9–13

As Jesus was walking along, he saw a man called Matthew sitting at the tax booth; and he said to him, "Follow me." And he got up and followed him.

And as he sat at dinner in the house, many tax-collectors and sinners came and were sitting with him and his disciples. When the Pharisees saw this, they said to his disciples, "Why does your teacher eat with tax-collectors and sinners?" But when he heard this, he said, "Those who are well have no need of a physician, but those who are sick. Go and learn what this means, 'I desire mercy, not sacrifice.' For I have come to call not the righteous but sinners."

- Jesus is inclusive; even "tax collectors and sinners" are welcomed. They represent those whose professions and social status are not respectable. But Jesus shows that he has come for all people, without exception, and especially the weak and the vulnerable, the "sick" and the "sinner."

- How inclusive and compassionate Jesus is in his ministry! I ask myself if I am prejudiced against any individuals or groups. Lord, help me become more like you in thought, word, and deed. Make me large-hearted.

Wednesday September 22

Luke 9:1–6

Then Jesus called the twelve together and gave them power and authority over all demons and to cure diseases, and he sent them out to proclaim the kingdom of God and to heal. He said to them, "Take nothing for your journey, no staff, nor bag, nor bread, nor money—not even an extra tunic. Whatever house you enter, stay there, and leave from there. Wherever they do not welcome you, as you are leaving that town shake the dust off your feet as a testimony against them." They departed and went through the villages, bringing the good news and curing diseases everywhere.

- This is a very frightening text if taken literally. It seems to mean that people who offer themselves fully to the Lord will be provided for by God through the kindness of others. St. Francis of Assisi gave up his inheritance through his wonderful relationship with the Lord. Many good people who set out to do things for God frequently have to resort to the prayer—if God wants it, he will provide.

- If we can live in the spirit of realizing that God does provide everything that we have, then we learn that there is nothing we have not received, and the prayer of thanksgiving takes on a deeper meaning.

Thursday September 23

Luke 9:7–9

Now Herod the ruler heard about all that had taken place, and he was perplexed, because it was said by some that John had been raised from the dead, by some that Elijah had appeared, and by others that one of the ancient prophets had arisen. Herod said, "John I beheaded; but who is this about whom I hear such things?" And he tried to see him.

- The Gospel today brings to light a very important point: to simply know about somebody is very different from actually knowing them personally. Through the gift of grace we can know Jesus, and our prayer is our communication with a friend, not with an acquaintance. If you are blessed in having some close friends, then you understand the difference. Recall the words of Jesus, "I do not call you servants any longer . . . I have called you friends" (John 15:15). You are never alone when you return his offer of friendship.

Friday September 24
Luke 9:18–22

Once when Jesus was praying alone, with only the disciples near him, he asked them, "Who do the crowds say that I am?" They answered, "John the Baptist; but others, Elijah; and still others, that one of the ancient prophets has arisen." He said to them, "But who do you say that I am?" Peter answered, "The Messiah of God."

He sternly ordered and commanded them not to tell anyone, saying, "The Son of Man must undergo great suffering, and be rejected by the elders, chief priests, and scribes, and be killed, and on the third day be raised."

- Did you ever wonder about what Jesus talked about when he was with his Father in prayer? Here we might assume that he was talking about his mission and so, when he was finished, he asked the apostles what people thought about him. Peter gives him a strange answer. But the apostles themselves are clear that he was sent by God as the Messiah, and Peter is able to say this in true belief.

- Our life of faith is based on the fact that we ourselves have made this confession of faith in Jesus. The Lord appreciates very much our act of faith in him, especially when we thank him for the depth of the love he has shown through his Passion, death, and resurrection. This is the space out of which we make our prayer to God—from a place of thanksgiving in our hearts.

Saturday September 25
Luke 9:43b–45

While everyone was amazed at all that he was doing, he said to his disciples, "Let these words sink into your ears: The Son of Man is going to be betrayed into human hands." But they did not understand this saying; its meaning was concealed from them, so that they could not perceive it. And they were afraid to ask him about this saying.

- The disciples need some inspiration points here! They cannot take in the fact that Jesus will be betrayed. Why would anyone betray him when he is doing so much good and is at the height of his powers and so popular? But when I feel myself betrayed, then I am glad that his life took this form. So many people experience betrayal, and the lives of others are cut short, as his was, by the malice of evil people. I am strengthened by the fact that the Son of God knows the anguish from personal experience and that he has grappled with it and brought great good out of it by his love.

- Lord, when things go badly wrong and I am discouraged, remind me of your Passion. Then I will be able to continue, in the belief that you have radically defeated the evil of the world from the inside.

September 26—October 2, 2021

Something to think and pray about each day this week:

There is an essential wisdom in . . . the constant challenge to find the balance between having sustainability (keeping ourselves strong, safe, and well) and output (impacting on the world and those around us) is one that we face daily, both as individuals and as groups of people.

If we focus too much on ourselves and our own sustainability, we can become self-obsessed and introspective. We won't let our voices of love, joy, and mercy be heard by those who might just need to hear them.

Too much volume and output into the world without taking care of sustainability might mean that we will be prone to burn-out. We might also put people off because our own volume and actions might crowd out the voices or actions of others; we might just miss some of the richness others have to offer.

—Brendan McManus, SJ, and Jim Deeds, *Deeper into the Mess:*
Praying Through Tough Times

The Presence of God
At any time of the day or night we can call on Jesus.
He is always waiting, listening for our call.
What a wonderful blessing. No phone needed, no e-mails, just a whisper.

Freedom
If God were trying to tell me something, would I know?
If God were reassuring me or challenging me, would I notice?
I ask for the grace to be free of my own preoccupations
and open to what God may be saying to me.

Consciousness
Help me, Lord, to become more conscious of your presence. Teach me
to recognize your presence in others. Fill my heart with gratitude for the
times your love has been shown to me through the care of others.

The Word
In this expectant state of mind, please turn to the text for the day with
confidence. Believe that the Holy Spirit is present and may reveal whatever the passage has to say to you. Read reflectively, listening with a third
ear to what may be going on in your heart. (*Please turn to the Scripture on
the following pages. Inspiration points are there, should you need them. When
you are ready, return here to continue.*)

Conversation
Conversation requires talking and listening.
As I talk to Jesus, may I also learn to pause and listen.
I picture the gentleness in his eyes and the love in his smile.
I can be totally honest with Jesus as I tell him my worries and cares.
I will open my heart to Jesus as I tell him my fears and doubts.
I will ask him to help me place myself fully in his care, knowing that he
always desires good for me.

Conclusion
I thank God for these moments we have spent together and for any insights I have been given concerning the text.

Sunday September 26
Twenty-Sixth Sunday in Ordinary Time
Mark 9:38–43, 45, 47–48

John said to him, "Teacher, we saw someone casting out demons in your name, and we tried to stop him, because he was not following us." But Jesus said, "Do not stop him; for no one who does a deed of power in my name will be able soon afterward to speak evil of me. Whoever is not against us is for us. For truly I tell you, whoever gives you a cup of water to drink because you bear the name of Christ will by no means lose the reward.

"If any of you put a stumbling-block before one of these little ones who believe in me, it would be better for you if a great millstone were hung around your neck and you were thrown into the sea. If your hand causes you to stumble, cut it off; it is better for you to enter life maimed than to have two hands and to go to hell, to the unquenchable fire. . . . And if your foot causes you to stumble, cut it off; it is better for you to enter life lame than to have two feet and to be thrown into hell. . . . And if your eye causes you to stumble, tear it out; it is better for you to enter the kingdom of God with one eye than to have two eyes and to be thrown into hell, where their worm never dies, and the fire is never quenched."

- Discipleship is not some personal privilege to be jealously guarded. We have no monopoly on Jesus. Appreciation of the good deeds done by others is essential. In his kingdom, power-seeking and rivalry have no place: they are obstacles and causes of scandal.

- Lord, self-renunciation and attention to the needs of our brothers and sisters are the hallmarks of belonging to you. You call me to be a stepping stone for others, not a stumbling block.

Monday September 27
Luke 9:46–50

An argument arose among them as to which one of them was the greatest. But Jesus, aware of their inner thoughts, took a little child and put it by his side, and said to them, "Whoever welcomes this child in my name welcomes me, and whoever welcomes me welcomes the one who sent me; for the least among all of you is the greatest."

John answered, "Master, we saw someone casting out demons in your name, and we tried to stop him, because he does not follow with us." But Jesus said to him, "Do not stop him; for whoever is not against you is for you."

- Certificates, titles, recognition, and honors come with the years and may mislead people who don't know what really matters. Being in Jesus' company reminded the disciples of his perspective. What will help me receive Jesus' message now? What does being like a child mean to me?

- John betrays a common human instinct: he separates and distinguishes himself from someone he does not associate with. I engage with Jesus, who saw things differently, and review my ways of thinking about who is "in" and who is "out."

Tuesday September 28
Luke 9:51–56

When the days drew near for him to be taken up, he set his face to go to Jerusalem. And he sent messengers ahead of him. On their way they entered a village of the Samaritans to make ready for him; but they did not receive him, because his face was set toward Jerusalem. When his disciples James and John saw it, they said, "Lord, do you want us to command fire to come down from heaven and consume them?" But he turned and rebuked them. Then they went on to another village.

- The disciples thought, "If only everybody were like us," as they asked Jesus to teach a lesson to the obstinate Samaritans. Even as he had set his face to Jerusalem, Jesus recognized how his followers did not understand his heart. Help me, Jesus, to follow you in humility, to seek your way. Let the logic of my head be tempered by the compassion of your heart.

Wednesday September 29
Ss. Michael, Gabriel and Raphael, Archangels
John 1:47–51

When Jesus saw Nathanael coming toward him, he said of him, "Here is truly an Israelite in whom there is no deceit!" Nathanael asked him,

"Where did you come to know me?" Jesus answered, "I saw you under the fig tree before Philip called you." Nathanael replied, "Rabbi, you are the Son of God! You are the King of Israel!" Jesus answered, "Do you believe because I told you that I saw you under the fig tree? You will see greater things than these." And he said to him, "Very truly, I tell you, you will see heaven opened and the angels of God ascending and descending upon the Son of Man."

- If I came toward you, Lord, what would you say of me? I tremble at the thought. I would wish to show a heart without deceit, and I remember the words of Rumi, the Sufi poet: "In the presence of His Glory, closely watch your heart, so your thoughts won't shame you, for He sees guilt, opinion, and desire as plainly as a hair in pure milk."

Thursday September 30
Luke 10:1–12

After this the Lord appointed seventy others and sent them on ahead of him in pairs to every town and place where he himself intended to go. He said to them, "The harvest is plentiful, but the laborers are few; therefore ask the Lord of the harvest to send out laborers into his harvest. Go on your way. See, I am sending you out like lambs into the midst of wolves. Carry no purse, no bag, no sandals; and greet no one on the road. Whatever house you enter, first say, 'Peace to this house!' And if anyone is there who shares in peace, your peace will rest on that person; but if not, it will return to you. Remain in the same house, eating and drinking whatever they provide, for the laborer deserves to be paid. Do not move about from house to house. Whenever you enter a town and its people welcome you, eat what is set before you; cure the sick who are there, and say to them, 'The kingdom of God has come near to you.' But whenever you enter a town and they do not welcome you, go out into its streets and say, 'Even the dust of your town that clings to our feet, we wipe off in protest against you. Yet know this: the kingdom of God has come near.' I tell you, on that day it will be more tolerable for Sodom than for that town."

- Jesus wanted his disciples to be also apostles; he sent them to take to others what they had heard and experienced. He sent them in pairs, not alone, to all the towns and villages. I read Jesus' instructions slowly and hear him sending me to take the Good News to others, like a sheep among wolves, depending only on him and the power of his word.

- Let your first words be, "Peace to this house!" The spreading of the gospel brings peace, and Jesus once said that peacemakers are blessed because they are children of God. I look at my own life and pray that I may not be deaf to this call to be a peacemaker in this violent and intolerant world.

Friday October 1
Luke 10:13–16

"Woe to you, Chorazin! Woe to you, Bethsaida! For if the deeds of power done in you had been done in Tyre and Sidon, they would have repented long ago, sitting in sackcloth and ashes. But at the judgment it will be more tolerable for Tyre and Sidon than for you. And you, Capernaum, will you be exalted to heaven? No, you will be brought down to Hades.

"Whoever listens to you listens to me, and whoever rejects you rejects me, and whoever rejects me rejects the one who sent me."

- Today's reading reminds us of an aspect we often overlook. Jesus from time to time speaks clearly of judgment: we will be judged according to our deeds and to our reaction to God's many gifts to us. We will only be saved if we want, and God, however merciful, cannot make us do what we refuse to choose.

Saturday October 2
Matthew 18:1–5, 10

At that time the disciples came to Jesus and asked, "Who is the greatest in the kingdom of heaven?" He called a child, whom he put among them, and said, "Truly I tell you, unless you change and become like children, you will never enter the kingdom of heaven. Whoever becomes humble like this child is the greatest in the kingdom of heaven. Whoever welcomes one such child in my name welcomes me. . . . Take care that you do not despise one of these little ones; for, I tell you, in heaven their angels continually see the face of my Father in heaven."

- Jesus sets the bar for entrance into the kingdom quite high: we must change and become like little children. Where do I need to change most? Ours is a world of narcissists, where so many are engrossed by themselves and their importance, so that being like a child is really countercultural. I ask for light and wisdom to see where and how I can become like a little child.

- Jesus warns us to respect children. I let myself feel sorrow at the scandal of child abuse, within and without the Church. I pray for the victims and the abusers, and for our leaders, humbly and compassionately. I consider how I look at the children present in my life.

The Twenty-Seventh Week in Ordinary Time
October 3–9, 2021

Something to think and pray about each day this week:

We are part of the unfathomable weave of the universe, immersed in its deep mystery. Its dance has already begun: it has always been in process. Each of us has a role in it. Jesus and his Father are working (John 4:34) for the good of all Creation, and we can tune in to their signals and do likewise. Thomas Merton says that every moment and every event in every person's life plants seeds of spiritual vitality in their hearts. This is the divine at work on Earth: this is grace, and grace is everywhere. All is sacred, and so are we. We must not desecrate our Common Home. We belong to the great Creation Story, to a whole that is infinitely greater than ourselves. We are called even now to share with all of Creation "in the freedom of the children of God" (Romans 8:21).

So let's put on our dancing shoes and learn the steps of the cosmic dance!

"See, the home of God is among mortals. God will dwell with them and they will be God's people." (Revelation 21:3)

—Brian Grogan, SJ, *Creation Walk: The Amazing Story of
a Small Blue Planet*

The Presence of God

"I am standing at the door, knocking," says the Lord. What a wonderful privilege that the Lord of all creation desires to come to me. I welcome his presence.

Freedom

I will ask God's help
to be free from my own preoccupations,
to be open to God in this time of prayer,
to come to know, love, and serve God more.

Consciousness

In God's loving presence I unwind the past day,
starting from now and looking back, moment by moment.
I gather in all the goodness and light, in gratitude.
I attend to the shadows and what they say to me,
seeking healing, courage, and forgiveness.

The Word

Now I turn to the Scripture set out for me this day. I read slowly over the words and see if any sentence or sentiment appeals to me. (*Please turn to the Scripture on the following pages. Inspiration points are there, should you need them. When you are ready, return here to continue.*)

Conversation

Sometimes I wonder what I might say
if I were to meet you in person, Lord.
I think I might say, "Thank you"
because you are always there for me.

Conclusion

I thank God for these moments we have spent together and for any insights I have been given concerning the text.

Sunday October 3
Twenty-Seventh Sunday in Ordinary Time
Mark 10:2–16

Some Pharisees came, and to test him they asked, "Is it lawful for a man to divorce his wife?" He answered them, "What did Moses command you?" They said, "Moses allowed a man to write a certificate of dismissal and to divorce her." But Jesus said to them, "Because of your hardness of heart he wrote this commandment for you. But from the beginning of creation, 'God made them male and female.' 'For this reason a man shall leave his father and mother and be joined to his wife, and the two shall become one flesh.' So they are no longer two, but one flesh. Therefore what God has joined together, let no one separate."

Then in the house the disciples asked him again about this matter. He said to them, "Whoever divorces his wife and marries another commits adultery against her; and if she divorces her husband and marries another, she commits adultery."

People were bringing little children to him in order that he might touch them; and the disciples spoke sternly to them. But when Jesus saw this, he was indignant and said to them, "Let the little children come to me; do not stop them; for it is to such as these that the kingdom of God belongs. Truly I tell you, whoever does not receive the kingdom of God as a little child will never enter it." And he took them up in his arms, laid his hands on them, and blessed them.

- Jesus' teaching on marriage and the inadmissibility of divorce may be a joyful message to those who receive from God the wonderful gift of marital union but a source of anguish for those whose attempt at marriage has failed. In *Amoris Laetitia*, Pope Francis invites Christian families "to be a sign of mercy and closeness wherever family life remains imperfect or lacks peace and joy." He offers "an invitation to mercy and the pastoral discernment of those situations that fall short of what the Lord demands of us" (5–6). Mercy is the love that all of us need to experience, regardless of our life history or track record.

- The teaching on marriage and adultery needs to be read alongside Jesus' reminder that the child, and the child's receptiveness to love, is the "key" to the kingdom of God. The passage is less about the regulations for ordering relationships and more of a glimpse or vision of God's loving plan for his children. And this plan remains "good news" for everyone, not just the fortunate ones.

Monday October 4
Luke 10:25–37

Just then a lawyer stood up to test Jesus. "Teacher," he said, "what must I do to inherit eternal life?" He said to him, "What is written in the law? What do you read there?" He answered, "You shall love the Lord your God with all your heart, and with all your soul, and with all your strength, and with all your mind; and your neighbor as yourself." And he said to him, "You have given the right answer; do this, and you will live."

But wanting to justify himself, he asked Jesus, "And who is my neighbor?" Jesus replied, "A man was going down from Jerusalem to Jericho, and fell into the hands of robbers, who stripped him, beat him, and went away, leaving him half dead. Now by chance a priest was going down that road; and when he saw him, he passed by on the other side. So likewise a Levite, when he came to the place and saw him, passed by on the other side. But a Samaritan while traveling came near him; and when he saw him, he was moved with pity. He went to him and bandaged his wounds, having poured oil and wine on them. Then he put him on his own animal, brought him to an inn, and took care of him. The next day he took out two denarii, gave them to the innkeeper, and said, 'Take care of him; and when I come back, I will repay you whatever more you spend.' Which of these three, do you think, was a neighbor to the man who fell into the hands of the robbers?" He said, "The one who showed him mercy." Jesus said to him, "Go and do likewise."

- The Samaritans were a breakaway group within Judaism—so Jesus' championing of the Samaritan traveler makes it clear that God's command to love has a broad extension. (So unpopular were the Samaritans that some modern experts believe the lawyer could not bring himself to even use the word, "Samaritan.") Also, some experts observe that the beaten-up traveler might have appeared dead—so that the priest and the Levite feared ritual defilement by approaching a corpse.

- Today is the feast of St. Francis, a saint who is a universal favorite because when we look at him we understand much better who Jesus was and what it means to be a follower of Jesus. Sometimes Francis is reduced to a romantic figure, a kind of thirteenth-century hippie. I ask myself what attracts me most in this saint, and I pray to become, like him, someone who reflects Jesus in my life.

Tuesday October 5
Luke 10:38–42

Now as they went on their way, he entered a certain village, where a woman named Martha welcomed him into her home. She had a sister named Mary, who sat at the Lord's feet and listened to what he was saying. But Martha was distracted by her many tasks; so she came to him and asked, "Lord, do you not care that my sister has left me to do all the work by myself? Tell her then to help me." But the Lord answered her, "Martha, Martha, you are worried and distracted by many things; there is need of only one thing. Mary has chosen the better part, which will not be taken away from her."

- Most significant in this story is the attitude taken by Mary, sitting attentively at the feet of Jesus, listening to what he is saying. As a true disciple, Mary recognizes that Jesus has far more to offer her in terms of spiritual nourishment than she or Martha can offer him. Each of us has to find the balance between service of the kingdom and moments of serious attentiveness to God. Both the active and contemplative dimensions of Christian life are necessary.

Wednesday October 6
Luke 11:1–4

He was praying in a certain place, and after he had finished, one of his disciples said to him, "Lord, teach us to pray, as John taught his disciples." He said to them, "When you pray, say:

'Father, hallowed be your name.
Your kingdom come.
Give us each day our daily bread.
And forgive us our sins,
for we ourselves forgive everyone indebted to us.
And do not bring us to the time of trial.'"

- The disciples were looking outward at John and his disciples, at Jesus in prayer. Jesus suggests to them that their prayer might begin by looking in, by starting with our most important relationships. To call God "Father" is to recognize where my life comes from and establishes me in relation to others. If I focus on my needs, it is so that I might grow in trust as I recognize who is ready to answer them.

Thursday October 7
Luke 11:5–13

And he said to them, "Suppose one of you has a friend, and you go to him at midnight and say to him, 'Friend, lend me three loaves of bread; for a friend of mine has arrived, and I have nothing to set before him.' And he answers from within, 'Do not bother me; the door has already been locked, and my children are with me in bed; I cannot get up and give you anything.' I tell you, even though he will not get up and give him anything because he is his friend, at least because of his persistence he will get up and give him whatever he needs.

"So I say to you, Ask, and it will be given to you; search, and you will find; knock, and the door will be opened for you. For everyone who asks receives, and everyone who searches finds, and for everyone who knocks, the door will be opened. Is there anyone among you who, if your child asks for a fish, will give a snake instead of a fish? Or if the child asks for an egg, will give a scorpion? If you then, who are evil, know how to give good gifts to your children, how much more will the heavenly Father give the Holy Spirit to those who ask him!"

- In this parable, Jesus gives the example of a friend who is reluctant to be disturbed but who gives in under persistent requests. The message is a simple one: keep trying, persisting until you get a result.

- "The Father will give the Holy Spirit." Do I thank the Father for his gifts? Do I thank him for this gift? For Luke, the Holy Spirit is the supreme gift of God to believers; the source of all "good things." How frequently do I pray for a greater outpouring of the Holy Spirit in my heart and life?

Friday October 8
Luke 11:15–26

But some of them said, "He casts out demons by Beelzebul, the ruler of the demons." Others, to test him, kept demanding from him a sign from heaven. But he knew what they were thinking and said to them, "Every kingdom divided against itself becomes a desert, and house falls on house. If Satan also is divided against himself, how will his kingdom stand?—for you say that I cast out the demons by Beelzebul. Now if I cast out the demons by Beelzebul, by whom do your exorcists cast them out? Therefore they will be your judges. But if it is by the finger of God that I cast out the demons, then the kingdom of God has come to you. When a strong man, fully armed, guards his castle, his property is safe. But when one stronger than he attacks him and overpowers him, he takes away his armor in which he trusted and divides his plunder. Whoever is not with me is against me, and whoever does not gather with me scatters.

"When the unclean spirit has gone out of a person, it wanders through waterless regions looking for a resting-place, but not finding any, it says, 'I will return to my house from which I came.' When it comes, it finds it swept and put in order. Then it goes and brings seven other spirits more evil than itself, and they enter and live there; and the last state of that person is worse than the first."

- How could anyone say that Jesus was casting out demons through the power of the prince of demons? The hardness of heart, so evident all around us and within us, remains a great mystery: how can we resist the truth, goodness, and justice, finding empty excuses to justify our hardness of heart? How can so much human suffering, so much ecological degradation leave us unmoved? I ask the Lord for an open heart and for light to see the hardness in me.

- Jesus gives us a clear warning: an empty heart is there for the taking. You cannot live a meaningful life if you never choose, never opt for what you believe in.

Saturday October 9

Luke 11:27–28

While he was saying this, a woman in the crowd raised her voice and said to him, "Blessed is the womb that bore you and the breasts that nursed you!" But he said, "Blessed rather are those who hear the word of God and obey it!"

- I join this woman in her praise of the mother of Jesus, the woman who brought him up, taught him how to relate to others, educated his heart to become so compassionate, and was the first one to talk to him about God and prayer. I remember that she is also my mother.

- I wonder at the power of Jesus' reply. Mary's greatness comes from her openness and obedience to God's word. I ask her to help me be like her in this.

October 10–16, 2021

Something to think and pray about each day this week:

Jalal ad-Din Muhammad Rumi was born in 1207 in Afghanistan, educated in the Sufi stream of Islam in Syria, and died in Turkey in 1273. While Rumi honored the prophet Muhammad, he combined that with the intuitive love of God and neighbor that he encountered in Sufism.

In Rumi's poetry about Jesus we find truths that are a central part of our Christian faith:

> I called through your door.
> "The mystics are gathering in the street. Come out!"
> "Leave me alone! I'm sick."
> "I don't care if you're dead. Jesus is here and he wants to resurrect
> somebody!"

Rumi's poetry is a reminder that we can learn from other faith traditions about what is true, good, and beautiful. *Laudato Si'* was written by Pope Francis in May of 2015. It was by a happy coincidence launched on the first day of Ramadan! He is the first pope ever to quote in a Church Encyclical a ninth-century Muslim scholar and mystic, Ali al-Khawas.

"The universe unfolds in God, who fills it completely. Hence there is a mystical meaning to be found in a leaf, in a mountain trail, in a dewdrop, in a poor person's face." (Ali al-Khawas in *Laudato Si'*, 233)

These powerful words remind us that we can discover God in all things. It echoes the motto of St. Ignatius that is lived by today's Jesuits. We need to go the extra mile and deepen our interfaith dialogue into a relationship that celebrates our shared spiritual traditions.

—John Cullen, *Alert, Aware, Attentive*

The Presence of God
Dear Jesus, I come to you today longing for your presence. I desire to love you as you love me. May nothing ever separate me from you.

Freedom
Lord, grant me the grace to be free from the excesses of this life. Let me not get caught up with the desire for wealth. Keep my heart and mind free to love and serve you.

Consciousness
Where do I sense hope, encouragement, and growth in my life? By looking back over the past few months, I may be able to see which activities and occasions have produced rich fruit. If I do notice such areas, I will determine to give those areas both time and space in the future.

The Word
God speaks to each of us individually. I listen attentively to hear what he is saying to me. Read the text a few times, then listen. (*Please turn to the Scripture on the following pages. Inspiration points are there, should you need them. When you are ready, return here to continue.*)

Conversation
What is stirring in me as I pray? Am I consoled, troubled, left cold? I imagine Jesus standing or sitting at my side, and I share my feelings with him.

Conclusion
Glory be to the Father, and to the Son, and to the Holy Spirit,
As it was in the beginning, is now, and ever shall be,
World without end. Amen.

Sunday October 10
Twenty-Eighth Sunday in Ordinary Time
Mark 10:17–30

As he was setting out on a journey, a man ran up and knelt before him, and asked him, "Good Teacher, what must I do to inherit eternal life?" Jesus said to him, "Why do you call me good? No one is good but God alone. You know the commandments: 'You shall not murder; You shall not commit adultery; You shall not steal; You shall not bear false witness; You shall not defraud; Honor your father and mother.'" He said to him, "Teacher, I have kept all these since my youth." Jesus, looking at him, loved him and said, "You lack one thing; go, sell what you own, and give the money to the poor, and you will have treasure in heaven; then come, follow me." When he heard this, he was shocked and went away grieving, for he had many possessions.

Then Jesus looked around and said to his disciples, "How hard it will be for those who have wealth to enter the kingdom of God!" And the disciples were perplexed at these words. But Jesus said to them again, "Children, how hard it is to enter the kingdom of God! It is easier for a camel to go through the eye of a needle than for someone who is rich to enter the kingdom of God." They were greatly astounded and said to one another, "Then who can be saved?" Jesus looked at them and said, "For mortals it is impossible, but not for God; for God all things are possible."

Peter began to say to him, "Look, we have left everything and followed you." Jesus said, "Truly I tell you, there is no one who has left house or brothers or sisters or mother or father or children or fields, for my sake and for the sake of the good news, who will not receive a hundredfold now in this age—houses, brothers and sisters, mothers and children, and fields, with persecutions—and in the age to come eternal life."

- Thank you, Lord, for this most consoling of images. I was not brought into this world to help you out of a mess. You above all are the one who is working. Your dynamism, active in nature from the beginning of time, should humble me. You are the force of growth, and if you privilege me with the chance to add incrementally to that growth, that is your gift to me, not mine to you.

Monday October 11
Luke 11:29–32

When the crowds were increasing, he began to say, "This generation is an evil generation; it asks for a sign, but no sign will be given to it except the sign of Jonah. For just as Jonah became a sign to the people of Nineveh, so the Son of Man will be to this generation. The queen of the South will rise at the judgment with the people of this generation and condemn them, because she came from the ends of the earth to listen to the wisdom of Solomon, and see, something greater than Solomon is here! The people of Nineveh will rise up at the judgment with this generation and condemn it, because they repented at the proclamation of Jonah, and see, something greater than Jonah is here!"

- For Jesus, it is the repentance of the people of Nineveh that is significant here. If they have wisdom to recognize the authority of the prophet Jonah and repent, then surely Jesus' generation should be able to do the same, given that Jesus is even greater than Jonah.

- The same applies to the Queen of Sheba, who came a long way to look upon the greatness of Israel's king.

- Foreigners like the Queen of Sheba and the Ninevites are better able to see the truth than the holy Israelites! Perhaps I too have a robust sense of my religious identity, of what is special and holy. But is it getting in the way?

Tuesday October 12
Luke 11:37–41

While he was speaking, a Pharisee invited him to dine with him; so he went in and took his place at the table. The Pharisee was amazed to see that he did not first wash before dinner. Then the Lord said to him, "Now you Pharisees clean the outside of the cup and of the dish, but inside you are full of greed and wickedness. You fools! Did not the one who made the outside make the inside also? So give for alms those things that are within; and see, everything will be clean for you."

- When Jesus and his followers eat and drink with those declared sinners and outcasts, God's kingdom comes about: a moment of liberation. Jews and Gentiles eat together at the same table, without fear of contamination.

- Pope Francis says that the person receiving the Eucharist ought to take on the mentality of Jesus and live for him and for others. "One who is nourished by the Eucharist assimilates the Lord's very mentality. He is Bread broken for us and those who receive it become in turn broken bread, which is not leavened with pride, but is given to others: they stop living for themselves, for success, to gain something or to become someone, but live for Jesus and like Jesus, that is, for others."

Wednesday October 13
Luke 11:42–46

"But woe to you Pharisees! For you tithe mint and rue and herbs of all kinds, and neglect justice and the love of God; it is these you ought to have practiced, without neglecting the others. Woe to you Pharisees! For you love to have the seat of honor in the synagogues and to be greeted with respect in the market-places. Woe to you! For you are like unmarked graves, and people walk over them without realizing it."

One of the lawyers answered him, "Teacher, when you say these things, you insult us too." And he said, "Woe also to you lawyers! For you load people with burdens hard to bear, and you yourselves do not lift a finger to ease them."

- Jesus unmasked the lack of heart in the law-abiding Pharisees. He focused on what is inside a person, in the human heart. The Pharisee, in sharp contrast, is primarily concerned with external observance of rules and regulations, such as the ritual washing before a meal.

- What is my focus? Do I need help, honest feedback from a friend to clarify my heart? You know my heart, Lord. You know the movements and thoughts under the surface of my behavior. Teach me to live first of all in your presence, free from seeking human respect.

Thursday October 14
Luke 11:47–54

"Woe to you! For you build the tombs of the prophets whom your ancestors killed. So you are witnesses and approve of the deeds of your ancestors; for they killed them, and you build their tombs. Therefore also the Wisdom of God said, 'I will send them prophets and apostles, some of whom they will kill and persecute,' so that this generation may be charged with the blood of all the prophets shed since the foundation of the world, from the blood of Abel to the blood of Zechariah, who perished between the altar and the sanctuary. Yes, I tell you, it will be charged against this generation. Woe to you lawyers! For you have taken away the key of knowledge; you did not enter yourselves, and you hindered those who were entering."

When he went outside, the scribes and the Pharisees began to be very hostile toward him and to cross-examine him about many things, lying in wait for him, to catch him in something he might say.

- Violence in religion is a hot topic for all times, including our own. It is not so easy to dismiss the topic nor see it only in "the others." Yet justifying violence by reference to God or his will ranks as one of the most serious forms of blasphemy. We humbly acknowledge that we form part of this violent history; as I ask for pardon and mercy, I recall that Jesus himself was a victim of religiously inspired violence.

- Today I pray for the Christian communities who are suffering persecution in so many parts of the world. I pray especially for the Christians in the Middle East, where Christianity first appeared and where it is running the real risk of disappearing.

Friday October 15
Luke 12:1–7

Meanwhile, when the crowd gathered in thousands, so that they trampled on one another, he began to speak first to his disciples, "Beware of the yeast of the Pharisees, that is, their hypocrisy. Nothing is covered up that will not be uncovered, and nothing secret that will not become known. Therefore whatever you have said in the dark will be heard in the light, and what you have whispered behind closed doors will be proclaimed from the housetops.

"I tell you, my friends, do not fear those who kill the body, and after that can do nothing more. But I will warn you whom to fear: fear him who, after he has killed, has authority to cast into hell. Yes, I tell you, fear him! Are not five sparrows sold for two pennies? Yet not one of them is forgotten in God's sight. But even the hairs of your head are all counted. Do not be afraid; you are of more value than many sparrows."

- I am a member of that great crowd that comes to hear the Word of God—I am part of the Sacred Space community. For a few moments I pray for the other members of this community, and I ask that it may continue to grow all over the world.

- A hypocrite was a person whose life was not in tune with the ways of God. A simple way to be part of God's music is to trust God and not be afraid. I ask God that I may not live out of fear but out of belief that I am limitlessly valued by God.

Saturday October 16
Luke 12:8–12

"And I tell you, everyone who acknowledges me before others, the Son of Man also will acknowledge before the angels of God; but whoever denies me before others will be denied before the angels of God. And everyone who speaks a word against the Son of Man will be forgiven; but whoever blasphemes against the Holy Spirit will not be forgiven. When they bring you before the synagogues, the rulers, and the authorities, do not worry about how you are to defend yourselves or what you are to say; for the Holy Spirit will teach you at that very hour what you ought to say."

- It is not always easy to declare oneself openly for Jesus in the presence of others. Sometimes this is because we deem it counterproductive, but at other times it is because we are fearful of what others might think about us. Today I ask for the gift of light and for fortitude, to be able to live in integrity before Jesus and before others.

- Everyone who says a word against the Son of Man will be forgiven, but he who blasphemes against the Holy Spirit will not be forgiven. Jesus means that if we continually resist the promptings of the Holy Spirit we will end up hardening our hearts to an extent that we are closed even to receive forgiveness. I pray insistently for the grace to keep an open heart, ready to listen and trust.

The Twenty-Ninth Week in Ordinary Time
October 17–23, 2021

Something to think and pray about each day this week:

The wilderness is a strong image. There are many different ways to imagine a wilderness. It could remind us, on the one hand, of walking in the countryside or in wide open spaces, with animals scurrying around us in the sun or the rain. It could remind us of the silence of the many winding roads that don't seem to go any particular place, giving us time to think and pray. This is a positive experience of being in the wilderness. However, the wilderness can also be a place of desolation for us. It can be an internal landscape of worry, problems, sin, and perceived distance from God. Being in the wilderness can be uncomfortable or worse.

Our job, it seems, is to bear with ourselves being in that wilderness. Wilderness times are an inevitable part of the story of life.

We see this in the Gospels when Jesus is driven into the wilderness. However, we are told that the wilderness was not the end of his journey. He emerged from that wilderness and came out the other side. Not only that, but he grew in the wilderness; he learned something about his life and his mission. We are told that he came out filled with the Spirit of God.

Emerging from the wilderness feels like a remote prospect when we are right in the middle of it. However, our emergence is as inevitable as the rising of the sun on a new day. We are invited to trust that God is with us in the wilderness and that we will emerge with deeper insights into ourselves, the world, and our place in it. We need not worry or despair; it is God, after all, who ultimately straightens all paths out of the wilderness.

—Brendan McManus, SJ, and Jim Deeds, *Deeper Into the Mess:
Praying Through Tough Times*

The Presence of God
As I sit here, the beating of my heart,
the ebb and flow of my breathing, the movements of my mind
are all signs of God's ongoing creation of me.
I pause for a moment and become aware
of this presence of God within me.

Freedom
Everything has the potential to draw from me a fuller love and life.
Yet my desires are often fixed, caught, on illusions of fulfillment.
I ask that God, through my freedom, may orchestrate my desires in a
vibrant loving melody rich in harmony.

Consciousness
I ask, how am I within myself today? Am I particularly tired, stressed,
or off-form? If any of these characteristics apply, can I try to let go of the
concerns that disturb me?

The Word
I read the word of God slowly, a few times over, and I listen to what
God is saying to me. (*Please turn to the Scripture on the following pages.
Inspiration points are there, should you need them. When you are ready,
return here to continue.*)

Conversation
I begin to talk with Jesus about the Scripture I have just read. What part
of it strikes a chord in me? Perhaps the words of a friend or a story I have
heard recently will slowly rise to the surface of my consciousness. If so,
does the story throw light on what the Scripture passage may be trying
to say to me?

Conclusion
Glory be to the Father, and to the Son, and to the Holy Spirit,
As it was in the beginning, is now, and ever shall be,
World without end. Amen.

Sunday October 17
Twenty-Ninth Sunday in Ordinary Time
Mark 10:35–45

James and John, the sons of Zebedee, came forward to him and said to him, "Teacher, we want you to do for us whatever we ask of you." And he said to them, "What is it you want me to do for you?" And they said to him, "Grant us to sit, one at your right hand and one at your left, in your glory." But Jesus said to them, "You do not know what you are asking. Are you able to drink the cup that I drink, or be baptized with the baptism that I am baptized with?" They replied, "We are able." Then Jesus said to them, "The cup that I drink you will drink; and with the baptism with which I am baptized, you will be baptized; but to sit at my right hand or at my left is not mine to grant, but it is for those for whom it has been prepared."

When the ten heard this, they began to be angry with James and John. So Jesus called them and said to them, "You know that among the Gentiles those whom they recognize as their rulers lord it over them, and their great ones are tyrants over them. But it is not so among you; but whoever wishes to become great among you must be your servant, and whoever wishes to be first among you must be slave of all. For the Son of Man came not to be served but to serve, and to give his life a ransom for many."

- This lovely dialogue leads us deep into Jesus' way of teaching. It starts with the sort of untamed desire that lies behind many of our prayers. Jesus leads James and John into the implications of what they are asking. He does not throw suffering at them but invites them to share his cup.

- Invite me too, Lord. I would prefer to serve with you than to sit on a throne.

Monday October 18
St. Luke, Evangelist
Luke 10:1–9

After this the Lord appointed seventy others and sent them on ahead of him in pairs to every town and place where he himself intended to go. He said to them, "The harvest is plentiful, but the laborers are few; therefore ask the Lord of the harvest to send out laborers into his harvest.

Go on your way. See, I am sending you out like lambs into the midst of wolves. Carry no purse, no bag, no sandals; and greet no one on the road. Whatever house you enter, first say, 'Peace to this house!' And if anyone is there who shares in peace, your peace will rest on that person; but if not, it will return to you. Remain in the same house, eating and drinking whatever they provide, for the laborer deserves to be paid. Do not move about from house to house. Whenever you enter a town and its people welcome you, eat what is set before you; cure the sick who are there, and say to them, 'The kingdom of God has come near to you.'"

- "Greet no one on the road." The single-minded urgency of the gospel requires a suspension of social norms, even of basic traveler's courtesy. What does my own spiritual "journey" look like? Does it have something of the same intensity and focus that makes people take notice of something unusual? Do I come across as a person on a mission?

- "The kingdom of God has come near to you." Take some time to imagine yourself hearing these words, spoken to you. By whom? Now take some time to imagine yourself speaking these words. To whom do you speak them?

Tuesday October 19
Luke 12:35–38

"Be dressed for action and have your lamps lit; be like those who are waiting for their master to return from the wedding banquet, so that they may open the door for him as soon as he comes and knocks. Blessed are those slaves whom the master finds alert when he comes; truly I tell you, he will fasten his belt and have them sit down to eat, and he will come and serve them. If he comes during the middle of the night, or near dawn, and finds them so, blessed are those slaves."

- A number of parables, including this one from Luke, remind us that the Christian life is, on some level, a matter of conscious choice, of being awake and "alert."

- The theologian Karl Barth has a lovely description of what salvation in Christ means: "The prisoner has become the watchman." Yes, the prisoner has been liberated; but he has been liberated only so that he can take his place in the watchtower, waiting for the return of the Messiah so that he can announce it.

- The master will sit the servants down and wait on them—this is exactly what happens with the banquet laid out for us by the Father. In the story of the Lost Son (Luke 15:11–32) Jesus tells of a father anxiously waiting for his prodigal son, scanning the horizon for his return. The Father is alert, mindful of his beloved children; we are asked in turn to be mindful of our loving Father.

Wednesday October 20
Luke 12:39–48

"But know this: if the owner of the house had known at what hour the thief was coming, he would not have let his house be broken into. You also must be ready, for the Son of Man is coming at an unexpected hour."

Peter said, "Lord, are you telling this parable for us or for everyone?" And the Lord said, "Who then is the faithful and prudent manager whom his master will put in charge of his slaves, to give them their allowance of food at the proper time? Blessed is that slave whom his master will find at work when he arrives. Truly I tell you, he will put that one in charge of all his possessions. But if that slave says to himself, 'My master is delayed in coming,' and if he begins to beat the other slaves, men and women, and to eat and drink and get drunk, the master of that slave will come on a day when he does not expect him and at an hour that he does not know, and will cut him in pieces, and put him with the unfaithful. That slave who knew what his master wanted, but did not prepare himself or do what was wanted, will receive a severe beating. But one who did not know and did what deserved a beating will receive a light beating. From everyone to whom much has been given, much will be required; and from one to whom much has been entrusted, even more will be demanded."

- The disciples still haven't understood Jesus' message about being ready. The drama of Jesus' parable is perhaps a bit exaggerated to stress its importance. Peter is trying to figure out if the story is supposed to refer directly to himself and the other apostles or if Jesus means the relationship between God and Israel in general. Both are implied.

- When it comes to leadership and those who are in authority in the community of believers, the parable points out how much more they have to account for because of their trusted positions of power.

- I could pray around the questions of where my own responsibilities lie and whether I fulfill them in a loving and committed way.

Thursday October 21
Luke 12:49–53

"I came to bring fire to the earth, and how I wish it were already kindled! I have a baptism with which to be baptized, and what stress I am under until it is completed! Do you think that I have come to bring peace to the earth? No, I tell you, but rather division! From now on, five in one household will be divided, three against two and two against three; they will be divided:

> father against son
> and son against father,
> mother against daughter
> and daughter against mother,
> mother-in-law against her daughter-in-law
> and daughter-in-law against mother-in-law."

- Jesus is passionate about his mission. Not only does he know what it is and the suffering it entails, but he also embraces it enthusiastically. My own mission as a Christian somehow partakes of Jesus' mission, bringing fire on earth. I ask for the grace to have more clarity about what God is calling me to do, and to do it with Jesus, with passion and energy.

- Jesus shed his blood to reconcile us with God and among ourselves. Yet the radicality of his message leads inevitably to division, between those who accept it and those who resist it. Often these divisions run across families. I pray that I may know how to bear the division that being faithful to Jesus and his message can bring to my life. I pray for my family and friends, that Jesus can be for them the source of unity rather than division.

Friday October 22
Luke 12:54–59

He also said to the crowds, "When you see a cloud rising in the west, you immediately say, 'It is going to rain'; and so it happens. And when you see the south wind blowing, you say, 'There will be scorching heat'; and it happens. You hypocrites! You know how to interpret the appearance of earth and sky, but why do you not know how to interpret the present time?

"And why do you not judge for yourselves what is right? Thus, when you go with your accuser before a magistrate, on the way make an effort to settle the case, or you may be dragged before the judge, and the judge hand you over to the officer, and the officer throw you in prison. I tell you, you will never get out until you have paid the very last penny."

- We seem to be living in a world that is very flat, that finds it next to impossible to think beyond the pragmatic and the immediate. Jesus challenges us to "interpret the present time" and behave wisely.

- I am called to be merciful, as I consider how the merciful Father deals with me, a sinner who fails in so many things. I can never be the one to throw the first stone, and I feel called to be compassionate, toward myself first, and to others.

Saturday October 23

Luke 13:1–9

At that very time there were some present who told him about the Galileans whose blood Pilate had mingled with their sacrifices. He asked them, "Do you think that because these Galileans suffered in this way they were worse sinners than all other Galileans? No, I tell you; but unless you repent, you will all perish as they did. Or those eighteen who were killed when the tower of Siloam fell on them—do you think that they were worse offenders than all the others living in Jerusalem? No, I tell you; but unless you repent, you will all perish just as they did."

Then he told this parable: "A man had a fig tree planted in his vineyard; and he came looking for fruit on it and found none. So he said to the gardener, 'See here! For three years I have come looking for fruit on this fig tree, and still I find none. Cut it down! Why should it be wasting the soil?' He replied, 'Sir, let it alone for one more year, until I dig round it and put manure on it. If it bears fruit next year, well and good; but if not, you can cut it down.'"

- The story about the fig tree is about God's patience and our need for time to repent and grow in our faith and prayer. It is about the "God of the many chances." The God of Jesus never lets us go and always believes in our future. All of us carry particular faults and failings through life, and even though we try our best, we find that they stay with us. God knows this and sees our efforts to change and be renewed. Prayer helps us believe in ourselves as God believes in us.

- In our various desires and activities we can be with God—or not be with him. We can love him fully or find ourselves tempted from God's path. Jesus calls us all the time to change so that we live out of the best side of ourselves and change so that we become more like him. At the Eucharist we pray, "May we come to share in the divinity of Christ who humbled himself to share in our humanity."

The Thirtieth Week in Ordinary Time
October 24–30, 2021

Something to think and pray about each day this week:

A young man in his late twenties—he enjoyed buying clothes. By no means wealthy, he bought in bargain shops. Wanting to appear better, he would transfer the clothes to a designer shop bag and go home with that. He even joked about it—a way of boasting or living up to appearances. Somehow the label gave him a lift about himself and how he might be seen by some others, a sort of living up to society's or others' expectations. He knew others who did the same.

Maybe this is about feeling good about the self in some aspect; ways we may pretend so as to impress. It is part of the drive in us all to feel good about ourselves. We try many ways to do this, often in the wrong places. We can look to where we live, where we are educated, to give a boast about ourselves, as we often look down on others for, for example, color of skin, race, religion. But these do not give a lasting self-love.

A lasting good image fits in with what Jesus says: "Love your neighbor as yourself."

To grow in this self-love, there are many helps: a grateful acceptance of our good personality, qualities, and gifts; the love of others who accept us as we are; a realistic view of faults and failings; the grace of forgiving ourselves; some success in life, among others—all these contribute to a strong love of self.

There is also the self-love from our faith: that God loves us unconditionally, that Jesus died and rose for us, and if so, why should I love myself less? That we are precious in the eyes of God and carved in love on the palm of God's hands.

A prayer that enhances our self-esteem is to thank God regularly, daily or hourly, for something good in life or about the self. If we can be grateful, our self-esteem and love of self is enhanced, and one big thanks each day is to be grateful for being a loved child of God.

—Donal Neary, SJ, *The Sacred Heart Messenger*,
May 2020

The Presence of God
"Be still, and know that I am God!" Lord, may your spirit guide me to seek your loving presence more and more, for it is there I find rest and refreshment from this busy world.

Freedom
By God's grace I was born to live in freedom. Free to enjoy the pleasures he created for me. Dear Lord, grant that I may live as you intended, with complete confidence in your loving care.

Consciousness
How am I today?
Where am I with God? With others?
Do I have something to be grateful for? Then I give thanks.
Is there something I am sorry for? Then I ask forgiveness.

The Word
God speaks to each of us individually. I need to listen, to hear what he is saying to me. Read the text a few times, then listen. (*Please turn to the Scripture on the following pages. Inspiration points are there, should you need them. When you are ready, return here to continue.*)

Conversation
How has God's word moved me? Has it left me cold?
Has it consoled me or moved me to act in a new way?
I imagine Jesus standing or sitting beside me.
I turn and share my feelings with him.

Conclusion
I thank God for these moments we have spent together and for any insights I have been given concerning the text.

Sunday October 24
Thirtieth Sunday in Ordinary Time
Mark 10:46–52

They came to Jericho. As he and his disciples and a large crowd were leaving Jericho, Bartimaeus son of Timaeus, a blind beggar, was sitting by the roadside. When he heard that it was Jesus of Nazareth, he began to shout out and say, "Jesus, Son of David, have mercy on me!" Many sternly ordered him to be quiet, but he cried out even more loudly, "Son of David, have mercy on me!" Jesus stood still and said, "Call him here." And they called the blind man, saying to him, "Take heart; get up, he is calling you." So throwing off his cloak, he sprang up and came to Jesus. Then Jesus said to him, "What do you want me to do for you?" The blind man said to him, "My teacher, let me see again." Jesus said to him, "Go; your faith has made you well." Immediately he regained his sight and followed him on the way.

- Like the people who scolded Bartimaeus, telling him to be quiet and not bring shame on them, I may sometimes prefer to keep the less presentable parts of my life out of Jesus' sight. Thinking of this scene, I realize that Jesus wants to stop, listen to my plea for help, and cure me.

- Bartimaeus threw off his cloak—his only protection—and, being blind, risked not finding it again. I allow myself to be before Jesus, unshrouded, seen as I am, trustingly expressing my need.

Monday October 25
Luke 13:10–17

Now he was teaching in one of the synagogues on the sabbath. And just then there appeared a woman with a spirit that had crippled her for eighteen years. She was bent over and was quite unable to stand up straight. When Jesus saw her, he called her over and said, "Woman, you are set free from your ailment." When he laid his hands on her, immediately she stood up straight and began praising God. But the leader of the synagogue, indignant because Jesus had cured on the sabbath, kept saying to the crowd, "There are six days on which work ought to be done; come on those days and be cured, and not on the sabbath day." But the Lord answered him and said, "You hypocrites! Does not each of you on the sabbath untie his ox or his donkey from the manger, and lead it away to give it water? And ought not this woman, a daughter of Abraham whom Satan bound for eighteen long years, be set free from this bondage on the sabbath day?" When he said this, all his opponents were put to shame; and the entire crowd was rejoicing at all the wonderful things that he was doing.

- For Jesus, mercy and compassion are paramount, trumping all other considerations. This is certainly a very challenging position. I imagine myself present in the synagogue and observe my spontaneous reaction during the argument between Jesus and the head of the synagogue. I ask for a heart that is like the heart of Jesus, always compassionate and ready to defend the poor and suffering.

- I wonder at how easily religion can become a source of hard-heartedness rather than Christlike mercy. I ask for light to be aware of my prejudices and of the rationalizations that justify them.

Tuesday October 26
Luke 13:18–21

He said therefore, "What is the kingdom of God like? And to what should I compare it? It is like a mustard seed that someone took and sowed in the garden; it grew and became a tree, and the birds of the air made nests in its branches."

And again he said, "To what should I compare the kingdom of God? It is like yeast that a woman took and mixed in with three measures of flour until all of it was leavened."

- Jesus was so optimistic when he spoke of the kingdom! For him, even a small beginning was sufficient, for he was convinced that it was the kingdom of God, so that it shared his power and dynamism. As I look around my world, I ask whether I share this conviction, or whether I find myself acting like a prophet of doom and gloom.

- The yeast can change the dough only if it is one with it. Even if the separation is minimal, it will be ineffective. Engagement and presence rather than size seems to be what matters for Jesus. I pray for a Church and a Christian community that are totally engaged with and in the world, like the yeast in the dough.

Wednesday October 27
Luke 13:22–30

Jesus went through one town and village after another, teaching as he made his way to Jerusalem. Someone asked him, "Lord, will only a few be saved?" He said to them, "Strive to enter through the narrow door; for many, I tell you, will try to enter and will not be able. When once the owner of the house has got up and shut the door, and you begin to stand outside and to knock at the door, saying, 'Lord, open to us,' then in reply he will say to you, 'I do not know where you come from.' Then you will begin to say, 'We ate and drank with you, and you taught in our streets.' But he will say, 'I do not know where you come from; go away from me, all you evildoers!' There will be weeping and gnashing of teeth when you see Abraham and Isaac and Jacob and all the prophets in the kingdom of God, and you yourselves thrown out. Then people will come from east and west, from north and south, and will eat in the kingdom of God. Indeed, some are last who will be first, and some are first who will be last."

- "Lord, will only a few be saved?" How easy it is to distract ourselves from the real challenges by asking very interesting but ultimately irrelevant questions. Jesus' reply points to what really matters: "Strive to enter through the narrow door; for many, I tell you, will try to enter and will not be able." Am I ready to do what is right, even when it costs?

- Jesus warns us off any false sense of entitlement: like some of the Jews he encountered, we can feel too comfortable in the belief that God is somehow obliged to save us. What counts is not our past exploits or successes but being with the Master at all times. I ask for humility and inner freedom.

Thursday October 28
Ss. Simon and Jude, Apostles
Luke 6:12–16

Now during those days he went out to the mountain to pray; and he spent the night in prayer to God. And when day came, he called his disciples and chose twelve of them, whom he also named apostles: Simon, whom he named Peter, and his brother Andrew, and James, and John, and Philip, and Bartholomew, and Matthew, and Thomas, and James son of Alphaeus, and Simon, who was called the Zealot, and Judas son of James, and Judas Iscariot, who became a traitor.

- Jesus made his decision following a night spent in prayer to God. When did I last pray before making a decision? Do I refer all my decisions to God as a wise and loving parent?

- Lord, you have inscribed me on the palm of your hands. You always keep me in your mind and heart. In this Sacred Space of prayer I ask now for your help and your guidance in all that I attempt to do, no matter how trivial it seems.

Friday October 29
Luke 14:1–6

On one occasion when Jesus was going to the house of a leader of the Pharisees to eat a meal on the sabbath, they were watching him closely. Just then, in front of him, there was a man who had dropsy. And Jesus asked the lawyers and Pharisees, "Is it lawful to cure people on the sabbath, or not?" But they were silent. So Jesus took him and healed him, and sent him away. Then he said to them, "If one of you has a child or an ox that has fallen into a well, will you not immediately pull it out on a sabbath day?" And they could not reply to this.

- The sabbath was an occasion for a holy or religious meal. This sabbath meal is invaded by a sick man who seems to be hoping for healing. No words are spoken between him and Jesus, but the movement in the incident is to put compassion before the law. This is a constant theme of Jesus throughout his life and the Gospels. Maybe prayer can be a time to bring to God the people in our mind and for us to see them with the compassionate eye of Jesus. Compassion reaches deeply into our hearts, both the giver and the one who receives it. All of us are the stronger for finding compassion between us and another, and the other is stronger too.

Saturday October 30

Luke 14:1, 7–11

On one occasion when Jesus was going to the house of a leader of the Pharisees to eat a meal on the sabbath, they were watching him closely. . . . When he noticed how the guests chose the places of honor, he told them a parable. "When you are invited by someone to a wedding banquet, do not sit down at the place of honor, in case someone more distinguished than you has been invited by your host; and the host who invited both of you may come and say to you, 'Give this person your place,' and then in disgrace you would start to take the lowest place. But when you are invited, go and sit down at the lowest place, so that when your host comes, he may say to you, 'Friend, move up higher'; then you will be honored in the presence of all who sit at the table with you. For all who exalt themselves will be humbled, and those who humble themselves will be exalted."

• We are often surprised and even shocked at the lengths people go to in order to be honored. In our efforts to be acknowledged, we can end up humiliating ourselves. This hunger for honor is a powerful force deep within us, and we need God's help to be free of our need to flaunt our own importance before others. St. Ignatius suggests that we ask insistently for the grace to be able to make the same choices Jesus made: to ask to be like him in refusing honors, and to choose to be humble and even humiliated as he was. I ask for the freedom to accept humiliations calmly and gracefully when they come.

The Thirty-First Week in Ordinary Time
October 31—November 6, 2021

Something to think and pray about each day this week:

They say that the difference between confidence and arrogance is that the confident person will say, "I can do it," whereas the arrogant person will say, "Only I can do it."

It's a very dangerous day when we learn the words "them" and "us." It's happening in Europe with the rise of the far right. Sometimes a change of perspective helps—to literally walk in the others' shoes. I was reading a true but bizarre story of the far-right Hungarian politician Csanad Szegedi whose discovery that his grandmother had been a Holocaust survivor prompted a radical about-turn in his thinking. He has since renounced his anti-semitism and works to teach people from his experience. And yet, something in our DNA has hardwired us to see the world not as one big "us" but as an innocent "us" versus a guilty "them."

It's strange how we struggle to acquire and hold on to things, even with God. We can be so jealous of our patch, our area of responsibility, no matter how small, and we guard it so carefully. We all too easily pit ourselves against others also; we versus they, ours versus theirs, labeling others as strangers or with chilling put-downs.

At the root of such behavior are envy and jealousy. At their heart is sadness, when you wallow in sadness at another's joys and God-given abilities. The temptation to exclude is no more legitimate within the Church than outside it. We are all so different and at varying points on the path. No one has the right to discount or despise. God's family is broad because God isn't choosy—we are.

—Fr. Tom Cox, *The Sacred Heart Messenger,*
May 2020

The Presence of God

"I am standing at the door, knocking," says the Lord. What a wonderful privilege that the Lord of all creation desires to come to me. I welcome his presence.

Freedom

Leave me here freely all alone. / In cell where never sunlight shone. / Should no one ever speak to me. / This golden silence makes me free!

> —Part of a poem by Bl. Titus Brandsma, written while he was a prisoner at Dachau concentration camp.

Consciousness

How am I really feeling? Lighthearted? Heavy-hearted? I may be very much at peace, happy to be here. Equally, I may be frustrated, worried, or angry.

I acknowledge how I really am. It is the real me whom the Lord loves.

The Word

I take my time to read the word of God slowly, a few times, allowing myself to dwell on anything that strikes me. (*Please turn to the Scripture on the following pages. Inspiration points are there, should you need them. When you are ready, return here to continue.*)

Conversation

Do I notice myself reacting as I pray with the word of God? Do I feel challenged, comforted, angry? Imagining Jesus sitting or standing by me, I speak out my feelings, as one trusted friend to another.

Conclusion

Glory be to the Father, and to the Son, and to the Holy Spirit,
As it was in the beginning, is now, and ever shall be,
World without end. Amen.

Sunday October 31
Thirty-First Sunday in Ordinary Time
Mark 12:28b–34

One of the scribes came near and heard them disputing with one another, and seeing that he answered them well, he asked him, "Which commandment is the first of all?" Jesus answered, "The first is, 'Hear, O Israel: the Lord our God, the Lord is one; you shall love the Lord your God with all your heart, and with all your soul, and with all your mind, and with all your strength.' The second is this, 'You shall love your neighbor as yourself.' There is no other commandment greater than these." Then the scribe said to him, "You are right, Teacher; you have truly said that 'he is one, and besides him there is no other'; and 'to love him with all the heart, and with all the understanding, and with all the strength,' and 'to love one's neighbor as oneself'—this is much more important than all whole burnt-offerings and sacrifices." When Jesus saw that he answered wisely, he said to him, "You are not far from the kingdom of God." After that no one dared to ask him any question.

- The first commandment is to love God with all we have—not only with our hearts, but with all our limbs. We need to be embracing the Almighty in all we do. We are called to give him total love in a spirit of adoration.

- There are two commandments, even if they merge together. We have to love the neighbor (all humankind) as being part of ourselves. Especially their sufferings need to impinge on us. Our love should be not only for those who please us but also for those we don't like and who may be hostile to us.

- The most important thing in life is to have a loving heart, which is very demanding.

Monday November 1
The Solemnity of All Saints
Matthew 5:1–12a

When Jesus saw the crowds, he went up the mountain; and after he sat down, his disciples came to him. Then he began to speak, and taught them, saying:

"Blessed are the poor in spirit, for theirs is the kingdom of heaven.

"Blessed are those who mourn, for they will be comforted.

"Blessed are the meek, for they will inherit the earth.

"Blessed are those who hunger and thirst for righteousness, for they will be filled.

"Blessed are the merciful, for they will receive mercy.

"Blessed are the pure in heart, for they will see God.

"Blessed are the peacemakers, for they will be called children of God.

"Blessed are those who are persecuted for righteousness' sake, for theirs is the kingdom of heaven.

"Blessed are you when people revile you and persecute you and utter all kinds of evil against you falsely on my account. Rejoice and be glad, for your reward is great in heaven, for in the same way they persecuted the prophets who were before you."

- A child was once asked for a definition of a saint. She said, "A stained-glass window!" Asked why, she explained, "The different colors let in the light, and every saint is a different color of God." Every one of our unknown saints colored God in a new way in his or her corner of the globe. On All Saints Day we are grateful for the lives of so many people of every age, church, and century who have lived as best they could within the vision and spirit of the gospel of Jesus Christ.

Tuesday November 2
The Commemoration of All the Faithful Departed (All Souls)
John 6:37–40

"Everything that the Father gives me will come to me, and anyone who comes to me I will never drive away; for I have come down from heaven, not to do my own will, but the will of him who sent me. And this is the will of him who sent me, that I should lose nothing of all that he has given me, but raise it up on the last day. This is indeed the will of my Father, that all who see the Son and believe in him may have eternal life; and I will raise them up on the last day."

- It is the will of God that nothing should be lost; may I look on everything that is good as a gift from God and an invitation to embrace the life that God offers.

- So much is offered to God each day! I pray that all people who are blessed may realize that their identity and destiny lie in God.

Wednesday November 3
Luke 14:25–33

Now large crowds were traveling with him; and he turned and said to them, "Whoever comes to me and does not hate father and mother, wife and children, brothers and sisters, yes, and even life itself, cannot be my disciple. Whoever does not carry the cross and follow me cannot be my disciple. For which of you, intending to build a tower, does not first sit down and estimate the cost, to see whether he has enough to complete it? Otherwise, when he has laid a foundation and is not able to finish, all who see it will begin to ridicule him, saying, 'This fellow began to build and was not able to finish.' Or what king, going out to wage war against another king, will not sit down first and consider whether he is able with ten thousand to oppose the one who comes against him with twenty thousand? If he cannot, then, while the other is still far away, he sends a delegation and asks for the terms of peace. So, therefore, none of you can become my disciple if you do not give up all your possessions."

- Jesus jolts us into thinking about the freedom we need; he wants us to resist anything that causes us to settle, to nest, to preen or plump for comfort. I ask God to help me grow in freedom. As I notice where I opt for security, am stuck, or have begun to put down roots, I pray that I may want only what God wants for me.

- Jesus wants us to know the scale of the task ahead of us; when it seems too much for us, what are we to do? To whom can we turn for help? I ask God to keep me in mind of my own need, that I may have the humility and trust always to seek help.

Thursday November 4
Luke 15:1–10

Now all the tax-collectors and sinners were coming near to listen to him. And the Pharisees and the scribes were grumbling and saying, "This fellow welcomes sinners and eats with them."

So he told them this parable: "Which one of you, having a hundred sheep and losing one of them, does not leave the ninety-nine in the wilderness and go after the one that is lost until he finds it? When he has found it, he lays it on his shoulders and rejoices. And when he comes home, he calls together his friends and neighbors, saying to them, 'Rejoice with me, for I have found my sheep that was lost.' Just so, I tell you, there will be more joy in heaven over one sinner who repents than over ninety-nine righteous people who need no repentance.

"Or what woman having ten silver coins, if she loses one of them, does not light a lamp, sweep the house, and search carefully until she finds it? When she has found it, she calls together her friends and neighbors, saying, 'Rejoice with me, for I have found the coin that I had lost.' Just so, I tell you, there is joy in the presence of the angels of God over one sinner who repents."

- Think of the trouble you take to find something you have lost. The search is more thorough when what we have lost is very valuable. Jesus gives us two examples of people searching for what is precious to them, and we hear of the joy that comes when they find it. He uses these examples to explain to us the sense of how God seeks us, and how joyful God is when our friendship with him is renewed. His searching for us cost him more than just the search—it cost him his life.

- When we spend some time realizing the value Jesus puts on our friendship, we can realize how precious we are to him.

Friday November 5
Luke 16:1–8

Then Jesus said to the disciples, "There was a rich man who had a manager, and charges were brought to him that this man was squandering his property. So he summoned him and said to him, 'What is this that I hear about you? Give me an account of your management, because you cannot be my manager any longer.' Then the manager said to himself, 'What will I do, now that my master is taking the position away from me? I am not strong enough to dig, and I am ashamed to beg. I have decided what to do so that, when I am dismissed as manager, people may welcome me into their homes.' So, summoning his master's debtors one by one, he asked the first, 'How much do you owe my master?' He answered, 'A hundred jugs of olive oil.' He said to him, 'Take your bill, sit down quickly, and make it fifty.' Then he asked another, 'And how much do you owe?' He replied, 'A hundred containers of wheat.' He said to him, 'Take your bill and make it eighty.' And his master commended the dishonest manager because he had acted shrewdly; for the children of this age are more shrewd in dealing with their own generation than are the children of light."

- If I am in debt, it would be such a relief to have the bank manager cut the debt in half. God has already canceled my debt. I am now free before God, and very grateful.
- How am I managing the gifts God has given me? They are meant to be at the service of those who are most needy.

Saturday November 6
Luke 16:9–15

"And I tell you, make friends for yourselves by means of dishonest wealth so that when it is gone, they may welcome you into the eternal homes.

"Whoever is faithful in a very little is faithful also in much; and whoever is dishonest in a very little is dishonest also in much. If then you have not been faithful with the dishonest wealth, who will entrust to you the true riches? And if you have not been faithful with what belongs to another, who will give you what is your own? No slave can serve two masters; for a slave will either hate the one and love the other, or be devoted to the one and despise the other. You cannot serve God and wealth."

The Pharisees, who were lovers of money, heard all this, and they ridiculed him. So he said to them, "You are those who justify yourselves in the sight of others; but God knows your hearts; for what is prized by human beings is an abomination in the sight of God."

- To walk the narrow path of faithfulness and justice is not easy—to be true to oneself and honest with one another is a task we must work at. Jesus tells us that we cannot serve two masters; we cannot sit on the fence. We must come down on the side of righteousness or be bereft of all that is good.
- You ask us to believe in you, Lord, to trust in your goodness and care for each one. Look into our hearts, Lord, and remove everything that causes us to stumble or fall, and as we walk through life, help us keep our eyes on you.

The Thirty-Second Week in Ordinary Time
November 7–13, 2021

Something to think and pray about each day this week:

We all run into relationship hurdles at some point in our lives, perhaps on a continuous basis. At times, we can be very sensitive to minor disturbances, which can lead to mental health problems. A disagreement, an uncomfortable silence, or a raw tension can tip us over the edge toward insomnia, anxiety, and vulnerable moods. The reality is that these are normal interactions we must try to live with. To smile in the acknowledgment that not everyone likes us may be an important first step toward wellness.

Our use of touch is a key way to improve our relationship with others. We have a vital need for it, from our earliest moments to the end of our days. A handshake, "high five," or friendly pat on the shoulder can draw us close to others. A hug, hand to hold, or gentle kiss can draw us even closer. We would do well to reach out a little further the next time we are with someone, and to notice how we feel afterward.

Moreover, taking chances on revealing ourselves is necessary for emotional intimacy. We need courage to share something personal, look the person in the eyes, build trust, and go on a journey together. A silent presence can sometimes be enough; I recall an image of my grandparents walking in the park, holding hands without saying a word, and smelling the roses. When we are thankful for our relationships, we are more ready to respond to deeper invitations of love.

Pope Francis has pointed out how easy it is to caress each other. What are we afraid of? I used to hesitate to kiss my grandmother when I saw her every day. I clearly loved her through my words and other deeds, but I seemed to have saved my kisses for only special occasions. So, I followed the pope's advice and started to do it, and it has now become second nature. Every day is a special day and an opportunity to show our love in the world.

—Gavin Thomas Murphy, *Bursting Out in Praise:*
Spirituality & Mental Health

The Presence of God

"Come to me, all you who are weary and are carrying heavy burdens, and I will give you rest." Here I am, Lord. I come to seek your presence. I long for your healing power.

Freedom

"In these days, God taught me as a schoolteacher teaches a pupil" (St. Ignatius).

I remind myself that there are things God has to teach me yet, and I ask for the grace to hear those things and let them change me.

Consciousness

Help me, Lord, to be more conscious of your presence. Teach me to recognize your presence in others.

Fill my heart with gratitude for the times your love has been shown to me through the care of others.

The Word

God speaks to each of us individually. I listen attentively to hear what he is saying to me. Read the text a few times, then listen. (*Please turn to the Scripture on the following pages. Inspiration points are there, should you need them. When you are ready, return here to continue.*)

Conversation

Conversation requires talking and listening.

As I talk to Jesus, may I also learn to be still and listen.

I will open my heart to him as I tell him of my fears and my doubts.

I will ask him to help me place myself fully in his care and to abandon myself to him, knowing that he always wants what is best for me.

Conclusion

I thank God for these moments we have spent together and for any insights I have been given concerning the text.

Sunday November 7
Thirty-Second Sunday in Ordinary Time
Mark 12:38–44

As he taught, he said, "Beware of the scribes, who like to walk around in long robes, and to be greeted with respect in the market-places, and to have the best seats in the synagogues and places of honor at banquets! They devour widows' houses and for the sake of appearance say long prayers. They will receive the greater condemnation."

He sat down opposite the treasury, and watched the crowd putting money into the treasury. Many rich people put in large sums. A poor widow came and put in two small copper coins, which are worth a penny. Then he called his disciples and said to them, "Truly I tell you, this poor widow has put in more than all those who are contributing to the treasury. For all of them have contributed out of their abundance; but she out of her poverty has put in everything she had, all she had to live on."

- Our age, even more than the time of Jesus, is so obsessed with image that it becomes the most important feature for our leaders, even more than their message or vision. I listen to Jesus' words, which are such a real challenge to this culture, and to his warning to beware not to be taken in by these antics.

- Jesus proclaims that the woman who put in two small copper coins had given more than all the rich people. In a very real way it is a summary of the whole gospel, for God looks at the heart and its readiness to give generously. Do I measure my worth by my external success, or am I free to look at my heart and be ready to be generous even in my poverty? I ask God to help me look at myself and at others as he looks at us.

Monday November 8
Luke 17:1–6

Jesus said to his disciples, "Occasions for stumbling are bound to come, but woe to anyone by whom they come! It would be better for you if a millstone were hung around your neck and you were thrown into the sea than for you to cause one of these little ones to stumble. Be on your guard! If another disciple sins, you must rebuke the offender, and if there is repentance, you must forgive. And if the same person sins against you seven times a day, and turns back to you seven times and says, 'I repent,' you must forgive."

The apostles said to the Lord, "Increase our faith!" The Lord replied, "If you had faith the size of a mustard seed, you could say to this mulberry tree, 'Be uprooted and planted in the sea,' and it would obey you."

- Jesus allows for our personal failings but warns against causing difficulties for others. I consider how I give a good example, am considerate and loving. I ask God's help to be neither proud nor careless.

- Living among others calls for care and attention to how I am in my relationships; I ask God to help me see how I help others to grow by how I give attention and by how I forgive.

Tuesday November 9
The Dedication of the Lateran Basilica
John 2:13–22

The Passover of the Jews was near, and Jesus went up to Jerusalem. In the temple he found people selling cattle, sheep, and doves, and the money-changers seated at their tables. Making a whip of cords, he drove all of them out of the temple, both the sheep and the cattle. He also poured out the coins of the money-changers and overturned their tables. He told those who were selling the doves, "Take these things out of here! Stop making my Father's house a market-place!" His disciples remembered that it was written, "Zeal for your house will consume me." The Jews then said to him, "What sign can you show us for doing this?" Jesus answered them, "Destroy this temple, and in three days I will raise it up." The Jews then said, "This temple has been under construction for forty-six years, and will you raise it up in three days?" But he was speaking of the temple of his body. After he was raised from the dead, his disciples remembered that he had said this; and they believed the Scripture and the word that Jesus had spoken.

- The Lateran Basilica is the pope's cathedral, and today's feast reminds us that as believers we are members of the People of God, the universal Church. This can sometimes become a source of frustration and even anger, but it is also the source of so much gratitude and consolation: I received the faith because it was kept alive in the Church, which is the church of sinners but also of saints. May I be able to keep it alive and pass it on to others who come after me. I pray in a special way for Pope Francis and his mission as our universal shepherd.

Wednesday November 10
Luke 17:11–19

On the way to Jerusalem Jesus was going through the region between Samaria and Galilee. As he entered a village, ten lepers approached him. Keeping their distance, they called out, saying, "Jesus, Master, have mercy on us!" When he saw them, he said to them, "Go and show yourselves to the priests." And as they went, they were made clean. Then one of them, when he saw that he was healed, turned back, praising God with a loud voice. He prostrated himself at Jesus' feet and thanked him. And he was a Samaritan. Then Jesus asked, "Were not ten made clean? But the other nine, where are they? Was none of them found to return and give praise to God except this foreigner?" Then he said to him, "Get up and go on your way; your faith has made you well."

- The healed man finds it in his heart to praise God. His first words are trustful petition: petition and thanks are fundamental movements of prayer. We engage one or the other, sometimes both. Asking for what we want, giving praise for what we are grateful for—these are the essentials of prayer.

- The lepers were able to recognize their need and call on Jesus to help them. I consider how ready I am to see my needs and to ask for the help I require.

Thursday November 11
Luke 17:20–25

Once Jesus was asked by the Pharisees when the kingdom of God was coming, and he answered, "The kingdom of God is not coming with things that can be observed; nor will they say, 'Look, here it is!' or 'There it is!' For, in fact, the kingdom of God is among you."

Then he said to the disciples, "The days are coming when you will long to see one of the days of the Son of Man, and you will not see it. They will say to you, 'Look there!' or 'Look here!' Do not go, do not set off in pursuit. For as the lightning flashes and lights up the sky from one side to the other, so will the Son of Man be in his day. But first he must endure much suffering and be rejected by this generation."

- The disciples eagerly await the coming of the kingdom. For us, the death and resurrection of Jesus mean that the kingdom is already within our reach: "In fact, the kingdom of God is among you." It is already present through the teaching and healing ministry of Jesus.

- Wherever we give or receive true love, kindness, gentleness, compassion, and generosity, we experience the kingdom.

Friday November 12
Luke 17:26–37

"Just as it was in the days of Noah, so too it will be in the days of the Son of Man. They were eating and drinking, and marrying and being given in marriage, until the day Noah entered the ark, and the flood came and destroyed all of them. Likewise, just as it was in the days of Lot: they were eating and drinking, buying and selling, planting and building, but on the day that Lot left Sodom, it rained fire and sulphur from heaven and destroyed all of them—it will be like that on the day that the Son of Man is revealed. On that day, anyone on the housetop who has belongings in the house must not come down to take them away; and likewise anyone in the field must not turn back. Remember Lot's wife. Those who try to make their life secure will lose it, but those who lose their life will keep it. I tell you, on that night there will be two in one bed; one will be taken and the other left. There will be two women grinding meal together; one will be taken and the other left." Then they asked him, "Where, Lord?" He said to them, "Where the corpse is, there the vultures will gather."

- In this month of November, the Church suggests that we recall those who have gone before us and that we think of our own passing from this life, and also, as this text reminds us, of the eventual ending of the world.

- As we know from experience, many overwhelming events catch us by surprise, just when we think that ordinary life will continue as usual. These moments often cause us to stop and think, What is it all about, and what are we really living for? God gives us the help to live to him and not be caught by surprise.

Saturday November 13
Luke 18:1–8

Then Jesus told them a parable about their need to pray always and not to lose heart. He said, "In a certain city there was a judge who neither feared God nor had respect for people. In that city there was a widow who kept coming to him and saying, 'Grant me justice against my opponent.' For a while he refused; but later he said to himself, 'Though I have no fear of God and no respect for anyone, yet because this widow keeps bothering me, I will grant her justice, so that she may not wear me out by continually coming.' And the Lord said, "Listen to what the unjust judge says. And will not God grant justice to his chosen ones who cry to him day and night? Will he delay long in helping them? I tell you, he will quickly grant justice to them. And yet, when the Son of Man comes, will he find faith on earth?"

- Jesus tells us we "need to pray continually and never lose heart." The simple parable has a clear message: Jesus is not comparing God to an unjust judge but tells us that if perseverance obtains justice from an unjust judge, how much more from a good and loving father?

- We need never to lose heart: this is certainly one of the bigger challenges for our faith. Persevering in prayer teaches me that God does not need to be informed of my needs. It is rather I who will notice that I am learning to trust God more, as I become more open to whatever he asks of me and my loved ones, for he wants nothing but what is good for me. I thank God for his loving care and ask for the gift of persevering prayer.

November 14–20, 2021

Something to think and pray about each day this week:

Our efforts may seem small and futile, but many Gospel episodes reveal the recurring motif, that God has an eye for small people and small things. Think of the widow's mite and the multiplication of the loaves and fish (Mark 12:41–44; 8:1–9). At Cana dull water is turned into the best of wine (John 2:1–12); at the Last Supper lowly bread and wine become the body and blood of the Lord (Luke 22:19–20). The life of each person, no matter how hidden, has its influence on all others (Romans 14:7). Any good deed, however small, that is done in love has an eternal quality, because love does not come to an end (1 Corinthians 13:8) and we will reap its reward at harvest time (Galatians 6:9). This grounds our hope that our tiny contributions on behalf of our sick planet carry their own symbolic value. Julian of Norwich expresses this hope:

> God showed me a little thing, the size of a hazel nut, lying in the palm of my hand. I looked upon it and thought, "What may this be?" And I was answered, "It is all that is made." I marveled how it might last, for I thought it might suddenly have fallen to nothing for smallness. And I was answered, "It lasts and ever shall, for God loves it. And so have all things their beginning by the love of God." In this little thing I saw three truths: the first is that God made it; the second that God loves it; and the third that God keeps it safe.

> Brian Grogan, SJ, *Creation Walk: The Amazing Story of a Small Blue Planet*

The Presence of God
"Be still, and know that I am God." Lord, your words lead us to the calmness and greatness of your presence.

Freedom
I am free. When I look at these words in writing, they seem to create in me a feeling of awe. Yes, a wonderful feeling of freedom. Thank you, God.

Consciousness
At this moment, Lord, I turn my thoughts to you.
I will leave aside my chores and preoccupations.
I will take rest and refreshment in your presence, Lord.

The Word
The word of God comes down to us through the Scriptures. May the Holy Spirit enlighten my mind and my heart to respond to the Gospel teachings. (*Please turn to the Scripture on the following pages. Inspiration points are there, should you need them. When you are ready, return here to continue.*)

Conversation
Begin to talk with Jesus about the Scripture you have just read. What part of it strikes a chord in you? Perhaps the words of a friend—or some story you have heard recently—will slowly rise to the surface of your consciousness. If so, does the story throw light on what the Scripture passage might be trying to say to you?

Conclusion
Glory be to the Father, and to the Son, and to the Holy Spirit,
As it was in the beginning, is now, and ever shall be,
World without end. Amen.

Sunday November 14
Thirty-Third Sunday in Ordinary Time
Mark 13:24–32

"But in those days, after that suffering,

> the sun will be darkened,
> and the moon will not give its light,
> and the stars will be falling from heaven,
> and the powers in the heavens will be shaken.

Then they will see 'the Son of Man coming in clouds' with great power and glory. Then he will send out the angels, and gather his elect from the four winds, from the ends of the earth to the ends of heaven.

"From the fig tree learn its lesson: as soon as its branch becomes tender and puts forth its leaves, you know that summer is near. So also, when you see these things taking place, you know that he is near, at the very gates. Truly I tell you, this generation will not pass away until all these things have taken place. Heaven and earth will pass away, but my words will not pass away.

"But about that day or hour no one knows, neither the angels in heaven, nor the Son, but only the Father."

- It is good to find something in life that cannot pass away. We want that—we want it in love, in our friendships, and in our trusting in the future. The word of God spoken in love, always a light in life, will never pass away. By prayer we insert ourselves into the reality of that word and that love.

Monday November 15
Luke 18:35–43

As he approached Jericho, a blind man was sitting by the roadside begging. When he heard a crowd going by, he asked what was happening. They told him, "Jesus of Nazareth is passing by." Then he shouted, "Jesus, Son of David, have mercy on me!" Those who were in front sternly ordered him to be quiet; but he shouted even more loudly, "Son of David, have mercy on me!" Jesus stood still and ordered the man to be brought to him; and when he came near, he asked him, "What do you want me to do for you?" He said, "Lord, let me see again." Jesus said to him, "Receive your sight; your faith has saved you." Immediately he regained his sight and followed him, glorifying God; and all the people, when they saw it, praised God.

- "Jesus, Son of David, have mercy on me!" What a beautiful prayer, which I can so easily make my own today, and every day. I stand in the presence of Jesus and ask him insistently to have mercy on me in all my needs and frailties.

- I might also hear Jesus asking me, "What do you want me to do for you?" Am I as prompt as the blind man to answer; do I know as well as he what I desire from Jesus? I too can ask to see again, to see God's presence in my life and the life of the world, to see what the Lord wants me to do. I thank Jesus for his merciful and reassuring presence in my life.

Tuesday November 16
Luke 19:1–10

He entered Jericho and was passing through it. A man was there named Zacchaeus; he was a chief tax-collector and was rich. He was trying to see who Jesus was, but on account of the crowd he could not, because he was short in stature. So he ran ahead and climbed a sycamore tree to see him, because he was going to pass that way. When Jesus came to the place, he looked up and said to him, "Zacchaeus, hurry and come down; for I must stay at your house today." So he hurried down and was happy to welcome him. All who saw it began to grumble and said, "He has gone to be the guest of one who is a sinner." Zacchaeus stood there and said to the Lord, "Look, half of my possessions, Lord, I will give to the poor; and if I have defrauded anyone of anything, I will pay back four times as much." Then Jesus said to him, "Today salvation has come to this house, because he too is a son of Abraham. For the Son of Man came to seek out and to save the lost."

- We all like Zacchaeus, the shy man who did not want to attract any attention yet ended up getting far beyond his expectations. Jesus could see what he really desired in the depths of his heart and invited himself to Zacchaeus's house. All who saw this began to grumble, but Jesus faced this criticism by proclaiming that salvation had come to Zacchaeus's house. I try to imagine myself present in this scene: would I be like the diffident Zacchaeus, like the complaining crowd, or like the merciful and strong Jesus?

- After meeting Jesus, Zacchaeus promised to mend his ways. I ask Jesus for his help, as he comes to seek and save what is lost.

Wednesday November 17
Luke 19:11–28

As they were listening to this, he went on to tell a parable, because he was near Jerusalem, and because they supposed that the kingdom of God was to appear immediately. So he said, "A nobleman went to a distant country to get royal power for himself and then return. He summoned ten of his slaves, and gave them ten pounds, and said to them, 'Do business with these until I come back.' But the citizens of his country hated him and sent a delegation after him, saying, 'We do not want this man to rule over us.' When he returned, having received royal power, he ordered these slaves, to whom he had given the money, to be summoned so that he might find out what they had gained by trading. The first came forward and said, 'Lord, your pound has made ten more pounds.' He said to him, 'Well done, good slave! Because you have been trustworthy in a very small thing, take charge of ten cities.' Then the second came, saying, 'Lord, your pound has made five pounds.' He said to him, 'And you, rule over five cities.' Then the other came, saying, 'Lord, here is your pound. I wrapped it up in a piece of cloth, for I was afraid of you, because you are a harsh man; you take what you did not deposit, and reap what you did not sow.' He said to him, 'I will judge you by your own words, you wicked slave! You knew, did you, that I was a harsh man, taking what I did not deposit and reaping what I did not sow? Why then did you not put my money into the bank? Then when I returned, I could have collected it with interest.' He said to the bystanders, 'Take the pound from him and give it to the one who has ten pounds.' (And they said to him, 'Lord, he has ten pounds!') "I tell you, to all those who have, more will be given; but from those who have nothing, even what they have will be taken away. But as for these enemies of mine who did not want me to be king over them—bring them here and slaughter them in my presence."

After he had said this, he went on ahead, going up to Jerusalem.

- Jesus seeks people he can trust to take risks, sometimes even recklessly. Cowards will never build the kingdom. During his last encounter with his apostles, he told them to take the gospel to the whole world, an impossible mission if ever there was one. Yet he knew whom he had chosen, for they did just that, taking huge risks to spread the gospel. I ask for the grace to be generous in my response to God's generosity to me.

- "Because you have been trustworthy in a very small thing, take charge of ten cities." I ask for the grace not to underestimate the value of being faithful in small things, in my relationships, in carrying out my responsibilities, in my life of faith and service.

Thursday November 18
Matthew 14:22–33

Immediately he made the disciples get into the boat and go on ahead to the other side, while he dismissed the crowds. And after he had dismissed the crowds, he went up the mountain by himself to pray. When evening came, he was there alone, but by this time the boat, battered by the waves, was far from the land, for the wind was against them. And early in the morning he came walking toward them on the lake. But when the disciples saw him walking on the lake, they were terrified, saying, "It is a ghost!" And they cried out in fear. But immediately Jesus spoke to them and said, "Take heart, it is I; do not be afraid."

Peter answered him, "Lord, if it is you, command me to come to you on the water." He said, "Come." So Peter got out of the boat, started walking on the water, and came toward Jesus. But when he noticed the strong wind, he became frightened, and beginning to sink, he cried out, "Lord, save me!" Jesus immediately reached out his hand and caught him, saying to him, "You of little faith, why did you doubt?" When they got into the boat, the wind ceased. And those in the boat worshipped him, saying, "Truly you are the Son of God."

- Jesus took some time to be at prayer apart from others. His time with God did not close him to the world but inspired him to go to the help of the troubled disciples. The time that I spend at prayer builds me up in my relationship with God and strengthens me to act in God's name.

- Peter had courage when his eyes were on Jesus but foundered when he focused on himself and his situation. I ask God to help me keep Jesus before me.

Friday November 19

Luke 19:45–48

Then he entered the temple and began to drive out those who were selling things there; and he said, "It is written,

'My house shall be a house of prayer'
but you have made it a den of robbers."

Every day he was teaching in the temple. The chief priests, the scribes, and the leaders of the people kept looking for a way to kill him; but they did not find anything they could do, for all the people were spellbound by what they heard.

- We can feel the growing tension, as Jesus forcefully challenges the way things were done in the holiest place of Judaism. It is so easy to lose sight of the real value of religious actions and rituals, ending up sometimes in shameful compromises.

- The Gospels often draw a stark contrast between the attitude of the chief priests, the scribes, and leaders and that of the common people. The latter are always seen as more open to God's presence in Jesus, while the religious leaders are trying to eliminate him. I ask for a simple heart, open to novelty and able to wonder.

Saturday November 20

Luke 20:27–40

Some Sadducees, those who say there is no resurrection, came to him and asked him a question, "Teacher, Moses wrote for us that if a man's brother dies, leaving a wife but no children, the man shall marry the widow and raise up children for his brother. Now there were seven brothers; the first married, and died childless; then the second and the third married her, and so in the same way all seven died childless. Finally the woman also died. In the resurrection, therefore, whose wife will the woman be? For the seven had married her."

Jesus said to them, "Those who belong to this age marry and are given in marriage; but those who are considered worthy of a place in that age and in the resurrection from the dead neither marry nor are given in marriage. Indeed they cannot die any more, because they are like angels and are children of God, being children of the resurrection. And the fact that the dead are raised Moses himself showed, in the story about the bush, where he speaks of the Lord as the God of Abraham, the God of Isaac, and the God of Jacob. Now he is God not of the dead, but of the living; for to him all of them are alive." Then some of the scribes answered, "Teacher, you have spoken well." For they no longer dared to ask him another question.

- The question asked by the Sadducees is somewhat contrived, intended not to seek clarity but to present a tricky conundrum. It sometimes happens that people we encounter present us with big imponderables, sure that the answer will elude us too. I pray for the wisdom I need not to be drawn into traps of pride or intelligence and for the courage to live in the simplicity to which Jesus calls me.

- Jesus often shows the poor and simple as being exemplars of God's kingdom; I pray for the kind of intelligence that Jesus values, careful not to get caught up in clever distractions.

The Thirty-Fourth Week in Ordinary Time
November 21–27, 2021

Something to think and pray about each day this week:

In emphasizing the importance of the experience of the spirit, we should be aware that references to the experience of the spirit are fraught with ambiguity and open to many misunderstandings. To take account of this ambiguity, it may be helpful to outline what an experience of the spirit is not. Karl Rahner, who explicitly affirms the possibility of an experience of the spirit, sought to highlight what is distinctive in this experience. He pointed out that the experience of the spirit is not of the same order or on the same level as the experience of objects in the world. An experience of the spirit is not an encounter with an object alongside other objects, nor is it an item of information alongside other items of information, nor is it an explanation alongside other explanations. Further, it should be noted that the experience is not to be found in the normal course of events as some kind of external or supernatural intervention in the natural processes of biological evolution and human development. The spirit is already present and active in these natural processes of evolution; it is "we" who are absent or inattentive to this ongoing presence of the spirit. In other words, the spirit "breathes where it will" in many surprising ways: in the life of nature, in the movements of history, in prophets and holy persons, in holy things, in cultures and religions, in the creative arts and the insights of modern science, in the awakening of human consciousness and the discovery of human interiority. An experience of the spirit is more about the spirit finding us than about us creating the spirit. In other words, an experience of the spirit is not a human projection but a discovery of what is already there in the world, not a merely human construction but the active unraveling of a gift already given, not a projection but a making explicit of that with which we are already familiar.

—Dermot A. Lane, *Theology and Ecology in Dialogue*

The Presence of God

To be present is to arrive as one is and open up to the other.
At this instant, as I arrive here, God is present waiting for me.
God always arrives before me, desiring to connect with me
even more than my most intimate friend.
I take a moment and greet my loving God.

Freedom

Leave me here freely all alone. / In cell where never sunlight shone. /
Should no one ever speak to me. / This golden silence makes me free!

> —Part of a poem by Bl. Titus Brandsma, written while
> he was a prisoner at Dachau concentration camp

Consciousness

Where am I with God? With others?
Do I have something to be grateful for? Then I give thanks.
Is there something I am sorry for? Then I ask forgiveness.

The Word

I take my time to read the word of God slowly, a few times, allowing myself to dwell on anything that strikes me. (*Please turn to the Scripture on the following pages. Inspiration points are there, should you need them. When you are ready, return here to continue.*)

Conversation

How has God's word moved me? Has it left me cold?
Has it consoled me or moved me to act in a new way?
I imagine Jesus standing or sitting beside me;
I turn and share my feelings with him.

Conclusion

Glory be to the Father, and to the Son, and to the Holy Spirit,
As it was in the beginning, is now, and ever shall be,
World without end. Amen.

Sunday November 21
Our Lord Jesus Christ, King of the Universe
John 18:33b–37

Then Pilate entered the headquarters again, summoned Jesus, and asked him, "Are you the King of the Jews?" Jesus answered, "Do you ask this on your own, or did others tell you about me?" Pilate replied, "I am not a Jew, am I? Your own nation and the chief priests have handed you over to me. What have you done?" Jesus answered, "My kingdom is not from this world. If my kingdom were from this world, my followers would be fighting to keep me from being handed over to the Jews. But as it is, my kingdom is not from here." Pilate asked him, "So you are a king?" Jesus answered, "You say that I am a king. For this I was born, and for this I came into the world, to testify to the truth. Everyone who belongs to the truth listens to my voice."

- There is always a certain ambiguity in giving Jesus the title of king. This is partly due to the varying attitudes to kings throughout history and in different cultures. But the greatest ambiguity surfaces in today's reading. Jesus has to correct Pilate's understanding of Jesus' role: "My kingdom is not from this world" or "My kingdom does not belong to this world." In spite of this warning we have sometimes celebrated this feast in a (worldly) triumphalist manner that does not harmonize with Jesus' self-understanding.

- Why is it important to read a scene from the Passion today? Does it help us grasp what the kingship of Christ truly means? (Notice Jesus' stress on truth in this passage.) How can Jesus be both king and Suffering Servant?

Monday November 22
Luke 21:1–4

He looked up and saw rich people putting their gifts into the treasury; he also saw a poor widow put in two small copper coins. He said, "Truly I tell you, this poor widow has put in more than all of them; for all of them have contributed out of their abundance, but she out of her poverty has put in all she had to live on."

- How often do I feel I am not doing enough when I compare myself to others! Today Jesus invites me to ask myself how God, who knows my heart, looks at me and my efforts.

- The amount of what I do is not that important for God; what matters is my generosity, what lies in my heart. I ask God for an open heart, ready to give all, like this poor widow of the Gospel.

Tuesday November 23
Luke 21:5–11

When some were speaking about the temple, how it was adorned with beautiful stones and gifts dedicated to God, he said, "As for these things that you see, the days will come when not one stone will be left upon another; all will be thrown down."

They asked him, "Teacher, when will this be, and what will be the sign that this is about to take place?" And he said, "Beware that you are not led astray; for many will come in my name and say, 'I am he!' and, 'The time is near!' Do not go after them.

"When you hear of wars and insurrections, do not be terrified; for these things must take place first, but the end will not follow immediately." Then he said to them, "Nation will rise against nation, and kingdom against kingdom; there will be great earthquakes, and in various places famines and plagues; and there will be dreadful portents and great signs from heaven."

- Endings are sometimes welcomed, sometimes feared. Now that we are coming to the end of the Liturgical Year (Advent begins next Sunday), our Gospel readings will focus on the end times. Jesus begins by foretelling the end of the temple in Jerusalem (destroyed in AD 70). Given the significance of the temple for Jewish religion and culture, this could be seen as symbolizing the end of their messianic hopes. It certainly led to the Jewish diaspora and to the Rabbinic Judaism that we know today. Nothing could ever be the same again.

- Did I have to deal with painful endings during the past few years? Death of loved ones, failed relationships, job loss, breakdown of health, and so forth? Where was God for me during these crises? Were there also endings that I welcomed, that brought me freedom and opened up new opportunities?

Wednesday November 24
Luke 21:12–19

"But before all this occurs, they will arrest you and persecute you; they will hand you over to synagogues and prisons, and you will be brought before kings and governors because of my name. This will give you an opportunity to testify. So make up your minds not to prepare your defense in advance; for I will give you words and a wisdom that none of your opponents will be able to withstand or contradict. You will be betrayed even by parents and brothers, by relatives and friends; and they will put some of you to death. You will be hated by all because of my name. But not a hair of your head will perish. By your endurance you will gain your souls."

- These words of Jesus continue what he was saying in yesterday's Scripture about future events. He speaks of great suffering for those who follow him. This was especially fulfilled in the early years of the Church when there were so many martyrs.

- Many today are suffering because of lack of freedom to live their beliefs. For many it can be difficult today openly to profess their faith. It is important to pray for the Church and also for those who find it difficult to believe in a God of love.

Thursday November 25
Luke 17:11–19

On the way to Jerusalem Jesus was going through the region between Samaria and Galilee. As he entered a village, ten lepers approached him. Keeping their distance, they called out, saying, "Jesus, Master, have mercy on us!" When he saw them, he said to them, "Go and show yourselves to the priests." And as they went, they were made clean. Then one of them, when he saw that he was healed, turned back, praising God with a loud voice. He prostrated himself at Jesus' feet and thanked him. And he was a Samaritan. Then Jesus asked, "Were not ten made clean? But the other nine, where are they? Was none of them found to return and give praise to God except this foreigner?" Then he said to him, "Get up and go on your way; your faith has made you well."

- The men who were healed all realized their good fortune and rejoiced in it, recognizing where it came from. Only one took time to address himself to Jesus. Prayer is good when it consists of asking, receiving, recognizing, and appreciating, but something is missing when it does not involve a humble return to Jesus to give thanks.

Friday November 26
Luke 21:29–33

Then [Jesus] told them a parable: "Look at the fig tree and all the trees; as soon as they sprout leaves you can see for yourselves and know that summer is already near. So also, when you see these things taking place, you know that the kingdom of God is near. Truly I tell you, this generation will not pass away until all things have taken place. Heaven and earth will pass away, but my words will not pass away."

- The Lord's reference to the fig tree evokes his earlier parable about the tree that was given a second chance to bear fruit. Do I have the courage to start again when I fall by the wayside?

- How well do I read the signs of the times, the signs that tell me what is valuable and what is passing?

- Do I dread the second coming of the Lord? Or do I wait for it in joyful anticipation?

Saturday November 27
Luke 21:34–36

"Be on guard so that your hearts are not weighed down with dissipation and drunkenness and the worries of this life, and that day does not catch you unexpectedly, like a trap. For it will come upon all who live on the face of the whole earth. Be alert at all times, praying that you may have the strength to escape all these things that will take place, and to stand before the Son of Man."

- Do I ever suspect that my life may be somewhat superficial? That I am not in touch with my deepest self? That I tend to drift rather than live reflectively? Prayer, of course, helps us grow in knowledge of self and of God. It also invites us to journey inward to the "still point" of the soul. Do I always accept this invitation, or does fear—or lack of faith—hold me back?

- It is surprising how much of Jesus' advice about preparing for the Second Coming is also relevant to our day-to-day living. For example: "Be on guard so that your hearts are not weighed down with dissipation and drunkenness and the worries of this life." Is anything weighing me down right now? It may be something sinful, or it may not. Do I want to be free of this burden? Might Jesus be able and willing to help me? "Be alert at all times, praying"!